Making Jesus Unforgettable!

**An Extraordinary Way to Internalize
the Gospels — And Pray Always**

JOSEPH F. SMITH, MD

Print edition ISBN: 978-1-947635-36-4
Ebook edition ISBN: 978-1-947635-37-1

Published by Froelich Forbes Press

Cover illustration by Mek Frinchaboy

About the cover: Traditional representations of the four Gospels grace the cover: John's eagle, Luke's ox, Matthew's angel, and Mark's lion. They combine here to form a cross symbolizing Jesus, the unforgettable focus of this book.

DEDICATED TO
MY WONDERFUL WIFE, SHERON
and
VERY SPECIAL DAUGHTERS, EMILY and ANNA
with
SPECIAL THANKS TO MYRTLE

CONTENTS

INTRODUCTION 1

Landmark 1: Index Finger 11

Landmark 2: Bicycle 19

Landmark 3: Triangle 29

Landmark 4: Table 41

Landmark 5: Basketball 50

Landmark 6: Snowflake 88

Landmark 7: Rabbit's Foot 96

Landmark 8: Octopus 106

Landmark 9: Baseball Diamond 112

Landmark 10: Two Hands 119

Landmark 11: Soccer Ball 124

Landmark 12: Box of Donuts 132

Landmark 13: Young Teenager 141

Landmark 14: Tennis Court 148

Landmark 15: Pool Table 152

Landmark 16: Teenager Driving 165

Landmark 17: Cicadas 174

Landmark 18: Golf Course 178

Landmark 19: The Game "Go" 186

Landmark 20: Eye Appointment 194

Landmark 21: Casino 203

Landmark 22: Tutu 209

Landmark 23: Pasture 221

Landmark 24: Calendar Square 228

Landmark 25: U.S. Quarter   235

Landmark 26: Marathon   242

Landmark 27: Three Cubes   254

Landmark 28: Dominoes   261

Landmark 29: Winter Party   268

Landmark 30: Bag of Silver Coins   279

Landmark 31: New Year's Eve Party   285

Landmark 32: Ice   294

Landmark 33: Record Album   303

Landmark 34: Inferno   311

Landmark 35: Camera   320

Landmark 36: Yardstick   334

Landmark 37: Thermometer   347

Landmark 38: Revolver   360

Landmark 39: Birthday Cake   367

Landmark 40: Bed   375

Landmark 41: Pearl Harbor   380

Landmark 42: 42nd Street   385

Landmark 43: Race Car   395

Landmark 44: Football Jersey   409

Landmark 45: Steep Hill   419

Landmark 46: Chromosome   431

Landmark 47: 747 Airplane   443

Landmark 48: A Tree   449

Landmark 49: Forty-Niner   459

Note

As will soon be explained, the purpose of this book is to deepen one's relationship with Jesus by implementing a unique method for "internalizing" the Gospels of Matthew, Mark, Luke, and John. This is done in a chronological and parallel fashion (also to be explained in detail) utilizing a unique mnemonic system.

Each section ("unit") of the book has several components: (1) a mnemonic story, (2) the Gospel text from *The New American Bible*, and (3) a brief commentary on the Gospel text. The commentary section is a combination of my thoughts and reflections as well as some explanatory information from the following sources:

1. *The New American Bible*
2. *The New Jerome Biblical Commentary*
3. *The Ignatius Catholic Bible Study Series (Matthew, Mark, Luke, John)*
4. *Harper Collins Bible Dictionary*

INTRODUCTION

"Oh my God, I forgot!" How many times have you uttered these words in disgust, or thought them in silent frustration? If you are like me, it is more times than you would like to remember. There are many reasons we forget to do something or cannot recall specific information. They include lack of motivation, becoming distracted, or being assaulted by too much data in our high-tech world. Forgetting some things may be inconsequential: where you put your keys, the purpose of a game you are playing, or to return a call at work. Others may be more significant: where you parked your car, your purpose for being in school, or to call your spouse. Forgetting some things could be catastrophic: where you placed your priorities, your purpose in life, or to call on Jesus in prayer. It is my sincere hope that this book will help you to always remember these last three. I believe that if you follow the method outlined here you will always remember Jesus and develop a deep, everlasting relationship with Him. By travelling with Jesus in the unique way described in the following pages, He will be your constant companion.

Traveling is a big part of life for most of us. We all travel in one way or another every day. People go on adventures to exotic and exciting places. However, visiting foreign lands and "seeing the world" are journeys that only relatively few are able to enjoy. Shorter trips to visit family and friends are common. Many enjoy traveling to sandy beaches or mountain hideaways when time allows. Mundane travel is a part of daily life for most people. Trips to school, work, or the store are routine and typically not worthy of much discussion. However, traveling just a few steps or negotiating a flight of stairs may be a noteworthy accomplishment for someone with a disability. Travel is movement, something almost all of us do to some extent every day of our lives.

We can also travel without physical movement. As humans with highly developed brains, we have a form of transportation always available. Our thoughts can take us into the past to relive events and experiences. We can also journey into the future and imagine the likely, hopeful, improbable, and impossible.

Life itself is a journey. It can be a trip of brief duration or in excess of one hundred years. The road from cradle to grave is full of twists, turns, highs, and lows. There is no clear map to follow, and the journey can end unexpectedly at any moment. This journey we call life has a purpose. It should not be to become wealthy or successful. Life's purpose is not to make friends and be popular. It is not even to be happy. All of these things can be good, even wonderful, but they should not be our life's primary purpose. Our goal should be to live this temporary, worldly life in such a way as to gain eternal life with God and His Son, Jesus, our Savior.

The book itself is written as a journey. You will walk with Jesus as He walks toward the cross. You will be with Him and His disciples as the events of the four Gospels unfold. You will be present when Jesus dies upon the cross and later when He ascends to the Father. This travel guide will help you walk with Jesus as He moves throughout Palestine preaching and healing. It will be a spiritual adventure. You will think and pray about the life of Jesus as you witness it unfold. The life of Christ is the greatest journey ever traveled. You are about to experience it fully, firsthand.

PRAYER

We are told in Scripture to "pray always." In the Letter to the Ephesians, we read, "With all prayer and supplication, pray at every opportunity in the Spirit" (Eph 6:18). In his first Letter to the Thessalonians, Paul writes: "Rejoice always. Pray without ceasing. In all circumstances give thanks, for this is the will of God for you in Christ Jesus" (1 Thess 5:16–18).

In our busy lives, we certainly are not always praying in the typical sense of the word. Our minds cannot perpetually be concentrating on prayer to the point of ignoring other responsibilities. However, our life itself can be a prayer. How we speak, behave, and interact with others can be a form of prayer. These actions speak louder than our words. As St. Francis of Assisi taught his friars, "Pray always, and if necessary use words."

As you travel with Jesus through the following pages, you will internalize the events of His life. You will not just read the familiar Gospel accounts of His ministry, passion, death, and resurrection. The life of Jesus, which was a perpetual prayer, will become a permanent part of your memory. That's right; you will experience and remember the Gospels as you never have. The goal is to be so thoroughly familiar with this prayer that lasted thirty-three years that you can recall all or any part of it whenever you wish. Such an intimate familiarity with Jesus' life will be a fertile source of prayer. Hopefully, this strong internalization of the Gospels will have a positive effect on how you lead your life. Your life can become a constant prayer and a witness to others.

The small spiritual classic *The Way of the Pilgrim* instructs one to pray always using the "Jesus Prayer." The words, "Lord Jesus Christ, Son of God, have mercy on me, a sinner," are prayed with such frequency that they are eventually imprinted upon one's heart. Even if the practitioner is not constantly reciting the prayer consciously, its effect is manifest as one travels through life. My hope is that by internalizing Jesus' life as told by the evangelists, our lives can become a constant prayer. We will consciously pray by meditating on these events or unconsciously pray by living our lives in Christlike fashion.

Our intimate familiarity with Jesus will give us a constant traveling companion. We will always have a source of comfort when the road gets rough. We will be able to think of Jesus and clear our cluttered mind when life seems overwhelming. Perhaps most importantly, we will never get lost as we travel this life toward the eternal life to come.

THE LANDMARKS

The journey you are about to begin will be very memorable. In fact, one of the primary purposes for taking the trip is to identify Landmarks that you can remember when you want to meditate on any portion of the four Gospels. Recognizable landmarks are important and useful for any traveler. Having natural or artificial features as part of the landscape is of great help as you move from place to place. Your upcoming journey with Jesus will contain forty-nine distinct and memorable Landmarks. This may seem like a lot of reference points to recall, but there is a simple way to make all forty-nine Landmarks instantly come to mind just by thinking of the number each one has been assigned.

It is not by chance that there are forty-nine Landmarks. You may recognize that *49* is a square number, 7 x 7. The number 7 has a special significance throughout the Bible.

Even a cursory reading of the Old and New Testaments leaves you with an appreciation for the significance of the number 7. It appears more than 1,700 times in the Bible. Seven represents the idea of completeness or perfection. For starters, God "rested" on the seventh day after completing

His work of creation. Thus, there are seven days in a week. The Bible itself is easily divided into seven parts: The Law, Prophets, Writings, Gospels, Acts, Epistles, and Revelation. The Bible's most important city, Jerusalem, sits on seven hills. You will soon "internalize" the seven miracles Jesus performed on the Sabbath. Peter asked Jesus if one who is wronged was to offer forgiveness seven times. Jesus' well-known response was to forgive seventy-seven times, that is, to forgive without limit. Due to the significance of the number 7, it is fitting that your travels with Jesus be divided into forty-nine (7 x 7) sections with each of these forty-nine sections represented by an easily remembered Landmark.

Each of the Landmarks is a familiar object, place, situation, or concept, and you will encounter them in numerical order. Each Landmark will trigger the memory of a unique story that will be easy to recall. Thus, your entire journey with Jesus will be committed to memory by recalling forty-nine different stories. Each is made up of several units that represent the events of the Gospels—an encounter, teaching, miracle, or some other event in Jesus' life. Thus, when you think of a Landmark it will trigger a story you have stored in your memory. As you recall the story, each of its units will remind you of an important part of Jesus' journey to the cross and beyond.

Instead of being an observer, you will be an integral part, actually the star, of each of the forty-nine stories that make up this great journey. By participating in the action, you will be able to commit the stories to memory more easily.

Your travels with Jesus commence at the outset of His adult ministry. Thus it is a trip lasting about three years. You become part of the story of Jesus with the Gospel introductions, followed by the teachings and ministry of John the Baptist. It is there that you will meet Jesus for the first time. You will not leave His side until after the Great Commission and His ascension.

THE GOSPELS

No one knows the exact chronology of the events of Jesus' life on earth, but the exact order of events is not critical. What is crucial is the content of His teachings, His actions and interactions, and His death and resurrection on our behalf. The four Gospels provide us with this information in detail.

Each of the four evangelists had a purpose for writing their Gospel. They also had specific audiences to whom they wrote. Each Gospel is presented differently, with variations in the sequence of events. As you will see, this is especially the case in the Gospel of John.

In your journey, the events of Jesus' life will be presented in a particular order, but it is not a random order. The four Gospels have been blended or "harmonized" to present the journey and the Landmarks you will encounter. The order of events uses the Gospel of Mark as the basic framework. Mark is believed to be not only the oldest of the four Gospels, but also a source for Matthew and Luke. John's Gospel is quite different from the other three. It contains large blocks of unique material that often stand together in our journey.

The following point cannot be overemphasized. A Gospel harmonization does not replace each of the four individual Gospels. Matthew, Mark, Luke, and John are divinely inspired works with their own unique purpose and perspective. When they are harmonized, their individual structure and order of events is lost. Each Gospel was written by a different author, at a different time, to a different audience, for a different purpose. This should never be forgotten. Some of these differences will be discussed on our journey. However, for our key purposes of "internalization" and "constant prayer," a harmonization of the Gospels is useful. It allows us to commit all the Gospels to memory in a logical and orderly fashion. However, in doing so we must never forget the uniqueness and specific themes of the four individual, inspired masterpieces.

Before setting out on our great adventure, it is important to have a general appreciation for each individual Gospel. Since some of their uniqueness is lost in harmonization, let us now look at them separately.

The Gospels of Mark, Matthew, and Luke are often referred to collectively as the Synoptic Gospels. *Synoptic* means "seen together." When these three books are seen together, they clearly share much of the same material, often presented in roughly the same order. The three are clearly different in order and content from the Gospel of John.

Most biblical scholars believe that the Gospel of Mark was written first. Both Matthew and Luke likely had Mark's Gospel available to them and used it as one of their sources. In fact, of the 661 verses in Mark, Matthew incorporates 80 percent of them into his work, and Luke uses 65 percent. Both also loosely follow the order of events as presented by Mark. However, Matthew and Luke share a significant amount of material not found in Mark, 220 verses that are believed to have come from another source termed "Q" (from *quelle*, the German word meaning "source"). Finally, there is some material unique to just Matthew or just Luke, both of which are much longer than Mark. Matthew contains 1,068 verses, and Luke contains 1,149 verses.

Let us first consider Mark's Gospel. Mark was not an actual eyewitness to the events about which he wrote. It appears that Mark's initial intended audience was the early Christians being severely persecuted in Rome. Mark's words were encouragement for his readers to persist in their faith. He wrote with a sense of urgency. Events in his Gospel happen immediately. The kingdom of God is at hand, and it is time for action. Jesus is portrayed as an active healer who performs many miracles.

Initially, Jesus wanted to keep secret His true identity as the Messiah sent by God to save His sinful people. At times, Jesus clearly tells His closest followers to keep what He says just between them. Jesus often proclaimed the good news of the kingdom of heaven using parables. A parable is a short story that uses everyday circumstances and imagery that an audience can easily relate to. However, the true meanings of Jesus' parables sometimes remained hidden for many of His listeners.

For Mark, Jesus is clearly the Son of God, who also shows human emotion. Mark captures this with a simple, dramatic style, often with much detail. Much emphasis is placed on the final week of Jesus' life in Jerusalem. Mark's portrayal of the death and resurrection depicts Jesus as a suffering servant, a most unexpected type of Messiah.

Mark appears to have structured his Gospel in four parts. Parts one and four are relatively short. He begins with the ministry of John the Baptist, which includes the Baptism of Jesus. Jesus is now prepared for His ministry. Mark concludes with Jesus rising from the dead and eventually ascending into heaven. The disciples are now prepared for their ministry. In between are two long sections. The public ministry of Jesus is filled with many teachings and miracles. It concludes with Peter's declaration of faith in Jesus' true identity and purpose. This is followed by the extensive Passion narrative, which details the events leading up to and including Jesus' death on the cross.

Although the Gospel of Matthew precedes Mark in the Bible, it was authored afterward. Like Mark, Matthew was probably written prior to the destruction of Jerusalem in AD 70. This Gospel's original target audience appears to have been Jewish Christians, since many Jewish customs go unexplained. (Matthew uses so many references to the Hebrew Scriptures that familiarity with them seems presumed.) Jesus is portrayed as the Messiah sent by God to fulfill these Scriptures. Matthew is quite critical of the Jewish officials who do not believe in Jesus. Matthew wants his Jewish readers to grow stronger in their faith and participate in the growing church. However, Jesus was not just for the Jews. He was for the entire world. Further use of Hebrew Scripture is evident in how Matthew portrays Jesus. He is the fulfillment of God's promise to Abraham. Jesus is a "new Moses," who proposes a new law. He is also the long-awaited Son of David.

Many of Jesus' teachings are organized by Matthew into five teaching discourses. The first and most well-known is Jesus' Sermon on the Mount. In the missionary discourse, Jesus instructs His disciples prior to sending them out for the first time. Parables about the kingdom of heaven are grouped into a third body of teaching. Jesus gives His disciples (and us) important words to live by in the Sermon on Life in the Church. The final discourse was given while Jesus sat with His disciples on the Mount of Olives. It provides difficult information about future difficult times.

The author of the Gospel of Luke was a Gentile and a physician. He accomplished his stated goal of writing "an orderly account" about Jesus. He depicts Jesus as the fulfillment of God's divine plan and His promise to Israel. Although at the outset he addresses Theophilus ("lover of God"), he wrote to Israelites, Samaritans, and Gentile Christians. Luke's Gospel emphasizes that salvation is for everyone. He often focuses on the outcasts of society. Women also play a prominent role in Luke. This Gospel makes it clear that there are demands in being a disciple of Jesus. However, the Holy Spirit offers assistance. God's mercy is the ultimate source of salvation. More than the other Gospel writers, Luke emphasizes the importance of rejoicing and celebrating our God-given gifts.

The Gospel of John in many ways stands alone. It is not one of the Synoptics. However, like Matthew, John was an eyewitness to the Gospel events. In fact, he was part of Jesus' inner circle along with Peter and his brother James. John does not specifically refer to himself in the Gospel, but many believe he is the apostle referred to as "the disciple whom Jesus loved" (not a bad title to have). The Book of John is considered by most to be the last Gospel written, just prior to the turn of the first century. It includes a significant amount of material not found in the synoptics. In

John, Jesus makes several trips to Jerusalem. Events are often presented in a different order, making harmonization less than an exact science.

Like Matthew, the Gospel of John has a strongly Jewish overtone. His original audience was probably Jewish Christians and Jewish nonbelievers. The evangelist clearly states his purpose toward the end of the Gospel. Following the resurrection, John writes in 20:31: "But these are written that you may [come to] believe that Jesus is the Messiah, the Son of God, and that through this belief you may have life in his name." In achieving this purpose, John produces a very spiritual and theological Gospel. There is a strong emphasis on the divinity of Jesus and His relationship with the Father. Jesus was sent by the Father to do His will. Faith in Jesus and His mission is critical to obtaining eternal life.

John makes rich use of symbols and symbolic language. At various times, Jesus identifies Himself as a shepherd, vine, light, water, and bread. Jesus describes Himself as the bread of life in a long symbolic discourse. The Synoptic Gospels describe Jesus uttering similar words at the Lord's Supper. Again, the order and content are quite different in John.

Jesus does perform miracles in John's Gospel. However, they are referred to as "signs." John's emphasis is not the wonder and power of the miracle itself. These actions by Jesus are "signs" that connect Him with God. They are signs that the Father is working through the Son. In short, Jesus was God. John's prologue declares:

"In the beginning was the Word,
and the Word was with God,
and the Word was God" (Jn 1:1).

HOW TO USE THIS BOOK

You may now be asking, "How do I proceed on this walk with Jesus through the Gospels?" Most journeys have a variety of options as to how to reach the destination. This is no exception. However, we still must take one step at a time. When you sit down to read from the Gospels, you do not usually start at the beginning of Matthew and continue through to the end of John in a single sitting. Similarly, when you want to take a walk with Jesus you will rarely begin at Landmark 1 and continue walking through Landmark 49 without stopping. However, when picking up this book for the first time I do suggest walking through the Landmarks in order, although not without resting. In this way, you will gain a general familiarity with how the book is structured and the mnemonic stories associated with the Landmarks. While taking this long walk for the first time, you may want to start committing the Landmarks to memory. Perhaps a few minutes each day, either before or after your walk, review the Landmarks listed in the Table of Contents. Also, before resuming your walk where you last stopped, take a few moments to review one or more of the mnemonic stories associated with the Landmarks you have already passed. There may be some times when you just mentally review Landmarks or their stories and do not actually cover any new ground.

Once you have completed the walk for the first time, you have limitless options and a lifetime to explore them. One day, you may review one Landmark entirely. Or perhaps you will just focus on one or two units within a Landmark. You may choose to skip from one Landmark to one further down the road. You may want to explore the Sermon on the Mount and then read and pray on an aspect of the Passion, many Landmarks away. There will be times during the day when a particular Landmark comes to mind. Take a minute or two and recall its story, then meditate about being with Jesus during this particular part of His life. At any time, any part of the Gospels is just a thought away. If longer periods of time are available, consider walking through seven Landmarks in a single day. If you are able to do this for seven days, you will take the entire walk in a single week. Remember, there is no hurry. You have the rest of your life to enjoy the walk and deepen your relationship with Jesus. Over time, my hope is that the story of the Gospels will always be on your mind, either consciously or unconsciously. More importantly, as a result of this, the love of Jesus will always be in your heart. Let us now take that first step.

The first of the forty-nine Landmarks on your walk with Jesus will remind you of the number 1. Each of the Landmarks that follow will include an indicator to tell you where you are on the journey. For example, the eighth and twenty-ninth Landmarks are things that represent the numbers 8 and 29. The actual thing, situation, place, animal, sport, object, or person that functions as one of the forty-nine Landmarks is very important. It will allow you to vividly recall the mnemonic story associated with that particular Landmark. After you come upon a Landmark, you will encounter a series of people, objects, or actions ("units") that will forever be linked to that Landmark. To make each mnemonic story unforgettable, you will play a major role. You will then read the portion of each Gospel that pertains to this particular part of Jesus' life and ministry. Subsequent Landmarks will remind you of more events or teachings as described in the four Gospels. In this way, you will "chronologically" walk with Jesus throughout His adult life, death, resurrection, and ascension.

Finally, for each "unit" there will be some comments about the Gospel passages. Hopefully, these thoughts will be a stimulus for prayer, meditation, and contemplation on this particular "unit" on your walk with Jesus.

Landmark 1:

INDEX FINGER

Since one purpose of each Landmark is to represent where you are on the journey with Jesus, the first Landmark represents the number *1*. People will often raise an **index finger** to indicate that something is "number 1." A familiar example occurs after a sporting contest. A participant or observer raises an **index finger** to tell the world that they or their winning team is "number 1." At times, you may be asked how many there is of something. If the answer is "one," simply raising an **index finger** may suffice. We will take advantage of this common gesture and use an **index finger** for the first Landmark.

This first Landmark, and the subsequent forty-eight Landmarks, will be unforgettable. Thus, you will not form an image of a simple, everyday **index finger**. No, the first Landmark is several feet long and is not attached to a hand. This **finger** rises from the ground, like a flesh-covered tree trunk. There are distinct joints allowing the **finger** to bend when necessary. The **index finger** has a large shiny nail. It reflects the sun's bright light. When you come upon this large, detached digit, you will immediately think of the number *1*, and vice versa. When you think of the number *1*, you will see the gigantic **index finger**. In this first Landmark, you are a logger who has been ordered to cut down the treelike **index finger** growing from the ground. It sounds bloody and painful, but rest assured, it will be neither.

You are a logger extraordinaire, not just an average run-of-the-sawmill logger. You are in fact a **pro-logger**! Picture yourself clad in a heavy flannel shirt. Blue bib overalls cover your legs with straps that cross and fasten in the front. The large letter P is emblazoned across the front of the overalls. The P signifies your lofty status in the logging world, that of a **pro-logger**. Your outfit is topped off with a woolen cap that also sports the letter P. Like any **pro-logger**, you would not be caught without your pride and joy, a well-oiled heavy-duty chainsaw. Now see yourself dressed and ready for work standing beside your next job, the index finger! Being a **pro-logger** reminds you of the **Prologue**, the well-known theological beginning of the Gospel of John. THE PROLOGUE is the first unit to be associated with the first Landmark.

||||||||||||||||||||||||||||||||||||||||||||||||||||||||||||||||||||||||||||||||||||||||||||||||||||||||||

PROLOGUE

||||||||||||||||||||||||||||||||||||||||||||||||||||||||||||||||||||||||||||||||||||||||||||||||||||||||||

Jn 1:1–18

1 In the beginning was the Word,
and the Word was with God,
and the Word was God.
2 He was in the beginning with God.
3 All things came to be through him,
and without him nothing came to be.
What came to be 4 through him was life,
and this life was the light of the human race;
5 the light shines in the darkness,
and the darkness has not overcome it.

6 A man named John was sent from God. 7 He came for testimony, to testify to the light, so that all might believe through him. 8 He was not the light, but came to testify to the light. 9 The true light, which enlightens everyone, was coming into the world.

10 He was in the world,
and the world came to be through him,
but the world did not know him.
11 He came to what was his own,
but his own people did not accept him.

12 But to those who did accept him he gave power to become children of God, to those who believe in his name, 13 who were born not by natural generation nor by human choice nor by a man's decision but of God.

14 And the Word became flesh
and made his dwelling among us,
and we saw his glory,
the glory as of the Father's only Son,
full of grace and truth.

15 John testified to him and cried out, saying, "This was he of whom I said, 'The one who is coming after me ranks ahead of me because he existed before me.'" 16 From his fullness we have all received, grace in place of grace, 17 because while the law was given through Moses, grace and truth came through Jesus Christ.

18 No one has ever seen God. The only Son, God, who is at the Father's side, has revealed him.

Information of great importance often merits repeating! So it is with the opening of John's Gospel. The redundancy of the first verses of the Prologue emphasize basic theological truths about Jesus. He is the Word of God, and has been one with God for eternity. In the upcoming genealogies, Jesus' earthly ancestry is traced back to either Abraham or Adam. John, the more theological evangelist, prefers to begin with Jesus' lack of a beginning. In doing so, he repeats the first words of Genesis, "In the beginning ..." As we will see on our journey, the Word is one with God and was sent by God to fulfill all of Scripture. Genesis describes how God the Father, through His spoken Word, brought life to all things. He now sends His Word in the form of Jesus, so that we all may have eternal life with Him.

Genesis described how God began His creative work by bringing light into existence. This good light by its very existence separated itself from darkness. God now sends His eternal Word to be light for a world made dark by sin. Although uncreated, in essence Jesus was created in flesh to provide light so that we could see the Father's love. It is not possible for our finite brain to fully comprehend this mystery of an infinite God becoming truly man. The essence of God, and thus Jesus, remains beyond our full understanding. However, the guiding light of Jesus leads us to a greater understanding of the Father and His infinite love for us.

John's Prologue initially described Jesus' divine name and relationship with the Father. Then came the amazing assertion: "The Word became flesh!" Jesus became like us, minus the sin. The infinite Word of God entered the realm of time and "dwelt among us." The special presence of God had dwelt among the Israelites in the ark of the covenant and later in the Jerusalem Temple. Now in a mysterious, wonderful way, God humbly stooped to the level of humanity through His Son. Imagine yourself wanting to become an ant or a worm or something that we so often carelessly trample underfoot! In becoming a man, Jesus lived and felt our human condition. He was not a stranger to disappointment, loneliness, rejection, fear, sadness, and abuse. He felt physical pain and hunger. Jesus knew firsthand what it is like to be us.

STANDING BESIDE THE INDEX FINGER, with chainsaw growling hungrily, you begin to have second thoughts. It seems so wrong to cut down a Landmark, especially one that is a blood-filled finger. Instead, you grab the finger firmly around the nail with both hands and begin to pull. The finger begins to bend at its joints. You pull even harder. The fingertip is about to touch the ground when it strikes a small golden object. Looking down, you recognize the object to be a **genie's** lamp! That's right, a lamp where a **genie** resides after vaporizing and returning home through the spout. Could a **genie** possibly be inside? Before you can pick up the lamp, your question is answered. A white cloud begins to stream from the spout. Several seconds later, a colorfully dressed, bejeweled, smiling male **genie** stands before you. This scene with the **genie's** lamp and the **genie** himself causes you to remember the word *genealogy*. Both Matthew and Luke present a genealogy of Jesus, though they vary significantly and have different purposes. Thus, the next unit is THE GENEALOGY OF JESUS.

THE GENEALOGY OF JESUS

Mt 1:1–17

1 The book of the genealogy of Jesus Christ, the son of David, the son of Abraham.

2 Abraham became the father of Isaac, Isaac the father of Jacob, Jacob the father of Judah and his brothers. **3** Judah became the father of Perez and Zerah, whose mother was Tamar. Perez became the father of Hezron, Hezron the father of Ram, **4** Ram the father of Amminadab. Amminadab became the father of Nahshon, Nahshon the father of Salmon, **5** Salmon the father of Boaz, whose mother was Rahab. Boaz became the father of Obed, whose mother was Ruth. Obed became the father of Jesse, **6** Jesse the father of David the king.

David became the father of Solomon, whose mother had been the wife of Uriah. **7** Solomon became the father of Rehoboam, Rehoboam the father of Abijah, Abijah the father of Asaph. **8** Asaph became the father of Jehoshaphat, Jehoshaphat the father of Joram, Joram the father of Uzziah. **9** Uzziah became the father of Jotham, Jotham the father of Ahaz, Ahaz the father of Hezekiah. **10** Hezekiah became the father of Manasseh, Manasseh the father of Amos, Amos the father of Josiah. **11** Josiah became the father of Jechoniah and his brothers at the time of the Babylonian exile.

12 After the Babylonian exile, Jechoniah became the father of Shealtiel, Shealtiel the father of Zerubbabel, **13** Zerubbabel the father of Abiud. Abiud became the father of Eliakim, Eliakim the father of Azor, **14** Azor the father of Zadok. Zadok became the father of Achim, Achim the father of Eliud, **15** Eliud the father of Eleazar. Eleazar became the father of Matthan, Matthan the father of Jacob, **16** Jacob the father of Joseph, the husband of Mary. Of her was born Jesus who is called the Messiah.

17 Thus the total number of generations from Abraham to David is fourteen generations; from David to the Babylonian exile, fourteen generations; from the Babylonian exile to the Messiah, fourteen generations.

Lk 3:23–38

23 When Jesus began his ministry he was about thirty years of age. He was the son, as was thought, of Joseph, the son of Heli, **24** the son of Matthat, the son of Levi, the son of Melchi, the son of Jannai, the son of Joseph, **25** the son of Mattathias, the son of Amos, the son of Nahum, the son of Esli, the son of Naggai, **26** the son of Maath, the son of Mattathias, the son of Semein, the son of Josech, the son of Joda, **27** the son of Joanan, the son of Rhesa, the son of Zerubbabel, the son of Shealtiel, the son of Neri, **28** the son of Melchi, the son of Addi, the son of Cosam, the son of Elmadam, the son of Er, **29** the son of Joshua, the son of Eliezer, the son of Jorim, the son of Matthat, the son of Levi, **30** the son of Simeon, the son of Judah, the son of Joseph, the son of Jonam, the son of Eliakim, **31** the son of Melea, the son of Menna, the son of Mattatha, the son of Nathan, the son of David, **32** the son of Jesse, the son of Obed, the son of Boaz, the son of Sala, the son of Nahshon, **33** the son of Amminadab, the son of Admin, the son of Arni, the son of Hezron, the son of Perez, the son of Judah, **34** the son of Jacob, the son of Isaac, the son of Abraham, the son of Terah, the son of Nahor, **35** the son of Serug, the son of Reu, the son of Peleg, the son of Eber, the son of Shelah, **36** the son of Cainan, the son of Arphaxad, the son of Shem, the son of Noah, the son of Lamech, **37** the son of Methuselah, the son of Enoch, the son of Jared, the son of Mahalaleel, the son of Cainan, **38** the son of Enos, the son of Seth, the son of Adam, the son of God.

In recent years, more and more people have become interested in their family genealogy. In our computer age with ready access to multiple databases, accurate information about our ancestors and their ancestors, their ancestors, and their ancestors…is available. The evangelists Matthew and Luke had no such technology. However, their purpose was different not only from today's researchers, but also from each other. The evangelists' goals were more theological than strictly historical. Even a cursory reading of the two genealogies shows them to be quite different from each other in content and structure.

Matthew begins his Gospel (and genealogy) by declaring Jesus as Christ ("Anointed One") and King. He was the royal Son of David. Just as David restored the nation of Israel, Jesus would restore Israel and all nations as heirs to God's kingdom. In Matthew, Jesus' family tree begins with Abraham, to whom God had promised that "Kings shall stem from you" (Gen 17:6). Fourteen generations later comes David, who had received a similar prophesy, "Your house and your kingdom shall endure forever" (2 Sam 7:16). After another fourteen generations, there is no patriarch or beloved king. Here, Matthew mentions one of the lowest points in Israel's history. The Jews were conquered and exiled to Babylon. They came under foreign rule and were very much in need of a Savior. With the passing of another fourteen generations, the Jewish people were again being controlled by harsh invaders. However, now under Roman rule, the long-awaited Messiah had come. Though He was of royal descent and would be the fulfillment of Hebrew Scripture, Jesus would not be the Messiah that people expected. The unexpected way Matthew ends his genealogy provides a clue that Jesus would be different. Previously, the phrase "the father of" linked one generation to the next. However, Joseph was not described as "the father of" Jesus. Jesus was born of Mary. The father is God Himself!

Luke does not begin his Gospel with a genealogy, and he does not begin the genealogy with Abraham. Luke likely used different sources than Matthew to construct his genealogy. Luke also had a different purpose. He placed this list tracing Jesus' earthly beginning after Jesus' Baptism as He was about to begin His earthly ministry. By beginning the family tree with Adam, the father of mankind, Luke indicates that Jesus' ministry was for everyone. Jesus was the new Adam, who restores our relationship with God, a relationship that was tainted by disobedience and pride. Like Matthew, it was important for Luke that Jesus was shown to be the fulfillment of Scripture and a descendant of King David. Luke mentions that Jesus began His ministry at age 30, the age when David was anointed king.

YOU, THE PRO-LOGGER, ARE FROZEN with fear by the genie's appearance. You stand rooted to the ground like a sturdy tree. As you try to compose yourself, the genie thrusts an arm toward you. Before you can back away, you hear the friendly words "Hello, I'm Genie." The genie has **introduced** himself! You tentatively extend your hand and **introduce** yourself. "Hi, I'm Pro-Logger." These **introductions** represent the final unit associated with the first Landmark. It is THE INTRODUCTIONS found in the Gospels of Mark and Luke.

THE INTRODUCTIONS

Mk 1:1

1 The beginning of the gospel of Jesus Christ [the Son of God].

Lk 1:1–4

1 Since many have undertaken to compile a narrative of the events that have been fulfilled among us, 2 just as those who were eyewitnesses from the beginning and ministers of the word have handed them down to us, 3 I too have decided, after investigating everything accurately anew, to write it down in an orderly sequence for you, most excellent Theophilus, 4 so that you may realize the certainty of the teachings you have received.

Unlike the other synoptic evangelists, Mark did not include a genealogy of Jesus' human ancestors. He was more interested in developing the theme of Jesus as the Son of God. Mark wastes no time. He proclaims this good news in the first verse of his Gospel. The reader knows Jesus' identity immediately. However, in Mark's fast-paced narrative it is not long before he develops the theme of secrecy. Jesus' role as Messiah will unfold in gradual fashion for reasons we will soon discover. This major theme of Jesus being the Son of God comes full circle at the cross when the centurion, a gentile, proclaims "Truly this man was the Son of God!" (Mk 15:39).

Luke introduced his Gospel like typical historical works of his day. He started by stating several facts. Information had been previously written and compiled. He was a recipient of this information. Luke then explained what he had written. His introduction then concluded with an explanation of why he has done so. Luke added that his information is reliable, even though he was not an eyewitness to the events. His wish was that Theophilus ("lover of God") and all who seek the truth will come to have faith through what he has "accurately" written.

Landmark 2:

BICYCLE

The second Landmark is something that you will immediately associate with the number 2. You will then be able to call to mind several more units attached to this Landmark that proclaim the good news about Jesus.

The second Landmark is a two-wheeler, your basic **bicycle**. Nothing too fancy, not a multiple speed, thin-tired, slick racer. It is just two wheels on a simple frame with a seat and handlebars. Imagine yourself sitting on the seat of this basic **bicycle**. Without low gears, it takes some effort to pedal. However, you enjoy the exercise and scenery on the old, but reliable, two-wheeler. Now when you think of the number 2, this **bicycle** will come to mind.

Pedaling the bicycle suddenly gets more difficult. You have taken on a passenger, even though there is only one seat! Sitting on the handlebars and blocking your view is a man named **John**. Now imagine a relative, friend, acquaintance, or a well-known person named **John** sitting inconveniently on your handlebars. The ride on your two-wheeler is no longer enjoyable. It has become burdensome and dangerous with the addition of **John**. While you struggle to maintain balance and some degree of safety, **John** relaxes and takes in the view from his lofty perch. This precarious ride with **John** is a reminder of John the Baptist. More specifically, the next unit is the Ministry and Teaching of John the Baptist.

MINISTRY AND TEACHING OF JOHN
THE BAPTIST

Mt 3:1–12

1 In those days John the Baptist appeared, preaching in the desert of Judea 2 [and] saying, "Repent, for the kingdom of heaven is at hand!" 3 It was of him that the prophet Isaiah had spoken when he said:

"A voice of one crying out in the desert,
'Prepare the way of the Lord,
make straight his paths.'"

4 John wore clothing made of camel's hair and had a leather belt around his waist. His food was locusts and wild honey. 5 At that time Jerusalem, all Judea, and the whole region around the Jordan were going out to him 6 and were being baptized by him in the Jordan River as they acknowledged their sins.

7 When he saw many of the Pharisees and Sadducees coming to his baptism, he said to them, "You brood of vipers! Who warned you to flee from the coming wrath? 8 Produce good fruit as evidence of your repentance. 9 And do not presume to say to yourselves, 'We have Abraham as our father.' For I tell you, God can raise up children to Abraham from these stones. 10 Even now the ax lies at the root of the trees. Therefore every tree that does not bear good fruit will be cut down and thrown into the fire. 11 I am baptizing you with water, for repentance, but the one who is coming after me is mightier than I. I am not worthy to carry his sandals. He will baptize you with the holy Spirit and fire. 12 His winnowing fan is in his hand. He will clear his threshing floor and gather his wheat into his barn, but the chaff he will burn with unquenchable fire."

Mk 1:2–8

2 As it is written in Isaiah the prophet:

"Behold, I am sending my messenger ahead of you;
he will prepare your way.
3 A voice of one crying out in the desert:
'Prepare the way of the Lord,
make straight his paths.'"

4 John [the] Baptist appeared in the desert proclaiming a baptism of repentance for the forgiveness of sins. 5 People of the whole Judean countryside and all the inhabitants of Jerusalem were going out to him and were being baptized by him in the Jordan River as they acknowledged their sins. 6 John was clothed in camel's hair, with a leather belt around his waist. He fed on locusts

and wild honey. **7** And this is what he proclaimed: "One mightier than I is coming after me. I am not worthy to stoop and loosen the thongs of his sandals. **8** I have baptized you with water; he will baptize you with the holy Spirit."

Lk 3:1–18

1 In the fifteenth year of the reign of Tiberius Caesar, when Pontius Pilate was governor of Judea, and Herod was tetrarch of Galilee, and his brother Philip tetrarch of the region of Ituraea and Trachonitis, and Lysanias was tetrarch of Abilene, **2** during the high priesthood of Annas and Caiaphas, the word of God came to John the son of Zechariah in the desert. **3** He went throughout [the] whole region of the Jordan, proclaiming a baptism of repentance for the forgiveness of sins, **4** as it is written in the book of the words of the prophet Isaiah:

"A voice of one crying out in the desert:
'Prepare the way of the Lord,
make straight his paths.
5 Every valley shall be filled
and every mountain and hill shall be made low.
The winding roads shall be made straight,
and the rough ways made smooth,
6 and all flesh shall see the salvation of God.'"

7 He said to the crowds who came out to be baptized by him, "You brood of vipers! Who warned you to flee from the coming wrath? **8** Produce good fruits as evidence of your repentance; and do not begin to say to yourselves, 'We have Abraham as our father,' for I tell you, God can raise up children to Abraham from these stones. **9** Even now the ax lies at the root of the trees. Therefore every tree that does not produce good fruit will be cut down and thrown into the fire."

10 And the crowds asked him, "What then should we do?" **11** He said to them in reply, "Whoever has two cloaks should share with the person who has none. And whoever has food should do likewise." **12** Even tax collectors came to be baptized and they said to him, "Teacher, what should we do?" **13** He answered them, "Stop collecting more than what is prescribed." **14** Soldiers also asked him, "And what is it that we should do?" He told them, "Do not practice extortion, do not falsely accuse anyone, and be satisfied with your wages."

15 Now the people were filled with expectation, and all were asking in their hearts whether John might be the Messiah. **16** John answered them all, saying, "I am baptizing you with water, but one mightier than I is coming. I am not worthy to loosen the thongs of his sandals. He will baptize you with the holy Spirit and fire. **17** His winnowing fan is in his hand to clear his threshing floor and to gather the wheat into his barn, but the chaff he will burn with unquenchable fire." **18** Exhorting them in many other ways, he preached good news to the people.

Jn 1:19–28

19 And this is the testimony of John. When the Jews from Jerusalem sent priests and Levites [to him] to ask him, "Who are you?" **20** he admitted and did not deny it, but admitted, "I am not the Messiah." **21** So they asked him, "What are you then? Are you Elijah?" And he said, "I am not." "Are you the Prophet?" He answered, "No." **22** So they said to him, "Who are you, so we can give an answer to those who sent us? What do you have to say for yourself?" **23** He said:

"I am 'the voice of one crying out in the desert,
"Make straight the way of the Lord'"

as Isaiah the prophet said." **24** Some Pharisees were also sent. **25** They asked him, "Why then do you baptize if you are not the Messiah or Elijah or the Prophet?" **26** John answered them, "I baptize with water; but there is one among you whom you do not recognize, **27** the one who is coming after me, whose sandal strap I am not worthy to untie." **28** This happened in Bethany across the Jordan, where John was baptizing.

Now that the four evangelists have introduced us to Jesus, it is time that Jesus is introduced to the world. John the Baptist performed this role as the fulfillment of prophecies from Isaiah, Exodus, and Malachi. John was the chosen messenger who called for repentance because the long-awaited Messiah had finally arrived. The kingdom of heaven was truly at hand. God's promise of salvation was about to be played out by His Son, who was also the Son of Man, Jesus Christ. Though the genealogy of John the Baptist was not presented, he was described as the "son of Zechariah" and thus of priestly descent.

Luke firmly placed John (and thus Jesus) as coming along at a specific time and place in human history. By doing so, Luke was able to introduce the Roman leaders and their puppets who would become Jesus' enemies.

John's physical appearance and lifestyle were not typical of his priestly lineage. His outfit was reminiscent of Elijah, the great prophet who was expected to return before the Messiah's arrival. John the Baptist explained that he was not Elijah or Moses and that he was especially not the Messiah, whose type of Baptism would be radically different, as different as water is from fire.

John was a fiery yet humble man. Compared to Jesus, he saw himself as less esteemed than a lowly slave. However, this did not keep John from addressing the hypocrisy of the religious leaders. He called them vipers, a symbol of evil. To obtain salvation, neither status nor heritage (being a descendant of Abraham) are sufficient. Salvation will be made available to all—tax collectors, soldiers, and yes, even Gentiles. In preparing the way for the one who would make salvation possible for all, John emphasized the importance of repentance. Repentance is symbolized with the water of Baptism, and is made evident by the production of "good fruit." The image of the winnowing fan indicated that with preparation we will survive the separation at the Final Judgment.

EVENTUALLY IT HAD TO HAPPEN. If you ride a bicycle and cannot see where you are going, there is going to be an accident. Fortunately, neither you nor John, nor anyone else, is injured. In fact, after working up quite a sweat while pedaling for two, the accident was quite refreshing! How could that be? While blindly pedaling with John obstructing your view, you plunge into the chilly and briskly moving water of the local **river**. This dunking topples you from the bicycle. You and John then float downstream together, occasionally bobbing beneath the surface of the **river**. This plunge into the **river** and subsequent periodic dunkings help recall THE BAPTISM OF JESUS in the Jordan River.

THE BAPTISM OF JESUS

Mt 3:13–17

13 Then Jesus came from Galilee to John at the Jordan to be baptized by him. 14 John tried to prevent him, saying, "I need to be baptized by you, and yet you are coming to me?" 15 Jesus said to him in reply, "Allow it now, for thus it is fitting for us to fulfill all righteousness." Then he allowed him. 16 After Jesus was baptized, he came up from the water and behold, the heavens were opened [for him], and he saw the Spirit of God descending like a dove [and] coming upon him. 17 And a voice came from the heavens, saying, "This is my beloved Son, with whom I am well pleased."

Mk 1:9–11

9 It happened in those days that Jesus came from Nazareth of Galilee and was baptized in the Jordan by John. 10 On coming up out of the water he saw the heavens being torn open and the Spirit, like a dove, descending upon him. 11 And a voice came from the heavens, "You are my beloved Son; with you I am well pleased."

Lk 3:21–22

21 After all the people had been baptized and Jesus also had been baptized and was praying, heaven was opened 22 and the holy Spirit descended upon him in bodily form like a dove. And a voice came from heaven, "You are my beloved Son; with you I am well pleased."

Jesus had now taken His first steps on the long, winding, yet purposeful journey to the cross. He had walked the many miles from His home in Nazareth to the bank of the Jordan River. Jesus had arrived where John was baptizing many "for the forgiveness of sins." The Son of God, though born of woman, was without sin. Why would He begin His public ministry in such a contradictory fashion? As we will see time after time, Jesus frequently did the unexpected or paradoxical. His behavior was often seen as shocking to those privileged to see Him up close. The powerful, militaristic Messiah He was not!

Jesus had become man. By submitting to be baptized by John, He identified with us, the sinners that He had come to save. Jesus, the Son of God, had been sent to fulfill His Father's plan. He showed obedience to the fulfillment of this plan by submitting to the Baptism by John in the very waters the Israelites had crossed long ago to enter the Promised Land. His Father was "well pleased" with this action of solidarity and humility.

Luke describes Jesus in prayer with His Father after rising from the water. On our walk with Jesus, we will see Him in prayer at times of special significance. At this moment, the heavens were opened as if to show a closer connection between God and man, brought about by Jesus' action. From the heavens, the Spirit of God descended upon Jesus in the form of a dove. It is uncertain if this was a private event between Father and Son. Perhaps those nearby who were newly baptized with the eyes of faith were also able to see. Jesus, as the Son of God, and being one with God and the Holy Spirit, had already possessed the Spirit. However, this scene with all three persons of the Trinity present seems to be the perfect inauguration of Jesus' earthly ministry.

TAKEN BY THE CURRENT, YOU begin to float downstream. Soon you and John become separated, though you will see him again. For now, you continue down the river alone. Before long, the chilly water begins to take its toll. You start to shiver. Fatigue has set in. You need to swim to shore. With some effort, you reach the riverbank and climb out onto dry land. You begin to warm up instantly. The ground is not only dry, but quite warm. Actually, it is hot! You have come ashore in a **desert**. Looking around, you see parched land dotted with clumps of brush. As you walk across the **desert** toward a large cactus, the scalding sand burns your feet. This **desert** scene triggers your memory of JESUS' TEMPTATION IN THE DESERT immediately after His Baptism.

JESUS' TEMPTATION IN THE DESERT

Mt 4:1–11

1 Then Jesus was led by the Spirit into the desert to be tempted by the devil. **2** He fasted for forty days and forty nights, and afterwards he was hungry. **3** The tempter approached and said to him, "If you are the Son of God, command that these stones become loaves of bread." **4** He said in reply, "It is written:

'One does not live by bread alone,
but by every word that comes forth from the mouth of God.'"

5 Then the devil took him to the holy city, and made him stand on the parapet of the temple, **6** and said to him, "If you are the Son of God, throw yourself down. For it is written:

'He will command his angels concerning you
and 'with their hands they will support you,
lest you dash your foot against a stone.'"

7 Jesus answered him, "Again it is written, 'You shall not put the Lord, your God, to the test.'" **8** Then the devil took him up to a very high mountain, and showed him all the kingdoms of the world in their magnificence, **9** and he said to him, "All these I shall give to you, if you will prostrate yourself and worship me." **10** At this, Jesus said to him, "Get away, Satan! It is written:

'The Lord, your God, shall you worship
and him alone shall you serve.'"

11 Then the devil left him and, behold, angels came and ministered to him.

Mk 1:12–13

12 At once the Spirit drove him out into the desert, **13** and he remained in the desert for forty days, tempted by Satan. He was among wild beasts, and the angels ministered to him.

Lk 4:1–13

1 Filled with the holy Spirit, Jesus returned from the Jordan and was led by the Spirit into the desert **2** for forty days, to be tempted by the devil. He ate nothing during those days, and when they were over he was hungry. **3** The devil said to him, "If you are the Son of God, command this stone to become bread." **4** Jesus answered him, "It is written, 'One does not live by bread alone.'" **5** Then he took him up and showed him all the kingdoms of the world in a single instant. **6** The devil said to him, "I shall give to you all this power and their glory; for it has been handed over to me, and I may give it to whomever I wish. **7** All this will be yours, if you worship me." **8** Jesus said to him in reply, "It is written:

'You shall worship the Lord, your God,
and him alone shall you serve.'"

9 Then he led him to Jerusalem, made him stand on the parapet of the temple, and said to him, "If you are the Son of God, throw yourself down from here, **10** for it is written:

'He will command his angels concerning you,
to guard you,'

11 and:

'With their hands they will support you,
lest you dash your foot against a stone.'"

12 Jesus said to him in reply, "It also says, 'You shall not put the Lord, your God, to the test.'" **13** When the devil had finished every temptation, he departed from him for a time.

We just saw the Son of God's obedience to His Father by receiving the strengthening gift of the Spirit in Baptism. Jesus would now endure forty days in the desert. As a man of flesh and blood, He will experience physical suffering and mental temptations.

It is no coincidence that this period of testing and preparation for Jesus' upcoming ministry lasted forty days. It was a common theme for God to test the chosen for forty days. Noah and his family weathered the deluge inside the ark for forty days. Moses fasted on Mount Sinai for forty days. Likewise, Elijah fasted for forty days. The people of Nineveh were given forty days to repent after the preaching of Jonah. We, too, are given forty days of Lent each year to repent and prepare for the crucifixion and resurrection of Jesus. Lastly, it was not forty days, but forty years that the Israelites struggled in the desert before entering the Promised Land.

Though the Israelites repeatedly succumbed to temptation during their sojourn in the desert, Jesus did not. Satan initially tempted the hungry Jesus to produce bread from desert stones. Jesus refused and quoted Deuteronomy 8:3, reminding us that the Word of God provides true nourishment. Satan then turned to Scripture, and tempted Jesus by incorrectly quoting from Psalm 91. He suggested that Jesus test God. Jesus' response was again from Deuteronomy (6:16), saying that we are to put our trust in God, not test Him. Satan finally tried to tempt Jesus away from the difficult path of suffering that He was about to walk. It would be so much easier to be an earthly conqueror and lead a life of wealth and power. Jesus declined and chose to honor His Father and complete the mission for which He was sent. Worshiping the Lord God leads to an everlasting Kingdom, while the kingdoms of earth last but an instant.

WALKING THROUGH THE HOT, DRY desert is quite a contrast to your experience in the cool, refreshing river. You are careful not to step on a snake or back into a thorny cactus as you work your way across the desert. Finally, the end is in sight, but so is something else, which you find quite disturbing. A small **lamb** was apparently not as careful as you. Its white fleece is knotted and tangled, caught in a small prickly cactus. The helpless **lamb** is struggling to free itself, bleating in despair. You come to the rescue of the unfortunate **lamb**. After a few minutes of delicate effort, the **lamb** is free. It licks your scratched hands in appreciation and trots off. This encounter with the **lamb** symbolizes the final unit associated with the bicycle Landmark. It is when John the Baptist declares that Jesus is THE LAMB OF GOD.

THE LAMB OF GOD

Jn 1:29–34

29 The next day he saw Jesus coming toward him and said, "Behold, the Lamb of God, who takes away the sin of the world. **30** He is the one of whom I said, 'A man is coming after me who ranks ahead of me because he existed before me.' **31** I did not know him, but the reason why I came baptizing with water was that he might be made known to Israel." **32** John testified further, saying, "I saw the Spirit come down like a dove from the sky and remain upon him. **33** I did not know him, but the one who sent me to baptize with water told me, 'On whomever you see the Spirit come down and remain, he is the one who will baptize with the holy Spirit.' **34** Now I have seen and testified that he is the Son of God."

This unit, like many to follow, is found only in the Gospel of John. John the evangelist did not write about the Baptism of Jesus. Describing the sinless Son of God receiving a Baptism of repentance was not part of his picture of the Messiah. He chose to emphasize the superiority of Jesus by reiterating what he had said in the Prologue. Here, John the Baptist prophesizes that Jesus is the Lamb of God by quoting the powerful imagery from Isaiah 53:7–12. Jesus is the sacrificial lamb, whose blood would be shed for our protection from the Angel of Death. He would be led to slaughter on Calvary so that we might live. John the Baptist says that he knows this to be true, having seen Jesus receive the gift of the Spirit. It is this Spirit that will remain with Jesus, giving Him the strength for what lies ahead. John concludes by testifying that Jesus is the "Son of God," as Mark had proclaimed in his opening verse.

Landmark 3:

TRIANGLE

The next Landmark is now looming in the distance. As you approach, its familiar shape immediately makes you think of the number 3. It is the outline of a **triangle**, though not just any triangle. It is quite large, measuring three meters on each of its three sides. The triangle is made of aluminum, so it is both bright and light. Reaching out, you gently run your hand along its cool, smooth surface. You feel strangely drawn to the **triangle** and decide to hold on to it. With little effort, you hoist it overhead and continue to walk. Others see a strange sight when you pass by with a large, shiny aluminum **triangle** held aloft. However, for you the **triangle** held above your head feels quite natural. This large **triangle** is your third Landmark.

You are such a curiosity carrying the triangle above your head that several men begin to follow behind you. These **followers** ask numerous questions about you and your triangle. You patiently respond, but the questions persist. Soon the questioning turns to heckling, and you become annoyed. Finally, you can't stand it any longer. Turning, you face the **followers** and ask them to come closer. They do. Quickly, you lower the triangle, trapping them within its perimeter. They become silent. These **followers** are now attracted to the triangle and are overtaken by its mysterious spell. This story of the **followers** now within the triangle is the first unit associated with the triangle Landmark: Jesus' First Followers.

JESUS' FIRST FOLLOWERS

Jn 1:35–51

35 The next day John was there again with two of his disciples, **36** and as he watched Jesus walk by, he said, "Behold, the Lamb of God." **37** The two disciples heard what he said and followed Jesus.

38 Jesus turned and saw them following him and said to them, "What are you looking for?" They said to him, "Rabbi" (which translated means Teacher), "where are you staying?" **39** He said to them, "Come, and you will see." So they went and saw where he was staying, and they stayed with him that day. It was about four in the afternoon. **40** Andrew, the brother of Simon Peter, was one of the two who heard John and followed Jesus. **41** He first found his own brother Simon and told him, "We have found the Messiah" (which is translated Anointed). **42** Then he brought him to Jesus. Jesus looked at him and said, "You are Simon the son of John; you will be called Cephas" (which is translated Peter).

43 The next day he decided to go to Galilee, and he found Philip. And Jesus said to him, "Follow me." **44** Now Philip was from Bethsaida, the town of Andrew and Peter. **45** Philip found Nathanael and told him, "We have found the one about whom Moses wrote in the law, and also the prophets, Jesus, son of Joseph, from Nazareth." **46** But Nathanael said to him, "Can anything good come from Nazareth?" Philip said to him, "Come and see." **47** Jesus saw Nathanael coming toward him and said of him, "Here is a true Israelite. There is no duplicity in him." **48** Nathanael said to him, "How do you know me?" Jesus answered and said to him, "Before Philip called you, I saw you under the fig tree." **49** Nathanael answered him, "Rabbi, you are the Son of God; you are the King of Israel." **50** Jesus answered and said to him, "Do you believe because I told you that I saw you under the fig tree? You will see greater things than this." **51** And he said to him, "Amen, amen, I say to you, you will see the sky opened and the angels of God ascending and descending on the Son of Man."

This unit, like the final unit of Landmark 2, consists of material found only in John's Gospel. John the Baptist's testimony about Jesus continues the next day. While talking to two of his own disciples, John again identifies Jesus using the powerful yet humble title, Lamb of God. The two disciples Andrew, and likely John (the evangelist himself), are impressed by this endorsement. They are quick to follow Jesus. John was probably pleased, because his mission of preparation was bearing fruit. They followed Jesus to where He was staying during this visit to Jerusalem. After being with Jesus for several hours, Andrew could no longer contain his excitement. He had to share it. Naturally, he went to his brother Simon with the good news. Upon meeting Jesus, Simon's life, as well as his name, was forever changed. Simon became Cephas, or Peter. These names, meaning "rock" in Aramaic and Greek respectively, signified the rock he would become in the early Christian Church.

Before returning to Galilee the next day, Jesus added two more followers to His small but growing group. He first called Philip, who was likely already known to Peter and Andrew since they all came from Bethsaida. Philip, like Andrew on the previous day, was compelled to share his excitement. He found his friend Nathanael, also known as Bartholomew. At first, Nathanael seemed less impressed, but Jesus greeted him with a compliment. Nathanael is called "a true Israelite," someone descended from Jacob, the great patriarch. Jacob, like Simon, had also been given a new name (after his wrestling match with an angel), Israel, meaning "one who sees God." Jesus responded to Nathanael's query as to how He knew him with another reference from Scripture. Seeing Nathanael "under the fig tree" is a reference to the time of the Messiah (Zech 3:10). Nathanael had heard enough. He professed Jesus to be the Son of God. Jesus concludes this unit with another reference to Jacob and his "ladder vision" in Genesis 28. This ladder connected heaven and earth. Jesus, the Son of God, is now in the process of doing the same.

NOW YOU HAVE CREATED AN even stranger scene. Walking on, you pull the large aluminum triangle behind you with the men walking in step inside its perimeter. You forge forward, unburdened and untroubled. You are blinded to the spectacle, for you are on a mission. Your plan is to attend a **wedding** and present the triangle as a gift to your friend, the bride. Unfortunately, due to your encounter with the followers, you are running late. Finally, you, the triangle, and the followers arrive at the outdoor venue where the **wedding** is being held. Though late, you and your entourage go and stand up front with the **wedding** party. This rather rude **wedding** entrance is a reminder of the next unit: THE WEDDING AT CANA.

THE WEDDING AT CANA

Jn 2:1–12

1 On the third day there was a wedding in Cana in Galilee, and the mother of Jesus was there. 2 Jesus and his disciples were also invited to the wedding. 3 When the wine ran short, the mother of Jesus said to him, "They have no wine." 4 [And] Jesus said to her, "Woman, how does your concern affect me? My hour has not yet come." 5 His mother said to the servers, "Do whatever he tells you." 6 Now there were six stone water jars there for Jewish ceremonial washings, each holding twenty to thirty gallons. 7 Jesus told them, "Fill the jars with water." So they filled them to the brim. 8 Then he told them, "Draw some out now and take it to the headwaiter." So they took it. 9 And when the headwaiter tasted the water that had become wine, without knowing where it came from (although the servers who had drawn the water knew), the headwaiter called the bridegroom 10 and said to him, "Everyone serves good wine first, and then when people have drunk freely, an inferior one; but you have kept the good wine until now." 11 Jesus did this as the beginning of his signs in Cana in Galilee and so revealed his glory, and his disciples began to believe in him.

12 After this, he and his mother, [his] brothers, and his disciples went down to Capernaum and stayed there only a few days.

———————————

Jesus and His group of followers have now been together for three days. It is on this third day that Jesus' power over life is first manifest. At the end of this long journey, we will witness Jesus' power over death again made manifest after three days. Jesus' return from Jerusalem to Cana in Galilee was prompted by a prior social commitment. Cana was just several miles down the road from Nazareth, and Jesus wanted to honor the request for His presence at the wedding of a friend. Jesus responded to another request while at the wedding. His mother wanted to avoid embarrassing the bride and groom for running out of wine. Jesus did not want to steal the thunder at a friend's wedding with His first miracle, but He was obedient to His mother's request. Mary showed complete faith in her Son's ability to do whatever was necessary. As we will see time and again, faith in Jesus leads to great things. After the servants filled the large vessels, Jesus, the Word of God, turned the water into wine without a word. The jars, which normally contained water to fulfill Jewish washing rituals, now contained the fruit of the vine. Wine would become a symbol of the new covenant between God and His people. The old will become new through Jesus' actions. Jesus Himself is the new wine provided by the Father to make the final Messianic Banquet possible for us. Jesus does not just provide sufficient wine to allow the wedding feast to end without embarrassment or empty cups. His love and generosity provided an extravagant amount of superior wine. The stone jars full of wine would have been enough to fill five thousand cups. This is a number we will again encounter as it relates to Jesus' generous provision. This first miracle, as well as the later multiplication of the loaves, both foreshadow the momentous events of the Lord's Supper.

YOU HAVE MADE QUITE AN impression at the wedding. Your intrusion with the triangle-enclosed followers is seen as outrageous. This is especially true for the man who happens to be standing next to you. However, this is no ordinary man! It is none other than jolly old Saint **Nick**. He is attired in his red velvet suit with white trim. However, Saint **Nick** is jolly no more. His angry face is even redder than his suit. You have quickly gone right to the top of Saint **Nick's** naughty list. The presence of Saint **Nick**, and his reaction to you, helps recall the conversation between JESUS AND NICODEMUS.

||||||||||||||||||||||||||||||||||||||||||||||||||||||||||||||||||||||||||||||||||||||||||||||||||||||||||||||||||||||||||||||||||

JESUS AND NICODEMUS

||||||||||||||||||||||||||||||||||||||||||||||||||||||||||||||||||||||||||||||||||||||||||||||||||||||||||||||||||||||||||||||||||

Jn 3:1–21

1 Now there was a Pharisee named Nicodemus, a ruler of the Jews. 2 He came to Jesus at night and said to him, "Rabbi, we know that you are a teacher who has come from God, for no one can do these signs that you are doing unless God is with him." 3 Jesus answered and said to him, "Amen, amen, I say to you, no one can see the kingdom of God without being born from above." 4 Nicodemus said to him, "How can a person once grown old be born again? Surely he cannot reenter his mother's womb and be born again, can he?" 5 Jesus answered, "Amen, amen, I say to you, no one can enter the kingdom of God without being born of water and Spirit. 6 What is born of flesh is flesh and what is born of spirit is spirit. 7 Do not be amazed that I told you, 'You must be born from above.' 8 The wind blows where it wills, and you can

hear the sound it makes, but you do not know where it comes from or where it goes; so it is with everyone who is born of the Spirit." **9** Nicodemus answered and said to him, "How can this happen?" **10** Jesus answered and said to him, "You are the teacher of Israel and you do not understand this? **11** Amen, amen, I say to you, we speak of what we know and we testify to what we have seen, but you people do not accept our testimony. **12** If I tell you about earthly things and you do not believe, how will you believe if I tell you about heavenly things? **13** No one has gone up to heaven except the one who has come down from heaven, the Son of Man. **14** And just as Moses lifted up the serpent in the desert, so must the Son of Man be lifted up, **15** so that everyone who believes in him may have eternal life."

16 For God so loved the world that he gave his only Son, so that everyone who believes in him might not perish but might have eternal life. **17** For God did not send his Son into the world to condemn the world, but that the world might be saved through him. **18** Whoever believes in him will not be condemned, but whoever does not believe has already been condemned, because he has not believed in the name of the only Son of God. **19** And this is the verdict, that the light came into the world, but people preferred darkness to light, because their works were evil. **20** For everyone who does wicked things hates the light and does not come toward the light, so that his works might not be exposed. **21** But whoever lives the truth comes to the light, so that his works may be clearly seen as done in God.

On your walk with Jesus, you will meet a variety of religious figures. This first encounter with a Pharisee is quite different from the typical interactions Jesus will have with members of this Jewish sect. *Pharisee*, which means "separated one," defines their purpose. During this time of Roman occupation, they were particularly concerned with the impurity of all things Gentile. They were preoccupied, actually obsessed, with rituals to ensure "purity." Their laws concerning various rituals were often at the heart of their interactions with Jesus. Their Old Covenant judgmental mindset frequently conflicted with the New Covenant love and acceptance of Jesus.

The Pharisee Nicodemus was an exception. He recognized Jesus as a teacher "from God," though not "the Son of God." Jesus proceeded to teach him the now very familiar concept of being "born again" (or as sometimes translated, "from above"). Nicodemus was confused by this concept of a spiritual rebirth. Jesus' elaboration that this involves water and the Spirit, rather than a physical process, raised questions in his mind. As you travel with Jesus, you will hear more teachings about the gift of the Spirit that acts as the agent in this process of rebirth. Jesus said things to Nicodemus that probably made his head spin. Jesus was the "Son of Man" who had come down from heaven, and as such was the source of knowledge about heaven. His reference to being "lifted up" on the cross so that this heavenly gift of eternal life might be ours must have left Nicodemus speechless!

Jesus then uttered what is probably the most quoted verse in the Bible. The extent of God's love for us is overwhelming. It cannot be described in mere words. Like all love, it is best conveyed by action. What action could be more meaningful than total self-sacrifice? God our Creator gave totally of Himself for our sake through a literal sacrifice of His Son, Jesus Christ! Understanding the true meaning of this should leave us all speechless.

BEFORE SAINT NICK CAN ASK why you are at the wedding, you put the same question to him. "Why are you here **witnessing** wedding joys rather than supervising the making of toys?" Saint Nick replies that you have answered your own question. He was invited to be the official **witness.** This talk about **witnessing** and the role of Saint Nick as the official **witness** represents the next unit: THE FINAL WITNESS OF JOHN.

THE FINAL WITNESS OF JOHN

Jn 3:22–4:3

22 After this, Jesus and his disciples went into the region of Judea, where he spent some time with them baptizing. 23 John was also baptizing in Aenon near Salim, because there was an abundance of water there, and people came to be baptized, 24 for John had not yet been imprisoned. 25 Now a dispute arose between the disciples of John and a Jew about ceremonial washings. 26 So they came to John and said to him, "Rabbi, the one who was with you across the Jordan, to whom you testified, here he is baptizing and everyone is coming to him." 27 John answered and said, "No one can receive anything except what has been given him from heaven. 28 You yourselves can testify that I said [that] I am not the Messiah, but that I was sent before him. 29 The one who has the bride is the bridegroom; the best man, who stands and listens for

him, rejoices greatly at the bridegroom's voice. So this joy of mine has been made complete. **30** He must increase; I must decrease."

31 The one who comes from above is above all. The one who is of the earth is earthly and speaks of earthly things. But the one who comes from heaven [is above all]. **32** He testifies to what he has seen and heard, but no one accepts his testimony. **33** Whoever does accept his testimony certifies that God is trustworthy. **34** For the one whom God sent speaks the words of God. He does not ration his gift of the Spirit. **35** The Father loves the Son and has given everything over to him. **36** Whoever believes in the Son has eternal life, but whoever disobeys the Son will not see life, but the wrath of God remains upon him.

1 Now when Jesus learned that the Pharisees had heard that Jesus was making and baptizing more disciples than John **2** (although Jesus himself was not baptizing, just his disciples), **3** he left Judea and returned to Galilee.

John's ministry of baptizing and heralding the coming of Jesus did not end with Jesus at the Jordan. John continued to proclaim Jesus and His primacy. John was approached with a concern about Old Covenant ceremonial washings, the type of rituals for which the Cana water jars were used. This gave John another opportunity to humble himself and emphasize what was most important: Jesus. John was the best man, and Jesus was the bridegroom. It was in Jesus that everyone, including John's own disciples, should rejoice. It was Jesus (not John) who had come down from heaven. Though a great prophet and a man of God, John was as nothing compared to this man who was also God's Son. It is faith in the spirit-filled Jesus, made manifest at His Baptism, that leads to eternal life.

IT HAS BECOME CLEAR FROM the conversation with St. Nick and the disapproving looks of many of the guests that you are not welcome at the wedding. You decide it is best for all, including your friend the bride, that you make an exit. Leaving the triangle and your followers behind, you begin to walk away. Immediately, there is a firm tap on your shoulder accompanied by an authoritative order, "Stop!" You're shocked when you turn around and see several police officers. It feels like you are being **arrested**. The feeling is confirmed when an officer barks, "You are under **arrest** for inappropriate wedding behavior." You cannot believe that you are being **arrested** on such a charge. However, the tight steel handcuffs make you a believer. This surprising scene serves as a reminder of THE ARREST OF JOHN THE BAPTIST.

THE ARREST OF JOHN THE BAPTIST

Mt 4:12

12 When he heard that John had been arrested, he withdrew to Galilee.

Mk 1:14

14 After John had been arrested, Jesus came to Galilee proclaiming the gospel of God.

Lk 3:19–20

19 Now Herod the tetrarch, who had been censured by him because of Herodias, his brother's wife, and because of all the evil deeds Herod had committed, 20 added still another to these by [also] putting John in prison.

During this early stage of the journey, we have heard the powerful words of John the Baptist on several occasions. Preaching was his mission. He introduced the long-awaited Messiah. However, his words would lead to his death. Not his words of preparation, but words of condemnation. He had publicly criticized Herod Antipas for his adulterous marriage. Herod had divorced his wife to marry Herodius, who had been the wife of his half-brother Philip. According to Jewish Law, this was adultery, since Philip was still alive. The angry Herod had John thrown into prison for his criticism. Here he would remain until the evil Herod sent for his head. This imprisonment was Jesus' cue to return to Galilee and formally begin His ministry. Up to this point, Jesus had also attracted some followers. In fact, they had been doing some baptizing, as well.

HOW HUMILIATING! BEING ARRESTED AT a wedding had not been on your agenda. The painful handcuffs on your wrists just add injury to the insult. As you are escorted from the wedding by the officers, there is a sudden but welcome turn of events. Someone very unexpected is running to the rescue. It is a Japanese **samurai** warrior! Charging with long sword held aloft and a longer robe flowing in the breeze, he is a formidable sight. The officers run away, yelling in fear. Upon reaching you, the **samurai** stops, a broad smile covers his face, and he motions for you to extend your shackled wrists. You oblige. With one quick motion of the sword, the handcuffs are on the ground. The **samurai** represents the last unit you will associate with the triangle Landmark. *Samurai*, both now and in later units, is a soundalike reminder of "Samaritan." In this case, it helps you recall Jesus' encounter with THE SAMARITAN WOMAN. This occurs on Jesus' return to Galilee.

THE SAMARITAN WOMAN

Jn 4:4–42

4 He had to pass through Samaria. **5** So he came to a town of Samaria called Sychar, near the plot of land that Jacob had given to his son Joseph. **6** Jacob's well was there. Jesus, tired from his journey, sat down there at the well. It was about noon.

7 A woman of Samaria came to draw water. Jesus said to her, "Give me a drink." **8** His disciples had gone into the town to buy food. **9** The Samaritan woman said to him, "How can you, a Jew, ask me, a Samaritan woman, for a drink?" (For Jews use nothing in common with Samaritans.) **10** Jesus answered and said to her, "If you knew the gift of God and who is saying to you, 'Give me a drink,' you would have asked him and he would have given you living water." **11** [The woman] said to him, "Sir, you do not even have a bucket and the cistern is deep; where then can you get this living water? **12** Are you greater than our father Jacob, who gave us this cistern and drank from it himself with his children and his flocks?" **13** Jesus answered and said to her, "Everyone who drinks this water will be thirsty again; **14** but whoever drinks the water I shall give will never thirst; the water I shall give will become in him a spring of water welling up to eternal life." **15** The woman said to him, "Sir, give me this water, so that I may not be thirsty or have to keep coming here to draw water."

16 Jesus said to her, "Go call your husband and come back." **17** The woman answered and said to him, "I do not have a husband." Jesus answered her, "You are right in saying, 'I do not have a husband.' **18** For you have had five husbands, and the one you have now is not your husband. What you have said is true." **19** The woman said to him, "Sir, I can see that you are a prophet. **20** Our ancestors worshiped on this mountain; but you people say that the place to worship is in Jerusalem." **21** Jesus said to her, "Believe me, woman, the hour is coming when you will worship the Father neither on this mountain nor in Jerusalem. **22** You people worship what you do not understand; we worship what we understand, because salvation is from the Jews. **23** But the hour is coming, and is now here, when true worshipers will worship the Father in Spirit and truth; and indeed the Father seeks such people to worship him. **24** God is Spirit, and those who worship him must worship in Spirit and truth." **25** The woman said to him, "I know that the Messiah is coming, the one called the Anointed; when he comes, he will tell us everything." **26** Jesus said to her, "I am he, the one who is speaking with you."

27 At that moment his disciples returned, and were amazed that he was talking with a woman, but still no one said, "What are you looking for?" or "Why are you talking with her?" **28** The woman left her water jar and went into the town and said to the people, **29** "Come see a man who told me everything I have done. Could he possibly be the Messiah?" **30** They went out of the town and came to him. **31** Meanwhile, the disciples urged him, "Rabbi, eat." **32** But he said to them, "I have food to eat of which you do not know." **33** So the disciples said to one another, "Could someone have brought him something to eat?" **34** Jesus said to them, "My food is to do the will of the one who sent me and to finish his work. **35** Do you not say, 'In four months the harvest will be here'? I tell you, look up and see the fields ripe for the harvest. **36** The reaper is already receiving his payment and gathering crops for eternal life, so that the sower and reaper can rejoice together. **37** For here the saying is verified that 'One sows and another reaps.' **38** I sent you to reap what you have not worked for; others have done the work, and you are sharing the fruits of their work."

39 Many of the Samaritans of that town began to believe in him because of the word of the woman who testified, "He told me everything I have done." **40** When the Samaritans came to him, they invited him to stay with them; and he stayed there two days. **41** Many more began to believe in him because of his word, **42** and they said to the woman, "We no longer believe because of your word; for we have heard for ourselves, and we know that this is truly the savior of the world."

Between Jerusalem in Judea and Jesus' home of Nazareth in Galilee was the land of Samaria with its "unclean" residents. There had been animosity between Jews and Samaritans for many, many years. When this part of Palestine was conquered by the Assyrians more than seven hundred years earlier, most of the Jews were deported. Foreigners from five other areas (Babylon, Cuthah, Avva, Hamath, and Sepharvaim—2 Kings 17:24) settled the land. The Jews who were left behind intermarried with these pagan immigrants and adopted their customs. As a result, they and future generations had been considered "unclean." Jews typically avoided this tainted land in their travels by taking an indirect north-south route along the Jordan River. Not Jesus! In choosing to pass through Samaria with His followers, Jesus had sent several messages even before His formal ministry in Galilee began. The Old Law and its concerns about impurity were a thing of the past. More importantly, He had come as the Savior of all people, not just the Jews.

Jesus' encounter in Samaria proved to be a trifecta of impurity. His speaking in public with a woman who was not only a Samaritan but a known sinner must have raised some eyebrows. She was surely surprised when this Jewish man asked her for water. More surprising was His talk of "living water." However, the longer they talked the more she came to understand. Jesus' knowledge of her past led her to acknowledge Him as a prophet. Her marital history of five husbands paralleled Samaria's history of intermarrying with the five foreigners who had settled the land. When she spoke of her belief in a coming Messiah, Jesus kept no secret by responding "I am He." It was no coincidence that He spoke the words "I Am," the name for God long used by the Hebrew people. Finally, the disciples returned with food. The Samaritan woman ran off to become the often-cited "first missionary."

It was now the disciples' turn to be confused. The Samaritan woman had misunderstood Jesus regarding water. The disciples had misunderstood the meaning of food. Jesus was nourished by doing the will of His Father, who had sent Him into the world. He had begun to implement the Father's plan of "gathering crops for eternal life." This plan would soon begin in earnest in the familiar towns and countryside of Galilee.

Landmark 4:

TABLE

You now travel on to Landmark 4. It will be a common item that comes to mind when thinking of the number 4. It is something that almost everyone sees and uses every day. It is associated with the number 4 because it has four legs. It is a simple **table**. Imagine any **table** that you are familiar with or one you would like to have, just make sure it has four legs. This **table** is your fourth Landmark.

You are now thinking of the number 4 and its associated Landmark, the four-legged table. As you approach the table, you can see that something has been placed on it. Close inspection reveals it to be a rather odd item. It is a plastic **gallon** container that typically contains milk. To your surprise, there is no milk inside. The **gallon** jug is full of disc-shaped **mints**. Someone with a sweet tooth has stuffed the **gallon** container with **mints**. A **gallon** of **mints** sits upon the table. You are pleased to be reminded of the first unit associated with the fourth Landmark: THE BEGINNING OF THE GALILEAN (GALLON) MINISTRY (MINTS).

THE BEGINNING OF THE GALILEAN MINISTRY

Mt 4:12–17

12 When he heard that John had been arrested, he withdrew to Galilee. **13** He left Nazareth and went to live in Capernaum by the sea, in the region of Zebulun and Naphtali, **14** that what had been said through Isaiah the prophet might be fulfilled:

15 "Land of Zebulun and land of Naphtali,
the way to the sea, beyond the Jordan,
Galilee of the Gentiles,

16 the people who sit in darkness
have seen a great light,
on those dwelling in a land overshadowed by death
light has arisen."

17 From that time on, Jesus began to preach and say, "Repent, for the kingdom of heaven is at hand."

Mk 1:14–15

14 After John had been arrested, Jesus came to Galilee proclaiming the gospel of God: **15** "This is the time of fulfillment. The kingdom of God is at hand. Repent, and believe in the gospel."

Lk 4:14–15

14 Jesus returned to Galilee in the power of the Spirit, and news of him spread throughout the whole region. **15** He taught in their synagogues and was praised by all.

Jn 4:43–45

43 After the two days, he left there for Galilee. **44** For Jesus himself testified that a prophet has no honor in his native place. **45** When he came into Galilee, the Galileans welcomed him, since they had seen all he had done in Jerusalem at the feast; for they themselves had gone to the feast.

You have already heard Jesus begin His ministry of teaching. His words to His first followers in Jerusalem, to Nicodemus, and the Samaritan woman still echo in your ears. You have also witnessed His first miracle at the wedding feast in Cana. Now in Capernaum, some eighty miles from Jerusalem, Jesus begins His Galilean ministry. It is here in Galilee where most of Jesus' three years of public ministry take place.

Capernaum was a town of about 15,000 people on the northwest coast of the Sea of Galilee. It was in the "Land of Naphtali," one of the Twelve Tribes of ancient Israel. The people of this land had "walked in darkness" for many years after the Assyrian conquest 750 years earlier. Now with Jesus, "the light of the world," establishing a home base here for His ministry, the familiar words of Isaiah 8:23–9:2 were being fulfilled.

Though Jesus had been busy in Jerusalem, Cana, and Samaria, He returned to Galilee with renewed strength to begin this critical aspect of His ministry. He came with the strength of the Spirit bestowed upon Him by His Father at His Baptism in the Jordan. Though it had been physically draining, Jesus had gained emotional and spiritual strength from His forty-day trial in the desert.

Jesus' first words in Capernaum recorded by Mark and Matthew set the tone for His entire ministry. Jesus' coming marked the beginning of the "time of fulfillment." It was the time that had been hoped for and prophesized about for centuries. The kingdom of God (heaven) in the form of Jesus had broken into human history. Jesus came to proclaim and make possible our future entry into the kingdom with Him. In order to participate in this show of God's love, we need a "change of mind." We need to repent and believe in the Gospel, the good news that Jesus was soon to proclaim throughout Galilee.

YOU ARE SURPRISED TO FIND the gallon of mints. Though tempted to claim them, you realize that they must belong to someone. Finding their owner would be best. You decide to begin the search by making a phone **call**. However, you are without a cell phone or money to use the nearby pay phone for the **call**. You hesitate momentarily before realizing you can use one of the disc-shaped mints as a coin to make the **call**. You tilt the gallon jug, and out comes a mint. You walk over to the pay phone and place a **call**. This strange, but hopefully memorable scene of making a **call** represents the unit when JESUS CALLS THE FIRST DISCIPLES. (Note that this is a very different event from the description of Jesus' first followers in the previous Landmark.)

JESUS CALLS THE FIRST DISCIPLES

Mt 4:18–22

18 As he was walking by the Sea of Galilee, he saw two brothers, Simon who is called Peter, and his brother Andrew, casting a net into the sea; they were fishermen. 19 He said to them, "Come after me, and I will make you fishers of men." 20 At once they left their nets and followed him. 21 He walked along from there and saw two other brothers, James, the son of Zebedee, and his brother John. They were in a boat, with their father Zebedee, mending their nets.

He called them, **22** and immediately they left their boat and their father and followed him.

Mk 1:16–20

16 As he passed by the Sea of Galilee, he saw Simon and his brother Andrew casting their nets into the sea; they were fishermen. **17** Jesus said to them, "Come after me, and I will make you fishers of men." **18** Then they abandoned their nets and followed him. **19** He walked along a little farther and saw James, the son of Zebedee, and his brother John. They too were in a boat mending their nets. **20** Then he called them. So they left their father Zebedee in the boat along with the hired men and followed him.

Lk 5:1–11

1 While the crowd was pressing in on Jesus and listening to the word of God, he was standing by the Lake of Gennesaret. **2** He saw two boats there alongside the lake; the fishermen had disembarked and were washing their nets. **3** Getting into one of the boats, the one belonging to Simon, he asked him to put out a short distance from the shore. Then he sat down and taught the crowds from the boat. **4** After he had finished speaking, he said to Simon, "Put out into deep water and lower your nets for a catch." **5** Simon said in reply, "Master, we have worked hard all night and have caught nothing, but at your command I will lower the nets." **6** When they had done this, they caught a great number of fish and their nets were tearing. **7** They signaled to their partners in the other boat to come to help them. They came and filled both boats so that they were in danger of sinking. **8** When Simon Peter saw this, he fell at the knees of Jesus and said, "Depart from me, Lord, for I am a sinful man." **9** For astonishment at the catch of fish they had made seized him and all those with him, **10** and likewise James and John, the sons of Zebedee, who were partners of Simon. Jesus said to Simon, "Do not be afraid; from now on you will be catching men." **11** When they brought their boats to the shore, they left everything and followed him.

We know from prior units that Jesus already had several followers. Peter, Andrew, John, Philip, and Nathanael had spent time with Jesus in Jerusalem. They had heard His teaching and witnessed the miracle in Cana. Now at the outset of His Galilean ministry, Jesus issued a more formal call to four fishermen. Three of whom were from that original group.

These two sets of brothers had been leading busy lives as fishermen when they heard Jesus issue the formal call of "come after Me." Their response was immediate. They did not hesitate to leave their lives of security to follow the uncertain path of someone they had only recently met. The charisma and message of this man from Nazareth must have been overwhelming.

Luke's account of this unit is quite different from that of Matthew and Mark. However, it is strikingly similar to a much later appearance of Jesus described by John. In Luke's version of the call of the first disciples, Simon (Peter) takes center stage. Luke, more than the other evangelists, emphasizes the key role of Peter and focuses on his positive qualities. After witnessing Jesus' power over the fish of the sea, Peter was overwhelmed with his own inadequacy. Jesus then offered words of comfort and the invitation to join His special fishing expedition. Peter, and then James and John, were quick to respond to this life-changing request. They immediately left behind their worldly possessions to seek what no amount of money or all the fish in the sea could purchase.

AFTER PLACING THE CALL USING the mint as a coin, you patiently wait for someone to answer the phone. You are not sure who will pick up on the other end. However, nothing could have prepared you for what happens next. The ringing stops and the angry words, "Synagogue, **Demon** speaking" assault your eardrum. There must be a mistake! Again, even louder, you hear "Synagogue, **Demon** speaking!" Wow, there is a **demon** in the synagogue! You quickly hang up, but will not forget this frightening call using the mint as a coin. This very wrong number serves as a reminder of Jesus' CURE OF A DEMONIAC IN THE SYNAGOGUE.

|||||||||||||||||||||||||||||||||||||||||||||||||||||||||||||||||||||||||||||||||||||||||||||||||||||||||||||||||||||||||||||||||||||||||||

CURE OF A DEMONIAC IN THE SYNAGOGUE

|||||||||||||||||||||||||||||||||||||||||||||||||||||||||||||||||||||||||||||||||||||||||||||||||||||||||||||||||||||||||||||||||||||||||||

Mk 1:21–28

21 Then they came to Capernaum, and on the sabbath he entered the synagogue and taught. 22 The people were astonished at his teaching, for he taught them as one having authority and not as the scribes. 23 In their synagogue was a man with an unclean spirit; 24 he cried out, "What have you to do with us, Jesus of Nazareth?

Have you come to destroy us? I know who you are—the Holy One of God!" **25** Jesus rebuked him and said, "Quiet! Come out of him!" **26** The unclean spirit convulsed him and with a loud cry came out of him. **27** All were amazed and asked one another, "What is this? A new teaching with authority. He commands even the unclean spirits and they obey him." **28** His fame spread everywhere throughout the whole region of Galilee.

Lk 4:31–37

31 Jesus then went down to Capernaum, a town of Galilee. He taught them on the sabbath, **32** and they were astonished at his teaching because he spoke with authority. **33** In the synagogue there was a man with the spirit of an unclean demon, and he cried out in a loud voice, **34** "Ha! What have you to do with us, Jesus of Nazareth? Have you come to destroy us? I know who you are—the Holy One of God!" **35** Jesus rebuked him and said, "Be quiet! Come out of him!" Then the demon threw the man down in front of them and came out of him without doing him any harm. **36** They were all amazed and said to one another, "What is there about his word? For with authority and power he commands the unclean spirits, and they come out." **37** And news of him spread everywhere in the surrounding region.

———————————

In Capernaum and elsewhere, the synagogue was a place where faithful Jews gathered to pray and worship. An important component of worship was a reading from Hebrew Scripture followed by instruction. In Jesus' time, a rabbi was not necessarily present. A learned member of the local community would often instruct his friends and neighbors. Scribes frequently did the teaching. They did not simply write or copy words. Scribes were well-versed teachers of the Hebrew Scriptures. They could interpret the Law of Moses, but not on their own authority. The authority of Scripture spoke for itself.

Jesus was "a new man in town." In Capernaum, relatively few people would have known the carpenter from Galilee. On this particular Sabbath, many in the synagogue must have been wondering who this new teacher was. The power and authority of Jesus' words were astonishing. Even more astonishing was the fact that He backed up His words with action. Jesus' first exorcism demonstrated that He was no ordinary teacher. Exorcisms typically involved ritualistic actions, recited formulas, and perhaps even a few roots. Jesus merely said several words and evil forces were rendered helpless.

THE BAD EXPERIENCE OF USING the mint from the gallon jug to make a phone call is still troubling you. Now just looking at the mints leaves a bad taste in your mouth. You must get rid of them. They should be destroyed! As you consider the options, your beloved **mother-in-law** happens to walk by. (If you do not have a **mother-in-law** think of someone who is a **mother-in-law**.) You ask your **mother-in-law** for suggestions about how to destroy the mints. She immediately says she has an idea. You hand the jug of mints to her. This encounter recalls Jesus' CURING OF PETER'S MOTHER-IN-LAW.

CURING OF PETER'S MOTHER-IN-LAW

Mt 8:14–15

14 Jesus entered the house of Peter, and saw his mother-in-law lying in bed with a fever. 15 He touched her hand, the fever left her, and she rose and waited on him.

Mk 1:29–31

29 On leaving the synagogue he entered the house of Simon and Andrew with James and John. 30 Simon's mother-in-law lay sick with a fever. They immediately told him about her. 31 He approached, grasped her hand, and helped her up. Then the fever left her and she waited on them.

Lk 4:38–39

38 After he left the synagogue, he entered the house of Simon. Simon's mother-in-law was afflicted with a severe fever, and they interceded with him about her. 39 He stood over her, rebuked the fever, and it left her. She got up immediately and waited on them.

This first day of Jesus' Galilean ministry was a busy one. After teaching and then curing a demoniac in the synagogue, Jesus retreated to Peter's home in Capernaum. According to Mark, all four of His new disciples were present. It is uncertain whether Peter knew that he was bringing Jesus home to a mother-in-law sick in bed with a fever. Nonetheless, the "Divine Physician" made a house call. Jesus had just healed a man from an emotional and spiritual affliction by exorcising the offending demon. He now healed Peter's mother-in-law of her physical illness. Many people in Jesus' day would have believed that the fever was also caused by a demon. Luke describes how Jesus "rebuked" the fever, a familiar demon-defeating term. The power of Jesus' words was again demonstrated as it had been in the synagogue. Like the healing of the demoniac in the synagogue, Jesus' intervention was immediate and complete. This was the result in all of Jesus' healing miracles, with one very interesting exception. It would now only be a short time until Jesus became well-known in His new hometown.

YOU CAN HARDLY WAIT TO see what your mother-in-law does with the mints. Surprisingly, she pours them all out onto the floor. The mints scatter and roll in all directions. You find this odd and not a particularly good idea. You quickly change your mind. You failed to notice that your moth-er-in-law is wearing high-**heeled** shoes. When she begins to vigorously stomp, you see the rather imposing **heels** on her shoes. You now under-stand! With great force and precision, she brings her **heels** down on the small helpless mints. Squish, pop, splat, crunch! One by one, the **heels** transform the mints into powder. The destructive action of her **heels** helps recall the final unit tied to the table Landmark: OTHER HEALINGS.

||||||||||||||||||||||||||||||||||||||||||||||||||||||||||||||||||||||||||||||||||||||||||||||||||||||||||||||||||||||||||||

OTHER HEALINGS

||||||||||||||||||||||||||||||||||||||||||||||||||||||||||||||||||||||||||||||||||||||||||||||||||||||||||||||||||||||||||||

Mt 8:16–17

16 When it was evening, they brought him many who were possessed by demons, and he drove out the spirits by a word and cured all the sick, 17 to fulfill what had been said by Isaiah the prophet:

"He took away our infirmities
and bore our diseases."

Mk 1:32–34

32 When it was evening, after sunset, they brought to him all who were ill or possessed by demons. 33 The whole town was gathered at the door. 34 He cured many who were sick with various diseases, and he drove out many demons, not permitting them to speak because they knew him.

Lk 4:40–41

40 At sunset, all who had people sick with various diseases brought them to him. He laid his hands on each of them and cured them. **41** And demons also came out from many, shouting, "You are the Son of God." But he rebuked them and did not allow them to speak because they knew that he was the Messiah.

This unit takes place on Saturday evening. The sun had set and the Sabbath was over. People were now able to perform the "work" required to bring their sick, ailing relatives and friends to the Healer they had been hearing so much about. For Matthew, this fulfilled the prophecy of Isaiah 53:4, where the Messiah was portrayed as the "suffering servant" who removes infirmity and heals disease. Despite this prophecy, the Jewish people of Jesus' time were expecting something quite different. They hoped for a powerful king-like Messiah who would overthrow the harsh Roman occupation and restore the Twelve Tribes of Israel. They were not ready to accept a Messiah who would be killed in order to free them from the infirmities and disease of sin. Here Mark began to develop the theme of the "Messianic Secret." Jesus was not yet ready to reveal His identity as a suffering Messiah, though the demons already seemed to know His identity.

It was late and Jesus had a long and eventful day. Nonetheless, He still took time to minister to this large, ailing crowd. Likely tired, He could have quickly healed everyone at once. With a few words, all could have been restored to health and sent on their way. However, Jesus chose to have a personal encounter with all who came to Him in need.

Landmark 5:

BASKETBALL

You now arrive at Landmark 5. It is the first of several to incorporate the theme of a sport or game. You will associate the number 5 with a **basketball** since there are five players on a **basketball** team. This Landmark, which will help you recall several more units, is a brand-new bright orange **basketball**. See yourself bend over and pick up the **basketball**. Feel its stippled, grainy surface. The **basketball** is firm and ready to be dribbled for the first time.

With the new basketball in hand, you decide it is time to put it to use. The ball has been inflated properly, so it should bounce well. You begin to dribble. Immediately, you feel the urge to find a basketball court. However, first things first. Before setting off in search of a place to play with the fifth Landmark, you decide to offer a **prayer** of thanksgiving for the ball. Dropping to your knees, you continue to skillfully bounce the ball. A **prayer** of thanks for the new ball rolls off of your lips. Continuing to dribble, you stand and **pray**. After several minutes, you finally finish **praying**. Remarkably, you have kept dribbling without missing a beat. This **prayer** while dribbling the basketball represents the unit: JESUS IN PRAYER.

JESUS IN PRAYER

Mk 1:35–38

35 Rising very early before dawn, he left and went off to a deserted place, where he prayed. 36 Simon and those who were with him pursued him 37 and on finding him said, "Everyone is looking for you." 38 He told them, "Let us go on to the nearby villages that I may preach there also. For this purpose have I come."

Lk 4:42–43

42 At daybreak, Jesus left and went to a deserted place. The crowds went looking for him, and when they came to him, they tried to prevent him from leaving them. 43 But he said to them, "To the other towns also I must proclaim the good news of the kingdom of God, because for this purpose I have been sent."

―――――――――

Several times on your walk with Jesus, you will see Him in solitary prayer. Jesus communicated with His Father to be strengthened for what lay ahead. Like us, Jesus needed quiet time away from the world's distractions.

This unit is also a transition. Jesus had initiated His ministry of preaching and healing in Galilee. He had established Capernaum as a home base. He was now ready to "hit the road" and travel throughout Galilee with His new disciples. In this brief unit, Jesus restates His purpose. He is not a mighty, political Messiah sent to free Israel from Roman oppression. He has come to proclaim and bring about the kingdom of God in a very radical and unexpected way.

YOU ARE NOW OFF IN search of a basketball court. With all of the dribbling, you have worked up a drenching sweat. However, the main reason you are now soaked in perspiration is the hot **summer** day. The sweat continues to pour. Fear of dehydration creeps in. Perhaps this **summer** day is not the best time for a vigorous game of basketball. Just dribbling has become an effort. You decide to seek relief from the **summer** heat. **Summer** is a soundalike for "**summary**." This experience with the basketball in the heat of **summer** represents the next unit: A SUMMARY STATEMENT of Jesus' Preaching and Healing.

A SUMMARY STATEMENT

Mt 4:23–25

23 He went around all of Galilee, teaching in their synagogues, proclaiming the gospel of the kingdom, and curing every disease and illness among the people. 24 His fame spread to all of Syria,

and they brought to him all who were sick with various diseases and racked with pain, those who were possessed, lunatics, and paralytics, and he cured them. 25 And great crowds from Galilee, the Decapolis, Jerusalem, and Judea, and from beyond the Jordan followed him.

Mk 1:39

39 So he went into their synagogues, preaching and driving out demons throughout the whole of Galilee.

Lk 4:44

44 And he was preaching in the synagogues of Judea.

———————————

This unit is a brief summary of Jesus' ministry thus far. We heard Jesus inaugurate His Galilean ministry by announcing the nearness of the Kingdom. We saw Him exorcise a demon in the synagogue and heal Peter's mother-in-law with a gentle touch. Now, after spending time in prayer, Jesus began to expand His ministry to all of Galilee and surrounding Gentile lands. Jesus went out to the people, and they also traveled great distances to hear His words and receive healing. People came from the Roman province of Syria, which included Antioch, Damascus, Phoenicia, Tyre, Sidon, and Idumea. They also came from the ten largely Greek cities east of the Jordan known as the Decapolis. From the outset, it was clear that this Jewish man named Jesus had not come just for His own people. He had come for all.

WHILE STILL DRIBBLING AND SWEATING, you see relief from the heat looming on the horizon. It is a **mountain**, where cooler air surely awaits at the summit. You dribble on and soon reach the trailhead leading up the **mountain**. Amongst the trees, shielded from the sun, relief is almost immediate. The trek up the **mountain** while still dribbling the basketball is not as difficult as anticipated. The cooler altitude and **mountain** breeze are refreshing. By the time you reach the **mountaintop**, all of your perspiration has evaporated. The steady "thump, thump" of the bouncing ball continues as you take in the gorgeous **mountain** view. This **mountain** excursion represents the next unit, the monumental SERMON ON THE MOUNT.

The Sermon on the Mount is probably the most well-known teaching and instructional material ever spoken. You will take your time with its powerful words and internalize them thoroughly. The Sermon, which is found in Matthew, contains some of the same or similar teachings included in Luke's discourse, known as The Sermon on the Plain. Though each writer structured his writing for a particular audience with a particular purpose, we will combine them here just as we have material in previous units.

In this first of Matthew's five major discourses, Jesus, the "new Moses," delivers a new law, not on tablets of stone, but with simple, elegant words. The radical teachings in the Sermons on the Mount and the Plain emphasize the importance of showing love and justice toward all people.

For the purpose of internalizing this lengthy unit, the Sermons will be broken down into twenty-six "bite-size" pieces. Each of these bites will be represented by one of the twenty-six letters of the English alphabet. Thus by reciting the ABCs, you will internalize and have a way of meditating on the Sermon(s). Each of the twenty-six letters will be represented by an animal. In Noah-like fashion, you will gather these animals into your memory. Once you have rounded them up, each animal will remind you of a particular teaching in the Sermon on the Mount or Plain.

A Is for Alligator

THE FIRST ANIMAL IS ONE that most people are familiar with, at least from a safe distance. Picture an alligator swimming peacefully along the surface of a lake. Suddenly, a swarm of angry **bees** swoops down and stings the alligator many times on its long, wide mouth. The **bees** are relentless. After thrashing about in pain, the alligator submerges to escape the hostile **bees**. You have now linked in your mind the alligator with **bees**. These **bees** are a soundalike for **beatitudes**. This will cause you to think of THE BEATITUDES, which comprise the first part of the Sermon on the Mount.

THE BEATITUDES

Mt 5:1–12

1 When he saw the crowds, he went up the mountain, and after he had sat down, his disciples came to him. 2 He began to teach them, saying:

3 "Blessed are the poor in spirit,
for theirs is the kingdom of heaven.
4 Blessed are they who mourn,
for they will be comforted.
5 Blessed are the meek,
for they will inherit the land.
6 Blessed are they who hunger and thirst for righteousness,
for they will be satisfied.
7 Blessed are the merciful,
for they will be shown mercy.
8 Blessed are the clean of heart,
for they will see God.
9 Blessed are the peacemakers,
for they will be called children of God.
10 Blessed are they who are persecuted for the sake of righteousness,
for theirs is the kingdom of heaven.

11 Blessed are you when they insult you and persecute you and utter every kind of evil against you [falsely] because of me. 12 Rejoice and be glad, for your reward will be great in heaven. Thus they persecuted the prophets who were before you."

Lk 6:20–23

20 And raising his eyes toward his disciples he said:

"Blessed are you who are poor,
for the kingdom of God is yours.
21 Blessed are you who are now hungry,
for you will be satisfied.
Blessed are you who are now weeping,
for you will laugh.
22 Blessed are you when people hate you,
and when they exclude and insult you,
and denounce your name as evil
on account of the Son of Man.

23 Rejoice and leap for joy on that day! Behold, your reward will be great in heaven. For their ancestors treated the prophets in the same way."

The Beatitudes are a series of blessings, which when fulfilled lead to a reward to be received in the kingdom of God. Attitudes and behaviors in this life have significant repercussions in the life to come. The Beatitudes build upon one another. The first Beatitude, "Blessed are the poor in spirit," is a foundation for those that follow. The Sermon itself goes full circle, concluding with a parable teaching about the importance of a strong spiritual foundation.

"Blessed are the poor in spirit, for theirs is the kingdom of heaven."

To be poor in spirit does not mean to be depressed and miserable. Rather, it is an endorsement for being self-aware. Many people see themselves as strong, independent, and self-reliant. While these traits are good to a certain degree, we are all in need of God's provision. Being poor in spirit is to be aware of our limitations as well as the limitations of all things created by man. This understanding should endow us with a sense of humility and detachment from the things of this world. This in turn will lead us to seek the kingdom of heaven and its lasting rewards. We will be at peace seeking that for which we were created rather than that which we have created. When we are poor in spirit, we realize how dependent we are on God's love and mercy.

"Blessed are they who mourn, for they will be comforted."

If we are poor in spirit, we will be aware of how limited we are when we act alone. We are able to mourn our weakness and the inevitable sin that it causes. We are sad about all of the evil and injustice that permeates the world. We may cry about how unfair life can be at times. However, in spite of all of this misfortune we are comforted by our faith in God. We believe that in turning to Him we can overcome the trials of this world. By doing so, we will eventually enjoy the ultimate comforts of His kingdom.

"Blessed are the meek,
for they will inherit the land."

This is not an endorsement for weakness. God did not make us to be spineless doormats. Like those who are poor in spirit, the meek also possess the quality of humility. From meekness, not weakness, flows a sense of serenity and peace in times of trouble. Those who are meek rest comfortably in the strong arms of God and as a result are gentle and slow to anger. They are able to remain calm amidst the storms of life. Much good comes to those who possess this strength of meekness.

"Blessed are they who hunger and thirst for righteousness,
for they will be satisfied."

When we are righteous, we are obedient to the teachings of Jesus. We strive to lead lives of integrity and holiness. This is quite the opposite of being self-righteous, when we are faithful only to our own desires. In being righteous, we look beyond ourselves and deepen our relationship with God. By striving for righteousness, we exercise strength or fortitude, a gift of the Spirit (Is 11:2). This gift of strength enables us to pursue righteousness, even in times of trouble. With this strength comes a satisfaction not obtained with material gains.

"Blessed are the merciful,
for they will be shown mercy."

We are not able to fully comprehend the mercy shown to us by God. As you journey with Jesus, you will witness miracles and hear teachings that attest to God's great mercy. Nothing can compare to the mercy and forgiveness shown by Jesus' death on the cross. We are to strive to do the same. Not to die upon a cross, but to daily die to our pride as we forgive and show mercy and compassion to others. This show of compassion is one of life's great challenges. Keep in mind our hope of receiving compassion when it matters most, on Judgment Day.

"Blessed are the clean of heart,
for they will see God."

There have been amazing advances in our understanding of the human body and its awe-inspiring complexity since this Sermon was delivered. Our modern understanding of how the heart works was totally unknown in Jesus' time. The idea of the heart as an electrically driven muscular pump with chambers and valves connected to the rest of the body by miles of blood vessels would have been unbelievable. People two thousand years ago attributed what we now consider to be brain functions to the heart. It was the source of behavior and thought. The heart allowed people to worship God and follow His commands. It was where love of God and fellow man originated. Today, we still use the heart as a metaphor for love and caring. In Jesus' time, it was literally the center of all things human. Thus, to have a clean and pure heart was essential. A pure heart allowed one to think clearly, to focus on God and the important things in one's relationship with God. A pure heart was the source of insight and the key to understanding the Word of God. This made it possible to "see" God in one's neighbor.

"Blessed are the peacemakers,
for they will be called children of God."

In our world, there is turmoil at every turn. Nations fight one another. People within a single country are at one another's throats. There are religious wars, political battles, and economic skirmishes. Peace is an elusive concept. The task of being a peacemaker may seem impossible. However, as individuals we must not lose sight of what constitutes true peace. This is the peace that cannot be shaken or destroyed by outside forces. It is the inner peace that comes through our relationship with God while living the life for which we have been made. This can come about by practicing the preceding six Beatitudes. With the inner peace that comes through our relationship with God, we can then be peacemakers to others.

"Blessed are you when they insult you and persecute you and utter every kind of evil against you [falsely] because of me. Rejoice and be glad, for your reward will be great in heaven."

The Beatitudes conclude with a sobering expectation. Jesus tells His disciples and the crowd that in following Him they will face hardships. It is not *if* but *when*. By following the righteous path in a relationship with Jesus, enemies will be made. By taking the role of peacemaker, there will be encounters with those who want a piece of you. Jesus knows that in choosing Him, you are choosing pain and persecution. You are also choosing the reward of eternal life.

Luke's Sermon on the Plain contains only half the number of Beatitudes as Matthew's Sermon on the Mount (four vs. eight). However, Luke includes four "woes," which stand as opposites to his four Beatitudes.

Lk 6:24–26

> **24** "But woe to you who are rich,
> for you have received your consolation.
> **25** But woe to you who are filled now,
> for you will be hungry.
> Woe to you who laugh now,
> for you will grieve and weep.
> **26** Woe to you when all speak well of you,
> for their ancestors treated the false prophets in this way."

These woes are warnings against a life of ease and complacency. Jesus does not intend for those who have money in their pocket or food in their belly to be damned. Those who are in good spirits or praised are not necessarily in trouble. It is what we do with these gifts that matters. God wants us to be happy, but not to the exclusion or misery of others. We are to share what we have with those less fortunate. In turn, the Father will share the Kingdom with us. The things of this life are worthless in comparison with what awaits us in the kingdom of God.

B Is for Beaver

YOU KNOW THAT THIS BUSY sharp-toothed water rodent is a dam builder. However, you will now focus on the beaver's flat broad tail. Imagine this powerful tail repeatedly slapping against a large **block of salt**. Whack, whack, whack. The **salt block** is quickly reduced to a pile of fine crystals. Now visualize hundreds of busy beavers loudly pulverizing **salt blocks** with their tails. This activity of beavers blasting **salt blocks** recalls the next part of the Sermon, Jesus' WORDS ABOUT SALT.

||||||||||||||||||||||||||||||||||||||||||||||||||||||||||||||||||||||||||||||||||||||||||||||||||||||||||||||||||||||||||||||||||||||||||||||||||||||||

WORDS ABOUT SALT

||||||||||||||||||||||||||||||||||||||||||||||||||||||||||||||||||||||||||||||||||||||||||||||||||||||||||||||||||||||||||||||||||||||||||||||||||||||||

Mt 5:13

13 "You are the salt of the earth. But if salt loses its taste, with what can it be seasoned? It is no longer good for anything but to be thrown out and trampled underfoot."

Mk 9:49–50

49 "Everyone will be salted with fire. 50 Salt is good, but if salt becomes insipid, with what will you restore its flavor? Keep salt in yourselves and you will have peace with one another."

Lk 14:34–35

34 "Salt is good, but if salt itself loses its taste, with what can its flavor be restored? 35 It is fit neither for the soil nor for the manure pile; it is thrown out. Whoever has ears to hear ought to hear."

———————————

When you pick up a shaker and sprinkle salt on your food, the result is very predictable. The food tastes salty. In our modern world, it is doubtful that you have experienced otherwise. The salt reliably enhances the flavor. But two thousand years ago, conditions were different. Salt could lose its strength and could become impure. This would render it worse than useless. It had to be disposed of. When Jesus refers to His followers as "salt," it is a compliment as well as a challenge. They are to enhance the world, to make it a better place. However, to do that they have to be loyal to His teachings, they must maintain their strength and guard against impurity. This is difficult. In times of trouble, we, too, must remain salt for the world and not be shaken.

C Is for Cow

THE COW IN THIS UNIT is a dairy cow, so we will focus on its milk dispenser—the udder. See yourself preparing to milk your cow. You are sitting on a stool down at udder level with arms outstretched. Something amazing and unexpected then occurs! From the udder shines a bright **light**. It is not a blinding **light**. It is warm and comforting. Basking in the soothing **light**, you forget the utter strangeness of its source. This **light**-producing cow is a reminder of Jesus' TEACHING ABOUT LIGHT.

TEACHING ABOUT LIGHT

Mt 5:14–16

14 "You are the light of the world. A city set on a mountain cannot be hidden. **15** Nor do they light a lamp and then put it under a bushel basket; it is set on a lampstand, where it gives light to all in the house. **16** Just so, your light must shine before others, that they may see your good deeds and glorify your heavenly Father."

Lk 11:33–36

33 "No one who lights a lamp hides it away or places it [under a bushel basket], but on a lampstand so that those who enter might see the light. **34** The lamp of the body is your eye. When your eye is sound, then your whole body is filled with light, but when it is bad, then your body is in darkness. **35** Take care, then, that the light in you not become darkness. **36** If your whole body is full of light, and no part of it is in darkness, then it will be as full of light as a lamp illuminating you with its brightness."

John's Prologue describes Jesus as "the light of the world." Jesus now calls His disciples to be the same. For the Israelites of the Old Covenant, their shining light was their obedience to the Law of Moses. New Covenant disciples' light will be their good works. In this way, their identity (and ours) would be as easy to see as Jerusalem, which was built on Mount Zion. The intention of doing good deeds is not to shine the spotlight on ourselves. If that were the purpose, then good deeds would be a source of pride. Their purpose is to bring glory to God.

In the Gospel of Luke, Jesus alludes to the belief people had about their eyes. Instead of being receptors for light, the eyes were believed to be a source of light that allowed one to see the surrounding world. People also believed that if you were a good person, your interior self was good.

This interior goodness would become manifest as "good light" from one's "good eye" (as opposed to "evil eye"). A good person would shine "good" light that could lead others to God. Jesus teaches that a sure way to shine good light is to follow Him, for He is the source of light.

D Is for Dog

IMAGINE A DOG THAT HAS just enjoyed a large bowl of dog food. The poor dog is stuffed. Picture the dog lying on his back next to the empty bowl with a **full**, bloated, protruding belly. The dog's stomach is packed **full**. You can even hear some digestive rumblings. This scene of the dog's inflated, **full** belly reminds you of the word *fulfill*. Jesus now teaches that He did not come to abolish, but to FULFILL THE LAW AND PROPHETS.

FULFILL THE LAW AND PROPHETS

Mt 5:17–20

17 "Do not think that I have come to abolish the law or the prophets. I have come not to abolish but to fulfill. **18** Amen, I say to you, until heaven and earth pass away, not the smallest letter or the smallest part of a letter will pass from the law, until all things have taken place. **19** Therefore, whoever breaks one of the least of these commandments and teaches others to do so will be called least in the kingdom of heaven. But whoever obeys and teaches these commandments will be called greatest in the kingdom of heaven. **20** I tell you, unless your righteousness surpasses that of the scribes and Pharisees, you will not enter into the kingdom of heaven."

The phrase "The Law and the Prophets" refers to a large portion of what Christians now call the Old Testament. Just as the "Great War" could not be referred to as World War I until there was World War II, the term Old Testament would not make sense until there was a New Testament.

Following the Sermon, we will descend the mount with Jesus and continue following Him to the cross. We will see and hear much along the way that makes it clear that He is the fulfillment of the Old Testament and its prophecies. Jesus completes (fulfills) the Law and the Prophets. Old sacrificial practices become obsolete after the ultimate sacrifice of Jesus on the cross. Laws and rituals that had ordered one's behavior become secondary to our behavior toward others. This is a much more difficult task, but we will be given assistance. Upcoming parts of this Sermon describe some of these new expected behaviors. We will hear teachings about anger, adultery, divorce, swearing, retaliation, and loving one's enemies. All of these involve adherence to a higher standard than was previously taught. Jesus thus "perfects" the standards of the existing moral laws of the Jewish people. These new standards would apply to all who follow Jesus.

E Is for Elephant

THIS HUGE BEAST IS KNOWN for its memory. Its size and odd features make it unforgettable. An image often used to describe someone who is **angry** is that they "turn red." Metaphorically, the internal heat generated by **angry** feelings causes one to have a burning red glow. Unfortunately, our elephant is quite **angry**. Another elephant has stepped on its toes. Our elephant is now quite red. Every square inch of the elephant has turned red with **anger**. Picture this massive **angry** red beast, so **angry** that steam is billowing from its huge red trunk. The elephant's wrinkly rough skin is bright red. Seeing this large red elephant is a reminder of **anger**, specifically Jesus' TEACHING ABOUT ANGER.

|||||||||||||||||||||||||||||||||||||||||||||||||||||||||||||||||||||||||||||||||||||||||||||||||||||||||||||||||||||||||||||||||||||||||||||||||||||||||||||||||||

TEACHING ABOUT ANGER

|||||||||||||||||||||||||||||||||||||||||||||||||||||||||||||||||||||||||||||||||||||||||||||||||||||||||||||||||||||||||||||||||||||||||||||||||||||||||||||||||||

Mt 5:21–26

21 "You have heard that it was said to your ancestors, 'You shall not kill; and whoever kills will be liable to judgment.' 22 But I say to you, whoever is angry with his brother will be liable to judgment, and whoever says to his brother, 'Raqa,' will be answerable to the Sanhedrin, and whoever says, 'You fool,' will be liable to fiery Gehenna. 23 Therefore, if you bring your gift to the altar, and there recall that your brother has anything against you, 24 leave your gift there at the altar, go first and be reconciled with your brother, and then come and offer your gift. 25 Settle with your opponent quickly while on the way to court with him. Otherwise your opponent will hand you over to the judge, and the judge will hand you over to the

guard, and you will be thrown into prison. **26** Amen, I say to you, you will not be released until you have paid the last penny."

Lk 12:57–59

57 "Why do you not judge for yourselves what is right? **58** If you are to go with your opponent before a magistrate, make an effort to settle the matter on the way; otherwise your opponent will turn you over to the judge, and the judge hand you over to the constable, and the constable throw you into prison. **59** I say to you, you will not be released until you have paid the last penny."

———————

The sixth of the Ten Commandments that God gave Moses on Mount Sinai prohibited the killing of another person. Now on another mountain, Jesus went far beyond this command. He addressed the issue of anger and slander toward others. Possessing a human nature, Jesus knew we would all have times when we feel anger toward others. How we handle these feelings is what is important.

Jesus emphasized the need to deal with our anger by becoming reconciled with the object of our anger, "our brother." In doing so, we become reconciled with God. Through reconciliation, we will avoid negative judgments from secular and religious courts (the Sanhedrin in Jesus' time), but most importantly from God.

F Is for Flamingo

THIS LONG-LEGGED FLIGHTLESS BIRD IS not the most common animal that begins with *F*, but it is certainly one of the most memorable! Your only experience with this colorful bird may be seeing the plastic variety on someone's lawn. Imagine that scene, but with a live flamingo. Picture the flamingo venturing from the yard and walking next door. There our wandering bird finds another flamingo, but of the opposite sex. The two big birds commence to have a "flamingo **fling**," the details of which are left to your imagination. This **fling** triggers your recollection of Jesus' TEACHING ON ADULTERY.

TEACHING ON ADULTERY

Mt 5:27–28

27 "You have heard that it was said, 'You shall not commit adultery.' 28 But I say to you, everyone who looks at a woman with lust has already committed adultery with her in his heart."

Here Jesus addressed one of the Ten Commandments, but tightens its standard by focusing on the person's interior state rather than exterior behavior. Thoughts of impurity are to be avoided. The thoughts are not on par with the actual act of adultery, but Jesus did emphasize the importance of a pure mind. Certainly someone with a pure mind or heart is far less likely to actually engage in sinful behavior.

G Is for Giraffe

HERE IS ANOTHER MEMORABLE ANIMAL with long legs. However, it is the long neck that really makes the giraffe stand out. It is this long neck that also makes shaving such a challenge for the male giraffe! With so much area to cover with a razor, it is no wonder that the male giraffe frequently **cuts** his long neck. This is in spite of his big bulging eyes, which carefully watch the shaving process. A close inspection of his neck reveals many scabs, as well as fresh **cuts**. These **cuts** are a reminder of Jesus' words of hyperbole about **cutting**, specifically **cutting** off one's hand (along with removal of the eye) in order to **avoid sin**.

CUTTING TO AVOID SIN

Mt 5:29–30

29 "If your right eye causes you to sin, tear it out and throw it away. It is better for you to lose one of your members than to have your whole body thrown into Gehenna. 30 And if your right hand causes you to sin, cut it off and throw it away. It is better for you

to lose one of your members than to have your whole body go into Gehenna."

Jesus certainly did not endorse self-mutilation. On the contrary, we are to respect the body that we have been given during our brief time in this world. Jesus also taught about the need for inner purity. It is important to avoid temptation in order to achieve this goal. There are many opportunities to do (hands) or see (eyes) things that lead to sin. Regarding these behaviors that cause us to sin, it is as if Jesus is saying "Cut it out!"

H Is for Horse

IMAGINE A BIG, STRONG, BEAUTIFUL horse. The horse may be brown or black, male or female, but regardless of what your horse looks like, you will be more focused on its riders. That's right, the horse has two riders. Observe that the riders are facing in opposite directions! They are sitting back to back. One is looking forward. The other is looking tailward, taking in the scenery that they just passed by. They are sitting this way because of intense displeasure with each other. The riders no longer have the same view of things. They are in fact **divorced** from each other. The pair now sees things differently as they ride the "**divorce horse**." This unhappy scene recalls Jesus' TEACHING ON DIVORCE.

TEACHING ON DIVORCE

Mt 5:31–32

31 "It was also said, 'Whoever divorces his wife must give her a bill of divorce.' 32 But I say to you, whoever divorces his wife (unless the marriage is unlawful) causes her to commit adultery, and whoever marries a divorced woman commits adultery."

In the Sermon, Jesus spoke briefly about divorce. Later in Matthew, He said more in response to the Pharisees' attempt to trap him. Here Jesus pointed out the ease with which a divorce was obtained under the Old Covenant. A man was required to give his wife a "Bill of Divorce." The grounds for this were quite liberal and vague. According to Deuteronomy 24:1–4, divorce was allowable if the man (not the woman) was "displeased" with his wife "because he finds in her something indecent" (v. 1). For Jesus, this was no longer the standard. Divorce was now permissible only if the marriage was for some reason "unlawful" from its beginning. That is to say, if it was not truly a marriage from the outset.

I Is for Iguana

THE IGUANA IS A LIZARD found in warm tropical settings. However, imagine that one is sitting on your bed! This situation probably has your full attention. Before going to bed, you ask the iguana to make a solemn **oath**. The iguana is to **swear** not to bother you while you sleep, especially with its long tail or teeth. For the **oath**, you hold a Bible and the iguana dutifully places its scaly paw on the cover. The iguana then **swears an oath** to let you rest in peace. This strange scene represents the next unit: Jesus' TEACHING ON THE SWEARING OF OATHS.

TEACHING ON THE SWEARING OF OATHS

Mt 5:33–37

33 "Again you have heard that it was said to your ancestors, 'Do not take a false oath, but make good to the Lord all that you vow.' **34** But I say to you, do not swear at all; not by heaven, for it is God's throne; **35** nor by the earth, for it is his footstool; nor by Jerusalem, for it is the city of the great King. **36** Do not swear by your head, for you cannot make a single hair white or black. **37** Let your 'Yes' mean 'Yes,' and your 'No' mean 'No.' Anything more is from the evil one."

Here Jesus was not preaching against the use of profanity, but against swearing oaths. One of the Ten Commandments says not to swear an oath using the name of the Lord. Jesus extended this Old Covenant law by saying no oaths for personal gain should be sworn. Gospel examples of this include Herod's oath to Salome and later Peter swearing that he does not know Jesus. For Jesus, a person's good word should stand alone without the need for swearing. If one is honest, an oath is unnecessary.

J Is for Jaguar

YOU WILL NOW THINK OF a large, sleek, predatory member of the cat family, the jaguar. The jaguar is a beautiful, photogenic beast. Imagine that you are going to shoot one—with your camera, of course! Seeing a jaguar standing alone in a field, you aim your camera. The first picture is a beautiful close-up of its left **cheek**. You patiently wait, hoping the jaguar will turn its head so you can get a picture of the **other cheek**. Soon the jaguar does turn the **other cheek** and you snap the picture. How fortunate that the wild animal obliged and turned the **other cheek**. This **cheek turning** reminds us of Jesus' TEACHINGS ON RETALIATION.

||||||||||||||||||||||||||||||||||||||||||||||||||||||||||||||||||||||||||||||||||||||||||||||||||||||||||||||||||||

TEACHINGS ON RETALIATION

||||||||||||||||||||||||||||||||||||||||||||||||||||||||||||||||||||||||||||||||||||||||||||||||||||||||||||||||||||

Mt 5:38–39

38 "You have heard that it was said, 'An eye for an eye and a tooth for a tooth.' **39** But I say to you, offer no resistance to one who is evil. When someone strikes you on [your] right cheek, turn the other one to him as well."

Lk 6:29

29 "To the person who strikes you on one cheek, offer the other one as well."

———

Since the time of Moses, it had been Jewish tradition and law to repay one wrong with another (Ex 21:23–25). Justice should mirror the crime. Two wrongs made things right. Jesus as the "new law giver" had other thoughts about retaliation. He preached the radical idea of nonresistance, actually doing the opposite of what was expected. Jesus' phrase to "turn the other cheek" was not instruction to stand and passively take more abuse. This teaching was about how to try to avoid physical retaliation. There are ways of handling confrontation that lead to a softening, rather than a hardening of hearts.

K Is for Koala

WHEN YOU ARRIVE AT THE letter *K*, think of this small Australian marsupial (mammals with a pouch) munching on a leaf. You decide to approach the koala to get a closer look. The koala, sensing that you have a tastier treat, drops the leaf and awaits your arrival. You soon regret your curiosity. The little koala pounces and begins to hungrily devour your **coat** (or **cloak**). Though you vigorously try to shake off the koala, its teeth dig in for another bite of your **coat (cloak)**. This feeding frenzy directed at your **coat (cloak)** reminds you of Jesus' TEACHINGS ON NONRETALIATION, one of which involves a "**cloak**."

TEACHINGS ON NONRETALIATION

Mt 5:40–41

40 "If anyone wants to go to law with you over your tunic, hand him your cloak as well. **41** Should anyone press you into service for one mile, go with him for two miles."

Jesus experienced firsthand what we all have come to know. Life is full of controversy and unwanted demands. The needs and wants of others have a way of interfering with our own plans. Jesus continued His teaching on nonretaliation with specific examples and unexpected radical ways of handling these situations. We are to respond with generosity and kindness. This response will hopefully curb controversy before it spirals out of control. A loving response may also be the catalyst that changes the heart of another. Go the unexpected extra mile!

PERHAPS WHEN YOU THINK OF a lion, the image of a majestic beast, the "King of the Jungle," comes to mind. The lion's large size and mighty roar strikes fear in most hearts. However, if you think of the famous "Cowardly Lion," you have a very different image. The lion you will imagine here is somewhere between these extremes. Your lion has fallen on hard times. He has lost his friends. He has lost his pride. Your unkempt lion is **begging** with a tin cup beside a forest path. Imagine the lion, cup in paw, **begging** for help. Along the path is a long line of animals waiting to give to the **begging** lion. This sad scene recalls Jesus' TEACHING ON GIVING TO THOSE WHO ASK.

TEACHING ON GIVING TO THOSE WHO ASK

Mt 5:42

42 "Give to the one who asks of you, and do not turn your back on one who wants to borrow."

Lk 6:30

30 "Give to everyone who asks of you, and from the one who takes what is yours do not demand it back."

Jesus had just taught His radical ideas of nonresistance and retaliation. He wants us to follow His example and do the unexpected. We are to give to beggars and borrowers alike. This is often difficult. In tough times, we may have what we think is just enough to "get by!" It takes strong faith to give in such circumstances. However, Jesus called us to perform acts of generosity and kindness.

Jesus did not specifically address the issue of enabling—giving to those who ask who would be better served in other ways. Perhaps our time or words of encouragement would be more appropriate than money. We often ask God in prayer for specifics. God knows what is best for us and does not always respond as we would like. Prayer for guidance as to how to respond to those who ask may be necessary.

M Is for Monkey

THE MONKEY IS TYPICALLY A cute and friendly animal. However, the playful monkey does have **enemies**, particularly when the **enemy** is hungry. One of these **enemies** is the hawk, who may swoop down and grab a monkey-to-go with its sharp talons. Imagine a sweet little monkey standing alone in a field. Not far above, a hungry hawk circles the monkey waiting for the right moment to strike. Suddenly, the hawk flies straight down toward the monkey. However, the little monkey responds in a very unexpected way. He does not run or scream. The loving monkey holds out a large bunch of bananas for the hawk. The hungry bird is stunned by this act of **love**. The monkey actually **loves** this angry bird. This monkey's act of **love** for his **enemy** reminds you of Jesus' next teaching in the Sermon about LOVING ONE'S ENEMIES.

LOVING ONE'S ENEMIES

Mt 5:43–48

43 "You have heard that it was said, 'You shall love your neighbor and hate your enemy.' **44** But I say to you, love your enemies, and pray for those who persecute you, **45** that you may be children of your heavenly Father, for he makes his sun rise on the bad and the good, and causes rain to fall on the just and the unjust. **46** For if you love those who love you, what recompense will you have? Do not the tax collectors do the same? **47** And if you greet your brothers only, what is unusual about that? Do not the pagans do the same? **48** So be perfect, just as your heavenly Father is perfect."

Lk 6:27–28, 32–36

27 "But to you who hear I say, love your enemies, do good to those who hate you, **28** bless those who curse you, pray for those who mistreat you. ... **32** For if you love those who love you, what credit is that to you? Even sinners love those who love them. **33** And if you do good to those who do good to you, what credit is that to you? Even sinners do the same. **34** If you lend money to those from whom you expect repayment, what credit [is] that to you? Even sinners lend to sinners, and get back the same amount. **35** But rather, love your enemies and do good to them, and lend expecting nothing back; then your reward will be great and you will be children of the Most High, for he himself is kind to the ungrateful and the wicked. **36** Be merciful, just as [also] your Father is merciful."

In Jesus' day, Jews knew the command in the Old Covenant: "Love your neighbor as yourself" (Lev 19:18). This is just as difficult now as it was then. Showing love to those who are close to us is not always easy. To love our enemies seems impossible. Jesus explained that we have more neighbors than we realize. Everyone is to be our neighbor. This would have included the despised Samaritans and even the hated Romans. How challenging it was to separate the actions, like idol worship (Samaritans) and violent persecution (Romans) from the perpetrators of these behaviors! Jesus told us that God our Father loves all those that He has created. We are to do the same. He gave us the perfect example of doing so. God gave us Himself in the person of Jesus, His Son, who preached and lived out this most difficult demand. Jesus went to the cross for all people. This included those who loved, were indifferent, and even hated Him. With His help, we are to do the same.

N Is for Nightingale

THIS SMALL BIRD IS KNOWN for its beautiful nocturnal song. It is not so much the quality of the sound, but its timing that makes the nightingale's singing distinctive. This bird is one of the few that sings after sunset. It is typically the lonely male singing for a mate. Imagine a male nightingale singing in a tree. However, do not focus on the song. You are more interested in what the male nightingale is wearing over his brown feathers. Surprisingly, it is a military uniform! More specifically, it is the U.S. Army uniform worn by a **private**. The single stripe on his upper wing indicates that the nightingale is a **private**. This is a reminder of Jesus' TEACHING ABOUT PRIVATE WORKS AND PRAYER.

TEACHING ABOUT PRIVATE WORKS AND PRAYER

Mt 6:1–6

1 "[But] take care not to perform righteous deeds in order that people may see them; otherwise, you will have no recompense from your heavenly Father. 2 When you give alms, do not blow a trumpet before you, as the hypocrites do in the synagogues and in the streets to win the praise of others. Amen, I say to you, they have received their reward. 3 But when you give alms, do not let your left hand know what your right is doing, 4 so that your almsgiving may be secret. And your Father who sees in secret will repay you.

5 "When you pray, do not be like the hypocrites, who love to stand and pray in the synagogues and on street corners so that others may see them. Amen, I say to you, they have received their reward. 6 But when you pray, go to your inner room, close the door, and pray to your Father in secret. And your Father who sees in secret will repay you."

Jesus was not preaching about new spiritual disciplines. The so-called "works of mercy" of prayer and almsgiving had been Jewish practices for centuries. What was new and different was the mindset and environment in which they were to take place. Public displays to garner attention and praise are to be avoided. Almsgiving is for the benefit of the poor, not the ego of the giver. God sees our generosity. That is enough. Similarly, Jesus spoke of the personal relationship we have with God through private prayer. We need not make a public display of our individual prayer. Jesus showed by example with His habit of seeking solitude to pray to His Father. Praying in community with others remains important, but individual prayer should not be a spectator sport.

O Is for Ostrich

YOU NOW ENCOUNTER A SECOND long-legged bird (recall that F is for flamingo). You saw how the "flinging flamingo" behaved. Not so for the ostrich. In fact, this big bird behaves in quite the opposite fashion. The shy, introverted ostrich has its head buried in the sand. You see long legs and a long neck, but at the end of the neck the ostrich's head disappears into the soft sand. As you approach to see if the ostrich needs some help, you hear muffled sounds coming from the sand. Soon you realize that these are not cries for help. They are words of **prayer!** The ostrich is **praying**. Though it is difficult to make out all of the words, you understand enough to recognize the words "Our Father." The ostrich is **praying** with its head underground. This scene represents Jesus TEACHING THE CROWD HOW TO PRAY using words that have become very familiar to us.

‖‖

TEACHING THE CROWD HOW TO PRAY

‖‖

Mt 6:7–15

7 "In praying, do not babble like the pagans, who think that they will be heard because of their many words. 8 Do not be like them. Your Father knows what you need before you ask him.

9 "This is how you are to pray:

Our Father in heaven,
hallowed be your name,
10 your kingdom come,
your will be done,
on earth as in heaven.
11 Give us today our daily bread;
12 and forgive us our debts,
as we forgive our debtors;
13 and do not subject us to the final test,
but deliver us from the evil one.

14 If you forgive others their transgressions, your heavenly Father will forgive you. 15 But if you do not forgive others, neither will your Father forgive your transgressions."

Lk 11:1–8

1 He was praying in a certain place, and when he had finished, one of his disciples said to him, "Lord, teach us to pray just as John taught his disciples." 2 He said to them, "When you pray, say:

Father, hallowed be your name,
your kingdom come.
3 Give us each day our daily bread
4 and forgive us our sins

for we ourselves forgive everyone in debt to us,
and do not subject us to the final test."

5 And he said to them, "Suppose one of you has a friend to
whom he goes at midnight and says, 'Friend, lend me three loaves
of bread, 6 for a friend of mine has arrived at my house from a
journey and I have nothing to offer him,' 7 and he says in reply
from within, 'Do not bother me; the door has already been locked
and my children and I are already in bed. I cannot get up to give
you anything.' 8 I tell you, if he does not get up to give him the
loaves because of their friendship, he will get up to give him
whatever he needs because of his persistence."

Jesus had just told the crowd how one's relationship with God is
personal. The opening words of this prayer, "Our Father," now emphasize
how we are all united as the children of a single Father. The structure of
this prayer to our loving Father is one of praise and glorification followed
by supplication. We first acknowledge God's Fatherhood and offer words
of praise. Before asking God to fulfill our human needs, we concede that
our prayers may not always be answered in ways that we would like. With
the powerful words "your will be done," we submit to the wisdom of
God's eternal plan. We affirm our reliance on our Father's providence. We
ask for the "daily manna" to sustain us as it did the Israelites in the desert
centuries earlier. This implies that we should pray to our Father on a daily
basis. Frequent communication helps build this most important relationship. By requesting forgiveness for our sins ("debts"), we acknowledge
our human frailty and the need to forgive the weaknesses of others when
they affect us. To do this often requires a superhuman effort. The prayer
acknowledges our need for the Father's protection in avoiding sinful distractions as we strive daily to walk the path of righteousness.

In Luke, after teaching this prayer, Jesus told a parable emphasizing
the need to pray with perseverance. Though God our Father knows our
needs, daily prayer reinforces our dependence on Him. Just as a friend
will help a friend, how much more will God help His children! Jesus
teaches this important lesson again in a later unit with a parable about
a persistent widow.

P Is for Pig

PICTURE A PLUMP PIG WANDERING about its sty. The mud-covered pig is starving. In spite of its hunger and large growling belly, the pig continues to circle a slop-filled trough. The pig drools while eyeing the feast, yet it does not approach the trough. The pig is **fasting**. The food is tempting, but the **fast** must continue. The aroma is almost overwhelming. Yet, the **fast** goes on. You now recall Jesus' TEACHING ON FASTING with this unlikely image of a fasting pig.

||||||||||||||||||||||||||||||||||||||||||||||||||||||||||||||||||||||||||||||||||||||||||||||||||||||||||||||||||||||||||||||||||||

TEACHING ON FASTING

||||||||||||||||||||||||||||||||||||||||||||||||||||||||||||||||||||||||||||||||||||||||||||||||||||||||||||||||||||||||||||||||||||

Mt 6:16–18

16 "When you fast, do not look gloomy like the hypocrites. They neglect their appearance, so that they may appear to others to be fasting. Amen, I say to you, they have received their reward. 17 But when you fast, anoint your head and wash your face, 18 so that you may not appear to be fasting, except to your Father who is hidden. And your Father who sees what is hidden will repay you."

Jesus taught the crowd and His disciples a new way to practice an old form of prayer. Fasting is a prayer of action rather than words. Previously, sackcloth on the body and ashes on the head made it obvious to others who was not eating. This outward sign was a show of inner repentance. For some, however, it was just a way to attract attention and respect from others. Fasting became a way to focus on self rather than on God. Jesus presumes that His followers will still fast, but they should now go about it differently. They are to present with a clean appearance, wearing normal clothing and a smile. Only God, the One to whom you draw closer, will know you are fasting.

Q Is for Queen Bee

THERE ARE NOT MANY ANIMALS that begin with the letter Q. However, there is a female that does create quite a buzz. This is of course the queen bee. Imagine the queen bee sitting upon her royal throne. Piled up around the throne is her vast **treasure**. Many drones continue to bring her gold coins and precious jewels. They drop the **treasure** they have gathered for their queen and buzz off. The large pile of **treasure** continues to grow around the queen. This scene of **treasure** around the queen bee recalls the next teaching about earthly TREASURE AND GREED.

TREASURE AND GREED

Mt 6:19–24

19 "Do not store up for yourselves treasures on earth, where moth and decay destroy, and thieves break in and steal. **20** But store up treasures in heaven, where neither moth nor decay destroys, nor thieves break in and steal. **21** For where your treasure is, there also will your heart be.

22 "The lamp of the body is the eye. If your eye is sound, your whole body will be filled with light; **23** but if your eye is bad, your whole body will be in darkness. And if the light in you is darkness, how great will the darkness be.

24 "No one can serve two masters. He will either hate one and love the other, or be devoted to one and despise the other. You cannot serve God and mammon."

Lk 12:13–21

13 Someone in the crowd said to him, "Teacher tell my brother to share the inheritance with me." **14** He replied to him, "Friend, who appointed me as your judge and arbitrator?" **15** Then he said to the crowd, "Take care to guard against all greed, for though one may be rich, one's life does not consist of possessions."

16 Then he told them a parable. "There was a rich man whose land produced a bountiful harvest. **17** He asked himself, 'What shall I do, for I do not have space to store my harvest?' **18** And he said, 'This is what I shall do: I shall tear down my barns and build larger ones. There I shall store all my grain and other goods **19** and I shall say to myself, "Now as for you, you have so many good things stored up for many years, rest, eat, drink, be merry!"' **20** But God said to him, 'You fool, this night your life will be demanded of you; and the things you have prepared, to whom will they belong?' **21** Thus will it be for the one who stores up treasure for himself but is not rich in what matters to God."

Jesus implored His followers to concentrate on what is truly important in life. In the scope of eternity, material treasure is worthless. Our eye, the "lamp of the body," should be focused on treasure that is lasting, the treasure of heaven. We have the opportunity to convert earthly treasure to heavenly treasure by sharing our blessings with others. If not, excess possessions can easily become a distraction from our ultimate goal and purpose. Jesus emphasized that we cannot serve both God and money.

In Luke, Jesus told a parable about the dangers of being preoccupied with earthly treasure. Wealth can build walls (like those of a barn) between people, and even between family members. Money can also build a false sense of security. It will all be lost when we die. We can be secure (or insecure) in knowing that this will happen to us all.

R Is for Raccoon

LIKE IT OR NOT, GO ahead and picture a raccoon. It is large, determined, and hungry. The raccoon is sitting atop a trash can covered with a very secure lid. However, the big hungry raccoon has come prepared. It is wielding a sharp **ax**. With several swings of the **ax**, the raccoon slices through the lid. The **ax** is a soundalike for **anxiety**. This lid-busting **ax** represents the feeling of **anxiety**. This will help you recall Jesus' TEACHING ABOUT ANXIETY AND WORRY.

TEACHING ABOUT ANXIETY AND WORRY

Mt 6:25–34

25 "Therefore I tell you, do not worry about your life, what you will eat [or drink], or about your body, what you will wear. Is not life more than food and the body more than clothing? 26 Look at the birds in the sky; they do not sow or reap, they gather nothing into barns, yet your heavenly Father feeds them. Are not you more important than they? 27 Can any of you by worrying add a single

moment to your life-span? **28** Why are you anxious about clothes?
Learn from the way the wild flowers grow. They do not work or
spin. **29** But I tell you that not even Solomon in all his splendor was
clothed like one of them. **30** If God so clothes the grass of the field,
which grows today and is thrown into the oven tomorrow, will he
not much more provide for you, O you of little faith? **31** So do not
worry and say, 'What are we to eat?' or 'What are we to drink?' or
'What are we to wear?' **32** All these things the pagans seek. Your
heavenly Father knows that you need them all. **33** But seek first the
kingdom [of God] and his righteousness, and all these things will
be given you besides. **34** Do not worry about tomorrow; tomorrow
will take care of itself. Sufficient for a day is its own evil."

Lk 12:22–34

22 He said to [his] disciples, "Therefore I tell you, do not worry
about your life and what you will eat, or about your body and what
you will wear. **23** For life is more than food and the body more than
clothing. **24** Notice the ravens: they do not sow or reap; they have
neither storehouse nor barn, yet God feeds them. How much more
important are you than birds! **25** Can any of you by worrying add a
moment to your life-span? **26** If even the smallest things are beyond
your control, why are you anxious about the rest? **27** Notice how
the flowers grow. They do not toil or spin. But I tell you, not even
Solomon in all his splendor was dressed like one of them. **28** If God
so clothes the grass in the field that grows today and is thrown into
the oven tomorrow, will he not much more provide for you, O you of
little faith? **29** As for you, do not seek what you are to eat and what
you are to drink, and do not worry anymore. **30** All the nations of
the world seek for these things, and your Father knows that you
need them. **31** Instead, seek his kingdom, and these other things
will be given you besides. **32** Do not be afraid any longer, little flock,
for your Father is pleased to give you the kingdom. **33** Sell your
belongings and give alms. Provide money bags for yourselves that
do not wear out, an inexhaustible treasure in heaven that no thief
can reach nor moth destroy. **34** For where your treasure is, there
also will your heart be."

Unfortunately, anxiety and worry have become very common in our
hectic, fast-paced modern world. A frantic life is a breeding ground for
stress and the anxiety that often results. Anxiety disorders are among our
most common illnesses. Because of this, Jesus' teachings from two thousand years ago are particularly important for us today.

Jesus' words on worry expand on His previous teaching about greed
and money. For those blessed and entrusted with financial resources, ma-

terial possessions can paradoxically become a major worry. In seeking to acquire more while holding tightly to what one has, anxiety and spiritual poverty can occur. We become poor in what matters most. To prevent this, Jesus urged that we deposit our trust and resources in God. This is a difficult challenge, requiring faith in God's love for us and our well-being. In Luke, Jesus assured us that it is a risk worth taking when pointing out how much our loving Father cares for the birds and flowers.

By sharing our God-given gifts with others, everyone benefits. Givers, by following Jesus' word, become more detached from material possessions and worldly desires. They are less burdened. Recipients of this generosity become less anxious about their material poverty.

S Is for Snake

SNAKES ARE FRIGHTENING TO MANY people, but they are memorable. On your trip down the alphabet, when you arrive at the letter *S*, you see a slithering snake. Of course, this snake is special. Its fangs are tightly clamped down on a gavel! That's right, a gavel, a wooden mallet like a **judge** uses to call for order in the courtroom. Imagine the snake sliding along while pounding the ground with its gavel. A gavel will hopefully make you think of a **judge**. This will allow you to recall Jesus' TEACHING ABOUT JUDGING.

TEACHING ABOUT JUDGING

Mt 7:1–5

1 "Stop judging, that you may be judged. 2 For as you judge, so will you be judged, and the measure with which you measure will be measured out to you. 3 Why do you notice the splinter in your brother's eye, but do not perceive the wooden beam in your own eye? 4 How can you say to your brother, 'Let me remove that splinter from your eye,' while the wooden beam is in your eye? 5 You hypocrite, remove the wooden beam from your eye first; then you will see clearly to remove the splinter from your brother's eye."

Lk 6:37–42

37 "Stop judging and you will not be judged. Stop condemning and you will not be condemned. Forgive and you will be forgiven.

38 Give and gifts will be given to you; a good measure, packed together, shaken down, and overflowing, will be poured into your lap. For the measure with which you measure will in return be measured out to you." **39** And he told them a parable, "Can a blind person guide a blind person? Will not both fall into a pit? **40** No disciple is superior to the teacher; but when fully trained, every disciple will be like his teacher. **41** Why do you notice the splinter in your brother's eye, but do not perceive the wooden beam in your own? **42** How can you say to your brother, 'Brother, let me remove that splinter in your eye,' when you do not even notice the wooden beam in your own eye? You hypocrite! Remove the wooden beam from your eye first; then you will see clearly to remove the splinter in your brother's eye."

As humans, we are acutely aware of the faults and mistakes of others, yet often blind to our own shortcomings. It is much easier to see many external problems than to look at the problems within. It is also very difficult to see what is deep in the hearts of those we judge. In fact, only God truly sees all that goes into the behavior of others. Thus it is not our place to pass judgment on the "splinters" of others. Our own "beams" give us plenty to handle. Dealing with our own imperfections will likely make us more understanding and less preoccupied with the flaws of others. In fact, we will be better able to deal with others' "splinters" and perhaps even help remove them.

T Is for Turkey

THOSE WHO CELEBRATE THANKSGIVING EVERY November typically "invite" a turkey to their table. If given the choice, the turkey would surely decline the invitation. Imagine sitting down to this traditional meal with the large turkey on a platter in the middle of the table. Suddenly, the turkey's wing springs up as if to **ask** permission to speak. This is surprising. It is more shocking when the headless turkey actually **asks** a question! "Why must you eat a turkey every Thanksgiving?" it **asks**. This holiday table scene featuring the **"asking"** turkey represents Jesus' TEACHING ON ASKING, SEEKING, AND KNOCKING.

TEACHING ON ASKING,
SEEKING, AND KNOCKING

Mt 7:6–11

6 "Do not give what is holy to dogs, or throw your pearls before swine, lest they trample them underfoot, and turn and tear you to pieces.
7 "Ask and it will be given to you; seek and you will find; knock and the door will be opened to you. **8** For everyone who asks, receives; and the one who seeks, finds; and to the one who knocks, the door will be opened. **9** Which one of you would hand his son a stone when he asks for a loaf of bread, **10** or a snake when he asks for a fish? **11** If you then, who are wicked, know how to give good gifts to your children, how much more will your heavenly Father give good things to those who ask him."

Lk 11:9–13

9 "And I tell you, ask and you will receive; seek and you will find; knock and the door will be opened to you. **10** For everyone who asks, receives; and the one who seeks, finds; and to the one who knocks, the door will be opened. **11** What father among you would hand his son a snake when he asks for a fish? **12** Or hand him a scorpion when he asks for an egg? **13** If you then, who are wicked, know how to give good gifts to your children, how much more will the Father in heaven give the holy Spirit to those who ask him?"

Earlier in the Sermon, Jesus taught us how to pray with the words of the "Our Father." We learned to "ask" for "daily bread" and to "ask" for forgiveness. Here Jesus repeated the need to "ask," but also emphasized the need for perseverance in prayer. We need to keep asking. We also need to "seek." In seeking, if the door is closed we must "knock." Certainly, our heavenly Father will provide for us, since even a wicked man provides for his children. However, we must also keep in mind that our prayer, no matter how persistent, is not always answered in the way we ask or would like.

U Is for Unicorn

THE ONE-HORNED UNICORN IS A legendary animal. It is a white horse-like creature with a long horn sprouting from its forehead. We will focus our attention on the horn. It has a spiral shape and a sharply pointed tip. This distinctive horn is said to have healing powers. This unicorn's horn is even more special and memorable. It is made of **gold**! The **golden** horn is so bright that even a brief glance is blinding. This horn of **gold** recalls Jesus' teaching commonly referred to as THE GOLDEN RULE.

||||||||||||||||||||||||||||||||||||||||||||||||||||||||||||||||||||||||||||||||||||||||||||||||||||||||||||||

THE GOLDEN RULE

||||||||||||||||||||||||||||||||||||||||||||||||||||||||||||||||||||||||||||||||||||||||||||||||||||||||||||||

Mt 7:12

12 "Do to others whatever you would have them do to you. This is the law and the prophets."

Lk 6:31

31 "Do to others as you would have them do to you."

In much of the Sermon on the Mount, Jesus instructed how we can and should get along with one another. This included teachings on anger, adultery, retaliation, love, almsgiving, and judging. You now come to a very familiar passage often referred to as The Golden Rule. Like gold, this lesson is a very valuable nugget for leading a Christian life. Here Jesus combined ideas found in Tobit and Sirach, two of the so-called apocryphal books of the Bible. Tobit 4:15 advises, "Do to no one what you yourself dislike." Sirach 31:15 says to "recognize that your neighbor feels as you do." Jesus framed these ideas as a call to action. We are to act positively toward others, not just avoid negative behavior. What a different world this would be if people took this teaching to heart!

V Is for Vulture

THE VULTURE IS A LARGE bird of prey. It is often pictured with its bald head and sharp teeth feasting on a tasty carcass. You will see this image, but with a slight twist—actually a **narrow** twist. Imagine a field enclosed by a fence. For a vulture to gain entrance to the field, an extremely **narrow gate** must be negotiated. The large hungry vulture stands outside of the field since it is too big to pass through the **gate.** (It is also not smart enough to fly over the fence!) Now picture the vulture with its head and neck poking through the **gate.** Only this much of the vulture will fit through the **narrow gate.** However, the vulture is now able to enjoy its meal. This rather unpleasant scene recalls Jesus' words about THE NARROW GATE.

THE NARROW GATE

Mt 7:13–14

13 "Enter through the narrow gate; for the gate is wide and the road broad that leads to destruction, and those who enter through it are many. 14 How narrow the gate and constricted the road that leads to life. And those who find it are few."

Here on the mountain, Jesus alluded to the city gates of Jerusalem. These points of entry into Jerusalem were very familiar to His audience. Some gates were wide, allowing animals and other large objects to pass through. Others were narrow, only accommodating individuals.

In life, we all have many decisions to make. Some are small and inconsequential. Others are major and can be life-changing. As individuals in a variety of circumstances, many of our options and choices will be different from those others face. However, we all have one choice in common. It also happens to be the most important decision of all. It is the choice that affects all of our other life decisions. Do you choose the narrow gate and walk with Jesus, or do you choose the wider and easier gate and focus on the distractions of this world?

God has given us a very special gift. Sometimes it may feel like a blessing and at other times a burden. It is free will. We are able to make choices that determine our path in life. Of course, we do not have total control of the outcome, but we can choose the narrow gate. Though more difficult to negotiate, it will put us on the path that leads to the kingdom of heaven.

W Is for Wolf

MANY LETTERS AGO, WE LEARNED that D is for dog. We now see a wolf, a wild member of the dog family. Imagine a big hungry wolf. See its pointy ears. Its sharp teeth are dripping with saliva. This wolf is both fierce and smart. Now see the wolf slipping on the mask of a **sheep** to cover its face. This disguise will allow the wolf to sneak up on the **sheep** grazing in a nearby field. This scene is a reminder of Jesus' teaching about A WOLF IN SHEEP'S CLOTHING.

A WOLF IN SHEEP'S CLOTHING

Mt 7:15–20

15 "Beware of false prophets, who come to you in sheep's clothing, but underneath are ravenous wolves. 16 By their fruits you will know them. Do people pick grapes from thornbushes, or figs from thistles? 17 Just so, every good tree bears good fruit, and a rotten tree bears bad fruit. 18 A good tree cannot bear bad fruit, nor can a rotten tree bear good fruit. 19 Every tree that does not bear good fruit will be cut down and thrown into the fire. 20 So by their fruits you will know them."

Lk 6:43–45

43 "A good tree does not bear rotten fruit, nor does a rotten tree bear good fruit. 44 For every tree is known by its own fruit. For people do not pick figs from thornbushes, nor do they gather grapes from brambles. 45 A good person out of the store of goodness in his heart produces good, but an evil person out of a store of evil produces evil; for from the fullness of the heart the mouth speaks."

Jesus now issued a warning to His audience. His prophetic words told of some who will claim to be true prophets of God. They will be as destructive as a hungry wolf, though their words will make them seem as harmless as grazing sheep. However, it is not what they say that will be important. It is what they do. Do they choose the narrow gate? Do they bear good fruit? Jesus told His audience that they, too, must bear good fruit in preparation for the Final Judgment.

In Luke's parallel account, Jesus spoke of the heart as the source of moral behavior. To lead a good life, you must have a good heart. One develops such a heart by following the teachings Jesus put forth in this very Sermon.

X Is for Nothing at All

THERE IS NO ANIMAL TO remember here. It has been crossed off the list!

Y Is for Yak

MOST PEOPLE HAVE PROBABLY ONLY seen a yak in pictures. This large, hairy animal lives in the mountains of Asia. It resembles the American bison. The yak is a furry animal, often trained as a beast of burden to carry loads over rough mountain terrain. Now imagine your own **father** sitting upon the back of a yak. Your **father** is guiding the yak through the mountains. He tells it to go left, then right, to speed up, to slow down. The yak obeys every command given by your **father**. It very faithfully does the **will of your father**. This scene with the yak doing your **father's will** is a reminder of Jesus' teaching about THE WILL OF THE FATHER.

THE WILL OF THE FATHER

Mt 7:21–23

21 "Not everyone who says to me, 'Lord, Lord,' will enter the kingdom of heaven, but only the one who does the will of my Father in heaven. **22** Many will say to me on that day, 'Lord, Lord, did we not prophesy in your name? Did we not drive out demons in your name? Did we not do mighty deeds in your name?' **23** Then I will declare to them solemnly, 'I never knew you. Depart from me, you evildoers.'"

These words coming at the end of the Sermon seem rather harsh, but they actually do us a favor. They are a warning against self-deception. Our lives may be full of deeds that we and others see as great or wonderful. However, if our actions are not the will of the Father, come Judgment Day they will be seen as trivial. So how do we know the Father's will? The answer is found in the gift of Himself. The answer is found in Jesus. We do the will of the Father when we know Jesus and obey His teachings. By following Jesus, we will not deceive ourselves and become complacent. We will lead a life filled not only with right deeds, but with love.

Z Is for Zebra

LAST BUT NOT LEAST, "Z Is for Zebra." Like the other animals you have met on your trip through the alphabet, the zebra is special. It is a horse-like animal with black and white stripes. However, this zebra has chosen not to live in the herd with the other zebras. It wants to **build** its own house! You watch as the zebra begins the **building** process. It knows the foundation comes first. The industrious zebra chooses a solid piece of land and begins **building** its house. When the last shovel of dirt is removed, **building** continues with the laying of iron bars to strengthen the foundation. Then, with great care, the zebra pours and smooths out the cement. With this strong foundation in place, the zebra waits for the cement to harden. This important process demonstrates the need for a strong foundation, which is found in THE PARABLE OF THE BUILDERS.

THE PARABLE OF THE BUILDERS

Mt 7:24–29

24 "Everyone who listens to these words of mine and acts on them will be like a wise man who built his house on rock. **25** The rain fell, the floods came, and the winds blew and buffeted the house. But it did not collapse; it had been set solidly on rock. **26** And everyone who listens to these words of mine but does not act on them will be like a fool who built his house on sand. **27** The rain fell, the floods came, and the winds blew and buffeted the house. And it collapsed and was completely ruined."

28 When Jesus finished these words, the crowds were astonished at his teaching, **29** for he taught them as one having authority, and not as their scribes.

Lk 6:46–49

46 "Why do you call me, 'Lord, Lord,' but not do what I command? **47** I will show you what someone is like who comes to me, listens to my words, and acts on them. **48** That one is like a person building a house, who dug deeply and laid the foundation on rock; when the flood came, the river burst against that house but could not shake it because it had been well built. **49** But the one who listens and does not act is like a person who built a house on the ground without a foundation. When the river burst against it, it collapsed at once and was completely destroyed."

———————

You have come to the end of the Sermon on the Mount. Jesus now preached about the need for a strong beginning, or foundation. The image of a flood washing away a house with a weak foundation was one that some in Jesus' audience may have actually witnessed. Flash floods during the rainy season in Palestine were quite destructive. Jesus told His listeners to build a strong life using the teachings they had just heard. Hearing and then acting on Jesus' words will build a strong life that can withstand the storm of the Final Judgment. This type of construction takes significant effort, but it is the best investment you can make for eternity.

Landmark 6:

SNOWFLAKE

With the radical teachings of the Sermon on the Mount filling your heart and mind, it is time to move on to the sixth Landmark. It is a six-sided object familiar to most people. It is a big part of life for those living in cold climates. This Landmark is always different, but always has six sides. You may have guessed by now that it is a **snowflake**. This particular **snowflake** is very large by **snowflake** standards. It measures six inches along each of its six sides. All of the intricate details of this huge **snowflake** are clearly visible. You are now watching this giant **snowflake** slowly drift down from the sky. Watching the **snowflake** fall, you are in awe of its delicate beauty and amazing size.

You watch the giant snowflake fall from the cloudy sky. As it comes closer to the ground, you see that a man standing nearby has also been tracking its slow descent. The super-sized flake is falling straight toward his upturned face. The man's unflinching posture gives you the impression that he wants the snowflake to land on him. He gets his wish. The snowflake makes a direct hit and remains attached to his now smiling face. You rush over to see if he has been injured. To your amazement, just the opposite begins to occur. You immediately recognize the distorted, diseased, and eroded face of a poor **leper**. You then witness a miraculous healing. Soon after the snowflake makes contact, the **leper's** face begins to change. His features are gradually restored. The **leper's** skin is once again smooth, taut, and youthful. The **leper** has been healed. This immediately reminds you of the story of Jesus HEALING A LEPER.

HEALING A LEPER

Mt 8:1–4

1 When Jesus came down from the mountain, great crowds followed him. 2 And then a leper approached, did him homage, and said, "Lord, if you wish, you can make me clean." 3 He stretched out his hand, touched him, and said, "I will do it. Be made clean." His leprosy was cleansed immediately. 4 Then Jesus said to him, "See that you tell no one, but go show yourself to the priest, and offer the gift that Moses prescribed; that will be proof for them."

Mk 1:40–45

40 A leper came to him [and kneeling down] begged him and said, "If you wish, you can make me clean." 41 Moved with pity, he stretched out his hand, touched him, and said to him, "I do will it. Be made clean." 42 The leprosy left him immediately, and he was made clean. 43 Then, warning him sternly, he dismissed him at once. 44 Then he said to him, "See that you tell no one anything, but go, show yourself to the priest and offer for your cleansing what Moses prescribed; that will be proof for them." 45 The man went away and began to publicize the whole matter. He spread the report abroad so that it was impossible for Jesus to enter a town openly. He remained outside in deserted places, and people kept coming to him from everywhere.

Lk 5:12–16

12 Now there was a man full of leprosy in one of the towns where he was; and when he saw Jesus, he fell prostrate, pleaded with him, and said, "Lord, if you wish, you can make me clean." 13 Jesus stretched out his hand, touched him, and said, "I do will it. Be made clean." And the leprosy left him immediately. 14 Then he ordered him not to tell anyone, but "Go, show yourself to the priest and offer for your cleansing what Moses prescribed; that will be proof for them." 15 The report about him spread all the more, and great crowds assembled to listen to him and to be cured of their ailments, 16 but he would withdraw to deserted places to pray.

This is the first of three miraculous healings associated with the sixth Landmark. All three were quite different, but each miracle caused controversy. This theme of Jesus as a controversial and polarizing figure will continue to develop as He works His way toward the cross.

Imagine the courage it must have taken for this disfigured outcast to approach Jesus and beg for healing. Similarly, Jesus publicly touching the leper's diseased skin was not an everyday occurrence. Jesus responded with pity and compassion to the man's profession of faith. This "cleansing" in response to faith will be a common theme in future healings.

Here there is another example of the "Messianic Secret." Jesus was not ready for His identity as the Messiah to be widely known. People were not ready to embrace the type of Messiah that Jesus would prove to be.

After this miracle, Jesus showed that He was very much a Jew who was well-versed in Jewish tradition. He commanded the man to observe the Jewish Law as described in Leviticus 14. The healed man was to present himself to a priest and follow the prescribed ritual. Only then could he be fully restored to the community. Like the leper, we can be touched and healed by Jesus; we, too, must have faith and the desire to be made clean.

THE LEPER HAS BEEN HEALED. His face has been restored to its youthful radiance. There is just one small problem. Actually, a fairly large problem. The giant snowflake remains attached to his face. Using his newfound strength, the healed man is still unable to remove the snowflake. You decide to come to his assistance. Before doing so, you will need the proper attire and equipment. You begin to don the uniform of a Roman **centurion**, a Roman soldier who commanded one hundred soldiers. You quickly attach the breastplate, put on the feathered helmet, and grab a razor-sharp sword. Approaching the snowflake, you see that the face it partially covers has a look of fear. The healed leper is naturally quite concerned about what you, dressed as a Roman **centurion**, have in mind. He does not know that your intention is to remove the snowflake. When you are within several feet of the snowflake, you quickly draw your sword. With all of the skill of a true Roman **centurion**, you pierce the snowflake. You now hold the sword high with the snowflake dangling from its tip. Your brief adventure as a **centurion** recalls the next unit: THE HEALING OF THE CENTURION'S SLAVE.

THE HEALING OF THE CENTURION'S SLAVE

Mt 8:5–13

5 When he entered Capernaum, a centurion approached him and appealed to him, 6 saying, "Lord, my servant is lying at home paralyzed, suffering dreadfully." 7 He said to him, "I will come and cure him." 8 The centurion said in reply, "Lord, I am not worthy to have you enter under my roof; only say the word and my servant will be healed. 9 For I too am a person subject to authority, with soldiers subject to me. And I say to one, 'Go,' and he goes; and to another, 'Come here,' and he comes; and to my slave, 'Do this,' and he does it." 10 When Jesus heard this, he was amazed and said to those following him, "Amen, I say to you, in no one in Israel have I found such faith. 11 I say to you, many will come from the east and the west, and will recline with Abraham, Isaac, and Jacob at the banquet in the kingdom of heaven, 12 but the children of the kingdom will be driven out into the outer darkness, where there will be wailing and grinding of teeth." 13 And Jesus said to the centurion, "You may go; as you have believed, let it be done for you." And at that very hour [his] servant was healed.

Lk 7:1–10

1 When he had finished all his words to the people, he entered Capernaum. 2 A centurion there had a slave who was ill and about to die, and he was valuable to him. 3 When he heard about Jesus, he sent elders of the Jews to him, asking him to come and save the life of his slave. 4 They approached Jesus and strongly urged him to come, saying, "He deserves to have you do this for him, 5 for he loves our nation and he built the synagogue for us." 6 And Jesus went with them, but when he was only a short distance from the house, the centurion sent friends to tell him, "Lord, do not trouble yourself, for I am not worthy to have you enter under my roof. 7 Therefore, I did not consider myself worthy to come to you; but say the word and let my servant be healed. 8 For I too am a person subject to authority, with soldiers subject to me. And I say to one, 'Go,' and he goes; and to another, 'Come here,' and he comes; and to my slave, 'Do this,' and he does it." 9 When Jesus heard this he was amazed at him and, turning, said to the crowd following him, "I tell you, not even in Israel have I found such faith." 10 When the messengers returned to the house, they found the slave in good health.

46 Then he returned to Cana in Galilee, where he had made the water wine. Now there was a royal official whose son was ill in Capernaum. **47** When he heard that Jesus had arrived in Galilee from Judea, he went to him and asked him to come down and heal his son, who was near death. **48** Jesus said to him, "Unless you people see signs and wonders, you will not believe." **49** The royal official said to him, "Sir, come down before my child dies." **50** Jesus said to him, "You may go; your son will live." The man believed what Jesus said to him and left. **51** While he was on his way back, his slaves met him and told him that his boy would live. **52** He asked them when he began to recover. They told him, "The fever left him yesterday, about one in the afternoon." **53** The father realized that just at that time Jesus had said to him, "Your son will live," and he and his whole household came to believe. **54** [Now] this was the second sign Jesus did when he came to Galilee from Judea.

———————————

This unit is another healing miracle. The actual cure is less emphasized than the conversation between Jesus and the centurion. This Roman soldier, like the leper, was someone most Jews would have made every effort to avoid. Not only was the soldier a Gentile, he also represented the cruel oppression of Rome. However, this particular centurion was full of surprises. He cared about his ill servant. Most slaves were treated as mere possessions. The centurion also showed respect for Jewish beliefs. He knew Jesus would be "defiled" if He entered the home of a Gentile. Most importantly, this despised Roman soldier showed a faith that Jesus found amazing. Jesus took this opportunity to warn against complacency. Many people from other lands (non-Jews) would partake in the heavenly banquet. Simply being a Jew did not guarantee a seat at the table. What a stir this radical statement must have caused! It was ironic that Jesus, who healed this suffering servant, would Himself become "The Suffering Servant" sent to heal us all.

A very similar story is found in John's Gospel. It is THE HEALING OF THE ROYAL OFFICIAL'S SON. Both of these miracles are examples of Jesus "healing from a distance." It takes place in Cana rather than Capernaum, and the official is a Jew rather than a Gentile. However, both show great faith in the word of Jesus, who Himself is the Word of God.

THE LARGE SNOWFLAKE HAS REMAINED pierced on the tip of your extended sword. Repeated shaking has failed to free the flake. The motion has lodged it even more securely on the blade. The healed leper has an idea. He pulls a ripe **pear** from his pocket and takes aim. He throws the **pear**, but misses the snowflake. However, he now has a sliced **pear**! He takes another **pear** and lets it fly. This shot hits its target and the flake flutters to the ground. You and the man share the **pears** to celebrate his healing. The **pears** are a soundalike for "paralytic." They are a reminder of the unit where JESUS HEALS A PARALYTIC.

JESUS HEALS A PARALYTIC

Mt 9:1–8

1 He entered a boat, made the crossing, and came into his own town. 2 And there people brought to him a paralytic lying on a stretcher. When Jesus saw their faith, he said to the paralytic, "Courage, child, your sins are forgiven." 3 At that, some of the scribes said to themselves, "This man is blaspheming." 4 Jesus knew what they were thinking, and said, "Why do you harbor evil thoughts? 5 Which is easier, to say, 'Your sins are forgiven,' or to say, 'Rise and walk'? 6 But that you may know that the Son of Man has authority on earth to forgive sins" —he then said to the paralytic, "Rise, pick up your stretcher, and go home." 7 He rose and went home. 8 When the crowds saw this they were struck with awe and glorified God who had given such authority to human beings.

Mk 2:1–12

1 When Jesus returned to Capernaum after some days, it became known that he was at home. 2 Many gathered together so that there was no longer room for them, not even around the door, and he preached the word to them. 3 They came bringing to him a paralytic carried by four men. 4 Unable to get near Jesus because of the crowd, they opened up the roof above him. After they had broken through, they let down the mat on which the paralytic was lying. 5 When Jesus saw their faith, he said to the paralytic, "Child, your sins are forgiven." 6 Now some of the scribes were sitting there asking themselves, 7 "Why does this man speak that way? He is blaspheming. Who but God alone can forgive sins?" 8 Jesus immediately knew in his mind what they were thinking to themselves, so he said, "Why are you thinking such things in your hearts? 9 Which is easier, to say to the paralytic, 'Your sins are

forgiven,' or to say, 'Rise, pick up your mat and walk'? **10** But that you may know that the Son of Man has authority to forgive sins on earth"— **11** he said to the paralytic, "I say to you, rise, pick up your mat, and go home." **12** He rose, picked up his mat at once, and went away in the sight of everyone. They were all astounded and glorified God, saying, "We have never seen anything like this."

Lk 5:17–26

17 One day as Jesus was teaching, Pharisees and teachers of the law were sitting there who had come from every village of Galilee and Judea and Jerusalem, and the power of the Lord was with him for healing. **18** And some men brought on a stretcher a man who was paralyzed; they were trying to bring him in and set [him] in his presence. **19** But not finding a way to bring him in because of the crowd, they went up on the roof and lowered him on the stretcher through the tiles into the middle in front of Jesus. **20** When he saw their faith, he said, "As for you, your sins are forgiven." **21** Then the scribes and Pharisees began to ask themselves, "Who is this who speaks blasphemies? Who but God alone can forgive sins?" **22** Jesus knew their thoughts and said to them in reply, "What are you thinking in your hearts? **23** Which is easier, to say, 'Your sins are forgiven,' or to say, 'Rise and walk'? **24** But that you may know that the Son of Man has authority on earth to forgive sins"—he said to the man who was paralyzed, "I say to you, rise, pick up your stretcher, and go home." **25** He stood up immediately before them, picked up what he had been lying on, and went home, glorifying God. **26** Then astonishment seized them all and they glorified God, and, struck with awe, they said, "We have seen incredible things today."

This is the final healing miracle associated with the snowflake Landmark. There was controversy in the first two instances when Jesus associated with an unclean leper and then a Roman centurion. This final healing took controversy to a new level. This familiar story is recorded in Matthew, Mark, and Luke. However, it should not be confused with Jesus' "Healing a Paralytic on the Sabbath." That story, found only in John's Gospel, is coming soon.

Back in Capernaum, Jesus attracted a large crowd, just as He had following the healing of Peter's mother-in-law. The crowd gave the friends of the paralytic an opportunity to show their faith in Jesus. They literally had to "raise the roof" in order to obtain an audience with Jesus. Before healing the man's obvious physical infirmity, Jesus did something even more shocking: He forgave the man's sins! Jesus claimed the authority possessed by God alone. In exercising this power first, Jesus showed the priority of spiritual healing. Sin is more crippling than any physical disease! However, to many who heard these healing words, it was blasphemy. Jesus had made Himself God, a crime punishable by death. Was this the "beginning of the end" for Jesus?

Landmark 7:

RABBIT'S FOOT

If you asked a large group of people to name a number that they considered to be "lucky," many would respond with "Seven." Since we have now arrived at the seventh Landmark, it, too, will be associated with luck or good fortune. An object many consider to be lucky is a **rabbit's foot**. Yes, the little furry **foot of a rabbit**. Traditionally, it has been the left hind **foot of the rabbit**, but we need not split hares ("hairs"). Just firmly set in your mind that the seventh Landmark is a small furry **rabbit's foot**, which you are holding in your hand.

You have the seventh Landmark, the rabbit's foot, firmly in hand. It is now time to travel on and experience the units associated with this lucky Landmark. For safekeeping, you decide it would be best to put the rabbit's foot in your pants pocket. It is important that you are wearing pants! It is equally important that they are denim jeans. It is most important that they are **Levi's**. They are comfortable, faded, and well-worn **Levi's**. You carefully place the rabbit's foot in a side pocket of the **Levi's**. There is now a slight bulge in the pocket of the **Levi's**, but the rabbit's foot is now secure. All of this talk about your **Levi's** is a friendly reminder about THE CALL OF LEVI (MATTHEW).

THE CALL OF LEVI

Mt 9:9–13

9 As Jesus passed on from there, he saw a man named Matthew sitting at the customs post. He said to him, "Follow me." And he got up and followed him. **10** While he was at table in his house, many tax collectors and sinners came and sat with Jesus and his disciples. **11** The Pharisees saw this and said to his disciples, "Why does your teacher eat with tax collectors and sinners?" **12** He heard this and said, "Those who are well do not need a physician, but the sick do. **13** Go and learn the meaning of the words, 'I desire mercy, not sacrifice.' I did not come to call the righteous but sinners."

Mk 2:13–17

13 Once again he went out along the sea. All the crowd came to him and he taught them. **14** As he passed by, he saw Levi, son of Alphaeus, sitting at the customs post. He said to him, "Follow me." And he got up and followed him. **15** While he was at table in his house, many tax collectors and sinners sat with Jesus and his disciples; for there were many who followed him. **16** Some scribes who were Pharisees saw that he was eating with sinners and tax collectors and said to his disciples, "Why does he eat with tax collectors and sinners?" **17** Jesus heard this and said to them [that], "Those who are well do not need a physician, but the sick do. I did not come to call the righteous but sinners."

Lk 5:27–32

27 After this he went out and saw a tax collector named Levi sitting at the customs post. He said to him, "Follow me." **28** And leaving everything behind, he got up and followed him. **29** Then Levi gave a great banquet for him in his house, and a large crowd of tax collectors and others were at table with them. **30** The Pharisees and their scribes complained to his disciples, saying, "Why do you eat and drink with tax collectors and sinners?" **31** Jesus said to them in reply, "Those who are healthy do not need a physician, but the sick do. **32** I have not come to call the righteous to repentance but sinners."

———————————

Levi (or Matthew) was a Jew who worked for the governor that ruled over Galilee and the surrounding territory. This governor was Herod Antipas, one of the sons of the now deceased Herod the Great. Antipas was a representative of the oppressive Roman Empire and the evil Emperor Tiberius. Levi was essentially a traitor, a Jew working for the enemy. How shocking it must have been for Jesus' disciples to hear the words "follow me" directed at Levi.

Later, at Levi's house, Jesus and His disciples actually broke bread with Levi and other "sinners." The Pharisees were beside themselves! These pious sticklers of Jewish Law were appalled at Jesus' disregard for Jewish belief and customs. They considered these undesirables to be "sick" with sin. Jesus made it clear that as the Divine Physician He had come to heal those paralyzed by sin. Just as the man Jesus healed earlier was physically paralyzed, sinners are paralyzed in their relationship with God.

WITH THE RABBIT'S FOOT NESTLED deep inside your Levi's, you suddenly feel extremely energized. You have the urge to run **fast**, like a rabbit, of course. Perhaps you have never been a very **fast** runner. Well, now you are extremely **fast**! See yourself running **fast** with the rabbit's foot as the source of your newfound speed. You are a blur. Running past many people, you are too **fast** to be recognized. While running at this **fast**, exhilarating pace, you cannot help thinking about the unit that asks THE QUESTION ABOUT FASTING.

THE QUESTION ABOUT FASTING

Mt 9:14–17

14 Then the disciples of John approached him and said, "Why do we and the Pharisees fast [much], but your disciples do not fast?" **15** Jesus answered them, "Can the wedding guests mourn as long as the bridegroom is with them? The days will come when the bridegroom is taken away from them, and then they will fast. **16** No one patches an old cloak with a piece of unshrunken cloth, for its fullness pulls away from the cloak and the tear gets worse. **17** People do not put new wine into old wineskins. Otherwise the skins burst, the wine spills out, and the skins are ruined. Rather, they pour new wine into fresh wineskins, and both are preserved."

Mk 2:18–22

18 The disciples of John and of the Pharisees were accustomed to fast. People came to him and objected, "Why do the disciples of John and the disciples of the Pharisees fast, but your disciples do not fast?" **19** Jesus answered them, "Can the wedding guests fast while the bridegroom is with them? As long as they have the bridegroom with them they cannot fast. **20** But the days will come when the bridegroom is taken away from them, and then they will fast on that day. **21** No one sews a piece of unshrunken cloth on an old cloak. If he does, its fullness pulls away, the new from the old, and the tear gets worse. **22** Likewise, no one pours new wine into old wineskins. Otherwise, the wine will burst the skins, and both the wine and the skins are ruined. Rather, new wine is poured into fresh wineskins."

Lk 5:33–39

33 And they said to him, "The disciples of John fast often and offer prayers, and the disciples of the Pharisees do the same; but yours eat and drink." 34 Jesus answered them, "Can you make the wedding guests fast while the bridegroom is with them? 35 But the days will come, and when the bridegroom is taken away from them, then they will fast in those days." 36 And he also told them a parable. "No one tears a piece from a new cloak to patch an old one. Otherwise, he will tear the new and the piece from it will not match the old cloak. 37 Likewise, no one pours new wine into old wineskins. Otherwise, the new wine will burst the skins, and it will be spilled, and the skins will be ruined. 38 Rather, new wine must be poured into fresh wineskins. 39 [And] no one who has been drinking old wine desires new, for he says, 'The old is good.'"

Jesus was now a controversial figure. While dining with sinners at the home of a tax collector, He was asked why His disciples did not follow the Jewish custom of fasting. Were they somehow above the Law? Jesus began His response by referring to Himself as a bridegroom. One does not fast when the bridegroom is present. It is a time of celebration. Perhaps some of the questioners were aware of the implications of the bridegroom analogy. In the Hebrew Scriptures, Yahweh Himself was described as the Bridegroom of Israel (Is 62:5). Here Jesus made the first reference to the fate that awaited Him. A day would come in the near future when the bridegroom would be brutally taken away. Then the tradition of fasting would resume.

The second part of Jesus' response to the question about fasting was in the form of two short parables. A well-worn cloak and a much-used wineskin represented old traditional religious practices. These were the customs and forms of worship familiar and comfortable to the Jewish people. Unwashed cloth and fresh wineskins symbolized the new practices and ideas put forth by Jesus. He did not want to abolish all of Jewish tradition. Jesus wanted to preserve and expand on the old. As He proclaimed in the Sermon on the Mount, Jesus had come not to abolish, but to fulfill the Law.

WHILE RUNNING FAST, YOU ARE naturally not able to take in all of your surroundings. Many small things go unnoticed. Unfortunately, you also overlook a large man lying in the middle of the road. Splat! You trip over the man and suddenly are lying face down in the street beside the immobile man. Slowly, you pull yourself to your knees. Now standing, you look down at the man lying in the street. He still does not move. It is as if he is **paralyzed.** You reach down to help him. Still there is no movement. The man explains that he is in fact **paralyzed.** His **paralysis** is severe. He was unable to get out of your way and is now unable to grasp your extended hand. The **paralyzed** man goes on to say that he was on his way to church (it is the Sabbath) when he suddenly became **paralyzed.** With great effort on this Sabbath morning, you pull the **paralyzed** man to safety by the side of the road. This sad event represents the unit HEALING A PARALYTIC ON THE SABBATH. Note that this is a different event from the recent healing of the paralytic who was lowered through the roof in Capernaum.

HEALING A PARALYTIC ON THE SABBATH

Jn 5:1–18

1 After this, there was a feast of the Jews, and Jesus went up to Jerusalem. **2** Now there is in Jerusalem at the Sheep [Gate] a pool called in Hebrew Bethesda, with five porticoes. **3** In these lay a large number of ill, blind, lame, and crippled. [4] **5** One man was there who had been ill for thirty-eight years. **6** When Jesus saw him lying there and knew that he had been ill for a long time, he said to him, "Do you want to be well?" **7** The sick man answered him, "Sir, I have no one to put me into the pool when the water is stirred up; while I am on my way, someone else gets down there before me." **8** Jesus said to him, "Rise, take up your mat, and walk." **9** Immediately the man became well, took up his mat, and walked.

Now that day was a sabbath. **10** So the Jews said to the man who was cured, "It is the sabbath, and it is not lawful for you to carry your mat." **11** He answered them, "The man who made me well told me, 'Take up your mat and walk.'" **12** They asked him, "Who is the man who told you, 'Take it up and walk'?" **13** The man who was healed did not know who it was, for Jesus had slipped away, since there was a crowd there. **14** After this Jesus found him in the temple area and said to him, "Look, you are well; do not sin anymore, so that nothing worse may happen to you." **15** The man went and told the Jews that Jesus was the one who had made him well. **16** Therefore, the Jews began to persecute Jesus because he did this on a sabbath. **17** But Jesus answered them, "My Father is at

work until now, so I am at work." **18 For this reason the Jews tried
all the more to kill him, because he not only broke the sabbath but
he also called God his own father, making himself equal to God.**

―――――――――

This is another unit where Jesus found Himself embroiled in controversy. It is also the first of four consecutive units found exclusively in the
Gospel of John. This healing of a paralytic took place in Jerusalem rather
than Capernaum. It also occurred on the Sabbath, a day when work and
apparently miracle-working were frowned upon.

This unit consists of several scenes involving three sets of characters.
In the first scene, Jesus became aware of the paralytic's chronic condition
and asked if he wanted to be made well. Indeed, he did! The man realized
that he, like all of us, needed help. Jesus then uttered familiar words with
familiar results. The long-suffering man was instantly healed. Off he went,
with mat in hand. The man then encountered some questioning, legalistic
Jews. The ex-paralytic was unaware of Jesus' identity, just as we are often
not aware of His hidden interventions in our lives. The man was eventually able to identify Jesus as the one who had healed him on the Sabbath.
Jesus was then criticized for doing what was "unlawful." Jesus explained
that neither He nor His Father take days off from doing good. The Jews
were more enraged with this blasphemous statement. Blasphemy was the
capital crime for which Jesus was eventually charged and executed.

THOUGH YOU ARE TIRED FROM pulling the paralytic from the road,
you continue your very fast running. Soon you begin to slow down. You
come to a stop in front of a large **work** site. You have arrived at a tall
office building. A construction crew is hard at **work** outside the building. Through the windows, you can see many people inside **working** at
their desks. Everyone seems to be **working**. Just watching all of this **work**
makes you feel even more tired. It also makes you think of the next unit
associated with the rabbit's foot in your pocket: THE WORK OF THE SON.

THE WORK OF THE SON

Jn 5:19–30

19 Jesus answered and said to them, "Amen, amen, I say to you, a son cannot do anything on his own, but only what he sees his father doing; for what he does, his son will do also. **20** For the Father loves his Son and shows him everything that he himself does, and he will show him greater works than these, so that you may be amazed. **21** For just as the Father raises the dead and gives life, so also does the Son give life to whomever he wishes. **22** Nor does the Father judge anyone, but he has given all judgment to his Son, **23** so that all may honor the Son just as they honor the Father. Whoever does not honor the Son does not honor the Father who sent him. **24** Amen, amen, I say to you, whoever hears my word and believes in the one who sent me has eternal life and will not come to condemnation, but has passed from death to life. **25** Amen, amen, I say to you, the hour is coming and is now here when the dead will hear the voice of the Son of God, and those who hear will live. **26** For just as the Father has life in himself, so also he gave to his Son the possession of life in himself. **27** And he gave him power to exercise judgment, because he is the Son of Man. **28** Do not be amazed at this, because the hour is coming in which all who are in the tombs will hear his voice **29** and will come out, those who have done good deeds to the resurrection of life, but those who have done wicked deeds to the resurrection of condemnation.

30 "I cannot do anything on my own; I judge as I hear, and my judgment is just, because I do not seek my own will but the will of the one who sent me."

The Jews who were upset with Jesus for referring to God as His Father could not have been pleased with the description of the work He was sent to do. Here Jesus further identified Himself with the Father by explaining that His work was the work of God, His Father. Thus the same honor and respect given to God should have been accorded Jesus, His Son.

Jesus was working on behalf of God, so hearing and believing in Jesus' work will lead to salvation. Those who do not follow this teaching are subject to a judgment that will not go well. The work of Jesus was to give life, but also to render judgment. Just as Jesus sought to do "the will of the one who sent me," those who hear Jesus' words should do the same.

OBSERVING THE PEOPLE OUTSIDE AND inside working at various jobs gives you an idea. You decide to go inside the office building and see if there is a job available for you. Upon entering the spacious lobby, you see a large sign with the words "Job **Testing** Here." You walk over and tell the woman in charge that you would like to **test** for a position. She hands you a copy of the job **test** and points to the **testing** room. You anxiously enter the room. There are several other people sitting at small desks answering their **test** questions. You slide into an empty chair and begin the **test**. This **test** scene brings to mind the unit about THE TESTIMONY OF JESUS.

THE TESTIMONY OF JESUS

Jn 5:31–40

31 "If I testify on my own behalf, my testimony cannot be verified. **32** But there is another who testifies on my behalf, and I know that the testimony he gives on my behalf is true. **33** You sent emissaries to John, and he testified to the truth. **34** I do not accept testimony from a human being, but I say this so that you may be saved. **35** He was a burning and shining lamp, and for a while you were content to rejoice in his light. **36** But I have testimony greater than John's. The works that the Father gave me to accomplish, these works that I perform testify on my behalf that the Father has sent me. **37** Moreover, the Father who sent me has testified on my behalf. But you have never heard his voice nor seen his form, **38** and you do not have his word remaining in you, because you do not believe in the one whom he has sent. **39** You search the scriptures, because you think you have eternal life through them; even they testify on my behalf. **40** But you do not want to come to me to have life."

Jesus acknowledged that just His own testimony about His identity and purpose would not be enough for many. This was particularly true for the legalistic Jews who were already upset with His radical behavior and teaching. Jesus pointed out the recent testimony of John the Baptist about His identity. However, there was much more compelling evidence. The miracles He had performed were more powerful than the words of John. Also, more convincing than the words of the Baptist were the words and prophecies found in the Hebrew Scriptures. Jesus then referred to the words of the Father who had verified Jesus' Sonship at His Baptism.

YOU IMMEDIATELY DISCOVER THAT THE job test is not just challenging, it is unbelievably difficult! You are in **disbelief**. The first several questions seem impossible. You shake your head in **disbelief**. Looking around, you see others are also shaking their heads in **disbelief**. Leafing through the rest of the test, you continue to shake your head in **disbelief**. Your frustration and **disbelief** continue to grow. You stand and walk toward the exit muttering "unbelievable"! This little episode of great **disbelief** is the final unit you will associate with the seventh Landmark: THE DISBELIEF OF JESUS' HEARERS.

THE DISBELIEF OF JESUS' HEARERS

Jn 5:41–47

41 "I do not accept human praise; **42** moreover, I know that you do not have the love of God in you. **43** I came in the name of my Father, but you do not accept me; yet if another comes in his own name, you will accept him. **44** How can you believe, when you accept praise from one another and do not seek the praise that comes from the only God? **45** Do not think that I will accuse you before the Father: the one who will accuse you is Moses, in whom you have placed your hope. **46** For if you had believed Moses, you would have believed me, because he wrote about me. **47** But if you do not believe his writings, how will you believe my words?"

In spite of all the testimony about Jesus' identity, there were many who still did not believe that Jesus was more than just a great man. In spite of Jesus' works, the words of John, Scripture, and the Father Himself, many continued in a state of disbelief. Jesus certainly did not look, sound, or behave like the powerful, conquering Messiah people had expected!

Jesus knew that the Jews continued to revere and believe in the words of their great forefather, Moses. He pointed out that it was inconsistent to believe in Moses, but to reject Him, for it is Jesus about whom Moses wrote. Perhaps most ironic and unfortunate was that many were more interested in seeking glory for themselves than in attaining the far greater everlasting glory offered by Jesus.

Landmark 8:

OCTOPUS

You have arrived at the eighth Landmark. It is the first of a few Land-marks that will be represented by an animal. You have already met a zoo full of animals while listening to the Sermon on the Mount in the fifth Landmark. You will now spend time with a friendly octopus. With its eight long arms, it is easy to see why the eighth Landmark is an **octopus**. Picture a large **octopus** moving its eight arms. Each arm is covered with little suction cups. The **octopus** is waving hello to you. This friendly **octopus** will help you recall the next few units along your journey with Jesus.

The octopus has taken a brief break from its difficult job to wave hello. The job is particularly challenging since it is out of water. The oc-topus is busy **picking wheat** in a large field! You watch in amazement as its arms work with coordinated precision to **pick the wheat**. The octopus appears more efficient **picking wheat** than any machine you have ever seen. This efficient **wheat-picking** octopus is a reminder of the first unit you will associate with the eighth Landmark. Jesus' disciples were accused of breaking Sabbath law by **"picking" wheat** on the Sabbath. This is the unit entitled THE DISCIPLES AND THE SABBATH.

THE DISCIPLES AND THE SABBATH

Mt 12:1–8

1 At that time Jesus was going through a field of grain on the sabbath. His disciples were hungry and began to pick the heads of grain and eat them. 2 When the Pharisees saw this, they said to him, "See, your disciples are doing what is unlawful to do on the sabbath." 3 He said to them, "Have you not read what David did when he and his companions were hungry, 4 how he went into the house of God and ate the bread of offering, which neither he nor

his companions but only the priests could lawfully eat? **5** Or have
you not read in the law that on the sabbath the priests serving in
the temple violate the sabbath and are innocent? **6** I say to you,
something greater than the temple is here. **7** If you knew what this
meant, 'I desire mercy, not sacrifice,' you would not have condemned
these innocent men. **8** For the Son of Man is Lord of the sabbath."

Mk 2:23–28

23 As he was passing through a field of grain on the sabbath,
his disciples began to make a path while picking the heads of
grain. **24** At this the Pharisees said to him, "Look, why are they
doing what is unlawful on the sabbath?" **25** He said to them, "Have
you never read what David did when he was in need and he and
his companions were hungry? **26** How he went into the house of
God when Abiathar was high priest and ate the bread of offering
that only the priests could lawfully eat, and shared it with his
companions?" **27** Then he said to them, "The sabbath was made for
man, not man for the sabbath. **28** That is why the Son of Man is
lord even of the sabbath."

Lk 6:1–5

1 While he was going through a field of grain on a sabbath, his
disciples were picking the heads of grain, rubbing them in their
hands, and eating them. **2** Some Pharisees said, "Why are you doing
what is unlawful on the sabbath?" **3** Jesus said to them in reply,
"Have you not read what David did when he and those [who were]
with him were hungry? **4** [How] he went into the house of God, took
the bread of offering, which only the priests could lawfully eat, ate
of it, and shared it with his companions." **5** Then he said to them,
"The Son of Man is lord of the sabbath."

———————————

All three units associated with the eighth Landmark are found in all
three Synoptic Gospels. In this unit, Jesus again encountered the nit-picking
Pharisees. They were upset that His disciples had broken religious law. The
disciples were accused of "working" by picking a small amount of grain
to satisfy their hunger. Jesus responded with a story about their great King
David. Surely common sense should be a consideration. More importantly,
mercy and understanding should override excessive legalism. The Sabbath is
a day to give glory to God rather than point out the faults of others.

YOU ARE HAVING A HARD time believing what you are seeing. An octopus that can not only pick wheat, but do it so well! You want a closer look to see just how it is being done. As you draw near, the octopus stops working. It has something else for you to see. The big creature motions with all but one of its arms for you to come closer. It now uses these seven arms to point to its eighth arm lying motionless on the ground. This arm is small and weak compared to the others. It is severely **withered**. This arm could not handle the demands of wheat picking. As a result of inactivity, the arm has **withered**. The **withered** arm has become useless; it is a hindrance. The weak and **withered** arm of the octopus helps you recall the unit when Jesus heals THE MAN WITH THE WITHERED HAND.

THE MAN WITH THE WITHERED HAND

Mt 12:9–14

9 Moving on from there, he went into their synagogue. **10** And behold, there was a man there who had a withered hand. They questioned him, "Is it lawful to cure on the sabbath?" so that they might accuse him. **11** He said to them, "Which one of you who has a sheep that falls into a pit on the sabbath will not take hold of it and lift it out? **12** How much more valuable a person is than a sheep. So it is lawful to do good on the sabbath." **13** Then he said to the man, "Stretch out your hand." He stretched it out, and it was restored as sound as the other. **14** But the Pharisees went out and took counsel against him to put him to death.

Mk 3:1–6

1 Again he entered the synagogue. There was a man there who had a withered hand. **2** They watched him closely to see if he would cure him on the sabbath so that they might accuse him. **3** He said to the man with the withered hand, "Come up here before us." **4** Then he said to them, "Is it lawful to do good on the sabbath rather than to do evil, to save life rather than to destroy it?" But they remained silent. **5** Looking around at them with anger and grieved at their hardness of heart, he said to the man, "Stretch out your hand." He stretched it out and his hand was restored. **6** The Pharisees went out and immediately took counsel with the Herodians against him to put him to death.

Lk 6:6–11

6 On another sabbath he went into the synagogue and taught, and there was a man there whose right hand was withered. **7** The scribes and the Pharisees watched him closely to see if he would cure on the sabbath so that they might discover a reason to accuse him. **8** But he realized their intentions and said to the man with the withered hand, "Come up and stand before us." And he rose and stood there. **9** Then Jesus said to them, "I ask you, is it lawful to do good on the sabbath rather than to do evil, to save life rather than to destroy it?" **10** Looking around at them all, he then said to him, "Stretch out your hand." He did so and his hand was restored. **11** But they became enraged and discussed together what they might do to Jesus.

Jesus again created controversy by performing a healing miracle on the Sabbath. Not only was it the Sabbath, this miracle occurred inside a synagogue. Perhaps Jesus was back in the synagogue in Capernaum where He had previously exorcised a demon (Landmark 4). The Pharisees were blind to His compassion. Jesus indicated that one does not need to check the calendar prior to doing good works. For Jesus, doing good was keeping the Sabbath!

YOU ARE SADDENED TO SEE the withered arm of the octopus and offer to get some assistance. This alarms the octopus. It uses one of its healthy arms to pull you closer. The octopus then leans in and whispers a **secret** in your ear. "My withered arm must remain a **secret**," it says. The octopus is worried that if word gets out about the withered, nonfunctioning arm it could lose its wheat-picking job. "My situation must remain a **secret**!" You assure the big creature that the **secret** is safe with you. This incident about the **secret** of the octopus recalls JESUS' MESSIANIC SECRET.

JESUS' MESSIANIC SECRET

Mt 12:15–21

15 When Jesus realized this, he withdrew from that place. Many [people] followed him, and he cured them all, **16** but he warned them not to make him known. **17** This was to fulfill what had been spoken through Isaiah the prophet:

18 "Behold, my servant whom I have chosen,
my beloved in whom I delight;
I shall place my spirit upon him,
and he will proclaim justice to the Gentiles.
19 He will not contend or cry out,
nor will anyone hear his voice in the streets.
20 A bruised reed he will not break,
a smoldering wick he will not quench,
until he brings justice to victory.
21 And in his name the Gentiles will hope."

Mk 3:7–12

7 Jesus withdrew toward the sea with his disciples. A large number of people [followed] from Galilee and from Judea. **8** Hearing what he was doing, a large number of people came to him also from Jerusalem, from Idumea, from beyond the Jordan, and from the neighborhood of Tyre and Sidon. **9** He told his disciples to have a boat ready for him because of the crowd, so that they would not crush him. **10** He had cured many and, as a result, those who had diseases were pressing upon him to touch him. **11** And whenever unclean spirits saw him they would fall down before him and shout, "You are the Son of God." **12** He warned them sternly not to make him known.

Lk 6:17–19

17 And he came down with them and stood on a stretch of level ground. A great crowd of his disciples and a large number of the people from all Judea and Jerusalem and the coastal region of Tyre and Sidon **18** came to hear him and to be healed of their diseases; and even those who were tormented by unclean spirits were cured. **19** Everyone in the crowd sought to touch him because power came forth from him and healed them all.

It was still early in Jesus' ministry. At this point, people were not ready to accept that He was the Son of God, the long-awaited Messiah. Even His closest disciples were not yet fully aware of His identity and incredible purpose. It was still unbelievable for them. Jesus had much to do and say before it was time to clarify His identity.

Some angry religious leaders had already begun to plot Jesus' death. The "secret" of His identity had to be kept a bit longer. In the meantime, Jesus continued to be God's "chosen servant" as first described in Isaiah (42:1–4) and quoted by Matthew. During this time, He touched the lives of many as they sought to touch Him, perhaps even by the man with the once withered hand!

Landmark 9:

BASEBALL DIAMOND

The next Landmark will be associated with a sport, similar to how Landmark 5 was a basketball. Recall that a basketball team has five players. Since this is now our ninth Landmark and a baseball team has nine players, we will incorporate some baseball imagery. However, we will not use a baseball. Instead, the Landmark is the whole **baseball field**, otherwise known as a **baseball diamond**. You will have the opportunity to travel around the bases. You will start at home plate before proceeding to first, second, and third base. Begin by forming a clear picture of this **baseball diamond**. See yourself approaching home plate with a bat over your shoulder, ready to "play ball!"

Standing in the batter's box at home plate with a big wooden bat in hand, you are a menacing sight. The opposing pitcher is clearly frightened, fearing you will embarrass him with a long home run. You decide to take advantage of his concern. Taking the bat, you **point** to the distant left field stands. This **pointing** clearly indicates where you intend to send his first pitch. The rattled pitcher timidly **points** the ball in the same direction, as if to ask if hitting the ball over the left field fence is your plan. You calmly **point** your bat again and slowly nod your head. The pitcher is now so intimidated that he issues you an intentional walk. The umpire then **points** for you to go to first base. All of this **pointing**, first by you, then the pitcher, and finally the umpire, represents the first unit you will associate with the baseball diamond: JESUS APPOINTS THE TWELVE.

JESUS APPOINTS THE TWELVE

Mt 10:1–4

1 Then he summoned his twelve disciples and gave them authority over unclean spirits to drive them out and to cure every disease and every illness. 2 The names of the twelve apostles are these: first, Simon called Peter, and his brother Andrew; James, the son of Zebedee, and his brother John; 3 Philip and Bartholomew, Thomas and Matthew the tax collector; James, the son of Alphaeus, and Thaddeus; 4 Simon the Cananean, and Judas Iscariot who betrayed him.

Mk 3:13–19

13 He went up the mountain and summoned those whom he wanted and they came to him. 14 He appointed twelve [whom he also named apostles] that they might be with him and he might send them forth to preach 15 and to have authority to drive out demons: 16 [he appointed the twelve:] Simon, whom he named Peter; 17 James, son of Zebedee, and John the brother of James, whom he named Boanerges, that is, sons of thunder; 18 Andrew, Philip, Bartholomew, Matthew, Thomas, James the son of Alphaeus; Thaddeus, Simon the Cananean, 19 and Judas Iscariot who betrayed him.

Lk 6:12–16

12 In those days he departed to the mountain to pray, and he spent the night in prayer to God. 13 When day came, he called his disciples to himself, and from them he chose Twelve, whom he also named apostles: 14 Simon, whom he named Peter, and his brother Andrew, James, John, Philip, Bartholomew, 15 Matthew, Thomas, James the son of Alphaeus, Simon who was called a Zealot, 16 and Judas the son of James, and Judas Iscariot, who became a traitor.

Thus far on your walk with Jesus, you have seen Him attract many followers. In Landmark 4, you witnessed the call of the two sets of fishermen brothers to be the first apostles. Jesus now appoints the remainder of the Twelve who will be "sent out" with His authority and power.

For Matthew, this was the beginning of the "Missionary Discourse." In this Gospel, Jesus had apparently already chosen the Twelve, but in this passage they were introduced by name. More importantly, they were given the authority and power to more fully participate in Jesus' ministry. They had been witnessing Jesus drive out demons and heal the sick. Now they were able to do the same.

It is no coincidence that Jesus named twelve people to be His special followers. A united Israel had once consisted of twelve tribes. The "restored" Israel in the form of the Christian Church would begin with these twelve.

In Luke, Jesus was described as spending the night in prayer prior to the important selection of the Twelve. Jesus models for us the importance of prayer before making major life decisions. He then proceeded to choose a fairly diverse group, other than the obvious fact that they are all men. Fishermen, a tax collector, a zealot, two sets of brothers, Galileans, and a Judean were among the chosen.

YOU ARE NOW ON FIRST base. As you stand there smiling, the first base-man on the opposing team has a few choice words for you. His profanity is actually quite **blasphemous**. You find the **blasphemy** very offensive, but the first-base umpire is even more disturbed by the **blasphemous** outburst. As a result, the umpire awards you second base. More **blasphemy** from the first baseman earns him a seat on the bench. This **blasphemous** scene at first base recalls the unit about THE BLASPHEMY OF THE SCRIBES.

THE BLASPHEMY OF THE SCRIBES

Mt 12:22–24

22 Then they brought to him a demoniac who was blind and mute. He cured the mute person so that he could speak and see. **23** All the crowd was astounded, and said, "Could this perhaps be the Son of David?" **24** But when the Pharisees heard this, they said, "This man drives out demons only by the power of Beelzebul, the prince of demons."

Mk 3:20–22

20 He came home. Again [the] crowd gathered, making it impossible for them even to eat. **21** When his relatives heard of this they set out to seize him, for they said, "He is out of his mind." **22** The scribes who had come from Jerusalem said, "He is possessed by Beelzebul," and "By the prince of demons he drives out demons."

Lk 11:14–16

14 He was driving out a demon [that was] mute, and when the demon had gone out, the mute person spoke and the crowds were amazed. 15 Some of them said, "By the power of Beelzebul, the prince of demons, he drives out demons." 16 Others, to test him, asked him for a sign from heaven.

It was the scribes and Pharisees who accused Jesus of blasphemy. It was the charge that eventually led to His death. Here they themselves committed the sin of blasphemy! They made Jesus an agent of Satan by saying it was by the power of Beelzebul that He performed His good works. Jesus' family was not much kinder, saying that, "He is out of His mind."

THE FIRST BASEMAN IS NOW in the dugout, and you have arrived at second base. On second base, you are behind the pitcher. You have a good view of home plate where you started and hope to return. However, second base is an uncomfortable place. The base has been split into two pieces. It is literally **divided** in half. In order to be safely on the base, you must stand with your legs several feet apart with a foot on each half of the **divided** base. You have never seen a **divided** base before. Neither has the umpire, who comes over to inspect the situation. He realizes how unfair it is to make you stand on a **divided** base. Over loud protesting from the opposing team, the umpire tells you to leave the **divided** base and go to third base. This bizarre **divided** situation triggers memories of Jesus preaching about A HOUSE DIVIDED.

A HOUSE DIVIDED

Mt 12:25–32

25 But he knew what they were thinking and said to them, "Every kingdom divided against itself will be laid waste, and no town or house divided against itself will stand. 26 And if Satan drives out Satan, he is divided against himself; how, then, will his kingdom stand? 27 And if I drive out demons by Beelzebul, by whom do your own people drive them out? Therefore they will be your judges. 28 But if it is by the Spirit of God that I drive out

demons, then the kingdom of God has come upon you. **29** How can anyone enter a strong man's house and steal his property, unless he first ties up the strong man? Then he can plunder his house. **30** Whoever is not with me is against me, and whoever does not gather with me scatters. **31** Therefore, I say to you, every sin and blasphemy will be forgiven people, but blasphemy against the Spirit will not be forgiven. **32** And whoever speaks a word against the Son of Man will be forgiven; but whoever speaks against the holy Spirit will not be forgiven, either in this age or in the age to come."

Mk 3:23–30

23 Summoning them, he began to speak to them in parables, "How can Satan drive out Satan? **24** If a kingdom is divided against itself, that kingdom cannot stand. **25** And if a house is divided against itself, that house will not be able to stand. **26** And if Satan has risen up against himself and is divided, he cannot stand; that is the end of him. **27** But no one can enter a strong man's house to plunder his property unless he first ties up the strong man. Then he can plunder his house. **28** Amen, I say to you, all sins and all blasphemies that people utter will be forgiven them. **29** But whoever blasphemes against the holy Spirit will never have forgiveness, but is guilty of an everlasting sin." **30** For they had said, "He has an unclean spirit."

Lk 11:17–23

17 But he knew their thoughts and said to them, "Every kingdom divided against itself will be laid waste and house will fall against house. **18** And if Satan is divided against himself, how will his kingdom stand? For you say that it is by Beelzebul that I drive out demons. **19** If I, then, drive out demons by Beelzebul, by whom do your own people drive them out? Therefore they will be your judges. **20** But if it is by the finger of God that [I] drive out demons, then the kingdom of God has come upon you. **21** When a strong man fully armed guards his palace, his possessions are safe. **22** But when one stronger than he attacks and overcomes him, he takes away the armor on which he relied and distributes the spoils. **23** Whoever is not with me is against me, and whoever does not gather with me scatters."

Jesus refuted the blasphemous charge that He was an agent of Satan with several analogies about division. There is hope for those who blaspheme against Jesus. If repentant, they will be forgiven. However, there will be a different outcome for those who blaspheme against the Spirit.

THIRD BASE IS MUCH MORE welcoming. It is even stranger than your experiences at first or second base. Third is a much larger base. It needs to be large to accommodate the big **fruit tree** growing from its center. That's right! A large **tree** bearing a variety of luscious **fruit** has sprouted from the middle of the base. Scattered around the bottom of the **fruit tree** are oranges, apples, pears, bananas, and several other types of **fruit** you do not even recognize. You bend down and pick up several pieces of **fruit** and put them in your pockets. They will make a nice post-game snack. Touching the trunk of the **fruit tree**, you await the next pitch. You are eager to get back to home plate. This bountiful **fruit tree** at third base symbolizes the unit about A TREE AND ITS FRUIT.

A TREE AND ITS FRUIT

Mt 12:33–37

33 "Either declare the tree good and its fruit is good, or declare the tree rotten and its fruit is rotten, for a tree is known by its fruit. **34** You brood of vipers, how can you say good things when you are evil? For from the fullness of the heart the mouth speaks. **35** A good person brings forth good out of a store of goodness, but an evil person brings forth evil out of a store of evil. **36** I tell you, on the day of judgment people will render an account for every careless word they speak. **37** By your words you will be acquitted, and by your words you will be condemned."

Lk 6:43–45

43 "A good tree does not bear rotten fruit, nor does a rotten tree bear good fruit. **44** For every tree is known by its own fruit. For people do not pick figs from thornbushes, nor do they gather grapes from brambles. **45** A good person out of the store of goodness in his heart produces good, but an evil person out of a store of evil produces evil; for from the fullness of the heart the mouth speaks."

You have already heard Jesus speak in the Sermon on the Mount about knowing false prophets by the fruit they bear. In this unit, Matthew also included Jesus' teaching about abusive speech. Jesus warned that we will have to answer for how we speak. This focus on judgment is a common theme in Matthew.

Landmark 10:

TWO HANDS

The tenth Landmark is always close at hand. It is something you carry at all times. You also use it to carry things. It is also something you can always count on and is very "handy." The tenth Landmark is your **hands**, your ten fingers. Thus, simply looking at your **hands** will help to recall the next few units in the life of Jesus.

There are many languages spoken around the world. Almost all of these tongues appropriately require the use of one's tongue. You, however, are fluent in a language that does not. You can expertly speak using the tenth Landmark. That's right, you are very skilled communicating in **sign** language! You are so talented in this area that you are currently teaching at a school for hearing-impaired students. Imagine yourself in a classroom teaching in **sign** language. You enjoy teaching with your hands. However, your supervisor wants you to teach lip reading. She is against your **signing**. She has turned the entire school administration against your **signing**. You are considering resigning!

One morning while you are **signing** in front of your classroom, the supervisor arrives. She has once again come to protest against your **signing**. You politely **sign** to her that you will discuss the issue after lunch. This problem the supervisor has with your **signing** will call to mind Jesus' teaching AGAINST SEEKING FOR SIGNS.

AGAINST SEEKING FOR SIGNS

Mt 12:38–42

38 Then some of the scribes and Pharisees said to him, "Teacher, we wish to see a sign from you." 39 He said to them in reply, "An evil and unfaithful generation seeks a sign, but no sign will be given it

except the sign of Jonah the prophet. **40** Just as Jonah was in the belly of the whale three days and three nights, so will the Son of Man be in the heart of the earth three days and three nights. **41** At the judgment, the men of Nineveh will arise with this generation and condemn it, because they repented at the preaching of Jonah; and there is something greater than Jonah here. **42** At the judgment the queen of the south will arise with this generation and condemn it, because she came from the ends of the earth to hear the wisdom of Solomon; and there is something greater than Solomon here."

Lk 11:29–32

29 While still more people gathered in the crowd, he said to them, "This generation is an evil generation; it seeks a sign, but no sign will be given it, except the sign of Jonah. **30** Just as Jonah became a sign to the Ninevites, so will the Son of Man be to this generation. **31** At the judgment the queen of the south will rise with the men of this generation and she will condemn them, because she came from the ends of the earth to hear the wisdom of Solomon, and there is something greater than Solomon here. **32** At the judgment the men of Nineveh will arise with this generation and condemn it, because at the preaching of Jonah they repented, and there is something greater than Jonah here."

Jesus denies the faithless request of the scribes and Pharisees. He recounts the sign of Jonah, whose three days of darkness foreshadowed the darkness Jesus will soon endure. Jesus says He is greater than the prophets Jonah and Solomon. It has already been proclaimed that He is greater than John the Baptist.

MORNING CLASS IS OVER, AND it is time for lunch. First, you must wash the tenth Landmark (your hands) before going to the school cafeteria. Upon entering the bathroom, you get the surprise of your life! Hovering in the air above the sink is a ghost. We will call it a **spirit**. This **spirit** has the general shape of a small person draped in a white sheet. More specifically, a soiled, dirty, **unclean** sheet. Thus the **spirit** appears to be **unclean**. This **unclean spirit** very forcefully tells you not to wash your hands. The **unclean spirit** wants you to remain **unclean**. You oblige, turn away from the **unclean spirit**, open the door, and run screaming down the hall. This frightening experience with the **unclean spirit** helps recall the unit about THE RETURN OF AN UNCLEAN SPIRIT.

THE RETURN OF AN UNCLEAN SPIRIT

Mt 12:43–45

43 "When an unclean spirit goes out of a person it roams through arid regions searching for rest but finds none. **44** Then it says, 'I will return to my home from which I came.' But upon returning, it finds it empty, swept clean, and put in order. **45** Then it goes and brings back with itself seven other spirits more evil than itself, and they move in and dwell there; and the last condition of that person is worse than the first. Thus it will be with this evil generation."

Lk 11:24–26

24 "When an unclean spirit goes out of someone, it roams through arid regions searching for rest but, finding none, it says, 'I shall return to my home from which I came.' **25** But upon returning, it finds it swept clean and put in order. **26** Then it goes and brings back seven other spirits more wicked than itself who move in and dwell there, and the last condition of that person is worse than the first."

A large part of Jesus' ministry involved expelling unclean spirits. This should certainly have provided a sign for those who had just requested one. When one is made clean by Jesus, the sin or "demon" is gone. The empty space needs to be filled with goodness, with new life. This goodness can take various forms, such as renewed faith or love. When the space is filled, the "demon" (sin) has no place to reside should it try to return.

AFTER THE EXPERIENCE WITH THE unclean spirit, your heart is racing and your hands remain unwashed. Your growling stomach tells you to head for the school cafeteria. You arrive and find an empty table. Before taking the first bite of lunch, you say a **blessing**. You put your hands together, bow your head, and say the **blessing** quietly. When you finish the **blessing** and raise your head, you are surprised to see all of the students and faculty staring at you. They all realize they had forgotten to say a **blessing**. To your even greater surprise, everyone in the cafeteria offers a **blessing** in unison. This lunchtime scene of spoken **blessings** recalls Jesus' words about TRUE BLESSEDNESS.

TRUE BLESSEDNESS

Lk 11:27-28

27 While he was speaking, a woman from the crowd called out and said to him, "Blessed is the womb that carried you and the breasts at which you nursed." **28** He replied, "Rather, blessed are those who hear the word of God and observe it."

To be truly blessed, we do not need to be heroic. Jesus' mother was certainly blessed by her chosen role. We have also been chosen to hear and obey God's Word. In doing so, we are heroic in the eyes of God. We will be truly blessed. This beatitude, found outside the Sermon on the Mount, should be our goal and a source of hope.

YOU ARE STILL SITTING AT a table in the cafeteria. Feeling a bit lonely, you wish your family was there eating lunch with you. Though you are surrounded by your school family, it is not the same as being with your **true family**. No sooner than this thought crosses your mind, your **true family** (whoever that may consist of) appears at the cafeteria doors. You stand and wave to your **true family**, motioning to them to come join you. Your **true family** is happy to see you. They rush over to join you for lunch. You continue eating, enjoying your **true family** in the midst of your work family. This meal with your **true family** signifies the discussion about THE TRUE FAMILY OF JESUS.

THE TRUE FAMILY OF JESUS

Mt 12:46–50

46 While he was still speaking to the crowds, his mother and his brothers appeared outside, wishing to speak with him. **47** [Someone told him, "Your mother and your brothers are standing outside, asking to speak with you."] **48** But he said in reply to the one who told him, "Who is my mother? Who are my brothers?" **49** And stretching out his hand toward his disciples, he said, "Here are my mother and my brothers. **50** For whoever does the will of my heavenly Father is my brother, and sister, and mother."

Mk 3:31–35

31 His mother and his brothers arrived. Standing outside they sent word to him and called him. **32** A crowd seated around him told him, "Your mother and your brothers [and your sisters] are outside asking for you." **33** But he said to them in reply, "Who are my mother and [my] brothers?" **34** And looking around at those seated in the circle he said, "Here are my mother and my brothers. **35** [For] whoever does the will of God is my brother and sister and mother."

Lk 8:19–21

19 Then his mother and his brothers came to him but were unable to join him because of the crowd. **20** He was told, "Your mother and your brothers are standing outside and they wish to see you." **21** He said to them in reply, "My mother and my brothers are those who hear the word of God and act on it."

Out of concern for Jesus, His family came to see Him in Capernaum. Aside from His mother, who was just mentioned, it remains debatable as to who comprised Jesus' family. Jesus made it clear who He considered family. It is the same people He had just deemed as "Blessed." It is us, if we "hear the word of God and act on it." In saying this, Jesus was not denying His earthly family. Family ties were of great importance in the Jewish culture of Jesus' time. He was emphasizing the new family He was sent to establish.

Landmark 11:

SOCCER BALL

The next Landmark is now rolling your way. The eleventh Landmark is another type of ball. Recall that the fifth Landmark was a basketball because there are five players on a basketball team. Similarly, the eleventh Landmark is a **soccer ball** since eleven players fill the roster of a soccer team. It is a brand-new, shiny, black-and-white **soccer ball**, just waiting to be kicked for the first time. You let the **soccer ball** roll up onto your right foot and then lift it gently to your knee. After several seconds on your knee, you grab the **soccer ball** and stand ready to take the field. With this deft bit of **soccer ball** handling, it should be easy to remember that the **soccer ball** is the eleventh Landmark.

You have been holding the soccer ball long enough. The goal now is to get involved in a game. You start kicking the ball around the field, hoping your skills will attract some players. A large group of women all dressed in black soon approach you. It appears to be a gathering of grieving **widows**! Some are softly sobbing while others are loudly wailing. This group of sad **widows** is heart-wrenching. Imagine your surprise—no, your shock—when the **widows** ask if they can play soccer with you. The **widows** feel a lively afternoon game of soccer will provide a respite from their mourning. You readily agree. Soon a spirited game of soccer with the **widows** is underway. Imagine the bizarre scene of these **widows** playing soccer in their dressy black outfits. This scene will help you remember Jesus Raising the Widow's Son to Life.

RAISING THE WIDOW'S SON TO LIFE

Lk 7:11–17

11 Soon afterward he journeyed to a city called Nain, and his disciples and a large crowd accompanied him. 12 As he drew near to the gate of the city, a man who had died was being carried out, the only son of his mother, and she was a widow. A large crowd from the city was with her. 13 When the Lord saw her, he was moved with pity for her and said to her, "Do not weep." 14 He stepped forward and touched the coffin; at this the bearers halted, and he said, "Young man, I tell you, arise!" 15 The dead man sat up and began to speak, and Jesus gave him to his mother. 16 Fear seized them all, and they glorified God, exclaiming, "A great prophet has arisen in our midst," and "God has visited his people." 17 This report about him spread through the whole of Judea and in all the surrounding region.

In this miracle story, Luke describes an emotional Jesus. He felt pity for the widow. With her great loss, she now had no husband or son. After this event, Jesus was proclaimed a "Great Prophet." This title is a major theme for Luke. The story is also very similar to one involving Elijah, one of the greatest Jewish prophets. In the first book of Kings (1 Kg 17:10–23), Elijah raised the son of Zarephath's widow.

PLAYING SOCCER WITH THE WIDOWS has proven to be much more difficult than you could have ever imagined. Soon you are gasping for air and need to go to the sideline for a breather. What a mistake! There waiting for you with an indignant frown is your friend, John. Recall that you last saw John back in Landmark 2 after you both had tumbled from the bicycle into the cold river. He is now the widows' soccer coach! John begins to assault you with **questions.** His first **question** is why you left him alone in the river. He then **questions** why you are playing with his team. His last **question** is why you have left the playing field. Though you find the **questions** frustrating, they help you recall the unit concerning JOHN'S QUESTION TO JESUS.

JOHN'S QUESTION TO JESUS

Mt 11:2–6

2 When John heard in prison of the works of the Messiah, he sent his disciples to him 3 with this question, "Are you the one who is to come, or should we look for another?" 4 Jesus said to them in reply, "Go and tell John what you hear and see: 5 the blind regain their sight, the lame walk, lepers are cleansed, the deaf hear, the dead are raised, and the poor have the good news proclaimed to them. 6 And blessed is the one who takes no offense at me."

Lk 7:18–23

18 The disciples of John told him about all these things. John summoned two of his disciples 19 and sent them to the Lord to ask, "Are you the one who is to come, or should we look for another?" 20 When the men came to him, they said, "John the Baptist has sent us to you to ask, 'Are you the one who is to come, or should we look for another?'" 21 At that time he cured many of their diseases, sufferings, and evil spirits; he also granted sight to many who were blind. 22 And he said to them in reply, "Go and tell John what you have seen and heard: the blind regain their sight, the lame walk, lepers are cleansed, the deaf hear, the dead are raised, the poor have the good news proclaimed to them. 23 And blessed is the one who takes no offense at me."

John was in prison. What question was so important that he sent his disciples to ask Jesus? It was the most important question of all! "Are You the Messiah?" Jesus responded by pointing out His works on behalf of the impaired, the outcast, and the poor. Jesus the Messiah was not the powerful, conquering, liberating King that had been expected! Jesus was instead a blessing for the needy. He in turn had offered a blessing to those who accepted His unexpected Messianic role, "those who take no offense."

AFTER JOHN HAS EMBARRASSED YOU with his questions, it seems best not to go back onto the field. You find a seat in the stands with the people who have come to watch the widows play soccer. You decide to say a few **words about John** to all who will listen. Your **words about John** are loud and animated, but not harsh. However, you are somewhat disruptive to those within earshot. A few people seem interested in what you have to say about John, but most of the spectators are friends or family of the widows. They do not appreciate your **words**. Finally, because of your incessant **words about John**, you are asked to leave. Once again you are embarrassed, but will oblige. You feel you have done nothing wrong by uttering a few **words about John**. This episode in the stands at the soccer field is a reminder of JESUS' WORDS ABOUT JOHN.

JESUS' WORDS ABOUT JOHN

Mt 11:7–19

7 As they were going off, Jesus began to speak to the crowds about John, "What did you go out to the desert to see? A reed swayed by the wind? **8** Then what did you go out to see? Someone dressed in fine clothing? Those who wear fine clothing are in royal palaces. **9** Then why did you go out? To see a prophet? Yes, I tell you, and more than a prophet. **10** This is the one about whom it is written:

'Behold, I am sending my messenger ahead of you;
he will prepare your way before you.'

11 Amen, I say to you, among those born of women there has been none greater than John the Baptist; yet the least in the kingdom of heaven is greater than he. **12** From the days of John the Baptist until now, the kingdom of heaven suffers violence, and the violent are taking it by force. **13** All the prophets and the law prophesied up to the time of John. **14** And if you are willing to accept it, he is Elijah, the one who is to come. **15** Whoever has ears ought to hear.

16 "To what shall I compare this generation? It is like children who sit in marketplaces and call to one another, **17** 'We played the flute for you, but you did not dance, we sang a dirge but you did not mourn.' **18** For John came neither eating nor drinking, and they said, 'He is possessed by a demon.' **19** The Son of Man came eating and drinking and they said, 'Look, he is a glutton and a drunkard, a friend of tax collectors and sinners.' But wisdom is vindicated by her works."

Lk 7:24–35

24 When the messengers of John had left, Jesus began to speak to the crowds about John. "What did you go out to the desert to see—a reed swayed by the wind? **25** Then what did you go out to see? Someone dressed in fine garments? Those who dress luxuriously and live sumptuously are found in royal palaces. **26** Then what did you go out to see? A prophet? Yes, I tell you, and more than a prophet. **27** This is the one about whom scripture says:

'Behold, I am sending my messenger ahead of you,
he will prepare your way before you.'

28 I tell you, among those born of women, no one is greater than John; yet the least in the kingdom of God is greater than he." **29** (All the people who listened, including the tax collectors, and who were baptized with the baptism of John, acknowledged the righteousness of God; **30** but the Pharisees and scholars of the law, who were not baptized by him, rejected the plan of God for themselves.)

31 "Then to what shall I compare the people of this generation? What are they like? **32** They are like children who sit in the marketplace and call to one another,

'We played the flute for you, but you did not dance.
We sang a dirge, but you did not weep.'

33 For John the Baptist came neither eating food nor drinking wine, and you said, 'He is possessed by a demon.' **34** The Son of Man came eating and drinking and you said, 'Look, he is a glutton and a drunkard, a friend of tax collectors and sinners.' **35** But wisdom is vindicated by all her children."

Jesus praised John as a prophet, a second Elijah. He was God's messenger and also a great man. However, John was not as great as those in the kingdom of heaven. Jesus linked Himself with John in a short parable calling them both "children of wisdom." They had been sent for a purpose, but were ignored or rejected. However, their words of wisdom would prove to be true.

AS YOU WALK AWAY FROM the soccer field, another woman approaches you. She is not a widow. This woman is working the gate at the soccer field and asks if you will be returning. You are uncertain. Perhaps the woman wants to stamp your hand in case you decide to come back. The woman surprises you by coming closer with a large tube of **ointment**. You extend a hand, thinking the woman intends to apply a dab of **ointment** rather than stamp your hand. Surprisingly, the **woman with the ointment** begins to rub **ointment** all over your forehead and face! You do not resist the woman's rather forward behavior because the **ointment** feels cool and refreshing on your warm skin. This encounter with the **woman with the ointment** is a clear reminder of Jesus and THE WOMAN WITH THE OINTMENT.

THE WOMAN WITH THE OINTMENT

Lk 7:36–50

36 A Pharisee invited him to dine with him, and he entered the Pharisee's house and reclined at table. 37 Now there was a sinful woman in the city who learned that he was at table in the house of the Pharisee. Bringing an alabaster flask of ointment, 38 she stood behind him at his feet weeping and began to bathe his feet with her tears. Then she wiped them with her hair, kissed them, and anointed them with the ointment. 39 When the Pharisee who had invited him saw this he said to himself, "If this man were a prophet, he would know who and what sort of woman this is who is touching him, that she is a sinner." 40 Jesus said to him in reply, "Simon, I have something to say to you." "Tell me, teacher," he said. 41 "Two people were in debt to a certain creditor; one owed five hundred days' wages and the other owed fifty. 42 Since they were unable to repay the debt, he forgave it for both. Which of them will love him more?" 43 Simon said in reply, "The one, I suppose, whose larger debt was forgiven." He said to him, "You have judged rightly." 44 Then he turned to the woman and said to Simon, "Do you see this woman? When I entered your house, you did not give me water for my feet, but she has bathed them with her tears and wiped them with her hair. 45 You did not give me a kiss, but she has not ceased kissing my feet since the time I entered. 46 You did not anoint my head with oil, but she anointed my feet with ointment. 47 So I tell you, her many sins have been forgiven; hence, she has shown great love. But the one to whom little is forgiven, loves little." 48 He said to her, "Your sins are forgiven." 49 The others at table said to themselves, "Who is this who even forgives sins?" 50 But he said to the woman, "Your faith has saved you; go in peace."

Jesus dined with a Pharisee, a member of the group that had been very critical of Him. Pharisees were critical when Jesus dined with a tax collector, and Simon was now critical of Jesus at his own table for contact with the sinful ointment-bearing woman. Jesus proceeded to teach this self-righteous Pharisee a lesson in forgiveness. He told the "Parable of the Forgiving Creditor." Jesus then gave credit to the sinful woman by forgiving her sins. Once again, a show of faith led to forgiveness.

WITH YOUR FACE SLATHERED IN cool, refreshing ointment, you now stand in the parking lot adjacent to the soccer field. Though the lot contains only a few cars, you are far from being alone. There are many poor, downtrodden, homeless people in your midst. They have not come to watch the widows play soccer. These unfortunate people have come to see some other **women**. There is a group of women in the parking lot **ministering** to the spiritual and physical needs of these homeless people. Some **women are ministering** by preaching God's Word. The **ministry** of other **women** is to provide a nourishing meal. Still other **women minister** by providing healthcare to the sick and infirm. You are overwhelmed by the love and caring attitude of these **ministering women**. This helps you recall the unit about THE MINISTERING WOMEN.

THE MINISTERING WOMEN

Lk 8:1-3

1 Afterward he journeyed from one town and village to another, preaching and proclaiming the good news of the kingdom of God. Accompanying him were the Twelve 2 and some women who had been cured of evil spirits and infirmities, Mary, called Magdalene, from whom seven demons had gone out, 3 Joanna, the wife of Herod's steward Chuza, Susanna, and many others who provided for them out of their resources.

This brief unit contains a lot of information. Like the second unit of Landmark 5, it speaks in general of Jesus' wide travels spreading the Gospel. Whereas great crowds are mentioned previously, here individuals are specified. The twelve apostles represented all of Israel (twelve tribes). The women, though few, were very important in Jesus' ministry. Two of the women who were specifically mentioned by Luke would have been ignored by many. One had been possessed by demons; the other was associated with Herod. This diverse group of men and women indicates that we are all called to follow Jesus and participate in His ministry.

Landmark 12:

BOX OF DONUTS

You have already traveled a long way on your walk with Jesus. The sight of the upcoming twelfth Landmark reminds you that you have yet to stop for a meal. The twelfth Landmark is a **box** of twelve treats, but it would be hard to call it a typical meal. The longer you stand looking at this **box** containing a dozen **donuts**, the more your growling stomach convinces you that the twelfth Landmark is in fact a meal. Would it be wrong to eat a Landmark? That is the question you ponder as you begin to drool over the **box of donuts**.

After sitting for a few minutes with the box of donuts on your lap, you have reached a difficult decision. It would be wrong to eat a Landmark. However, you feel you must do something with them. To leave them as a temptation for someone else would be the ultimate donut do not! You decide to transform the twelve donuts from something edible to something wearable! This will require some **sewing**. It just so happens that you have some skill with a needle and thread, so you begin **sewing** the donuts together. The plan is to **sew** them into a necklace. You will craft a very unique piece of jewelry. The **sewing** is easy. The needle easily pierces the soft glazed surface of each donut. Soon your fingers are tired and sticky, but the **sewing** is complete. The donut necklace is ready to be worn. This bit of unusual **sewing** calls to mind Jesus' well-known PARABLE OF THE SOWER.

PARABLE OF THE SOWER

Mt 13:1–9

1 On that day, Jesus went out of the house and sat down by the sea. 2 Such large crowds gathered around him that he got into a boat and sat down, and the whole crowd stood along the shore.

3 And he spoke to them at length in parables, saying: "A sower went out to sow. 4 And as he sowed, some seed fell on the path, and birds came and ate it up. 5 Some fell on rocky ground, where it had little soil. It sprang up at once because the soil was not deep, 6 and when the sun rose it was scorched, and it withered for lack of roots. 7 Some seed fell among thorns, and the thorns grew up and choked it. 8 But some seed fell on rich soil, and produced fruit, a hundred or sixty or thirtyfold. 9 Whoever has ears ought to hear."

Mk 4:1–9

1 On another occasion he began to teach by the sea. A very large crowd gathered around him so that he got into a boat on the sea and sat down. And the whole crowd was beside the sea on land. 2 And he taught them at length in parables, and in the course of his instruction he said to them, 3 "Hear this! A sower went out to sow. 4 And as he sowed, some seed fell on the path, and the birds came and ate it up. 5 Other seed fell on rocky ground where it had little soil. It sprang up at once because the soil was not deep. 6 And when the sun rose, it was scorched and it withered for lack of roots. 7 Some seed fell among thorns, and the thorns grew up and choked it and it produced no grain. 8 And some seed fell on rich soil and produced fruit. It came up and grew and yielded thirty, sixty, and a hundredfold." 9 He added, "Whoever has ears to hear ought to hear."

Lk 8:4–8

4 When a large crowd gathered, with people from one town after another journeying to him, he spoke in a parable. 5 "A sower went out to sow his seed. And as he sowed, some seed fell on the path and was trampled, and the birds of the sky ate it up. 6 Some seed fell on rocky ground, and when it grew, it withered for lack of moisture. 7 Some seed fell among thorns, and the thorns grew with it and choked it. 8 And some seed fell on good soil, and when it grew, it produced fruit a hundredfold." After saying this, he called out, "Whoever has ears to hear ought to hear."

The parables are Jesus' most well-known form of teaching. They are familiar stories that help recall and internalize important aspects of Jesus' lessons. Part of what makes a parable memorable is its ending. It is typically unexpected. It goes against how things are usually seen or understood. This was true for Jesus' entire ministry. He certainly said and did the unexpected. Jesus was not the type of Messiah who had been anticipated for so many years. His life, like each of His parables, had a memorable and unexpected ending.

One reason that Jesus' parables were so effective is that His audience could easily relate to them. They could see themselves in the story. A parable about a sower was very familiar to their agrarian way of life. The listener could also relate to the various problems a farmer encountered while planting seeds. This parable offers encouragement as one deals with the predators, rocks, thorns, and hurts of everyday life. These obstacles can be overcome. We, the seeds, can obtain the Kingdom through Jesus, our Sower. The reward will be great in the rich soil of the kingdom of heaven.

YOUR HANDS ARE VERY STICKY after sewing together the donut necklace. As you continue to hold the gooey creation, you are having second thoughts about hanging it around your neck. Who could you bestow this sweet treat upon who would wear it in comfort? Your pet **porpoise** immediately comes to mind. That's right, you have a glistening wet baby **porpoise** for a pet. Your porpoise is the ideal candidate to wear your sticky creation. With your **porpoise** under one arm, you gently slide the donut necklace over its head. The **porpoise's** fin keeps the necklace from sliding too far down its sleek, slippery body. You now proudly hold the world's only pet **porpoise** wearing a necklace made from a dozen hand-sewn donuts! Gazing proudly at the **porpoise**, you recall how it relates to your journey with Jesus. The **porpoise** is another soundalike. *Porpoise* sounds like "purpose." It refers to a description of THE PURPOSE OF JESUS' PARABLES.

THE PURPOSE OF JESUS' PARABLES

Mt 13:10–15

10 The disciples approached him and said, "Why do you speak to them in parables?" **11** He said to them in reply, "Because knowledge of the mysteries of the kingdom of heaven has been granted to you, but to them it has not been granted. **12** To anyone who has, more will be given and he will grow rich; from anyone who has not, even what he has will be taken away. **13** This is why I speak to them in parables, because 'they look but do not see and hear but do not listen or understand.' **14** Isaiah's prophecy is fulfilled in them, which says:

'You shall indeed hear but not understand,

you shall indeed look but never see.
15 Gross is the heart of this people,
they will hardly hear with their ears,
they have closed their eyes,
lest they see with their eyes
and hear with their ears
and understand with their heart and be converted,
and I heal them.'"

Mk 4:10–12

10 And when he was alone, those present along with the Twelve questioned him about the parables. 11 He answered them, "The mystery of the kingdom of God has been granted to you. But to those outside everything comes in parables, 12 so that

'they may look and see but not perceive,
and hear and listen but not understand,
in order that they may not be converted and be forgiven.'"

Lk 8:9–10

9 Then his disciples asked him what the meaning of this parable might be. 10 He answered, "Knowledge of the mysteries of the kingdom of God has been granted to you; but to the rest, they are made known through parables so that 'they may look but not see, and hear but not understand.'"

—————————

Jesus explained to His disciples why He used parables when He taught. Without them, the people would often not understand His message. Unlike the disciples, they had not been granted knowledge of the Kingdom. It would later become the disciples' role to preach and help others understand God's kingdom.

YOUR LITTLE PORPOISE IS EVEN prouder of its new necklace than you are. It very much wants to swim out to sea and be seen. However, the porpoise does not want to risk damaging the donut necklace. So your porpoise politely asks you to take it aboard a **ship**—not just a small boat, but a large **ship**. You object, arguing that a **ship** is unnecessary and expensive. The porpoise is unrelenting. It must also be a fancy **ship** to match the fancy new necklace. Fortunately, a large **ship** is docked nearby. This brightly painted cruise **ship** dominates the horizon. With the porpoise under your arm, you walk to the nearby **ship**. This talk about a **ship** and seeing the large cruise **ship** recalls a special type of **ship: discipleship!** Specifically, it recalls the unit about THE PRIVILEGE OF DISCIPLESHIP.

<hr>

THE PRIVILEGE OF DISCIPLESHIP

Mt 13:16–17

16 "But blessed are your eyes, because they see, and your ears, because they hear. 17 Amen, I say to you, many prophets and righteous people longed to see what you see but did not see it, and to hear what you hear but did not hear it."

Lk 10:23–24

23 Turning to the disciples in private he said, "Blessed are the eyes that see what you see. 24 For I say to you, many prophets and kings desired to see what you see, but did not see it, and to hear what you hear, but did not hear it."

<hr>

Most Christians have probably wondered what it would have been like to live in Palestine during Jesus' time. How would we have reacted if we were living nearby and heard of this man, Jesus? Many have dreamed about being a close disciple of Jesus two thousand years ago. In this passage, Jesus put forth another beatitude. He told the disciples how blessed they were to be able to experience His ministry firsthand. Though we are not eyewitnesses to the historical Jesus, we can see evidence of His ministry all around us. Hopefully others can see this evidence in us and our actions.

IT IS NOW GETTING DARK. This makes it difficult to walk up the gangplank of the ship carrying a slippery porpoise under your arm. Your struggle has attracted the attention of some curious onlookers. Unfortunately, one of those most interested in your situation is the captain of the ship. He awaits you and your slippery pet at the top of the gangplank. The captain gruffly demands an **explanation** for your strange presentation. He wants an **explanation** as to why you are carrying a porpoise. He also wants an **explanation** of what the porpoise is wearing. You proceed to provide

explanations to his questions. You spend the most time **explaining** why you were the sewer of the donuts. These requests for **explanations**, particularly to **explain** your sewing, recall the unit when THE PARABLE OF THE SOWER IS EXPLAINED.

THE PARABLE OF THE SOWER IS EXPLAINED

Mt 13:18–23

18 "Hear then the parable of the sower. **19** The seed sown on the path is the one who hears the word of the kingdom without understanding it, and the evil one comes and steals away what was sown in his heart. **20** The seed sown on rocky ground is the one who hears the word and receives it at once with joy. **21** But he has no root and lasts only for a time. When some tribulation or persecution comes because of the word, he immediately falls away. **22** The seed sown among thorns is the one who hears the word, but then worldly anxiety and the lure of riches choke the word and it bears no fruit. **23** But the seed sown on rich soil is the one who hears the word and understands it, who indeed bears fruit and yields a hundred or sixty or thirtyfold."

Mk 4:13–20

13 Jesus said to them, "Do you not understand this parable? Then how will you understand any of the parables? **14** The sower sows the word. **15** These are the ones on the path where the word is sown. As soon as they hear, Satan comes at once and takes away the word sown in them. **16** And these are the ones sown on rocky ground who, when they hear the word, receive it at once with joy. **17** But they have no root; they last only for a time. Then when tribulation or persecution comes because of the word, they quickly fall away. **18** Those sown among thorns are another sort. They are the people who hear the word, **19** but worldly anxiety, the lure of riches, and the craving for other things intrude and choke the word, and it bears no fruit. **20** But those sown on rich soil are the ones who hear the word and accept it and bear fruit thirty and sixty and a hundredfold."

Lk 8:11–15

11 "This is the meaning of the parable. The seed is the word of God. **12** Those on the path are the ones who have heard, but the

devil comes and takes away the word from their hearts that they may not believe and be saved. **13** Those on rocky ground are the ones who, when they hear, receive the word with joy, but they have no root; they believe only for a time and fall away in time of trial. **14** As for the seed that fell among thorns, they are the ones who have heard, but as they go along, they are choked by the anxieties and riches and pleasures of life, and they fail to produce mature fruit. **15** But as for the seed that fell on rich soil, they are the ones who, when they have heard the word, embrace it with a generous and good heart, and bear fruit through perseverance."

The disciples had the privilege of having Jesus explain this parable to them. Through prayer, meditation, and spiritual reading, we the seeds can enrich our soil. In developing our personal relationship with Jesus, we can more fully hear and understand His Word. Hopefully, this current journey of internalizing the Gospels will deepen our relationship with Jesus and help us to bear much fruit.

ONCE YOU PROVIDE THE CAPTAIN with explanations to his questions, his demeanor quickly changes. He becomes quite pleasant and cooperative. He offers the use of an oil **lamp** to help navigate the darkness. You are pleased to receive the **lamp**, but express concern that it is nearly out of oil. The captain takes the **lamp** from you and proceeds to **measure** out some oil from a large barrel. He **measures** the oil carefully, so as not to spill any on the deck. He then fills the **lamp** with the **measured** oil and hands it to you. After expressing appreciation for the **lamp** and its carefully **measured** oil, you proceed to your cabin. This scene involving the **lamp** and the **measured** oil helps you recall THE PARABLES OF THE LAMP AND MEASURE.

THE PARABLES OF THE LAMP AND
MEASURE

Mk 4:21–25

21 He said to them, "Is a lamp brought in to be placed under a bushel basket or under a bed, and not to be placed on a lampstand? **22** For there is nothing hidden except to be made visible; nothing is secret except to come to light. **23** Anyone who has ears to hear ought to hear." **24** He also told them, "Take care what you hear. The measure with which you measure will be measured out to you, and still more will be given to you. **25** To the one who has, more will be given; from the one who has not, even what he has will be taken away."

Lk 8:16–18

16 "No one who lights a lamp conceals it with a vessel or sets it under a bed; rather, he places it on a lampstand so that those who enter may see the light. **17** For there is nothing hidden that will not become visible, and nothing secret that will not be known and come to light. **18** Take care, then, how you hear. To anyone who has, more will be given, and from the one who has not, even what he seems to have will be taken away."

In this short parable, the light provided by a lamp was likened to the enlightenment the disciples (and we) receive from Jesus' teaching. The hearers of God's Word are not to keep it to themselves. They are to let it shine before others in words and actions. We are to share the light of Jesus' teaching with others. If we keep the light of God's Word to ourselves ("in a basket"), we do not truly understand its meaning. If we don't share it with others, the light will be lost.

The parable of the measure is actually more like a saying. Though brief, it makes two important points. First, the measure (amount) we give others in the form of good words or works will come back to us from our loving Father in even greater amounts. Perhaps a cup of water to us, in God's system of measurement, is an ocean! At first glance, and seemingly unfair, are the words "to the one who has, more will be given" (Mk 4:25). However, when seen in spiritual terms, this should provide motivation. To those who seek God and have some spiritual insight, it can be increased with ongoing study and living the Word of God.

YOU AND YOUR PORPOISE, WITH the help of the brightly burning oil lamp, finally arrive at your cabin. It is late, and you are hungry. You have not had time for dinner and wonder if there is any food available at this late hour. Glancing down at the porpoise still tucked under your arm, you almost scream. Your pet's once slick, smooth skin is now covered with **seeds**. That's right, **seeds**! The poor porpoise is now encrusted with **seeds**. There are many varieties of **seeds**. Most notable are sesame **seeds**, poppy **seeds**, and sunflower **seeds**. You have no idea where the **seeds** came from, but they have appeared at a good time. Though it does not sound appetizing, you quickly begin plucking the **seeds** and popping them into your mouth. It takes many **seeds** to make a meal, but eventually you are full. This unlikely **seed** scene triggers your memory of Jesus' parable about THE SEED THAT GROWS OF ITSELF.

THE SEED THAT GROWS OF ITSELF

Mk 4:26–29

26 He said, "This is how it is with the kingdom of God; it is as if a man were to scatter seed on the land **27** and would sleep and rise night and day and the seed would sprout and grow, he knows not how. **28** Of its own accord the land yields fruit, first the blade, then the ear, then the full grain in the ear. **29** And when the grain is ripe, he wields the sickle at once, for the harvest has come."

Jesus returned to the theme of seeds and their growth. Previously, the focus was on the soil and how some seeds grew while others perished. We were the seeds. In this parable, the focus is on life. At all levels, from humans to grains of wheat, the growth and development of living things is miraculous. The more one knows about how life develops, particularly human life, the more the hand of God can be seen at work. In this parable, Jesus likened the growth process of the seed to the kingdom of God. The process may be hidden and slow, but it is ongoing. The Kingdom at the time of Jesus' earthly ministry was like a seed. Jesus was sent by God to nurture the seed, to guide it toward fulfillment.

YOUNG TEENAGER

The number of the next Landmark is often associated with bad luck. Some people will make great efforts to avoid anything associated with the number *13*. You, however, will embrace the thirteenth Landmark. It will help you internalize additional units of Jesus' teaching. Like the preceding Landmark of a dozen donuts, the thirteenth Landmark will focus on more of Jesus' parables.

Many preteens eagerly await their thirteenth birthday. This step into the challenging teenage years is a milestone along the path to adulthood. To commemorate this chronological rite of passage, our thirteenth Landmark will be a **thirteen-year-old** boy. Who this **thirteen-year-old** is and what he looks like is up to you. Recall way back at Landmark 2 when you imagined someone named John. In the same way, you will now imagine a **thirteen-year-old**. This can be someone you know now who is thirteen, or your memory of someone when they were this age, perhaps a friend or relative.

The thirteen-year-old you have chosen to be Landmark 13 has just gotten his first job. It is not a glamorous position. However, it is an opportunity to have some responsibility and begin earning a little money. It is a job pulling **weeds**. You first see the teen down on his hands and knees pulling **weeds** from the ground. You approach and ask him if he would like some assistance. It is a tough job. The **weeds** have long roots and are not surrendering without a fight. Though the boy is persistent, pulling the stubborn gnarly **weeds** is slow going (just the opposite of the efficient octopus of Landmark 8 picking wheat). You bend over and tell the thirteen-year-old that you want to help with the **weed** pulling. The smile you receive is one of welcome relief. This **weed** pulling and your offer to join in brings to mind Jesus' PARABLE OF THE WEEDS.

PARABLE OF THE WEEDS

Mt 13:24–30

24 He proposed another parable to them. "The kingdom of heaven may be likened to a man who sowed good seed in his field. 25 While everyone was asleep his enemy came and sowed weeds all through the wheat, and then went off. 26 When the crop grew and bore fruit, the weeds appeared as well. 27 The slaves of the householder came to him and said, 'Master, did you not sow good seed in your field? Where have the weeds come from?' 28 He answered, 'An enemy has done this.' His slaves said to him, 'Do you want us to go and pull them up?' 29 He replied, 'No, if you pull up the weeds you might uproot the wheat along with them. 30 Let them grow together until harvest; then at harvest time I will say to the harvesters, "First collect the weeds and tie them in bundles for burning; but gather the wheat into my barn."'"

This is another "Kingdom Parable." Before the kingdom of heaven becomes a reality for us (good seed/wheat), we need to experience this world (the field) and its evil (weeds). In spite of the weeds, the wheat can still flourish. Our relationship with Jesus (still the Sower) will allow us to bear fruit. In the previous parable, Jesus nurtured the seed, which represents the Kingdom. Here, we are the seed, which can enter into the Kingdom (the barn) with the help of Jesus.

THOUGH YOU HAVE VOLUNTEERED TO help the teenager, you have in mind a very different method for pulling weeds. The boy has already accumulated a fairly large pile of green weeds. Rather than bending down and assuming a pulling position, you walk over and carefully inspect the slowly growing pile. The teen is frustrated with your apparent waste of time. You explain that you have an idea that will make weed removal easier and more efficient. You have several secret weapons. The thirteen-year-old is now excited. This excitement quickly turns to disappointment when you pull the first weapon from your pants pocket. It is a bottle of **mustard**! "What are you going to do with **mustard**?" asks the now exasperated teen. You begin to liberally squirt the **mustard** on the pile of previously picked weeds. Soon the green pile is covered with yellow **mustard**. What a mess! The teenager is speechless. You, however, are quite pleased with the **mustard** mound you have created. This strange application of **mustard** signifies Jesus' well-known Parable of the Mustard Seed.

||||||||||||||||||||||||||||||||||||||||||||||||||||||||||||||||||||||||||||||||||||||||||||||||||||||||||||||||||||||||||||||

PARABLE OF THE MUSTARD SEED

||||||||||||||||||||||||||||||||||||||||||||||||||||||||||||||||||||||||||||||||||||||||||||||||||||||||||||||||||||||||||||||

Mt 13:31–32

31 He proposed another parable to them. "The kingdom of heaven is like a mustard seed that a person took and sowed in a field. 32 It is the smallest of all the seeds, yet when full-grown it is the largest of plants. It becomes a large bush, and the birds of the sky come and dwell in its branches.'"

Mk 4:30–32

30 He said, "To what shall we compare the kingdom of God, or what parable can we use for it? 31 It is like a mustard seed that, when it is sown in the ground, is the smallest of all the seeds on the earth. 32 But once it is sown, it springs up and becomes the largest of plants and puts forth large branches, so that the birds of the sky can dwell in its shade."

Lk 13:18–19

18 Then he said, "What is the kingdom of God like? To what can I compare it? 19 It is like a mustard seed that a person took and planted in the garden. When it was fully grown, it became a large bush and 'the birds of the sky dwelt in its branches.'"

This is Jesus' fourth parable involving seeds, either in a leading or supporting role. It is also another parable about the kingdom of heaven, with several more to come. A mustard seed is tiny, generally only one to two millimeters wide. When Jesus spoke this parable, the kingdom of God, like the mustard seed, was depicted as relatively small, yet it had begun in Jesus. It would slowly, steadily, and inevitably grow like a little mustard seed. Like the earlier seed that seemingly grew by itself (Landmark 12), God will nurture its growth. We need not be impatient or discouraged. It will be large enough in its fullness to accommodate all of us "birds."

THE HARDWORKING TEENAGE WEED-PULLER ASKS if you have lost your mind. You offer assurance that you have not and that the mustard masterpiece is step 1 of your plan. Step 2 involves a packet of **yeast** you pull from another pocket. "What in the world are you going to do with the **yeast**?" asks the boy incredulously. Tearing open the packet, you begin to liberally sprinkle the **yeast** on the mustard-covered pile of weeds. Almost immediately, the pile begins to rise. The **yeast** causes the pile to rise as high as the top of your head! The boy shakes his head in amazement, and perhaps some fear. Now that the **yeast** has caused the original small pile of weeds to rise so significantly, what will you do next? Placing the empty **yeast** packet back in your pocket, you ask for a little more time and patience. This bizarre turn of events involving the **yeast** represents Jesus' PARABLE OF THE YEAST.

PARABLE OF THE YEAST

Mt 13:33

33 He spoke to them another parable. "The kingdom of heaven is like yeast that a woman took and mixed with three measures of wheat flour until the whole batch was leavened."

Lk 13:20–21

20 Again he said, "To what shall I compare the kingdom of God? **21** It is like yeast that a woman took and mixed [in] with three measures of wheat flour until the whole batch of dough was leavened."

This was another parable about the kingdom of God. Jesus again made a point by describing the action of something quite small. Yeast is a microorganism, a type of fungus. The yeast can be understood in two different ways. As a metaphor for the kingdom of God, it speaks of how something small can have a large effect. The yeast works in hidden ways. God's plan is also at work! In Jesus' day, yeast was considered unclean, something that was evil. From this perspective, to use it as a metaphor for the Kingdom was both unexpected and memorable. Just as yeast is hidden and at work in dough, the Kingdom is hidden, but will soon become manifest.

YOU HAVE VOLUNTEERED TO HELP the teenager pull weeds. Thus far, you have only created a large, yellow mess. The mustard-covered weeds are now somewhat congealed in the form of a big round sticky ball. The most important feature of this creation is its stickiness. Touching the tacky yellow surface, your finger sticks, as if held by a strong glue that does not want to let go. You are pleased with the results, but the teen calls it "**useless.**" You object and say you are about to demonstrate its **use.** The boy becomes angry and says, "I have no **use** for this silly sticky ball, and I have no **use** for you!" Being called **useless** is moderately painful, but you decide to proceed and demonstrate how to **use** the yellow masterpiece. You begin to roll the yellow sticky ball across the ground. The teen's attitude changes immediately. The excited words "I see how to **use** it now" are music to your ears. All of this banter about the **use** of the sticky mustard-covered ball of weeds recalls the unit describing JESUS' USE OF PARABLES.

JESUS' USE OF PARABLES

Mt 13:34–35

34 All these things Jesus spoke to the crowds in parables. He spoke to them only in parables, 35 to fulfill what had been said through the prophet:

"I will open my mouth in parables,
I will announce what has lain hidden from the foundation [of the world]."

Mk 4:33–34

33 With many such parables he spoke the word to them as they were able to understand it. 34 Without parables he did not speak to them, but to his own disciples he explained everything in private.

For Mark, this unit functioned as a summary statement reiterating Jesus' method of teaching to the crowd. It also reinforces how privileged (Landmark 12) the disciples were. They received private instruction from Jesus after the crowds dispersed. For Matthew, the unit helped break up the block of parables and inform us that the privileged disciples also received private instruction from Jesus.

YOUR CREATION IS NOW MAKING life easy for the teen. Rolling the sticky ball along the ground is like having a **weed** magnet! The **weeds** almost seem to jump from the ground to attach themselves to the ball. The grass somehow remains undisturbed. As the ball rolls along, more and more **weeds** adhere to its outer surface. Gradually, the yellow ball turns a dark shade of green. Several minutes later, all of the **weeds** have been pulled. You and the teen shake hands. The grass waves in appreciation, and the **weed** ball gives you a round of applause. The teen's second and more successful weed-pulling effort does not recall the parable of the weeds, which you have already heard, but THE EXPLANATION OF THE PARABLE OF THE WEEDS.

THE EXPLANATION OF THE PARABLE OF THE WEEDS

Mt 13:36–43

36 Then, dismissing the crowds, he went into the house. His disciples approached him and said, "Explain to us the parable of the weeds in the field." **37** He said in reply, "He who sows good seed is the Son of Man, **38** the field is the world, the good seed the children of the kingdom. The weeds are the children of the evil one, **39** and the enemy who sows them is the devil. The harvest is the end of the age, and the harvesters are angels. **40** Just as weeds are collected and burned [up] with fire, so will it be at the end of the age. **41** The Son of Man will send his angels, and they will collect out of his kingdom all who cause others to sin and all evildoers. **42** They will throw them into the fiery furnace, where there will be wailing and grinding of teeth. **43** Then the righteous will shine like the sun in the kingdom of their Father. Whoever has ears ought to hear."

Only Matthew includes the explanation of this parable. In explaining the parable, Jesus described the meaning of each element. Here it is important to note several more details. Here on earth, the Kingdom is a mixed bag. The good and not so good coexist. It is not our job to judge who is who, or what is what. Judgment will come in due time. It is our task to be patient with the process. It is our role to prepare for the harvest. Wailing and teeth grinding are to be avoided.

TENNIS COURT

The fourteenth Landmark also involves sports imagery, but not in the same way as Landmarks 5, 9, or 11. You would be hard-pressed to come up with a sport that had fourteen players on a team. Instead, we will invoke the concept of a fortnight, which is fourteen days. Major tennis tournaments, perhaps Wimbledon being the best example, are played over the course of fourteen days. For this reason, the fourteenth Landmark is a **tennis court**. Imagine yourself on a **tennis court**. It can be a grass **tennis court** if you would like to play Wimbledon. Feel the **tennis court** beneath your feet. With tennis racket in hand, you stare beyond the net at your opponent, who awaits your mighty serve. You are ready to play on the fourteenth Landmark, a beautiful **tennis court**. Here at the beginning of the fourteenth Landmark, two units will be combined.

You prepare to begin the tennis match by serving the first ball. There is just one small problem. You have no ball! Glancing around looking for a ball, you see something utterly unexpected. Sitting just outside of the line marking the edge of the court is an open **treasure** chest. A **treasure** of gold coins and precious jewels sparkles in the sun. Naturally, the **treasure** chest is a major distraction. You walk over to investigate. Could the treasure be real? You become mesmerized by the beauty and sheer quantity of the **treasure**. Soon the yelling of the crowd brings you back to reality. The fans have come to watch tennis, not to see you staring at the **treasure**. This amazing **treasure** by the tennis court recalls the first unit you will associate with the fourteenth Landmark: THE PARABLE OF THE HIDDEN TREASURE.

The booing of the tennis crowd has gotten your attention. It is time to set your mind on tennis, but you still have no ball. Being both resourceful and playful, you have an idea that should entertain the impatient crowd. You grab a huge **pearl** sitting atop the treasure. This massive white **pearl** appears to be about the size of a tennis ball, though it has no fuzz and is a

148

bit heavy. However, it should serve your purpose. You smile and the crowd gasps as you walk to the baseline with the **pearl**. This scene with the **pearl** represents THE PARABLE OF THE PEARL OF GREAT PRICE.

PARABLES OF THE HIDDEN TREASURE AND PEARL

Mt 13:44–46

44 "The kingdom of heaven is like a treasure buried in a field, which a person finds and hides again, and out of joy goes and sells all that he has and buys that field. **45** Again, the kingdom of heaven is like a merchant searching for fine pearls. **46** When he finds a pearl of great price, he goes and sells all that he has and buys it."

Found only in Matthew, these Kingdom parables emphasize that the riches of the kingdom of heaven far exceed our expectations. The Kingdom is worth giving up all of your material possessions. It is not practical for most of us to sell all we own. Some possessions are necessary. We can, however, practice detachment from material objects. Relative to the Kingdom, material objects have no value. For those who realize this, there can come great joy. They willingly detach themselves from material things. Let us pray that we become aware of and have the strength to detach ourselves from whatever stands between us and the Kingdom.

AS YOU PREPARE TO SERVE the pearl, second thoughts about this little stunt creep in. You begin to worry about smashing the pearl into the **net**. Even worse, what if it gets stuck in the **net**? Perhaps the oyster that made the pearl was caught in a **net**, but for the pearl to meet a similar fate would be tragic. It would undoubtedly diminish its **net** worth. You shake these negative thoughts from your head and prepare to serve. The racket strings strike the pearl with a heavy thud. Uh oh! You misjudged how hard to swing. The pearl is heading straight for the **net**. You pray the **net** will somehow be avoided. Another heavy thud tells you the **net** has caught your treasure. It is certainly your fault. This encounter with the **net** represents THE PARABLE OF THE NET.

THE PARABLE OF THE NET

Mt 13:47–50

47 "Again, the kingdom of heaven is like a net thrown into the sea, which collects fish of every kind. 48 When it is full they haul it ashore and sit down to put what is good into buckets. What is bad they throw away. 49 Thus it will be at the end of the age. The angels will go out and separate the wicked from the righteous 50 and throw them into the fiery furnace, where there will be wailing and grinding of teeth."

This Kingdom parable has a familiar theme. The net, which represents the Kingdom, collects all of the fish. In the sea swim many fish, both desirable and otherwise. Previously we saw that in the field, both wheat and weeds grow together, but are separated at the harvest. So, too, will the good and bad fish be divided. While we may flounder together in our current situation, let us be patient with our fellow fish. God will sort things out in the end.

YOU ARE STARING WITH EMBARRASSMENT at the pearl you have served into the net. The ball boys are in shock and slow to retrieve this unconventional ball. There are two ball boys. One is in fact a boy; the other is an **old** man! The **old** man is quite experienced at removing errant serves from the court, but he has never seen anything like this. Though an **old** man with **old** legs, he is still quite quick and agile. The young ball boy is **new** to the sport. He has some **new** ideas about how balls should be retrieved. This upsets the **old** man. However, the **newbie** and the **oldster** are doing their best to work as a team. You watch impatiently as the **old** man and the **newcomer** argue about how to extract the pearl from the net. Finally, they run out onto the court together to retrieve the pearl. All of these references to **old** and **new** refer to the parable about TREASURES OLD AND NEW.

TREASURES OLD AND NEW

Mt 13:51–53

51 "Do you understand all these things?" They answered, "Yes."
52 And he replied, "Then every scribe who has been instructed in
the kingdom of heaven is like the head of a household who brings
from his storeroom both the new and the old." **53** When Jesus
finished these parables, he went away from there.

Jesus concluded this block of teaching by asking His disciples if they
understood the parables He had just told them. Their response indicated
that the parables had been successful in conveying Jesus' message. Jesus
then told this short parable to encourage them to use this storytelling technique to teach others. New treasure, material about Jesus Himself, should
be used. Old treasure, information from the Hebrew Scriptures, is also an
important source to be taught and cherished.

POOL TABLE

The next Landmark, like the last, will use imagery associated with a sport. Some people may consider pool or pocket billiards a game, rather than a sport. Either way, the fifteen colorful balls that are used is why a **pool table** is the fifteenth Landmark. It is a beautiful handcrafted **pool table**. The wood is a deep rich mahogany. The felt is bright green. This **pool table** would be a handsome piece of furniture in any home. Upon seeing this **pool table**, it would be difficult to resist racking up the fifteen balls and shooting a game! However, before playing on the **pool table** you decide to look it over carefully. You examine its intricate carvings and feel the smooth polished surface of the wood. You breathe in the leather scent of each pocket. Inspect the taut, flawless green felt that covers the surface of the fifteenth Landmark, a beautiful **pool table**.

Despite having a pool table to play on, you decide to use the fifteenth Landmark for something else. It is likely that no one has ever used such a fine pool table as a raft. Yes, a raft, something you put in the water! In spite of strong **storm** warnings, you decide to do just that. Imagine pushing this beautifully carved felt-covered raft out into the water. A terrible **storm** is brewing. Just as you hop aboard the fancy wooden raft, the sky opens up. Rain pours down, drenching you and your green raft. You begin to use a pool stick to paddle into the heart of the **storm**. Within several minutes, the **storm** has intensified. Thunder roars and lightning flashes. You come to the conclusion that venturing out into this **storm** was not a good idea. Suddenly, the **storm** stops. There is no more rain, lightning, or thunder. All is **calm**. The sudden end of the **storm** and the **calming** of the water is overwhelming. You thank God for the relief and are reminded of JESUS CALMING THE STORM.

JESUS CALMING THE STORM

Mt 8:23–27

23 He got into a boat and his disciples followed him. **24** Suddenly a violent storm came up on the sea, so that the boat was being swamped by waves; but he was asleep. **25** They came and woke him, saying, "Lord, save us! We are perishing!" **26** He said to them, "Why are you terrified, O you of little faith?" Then he got up, rebuked the winds and the sea, and there was great calm. **27** The men were amazed and said, "What sort of man is this, whom even the winds and the sea obey?"

Mk 4:35–41

35 On that day, as evening drew on, he said to them, "Let us cross to the other side." **36** Leaving the crowd, they took him with them in the boat just as he was. And other boats were with him. **37** A violent squall came up and waves were breaking over the boat, so that it was already filling up. **38** Jesus was in the stern, asleep on a cushion. They woke him and said to him, "Teacher, do you not care that we are perishing?" **39** He woke up, rebuked the wind, and said to the sea, "Quiet! Be still!" The wind ceased and there was great calm. **40** Then he asked them, "Why are you terrified? Do you not yet have faith?" **41** They were filled with great awe and said to one another, "Who then is this whom even wind and sea obey?"

Lk 8:22–25

22 One day he got into a boat with his disciples and said to them, "Let us cross to the other side of the lake." So they set sail, **23** and while they were sailing he fell asleep. A squall blew over the lake, and they were taking in water and were in danger. **24** They came and woke him saying, "Master, master, we are perishing!" He awakened, rebuked the wind and the waves, and they subsided and there was a calm. **25** Then he asked them, "Where is your faith?" But they were filled with awe and amazed and said to one another, "Who then is this, who commands even the winds and the sea, and they obey him?"

This was the first in a series of six miracles performed by Jesus. In previous miracles, Jesus healed many people in response to their show of faith. Here the disciples' lack of faith was followed by a miracle showing Jesus' power over nature.

It was not unusual for violent storms to suddenly arise on the Sea of Galilee. Calm could quickly turn to chaos. Jesus' calm demeanor reflects the serenity we should strive for when surrounded by turmoil. A strong trust in God will help us maintain calmness in stormy situations. In the Hebrew Scriptures, a stormy sea symbolized chaos and the power of evil. Jesus rebuked the sea in the same way He rebuked demons. The sea became calm and the wind died down. Let us allow Jesus to take control of the storms in our life.

THE STORM IS OVER, BUT something feels wrong. You are not sure what it is. Soon you realize your feet are standing in the problem. During the storm, the pool table took on a liquid that is clearly not water. You recognize the distinct odor of **kerosene**! During the storm, your makeshift raft must have gone through a **kerosene** spill. This fuel cannot be good for the felt or the beautiful wood. You furiously begin using your feet to slosh the **kerosene** into the corner pockets of the pool table. Hopefully, the porous pockets will drain the **kerosene** out of your pricey raft. You seem to be having some success. **Kerosene** begins to slowly flow out from the corners of the table. The discovery of the unwanted **kerosene** is a soundalike reminder of the next unit. *Kerosene* sounds like "Gerasene," as in THE HEALING OF THE GERASENE DEMONIAC.

||||||||||||||||||||||||||||||||||||||||||||||||||||||||||||||||||||||||||||||||||||||||||||||||||||||||||||||||||||||||||||||||||||

THE HEALING OF THE GERASENE
(GADARENE) DEMONIAC

||||||||||||||||||||||||||||||||||||||||||||||||||||||||||||||||||||||||||||||||||||||||||||||||||||||||||||||||||||||||||||||||||||

Mt 8:28–34

28 When he came to the other side, to the territory of the Gadarenes, two demoniacs who were coming from the tombs met him. They were so savage that no one could travel by that road. **29** They cried out, "What have you to do with us, Son of God? Have you come here to torment us before the appointed time?" **30** Some distance away a herd of many swine was feeding. **31** The demons pleaded with him, "If you drive us out, send us into the herd of swine." **32** And he said to them, "Go then!" They came out and entered the swine, and the whole herd rushed down the steep bank into the sea where they drowned. **33** The swineherds ran away, and when they came to the town they reported everything, including what had happened to the demoniacs. **34** Thereupon the whole town came out to meet Jesus, and when they saw him they begged him to leave their district.

Mk 5:1–20

1 They came to the other side of the sea, to the territory of the Gerasenes. **2** When he got out of the boat, at once a man from the tombs who had an unclean spirit met him. **3** The man had been dwelling among the tombs, and no one could restrain him any longer, even with a chain. **4** In fact, he had frequently been bound with shackles and chains, but the chains had been pulled apart by him and the shackles smashed, and no one was strong enough to subdue him. **5** Night and day among the tombs and on the hillsides he was always crying out and bruising himself with stones.
6 Catching sight of Jesus from a distance, he ran up and prostrated himself before him, **7** crying out in a loud voice, "What have you to do with me, Jesus, Son of the Most High God? I adjure you by God, do not torment me!" **8** (He had been saying to him, "Unclean spirit, come out of the man!") **9** He asked him, "What is your name?" He replied, "Legion is my name. There are many of us." **10** And he pleaded earnestly with him not to drive them away from that territory.
11 Now a large herd of swine was feeding there on the hillside. **12** And they pleaded with him, "Send us into the swine. Let us enter them." **13** And he let them, and the unclean spirits came out and entered the swine. The herd of about two thousand rushed down a steep bank into the sea, where they were drowned. **14** The swineherds ran away and reported the incident in the town and throughout the countryside. And people came out to see what had happened. **15** As they approached Jesus, they caught sight of the man who had been possessed by Legion, sitting there clothed and in his right mind. And they were seized with fear. **16** Those who witnessed the incident explained to them what had happened to the possessed man and to the swine. **17** Then they began to beg him to leave their district. **18** As he was getting into the boat, the man who had been possessed pleaded to remain with him. **19** But he would not permit him but told him instead, "Go home to your family and announce to them all that the Lord in his pity has done for you."
20 Then the man went off and began to proclaim in the Decapolis what Jesus had done for him; and all were amazed.

Lk 8:26–39

26 Then they sailed to the territory of the Gerasenes, which is opposite Galilee. **27** When he came ashore a man from the town who was possessed by demons met him. For a long time he had not worn clothes; he did not live in a house, but lived among the tombs. **28** When he saw Jesus, he cried out and fell down before him; in a loud voice he shouted, "What have you to do with me, Jesus, son of the Most High God? I beg you, do not torment me!" **29** For he had ordered the unclean spirit to come out of the man. (It had taken hold of him many times, and he used to be bound with chains and shackles as a restraint, but he would break his bonds and be driven by the demon into deserted places.) **30** Then Jesus asked him, "What is your name?" He replied, "Legion," because many demons had entered him. **31** And they pleaded with him not to order them to depart to the abyss.

32 A herd of many swine was feeding there on the hillside, and they pleaded with him to allow them to enter those swine; and he let them. **33** The demons came out of the man and entered the swine, and the herd rushed down the steep bank into the lake and was drowned. **34** When the swineherds saw what had happened, they ran away and reported the incident in the town and throughout the countryside. **35** People came out to see what had happened and, when they approached Jesus, they discovered the man from whom the demons had come out sitting at his feet. He was clothed and in his right mind, and they were seized with fear. **36** Those who witnessed it told them how the possessed man had been saved. **37** The entire population of the region of the Gerasenes asked Jesus to leave them because they were seized with great fear. So he got into a boat and returned. **38** The man from whom the demons had come out begged to remain with him, but he sent him away, saying, **39** "Return home and recount what God has done for you." The man went off and proclaimed throughout the whole town what Jesus had done for him.

Jesus has now performed His first miracle in Gentile territory. This is another foreshadowing of the church's mission to minister to all people. Again the demon, not the person possessed, recognized and called Jesus by name, acknowledging Him as the Son of God. This story includes several jabs directed at the despised Romans. The demon(s)' name is Legion. A legion consisted of 5,000 Roman soldiers. The demons were sent into a nearby herd of unclean swine. Pigs were a symbol of Roman power and oppression. After entering the swine, they were promptly drowned, killing the demons in the process. In Mark and Luke, the healed man proclaimed Jesus throughout the area.

AS YOU CONTINUE TO SLOSH kerosene toward the corner pockets, it seems as if your effort is yielding poor results. The pockets are not draining well. They appear to be clogged. They are! You walk around the pool table and collect something very odd from the pockets. Each contains a small **jar**. It is not the **jar** itself that is bizarre. Each **jar** is filled with **blood**! This is a shocking find. As you carefully examine each **blood-filled jar**, several questions come to mind. Whose **blood** is in the **jars**? Why were they placed in the pockets? You decide to take the raft and the **jars of blood** back to shore for some answers. These **jars** and the **blood** are reminders of the two components of the next unit: JAIRUS'S (JARS) DAUGHTER AND THE WOMAN WITH THE HEMORRHAGE (BLOOD).

JAIRUS'S DAUGHTER AND THE WOMAN WITH THE HEMORRHAGE

Mt 9:18–26

18 While he was saying these things to them, an official came forward, knelt down before him, and said, "My daughter has just died. But come, lay your hand on her, and she will live." **19** Jesus rose and followed him, and so did his disciples. **20** A woman suffering hemorrhages for twelve years came up behind him and touched the tassel on his cloak. **21** She said to herself, "If only I can touch his cloak, I shall be cured." **22** Jesus turned around and saw her, and said, "Courage, daughter! Your faith has saved you." And from that hour the woman was cured.

23 When Jesus arrived at the official's house and saw the flute players and the crowd who were making a commotion, **24** he said, "Go away! The girl is not dead but sleeping." And they ridiculed him. **25** When the crowd was put out, he came and took her by the hand, and the little girl arose. **26** And news of this spread throughout all that land.

Mk 5:21–43

21 When Jesus had crossed again [in the boat] to the other side, a large crowd gathered around him, and he stayed close to the sea. **22** One of the synagogue officials, named Jairus, came forward. Seeing him he fell at his feet **23** and pleaded earnestly with him, saying, "My daughter is at the point of death. Please, come lay your hands on her that she may get well and live." **24** He went off with him, and a large crowd followed him and pressed upon him.

25 There was a woman afflicted with hemorrhages for twelve years. **26** She had suffered greatly at the hands of many doctors and had spent all that she had. Yet she was not helped but only grew worse. **27** She had heard about Jesus and came up behind him in the crowd and touched his cloak. **28** She said, "If I but touch his clothes, I shall be cured." **29** Immediately her flow of blood dried up. She felt in her body that she was healed of her affliction. **30** Jesus, aware at once that power had gone out from him, turned around in the crowd and asked, "Who has touched my clothes?" **31** But his disciples said to him, "You see how the crowd is pressing upon you, and yet you ask, 'Who touched me?'" **32** And he looked around to see who had done it. **33** The woman, realizing what had happened to her, approached in fear and trembling. She fell down before Jesus and told him the whole truth. **34** He said to her, "Daughter, your faith has saved you. Go in peace and be cured of your affliction."

35 While he was still speaking, people from the synagogue official's house arrived and said, "Your daughter has died; why trouble the teacher any longer?" **36** Disregarding the message that was reported, Jesus said to the synagogue official, "Do not be afraid; just have faith." **37** He did not allow anyone to accompany him inside except Peter, James, and John, the brother of James. **38** When they arrived at the house of the synagogue official, he caught sight of a commotion, people weeping and wailing loudly. **39** So he went in and said to them, "Why this commotion and weeping? The child is not dead but asleep." **40** And they ridiculed him. Then he put them all out. He took along the child's father and mother and those who were with him and entered the room where the child was. **41** He took the child by the hand and said to her, *"Talitha koum,"* which means, "Little girl, I say to you, arise!" **42** The girl, a child of twelve, arose immediately and walked around. [At that] they were utterly astounded. **43** He gave strict orders that no one should know this and said that she should be given something to eat.

Lk 8:40–56

40 When Jesus returned, the crowd welcomed him, for they were all waiting for him. **41** And a man named Jairus, an official of the synagogue, came forward. He fell at the feet of Jesus and begged him to come to his house, **42** because he had an only daughter, about twelve years old, and she was dying. As he went, the crowds almost crushed him. **43** And a woman afflicted with hemorrhages for twelve years, who [had spent her whole livelihood on doctors and] was unable to be cured by anyone, **44** came up behind him and touched the tassel on his cloak. Immediately her bleeding stopped. **45** Jesus then asked, "Who touched me?" While all were denying it, Peter said, "Master, the crowds are pushing and pressing in upon you." **46** But Jesus said, "Someone has touched me; for I know that power has gone out from me." **47** When the woman realized that she had not escaped notice, she came forward trembling. Falling down before him, she explained in the presence of all the people why she had touched him and how she had been healed immediately. **48** He said to her, "Daughter, your faith has saved you; go in peace."

49 While he was still speaking, someone from the synagogue official's house arrived and said, "Your daughter is dead; do not trouble the teacher any longer." **50** On hearing this, Jesus answered him, "Do not be afraid; just have faith and she will be saved." **51** When he arrived at the house he allowed no one to enter with him except Peter and John and James, and the child's father and mother. **52** All were weeping and mourning for her, when he said, "Do not weep any longer, for she is not dead, but sleeping." **53** And they ridiculed him, because they knew that she was dead. **54** But he took her by the hand and called to her, "Child, arise!" **55** Her breath returned and she immediately arose. He then directed that she should be given something to eat. **56** Her parents were astounded, and he instructed them to tell no one what had happened.

This unit is a good example of a literary technique often used by the evangelists, particularly Mark. The healing of the bleeding woman is "sandwiched" between Jesus' interactions with Jairus. The stories are connected in several other ways. Both involve females who were healed with a touch. The "unclean" woman touched Jesus and was healed. Jesus subsequently touched the young girl's unclean corpse. The healings are also connected by time. The woman's illness had begun when the girl was born, twelve years earlier.

This unit also describes the first time Jesus gathered together His "inner circle." It consisted of the two sets of fishermen brothers, Peter and his brother Andrew; and the sons of Zebedee, James and John. These four were with Jesus when the girl was returned to life. Later, they would be with Jesus at the transfiguration and in Gethsemane.

YOU ARE NOW BACK ON shore. The blood in the jars must be analyzed. It is very important that it be done anonymously. You do not want your identity known in case there has been foul play. The blood needs to arrive at the laboratory without anyone being able to trace it back to you. A brilliant two-step scheme comes to mind. First you must give the blood in the jars to a person who will not be able to recognize your face. You need someone who is **blind**. You are particularly fortunate, because at that moment **two blind men** happen to pass by. You ask the **blind men** to stop. After exchanging pleasantries with the **blind men**, you ask them for a favor. Would they be kind enough to deliver the jars to the man standing down at the street corner? The **blind men** are very accommodating. Without asking any questions, the **blind men** take the jars and proceed to the corner to make the delivery. This encounter with the **blind men** evokes memories of Jesus HEALING THE TWO BLIND MEN.

HEALING THE TWO BLIND MEN

Mt 9:27–31

27 And as Jesus passed on from there, two blind men followed [him], crying out, "Son of David, have pity on us!" 28 When he entered the house, the blind men approached him and Jesus said to them, "Do you believe that I can do this?" "Yes, Lord," they said to him. 29 Then he touched their eyes and said, "Let it be done for you according to your faith." 30 And their eyes were opened. Jesus warned them sternly, "See that no one knows about this." 31 But they went out and spread word of him through all that land.

This miracle story is found only in Matthew. Once again it tells of healing in response to faith. Though blind, the men could "see" that this was the "Son of David" and beg for healing. Jesus could have restored their sight without making physical contact. Instead, He chose to make a connection with the men by touching their eyes. Their response, like the healed demoniac in Gerasene, was to spread the good news about Jesus. They were so overcome by Jesus' healing touch they felt compelled to sing Jesus' praises to others, despite His request to refrain.

PART ONE OF YOUR PLAN to have the blood anonymously analyzed is complete. The blind men will not be able to identify you. Part two involves a man who regularly hangs out at the street corner. You know he is an undercover detective. He will certainly take the blood to a lab. You also know that he is **mute** and will be unable to tell anyone who gave him the blood. This will make it particularly difficult for anyone to trace you as its source. You watch the exchange to make sure it goes smoothly. The blind men approach the **mute** plainclothes detective. He takes the jars, sees the blood, and is of course speechless! You then follow the **mute** detective until you see him enter the nearby laboratory. This delivery to the **mute** detective refers to the unit where JESUS HEALS THE MUTE DEMONIAC.

JESUS HEALS THE MUTE DEMONIAC

Mt 9:32–36

> **32** As they were going out, a demoniac who could not speak was brought to him, **33** and when the demon was driven out the mute person spoke. The crowds were amazed and said, "Nothing like this has ever been seen in Israel." **34** But the Pharisees said, "He drives out demons by the prince of demons."
> **35** Jesus went around to all the towns and villages, teaching in their synagogues, proclaiming the gospel of the kingdom, and curing every disease and illness. **36** At the sight of the crowds, his heart was moved with pity for them because they were troubled and abandoned, like sheep without a shepherd.

Matthew mentions that some Pharisees witnessed this miracle. They repeated the same accusation leveled against Jesus when He healed the mute and blind demoniac in the ninth Landmark ("The Blasphemy of the Scribes"). In both cases, Jesus was accused of "driving out demons by the prince of demons."

This unit also contains a summary statement much like the one in Landmark 5 just prior to the Sermon on the Mount. The summary reinforced Jesus' activities of traveling, teaching, healing, and proclaiming the Kingdom. Jesus' ministry was constantly attracting large crowds. The multitudes filled Him with compassion. Using familiar agricultural imagery, Jesus first likened the crowd to untended sheep in need of a shepherd. Jesus would later describe Himself as the Good Shepherd.

THE JARS OF BLOOD ARE now inside the laboratory. You are still outside, but feel overwhelmed with curiosity. Looking at the sign on the building, you see that it is actually a "Research Laboratory." Curiosity now turns to anxiety. If this is a research lab rather than a testing facility, they will probably want nothing to do with the jars of blood. You decide to go in and find out. Inside, a woman wearing a vest emblazoned with a large letter R greets you. She hands you an identical vest with the letter R and asks you to put it on. Of course you ask why you must wear the **R-vest**. You are told the R stands for "Research" and everyone is required to wear an **R-vest** while inside this building. Looking around, you see that in fact everyone walking by is sporting the **R-vest**. Not wanting to look conspicuous, you quickly slip on the **R-vest**. Though snug, the **R-vest** is fairly fashionable. The **R-vest** is another soundalike. It reminds you of the word *harvest* and JESUS' TEACHING ABOUT THE HARVEST.

||||||||||||||||||||||||||||||||||||||||||||||||||||||||||||||||||||||||||||||||||||||||||||||||||||||||||||||||||||||||||||||||||||||||||

JESUS' TEACHING ABOUT THE HARVEST

||||||||||||||||||||||||||||||||||||||||||||||||||||||||||||||||||||||||||||||||||||||||||||||||||||||||||||||||||||||||||||||||||||||||||

Mt 9:37–38

37 Then he said to his disciples, "The harvest is abundant but the laborers are few; 38 so ask the master of the harvest to send out laborers for his harvest."

———————————

Jesus now likened the crowd to a harvest ready for reaping. His disciples were in training to be laborers to gather the harvest. Jesus intends for us to be laborers for the current harvest. To do this, we need Him to be our Shepherd.

IN SPITE OF THE R-VEST, you still feel that you are somewhere that you do not belong. You decide to look around anyway. You need to see if the blood in the jars is going to be analyzed. Walking down the hall, you are met with inquisitive looks and angry stares. The feeling of **rejection** is overwhelming. The hostility in the air is palpable. You have never experienced such intense feelings of **rejection**. Soon the **rejection** intensifies. In front of you is a door labeled "**Rejects**." Against your better judgment, you enter the **reject** room. Inside, your earlier worries about the jars of blood are confirmed. There they are, sitting on a table. However, the jars are now labeled. Across each has been scrawled the word *reject*. This story of **rejections**—first you, then the jars—is a reminder of JESUS' REJECTION AT NAZARETH.

JESUS' REJECTION AT NAZARETH

Mt 13:53–58

53 When Jesus finished these parables, he went away from there.
54 He came to his native place and taught the people in their synagogue. They were astonished and said, "Where did this man get such wisdom and mighty deeds? **55** Is he not the carpenter's son? Is not his mother named Mary and his brothers James, Joseph, Simon, and Judas? **56** Are not his sisters all with us? Where did this man get all this?" **57** And they took offense at him. But Jesus said to them, "A prophet is not without honor except in his native place and in his own house." **58** And he did not work many mighty deeds there because of their lack of faith.

Mk 6:1–6

1 He departed from there and came to his native place, accompanied by his disciples. **2** When the sabbath came he began to teach in the synagogue, and many who heard him were astonished. They said, "Where did this man get all this? What kind of wisdom has been given him? What mighty deeds are wrought by his hands! **3** Is he not the carpenter, the son of Mary, and the brother of James and Joses and Judas and Simon? And are not his sisters here with us?" And they took offense at him. **4** Jesus said to them, "A prophet is not without honor except in his native place and among his own kin and in his own house." **5** So he was not able to perform any mighty deed there, apart from curing a few sick people by laying his hands on them. **6** He was amazed at their lack of faith.
He went around to the villages in the vicinity teaching.

Lk 4:16–30

16 He came to Nazareth, where he had grown up, and went according to his custom into the synagogue on the sabbath day. He stood up to read **17** and was handed a scroll of the prophet Isaiah. He unrolled the scroll and found the passage where it was written:

18 "The Spirit of the Lord is upon me,
because he has anointed me
to bring glad tidings to the poor.

He has sent me to proclaim liberty to captives
and recovery of sight to the blind,
to let the oppressed go free,
19 and to proclaim a year acceptable to the Lord."

20 Rolling up the scroll, he handed it back to the attendant and sat down, and the eyes of all in the synagogue looked intently at him. **21** He said to them, "Today this scripture passage is fulfilled in your hearing." **22** And all spoke highly of him and were amazed at the gracious words that came from his mouth. They also asked, "Isn't this the son of Joseph?" **23** He said to them, "Surely you will quote me this proverb, 'Physician, cure yourself,' and say, 'Do here in your native place the things that we heard were done in Capernaum.'"
24 And he said, "Amen, I say to you, no prophet is accepted in his own native place. **25** Indeed, I tell you, there were many widows in Israel in the days of Elijah when the sky was closed for three and a half years and a severe famine spread over the entire land. **26** It was to none of these that Elijah was sent, but only to a widow in Zarephath in the land of Sidon. **27** Again, there were many lepers in Israel during the time of Elisha the prophet; yet not one of them was cleansed, but only Naaman the Syrian." **28** When the people in the synagogue heard this, they were all filled with fury. **29** They rose up, drove him out of the town, and led him to the brow of the hill on which their town had been built, to hurl him down headlong. **30** But he passed through the midst of them and went away.

———————————

Being rejected is a painful experience. It is especially difficult if your hometown is doing the rejecting. Wanting you dead would almost be the ultimate rejection. In this unit, Jesus escaped, though He will eventually experience the ultimate rejection. Both Mark and Matthew describe the rejection at Nazareth as taking place well into Jesus' public ministry. It occurred after many had seen or personally experienced His extraordinary teaching and healing power. Luke places this hometown rejection at a particularly difficult time, at the beginning of Jesus' public ministry. Immediately after describing His rejection in Nazareth, Luke tells about the cure of the demoniac in the synagogue. As you recall from Landmark 4, this caused a positive reaction among the people in Capernaum.

Luke includes the passage from Isaiah about being anointed with "the Spirit of the Lord." In Luke, this is particularly appropriate since it was at the beginning of Jesus' ministry, just after He had been baptized.

We all experience rejection in our lives. Given His experiences, Jesus clearly understands this. How comforting to know that Jesus never rejects us.

Landmark 16:

TEENAGER DRIVING

Recall a few Landmarks ago when you helped a thirteen-year-old who had just gotten a job pulling weeds. You will now meet another teenager. Since this is Landmark 16, this teen has just turned 16. Of course, that means that you are with a newly licensed driver! Picture an excited, but nervous **sixteen-year-old** girl behind the wheel of a car. This **sixteen-year-old** is the sixteenth Landmark. You are sitting in the passenger seat "riding shotgun." The young girl is heading down the highway with both hands tightly on the wheel, continuously scanning and glancing in the side and rear mirrors. This **sixteen-year-old** appears well on her way to becoming a good and safe driver.

Where is the sixteen-year-old girl going? Though just a teenager, the young girl feels ready to join the Army! You are accompanying her to the recruitment center. This underage patriot does not want to simply join the Army. The sixteen-year-old is hoping to be **commissioned** as an officer! Upon arrival, the officer on duty greets the excited young teen. He explains that he is unable to **commission** the eager recruit. **Commissioning** will have to wait. The officer then spends time discussing the requirements for being **commissioned** into the Army. The future officer seems to understand the **commissioning** process. This **commission** discussion reminds you of the unit about another type of **commissioning**: Jesus' COMMISSIONING AND INSTRUCTING THE APOSTLES.

COMMISSIONING AND INSTRUCTING
THE APOSTLES

Mt 10:5–16, 23–25

5 Jesus sent out these twelve after instructing them thus, "Do not go into pagan territory or enter a Samaritan town. **6** Go rather to the lost sheep of the house of Israel. **7** As you go, make this proclamation: 'The kingdom of heaven is at hand.' **8** Cure the sick, raise the dead, cleanse lepers, drive out demons. Without cost you have received; without cost you are to give. **9** Do not take gold or silver or copper for your belts; **10** no sack for the journey, or a second tunic, or sandals, or walking stick. The laborer deserves his keep. **11** Whatever town or village you enter, look for a worthy person in it, and stay there until you leave. **12** As you enter a house, wish it peace. **13** If the house is worthy, let your peace come upon it; if not, let your peace return to you. **14** Whoever will not receive you or listen to your words—go outside that house or town and shake the dust from your feet. **15** Amen, I say to you, it will be more tolerable for the land of Sodom and Gomorrah on the day of judgment than for that town.

16 "Behold, I am sending you like sheep in the midst of wolves; so be shrewd as serpents and simple as doves. ... **23** When they persecute you in one town, flee to another. Amen, I say to you, you will not finish the towns of Israel before the Son of Man comes. **24** No disciple is above his teacher, no slave above his master. **25** It is enough for the disciple that he become like his teacher, for the slave that he become like his master. If they have called the master of the house Beelzebul, how much more those of his household!"

Mk 6:7–11

7 He summoned the Twelve and began to send them out two by two and gave them authority over unclean spirits. **8** He instructed them to take nothing for the journey but a walking stick—no food, no sack, no money in their belts. **9** They were, however, to wear sandals but not a second tunic. **10** He said to them, "Wherever you enter a house, stay there until you leave from there. **11** Whatever place does not welcome you or listen to you, leave there and shake the dust off your feet in testimony against them."

Lk 9:1–5

1 He summoned the Twelve and gave them power and authority over all demons and to cure diseases, **2** and he sent them to proclaim the kingdom of God and to heal [the sick]. **3** He said to them, "Take nothing for the journey, neither walking stick, nor sack, nor food, nor money, and let no one take a second tunic. 4 Whatever house you enter, stay there and leave from there. 5 And as for those who do not welcome you, when you leave that town, shake the dust from your feet in testimony against them."

This description of the commissioning is found in all three Synoptic Gospels. In Matthew, it is the beginning of the lengthy "Missionary Discourse." Jesus gave the Twelve some basic instructions in preparation for their first mission trip. He also gave them something that would make it possible to go forward with little else. Jesus gave them power and authority! Armed with the power and authority of Jesus, excessive personal and material belongings were unnecessary. The newly commissioned disciples were to preach the coming of the Kingdom just as John the Baptist had done, and just as Jesus continued to do. The disciples were also warned about the possibility of rejection and how to handle it. In the not-too-distant future, Jesus would suffer the ultimate in rejection, His death upon the cross. In dying, Jesus showed the depth of His trust in God. The apostles were also to trust in God to provide for them on their mission.

AS THE FUTURE OFFICER TURNS to leave, the door bursts open. The shocked teen blurts out, "Mom, what are you doing here?" The mother had heard that her underage daughter was trying to join the Army. She had come to intervene. Her angry look and large **purse** give you and the officer cause for concern. She yells some unpleasant words at him. Her wrath is then directed at you for abetting her sixteen-year-old daughter. You try to maintain some composure, but strongly suspect you are about to be assaulted with a large, heavy **purse**. The mother steps closer with the **purse,** which is now swinging in large circles above her head. She releases the **purse**. Thwack! The **purse** strikes you squarely in the chest. Mother and daughter now exit the office, leaving the **purse** behind. This unpleasant scene with the **purse** reminds you of **persecution**, and more specifically, Jesus' teaching to the apostles about COURAGE UNDER PERSECUTION.

COURAGE UNDER PERSECUTION

Mt 10:26–33

26 "Therefore do not be afraid of them. Nothing is concealed that will not be revealed, nor secret that will not be known. 27 What I say to you in the darkness, speak in the light; what you hear whispered, proclaim on the housetops. 28 And do not be afraid of those who kill the body but cannot kill the soul; rather, be afraid of the one who can destroy both soul and body in Gehenna. 29 Are not two sparrows sold for a small coin? Yet not one of them falls to the ground without your Father's knowledge. 30 Even all the hairs of your head are counted. 31 So do not be afraid; you are worth more than many sparrows. 32 Everyone who acknowledges me before others I will acknowledge before my heavenly Father. 33 But whoever denies me before others, I will deny before my heavenly Father."

Lk 12:2–9

2 "There is nothing concealed that will not be revealed, nor secret that will not be known. 3 Therefore whatever you have said in the darkness will be heard in the light, and what you have whispered behind closed doors will be proclaimed on the housetops. 4 I tell you, my friends, do not be afraid of those who kill the body but after that can do no more. 5 I shall show you whom to fear. Be afraid of the one who after killing has the power to cast into Gehenna; yes, I tell you, be afraid of that one. 6 Are not five sparrows sold for two small coins? Yet not one of them has escaped the notice of God. 7 Even the hairs of your head have all been counted. Do not be afraid. You are worth more than many sparrows. 8 I tell you, everyone who acknowledges me before others the Son of Man will acknowledge before the angels of God. 9 But whoever denies me before others will be denied before the angels of God."

Jesus knew that those who spoke out and proclaimed Him would face persecution. He was very aware of what His disciples would encounter. In fact, He knew everything about them—hair color as well as hair count! Though difficult times are certain, so is the reward of being acknowledged by our heavenly Father. There is no reason to be fearful. Fear can be overcome by faith in Jesus. He is in control.

YOU HAVE RECOVERED FROM THE blow to the chest from the large, heavy purse. You have even forgiven the angry mother who slung the purse. Now you have to figure out how to return it without any further persecution. You decide to deliver the purse personally, but you will not go alone. The recruiter has many soldiers at his disposal. To return the purse, you decide to bring along an entire **division** of soldiers. That's right, a **division** of ten thousand troops! With the purse in hand and an entire **division** marching behind, you set out to return the purse. Admittedly, an entire **division** of soldiers is probably overkill. The recruiter is hoping that the vision and precision of an entire **division** will cause the mother to change her decision. This scene of you leading an entire **division** of soldiers represents JESUS AS A CAUSE OF DIVISION.

JESUS AS A CAUSE OF DIVISION

Mt 10:34–36

34 "Do not think that I have come to bring peace upon the earth. I have come to bring not peace but the sword. 35 For I have come to set

a man 'against his father,
a daughter against her mother,
and a daughter-in-law against her mother-in-law;
36 and one's enemies will be those of his household.'"

Lk 12:49–53

49 "I have come to set the earth on fire, and how I wish it were already blazing! 50 There is a baptism with which I must be baptized, and how great is my anguish until it is accomplished! 51 Do you think that I have come to establish peace on the earth? No, I tell you, but rather division. 52 From now on a household of five will be divided, three against two and two against three; 53 a father will be divided against his son and a son against his father, a mother against her daughter and a daughter against her mother, a mother-in-law against her daughter-in-law and a daughter-in-law against her mother-in-law."

Jesus was fully aware that His message was radical. He knew that His teachings and the demands required of discipleship were controversial. Many people, even close family members, disagreed and were divided over Jesus. This was symbolized by the sword.

Jesus did not wish to bring dissension. Earlier He had declared "Blessed are the peacemakers." However, He demanded absolute and undivided allegiance. This was not something all would be able to give. Those who did and those who did not would be separated by a great divide.

AFTER MARCHING FOR SEVERAL MILES with the division of troops, you arrive at the home of the sixteen-year-old. The sound of an entire division marching through the neighborhood is deafening. The sight of you leading the soldiers while carrying a large purse makes the scene quite memorable. You soon find the teen and parents nervously standing in their front yard. They are impressed and overwhelmed by the display of power. They are even more impressed by the trouble you went to just to return the purse. Your kindness has swayed the parents to allow their sixteen-year-old to join the Army, but under one **condition**. That condition depends on your **condition**! You must be in excellent physical **condition**. You find this **condition** strange, but decide to demonstrate your **conditioning**. For the next hour, your physical **conditioning** prowess is on display for the entire neighborhood. You sprint through the streets, lift weights, and perform many other **conditioning** drills. Everyone is amazed. When finished, you are short of breath and drenched in sweat, but there is no doubt that you are in superior **condition**. This strange **condition** followed by your display of **conditioning** triggers memories of JESUS' CONDITIONS OF DISCIPLESHIP.

JESUS' CONDITIONS OF DISCIPLESHIP

Mt 10:37–39

37 "Whoever loves father or mother more than me is not worthy of me, and whoever loves son or daughter more than me is not worthy of me; **38** and whoever does not take up his cross and follow after me is not worthy of me. **39** Whoever finds his life will lose it, and whoever loses his life for my sake will find it."

To be a follower of Jesus is a radical decision that has radical consequences. Jesus must be "number one." Our love for Him and desire to do the will of His (and our) Father must be our top priority. Jesus was not saying that we should disregard family. Throughout the Gospels, He preached the need to love family. We are to love non-family as well, for they are our "brothers." In loving our family and those entrusted to us, we not only love God, but also reflect His love to others.

Being a disciple of Jesus requires a total commitment. Material possessions can easily cause us to lose focus of what is truly important. God has loaned us earthly possessions to enjoy and use in the service of others. We must be constantly vigilant that we do not pursue transient things that will all pass away.

THE PURPOSE FOR DISPLAYING YOUR excellent physical condition was to help the officer obtain a recruit. However, you receive unexpected results. All who were witness to your display of conditioning begin to **reward** you. Soon the teenager, parents, and neighbors are all dropping money at your feet. This financial **reward** is humbling, but very much appreciated. You have inspired everyone to become more fit, and they feel that you should be **rewarded** for your effort. Their appreciation is **reward** enough, but to refuse their generosity would be rude. This **reward** is a reminder of Jesus' words about THE REWARDS OF DISCIPLESHIP.

THE REWARDS OF DISCIPLESHIP

Mt 10:40–42

40 "Whoever receives you receives me, and whoever receives me receives the one who sent me. 41 Whoever receives a prophet because he is a prophet will receive a prophet's reward, and whoever receives a righteous man because he is righteous will receive a righteous man's reward. 42 And whoever gives only a cup of cold water to one of these little ones to drink because he is a disciple— amen, I say to you, he will surely not lose his reward."

In Matthew, Jesus explained that when His disciples were preaching about Him and the Kingdom they were true ambassadors. They were acting in the name of Jesus and for Jesus. Since Jesus was sent by the Father to do His will, the disciples were also acting on behalf of God the Father. This was a big responsibility. It would be a great comfort to Jesus' disciples knowing the reward that awaited them. Reward also awaits those who receive Jesus' disciples.

THE PARENTS OF THE SIXTEEN-YEAR-OLD are now quite impressed for several reasons. Your excellent conditioning and thoughtfulness in returning the purse are both admirable. The fact that you also brought along a division of ten thousand soldiers is remarkable. Their position on allowing their sixteen-year-old to join the Army has changed as a result of your efforts. They are now willing to **send out** their sixteen-year-old with the officer and all the troops. The teen is still quite willing to be **sent out**. The entire neighborhood decides to join in and throw a major **send-off** party. The sixteen-year-old is overwhelmed. Few new soldiers are **sent out** with such fanfare. This elaborate **sending out** of the new recruit recalls Jesus' SENDING OUT OF THE TWELVE.

SENDING OUT OF THE TWELVE

Mt 10:5

5 Jesus sent out these twelve after instructing them thus.

Mk 6:12–13

12 So they set off and preached repentance. 13 They drove out many demons, and they anointed with oil many who were sick and cured them.

Lk 9:6

6 Then they set out and went from village to village proclaiming the good news and curing diseases everywhere.

Try to imagine how the Twelve must have felt after seeing and hearing all that Jesus had been doing and saying. They were being sent out to do the same! Sure, they had been given power, authority, and instruction, but what an awesome assignment! Imagine their reaction and deepening faith when people were healed by God acting through them!

CICADAS

The next Landmark is very small. You will need to be careful not to step on it. The opportunity to squash it underfoot occurs only every seventeen years. You may be familiar with the **cicada**, an insect that emerges from the ground in cycles of seventeen years. This little creature is approximately two inches long with a prominent eye on each side of its head and short antennae on top. The **cicada** is able to escape your foot since it can fly using its small, thin wings. Now imagine coming upon a large horde of **cicadas** as they fly up from the ground after a seventeen-year absence. These **cicadas** are Landmark 17.

You are fascinated by the cicadas since they appear only every seventeen years. It is exciting that you now have the chance to observe them. You decide to follow the cicadas as they emerge from the ground. Soon the swarm splits up. Half go in one direction and half go in another. You pick one group and continue to trail them. After a minute or so, they arrive at a cemetery. Then, as if drawn by a magnet, they all descend together around one tombstone. How strange. You walk over to read the name engraved in the stone. You are shocked and saddened to see the name **John**. It is your friend **John**, who you spent time with in Landmarks 2 and 11. The **death of John** brings you to tears. You had no idea that **John had died**. You decide to sit there amongst the cicadas and try to come to terms with the fact that your friend **John has died**. This sad scene is a reminder of the dramatic story about THE DEATH OF JOHN THE BAPTIST.

THE DEATH OF JOHN THE BAPTIST

Mt 14:3–12

3 Now Herod had arrested John, bound [him], and put him in prison on account of Herodias, the wife of his brother Philip, **4** for John had said to him, "It is not lawful for you to have her." **5** Although he wanted to kill him, he feared the people, for they regarded him as a prophet. **6** But at a birthday celebration for Herod, the daughter of Herodias performed a dance before the guests and delighted Herod **7** so much that he swore to give her whatever she might ask for. **8** Prompted by her mother, she said, "Give me here on a platter the head of John the Baptist." **9** The king was distressed, but because of his oaths and the guests who were present, he ordered that it be given, **10** and he had John beheaded in the prison. **11** His head was brought in on a platter and given to the girl, who took it to her mother. **12** His disciples came and took away the corpse and buried him; and they went and told Jesus.

Mk 6:17–29

17 Herod was the one who had John arrested and bound in prison on account of Herodias, the wife of his brother Philip, whom he had married. **18** John had said to Herod, "It is not lawful for you to have your brother's wife." **19** Herodias harbored a grudge against him and wanted to kill him but was unable to do so. **20** Herod feared John, knowing him to be a righteous and holy man, and kept him in custody. When he heard him speak he was very much perplexed, yet he liked to listen to him. **21** She had an opportunity one day when Herod, on his birthday, gave a banquet for his courtiers, his military officers, and the leading men of Galilee. **22** Herodias's own daughter came in and performed a dance that delighted Herod and his guests. The king said to the girl, "Ask of me whatever you wish and I will grant it to you." **23** He even swore [many things] to her, "I will grant you whatever you ask of me, even to half of my kingdom." **24** She went out and said to her mother, "What shall I ask for?" She replied, "The head of John the Baptist." **25** The girl hurried back to the king's presence and made her request, "I want you to give me at once on a platter the head of John the Baptist." **26** The king was deeply distressed, but because of his oaths and the guests he did not wish to break his word to her. **27** So he promptly dispatched an executioner with orders to bring back his head. He went off and beheaded him in the prison. **28** He brought in the head on a platter and gave it to the girl. The girl in turn gave it to her mother. **29** When his disciples heard about it, they came and took his body and laid it in a tomb.

The story of John's beheading by the evil Herod Antipas is a "flashback." It is an event that had already occurred. However, while the apostles were on their first missionary trip was a convenient time to tell the story. John had been imprisoned for speaking out about Herod's unlawful marriage. Herod's impulsive promise and the anger of Herodias led to his death. John, the forerunner of Jesus, was a truly righteous disciple of God. His death was a foreshadowing of Jesus' own death. The story of John's death follows units when Jesus taught the Twelve about discipleship. John's death emphasized that being a disciple of Jesus can be costly.

WHILE SITTING AT THE GRAVESIDE of your friend John, you become aware of a low droning sound. It gradually intensifies to the point where you can no longer focus on your thoughts about John. You turn and see the other half of the cicadas that had split from the original swarm. You also see what appears to be an **onion** flying through the air with the cicadas! As they approach, the cicadas appear to be flying in very tight formation. In fact, they are massed so closely together that they are carrying the **onion** upon their collective backs. The cicadas circle the tombstone of John while supporting the **onion**. Then suddenly the swarm separates and the **onion** plops down in front of the grave. It appears that they are paying their respects to John with the gift of an **onion**. Does the **onion** represent the many layers of his personality? Perhaps it is their way of shedding tears, since an **onion** causes many to cry. Whatever the reason, there sits the **onion** at the grave. The onion is a soundalike for "opinion." This represents the unit describing HEROD'S OPINION OF JESUS.

HEROD'S OPINION OF JESUS

Mt 14:1–2

1 At that time Herod the tetrarch heard of the reputation of Jesus 2 and said to his servants, "This man is John the Baptist. He has been raised from the dead; that is why mighty powers are at work in him."

Mk 6:14–16

14 King Herod heard about it, for his fame had become widespread, and people were saying, "John the Baptist has been raised from the dead; that is why mighty powers are at work in him." 15 Others were saying, "He is Elijah"; still others, "He is a prophet like any of the prophets." 16 But when Herod learned of it, he said, "It is John whom I beheaded. He has been raised up."

Lk 9:7–9

7 Herod the tetrarch heard about all that was happening, and he was greatly perplexed because some were saying, "John has been raised from the dead"; 8 others were saying, "Elijah has appeared"; still others, "One of the ancient prophets has arisen." 9 But Herod said, "John I beheaded. Who then is this about whom I hear such things?" And he kept trying to see him.

───────────

Up to this point in Jesus' ministry, His true identity to His disciples had been uncertain. We know that Jesus was the Messiah, the Son of God. At the time, it was not clear to those around Him. The Jewish people were expecting a great and powerful Messiah who would free them from the yoke of Roman oppression. Jesus, with His group of ragtag and seemingly "ordinary" disciples, did not seem to fit the bill. Complicating the picture were Jesus' attempts to keep His true identity a secret. All of this hardly seemed to be Messiah-like behavior. Many thought Jesus was just another prophet. Others felt He was not just any prophet, but the great Elijah himself. The Gospels describe this confusion and uncertainty. Matthew and Mark depict a guilty Herod believing that Jesus was John the Baptist, whom he had beheaded. Luke has Herod dismiss this notion and express the uncertainty he and others felt.

Landmark 18:

GOLF COURSE

You have arrived at the beautiful eighteenth Landmark. It is a **golf course**. The sprawling course with its eighteen lush, green manicured holes stretches to the horizon. It is a busy day on the **golf course**. It appears that there are golfers on each of the eighteen holes either hitting their ball or awaiting their turn. Since it is such a beautiful day, you decide to play eighteen holes on the eighteenth Landmark, a **golf course**.

You are approaching the first tee carrying a recently purchased golf bag and set of clubs. The new equipment is a bit heavy strapped across your shoulder. Despite the burden, you are very excited. Your excitement quickly turns to surprise and frustration when the strap on the bag breaks. The new bag and clubs crash to the ground. When you pick up the bag, the bottom falls out. The new clubs lie scattered at your feet. Now you are angry. You decide to **return** both bag and clubs. After gathering the defective bag and scratched clubs, you march to the nearby golf shop to **return** everything. Walking inside to make your **return**, you are greeted by an unfriendly sign reading "**No Returns**." Taking a deep breath, you tell the salesperson your bag and clubs must be **returned**! Unfortunately, a heated argument ensues about the **return** policy. This effort to **return** the bag and clubs represents the first unit associated with Landmark 18: THE RETURN OF THE APOSTLES.

THE RETURN OF THE APOSTLES

Mk 6:30–32

30 The apostles gathered together with Jesus and reported all they had done and taught. **31** He said to them, "Come away by yourselves to a deserted place and rest a while." People were coming and going in great numbers, and they had no opportunity even to eat. **32** So they went off in the boat by themselves to a deserted place.

Lk 9:10

10 When the apostles returned, they explained to him what they had done. He took them and withdrew in private to a town called Bethsaida.

―――――――――

The returning apostles eagerly told Jesus about their teaching and healing experiences. They were now active participants in His ministry. It is unclear how long their first journey lasted, but Jesus knew they were hungry, tired, and needed rest. They had returned to Capernaum where it was busy and hectic. Jesus suggested they retreat to a place of solitude. Mark describes them leaving by boat. Luke indicates that the area around Bethsaida was their destination. This would have been a short trip across the northern tip of the Sea of Galilee.

NOT ONLY DO YOU WANT to return your golf bag and clubs, you want a complete refund. The entire **$5,000** that you spent for the bag and clubs. That's right, you paid **$5,000** for this extremely nice golf gear, and you want every penny of it back. An exchange of equipment is offered, but you demand a full **$5,000** refund. The salesperson firmly repeats that the **$5,000** will not be returned. You dig into your pocket and produce the receipt for **$5,000** and place it on the counter. Once again, your request for the **$5,000** is rejected. This heated exchange over the **$5,000** signifies the unit when JESUS FEEDS THE FIVE THOUSAND.

JESUS FEEDS THE FIVE THOUSAND

Mt 14:13–21

13 When Jesus heard of it, he withdrew in a boat to a deserted place by himself. The crowds heard of this and followed him on foot from their towns. 14 When he disembarked and saw the vast crowd, his heart was moved with pity for them, and he cured their sick.

15 When it was evening, the disciples approached him and said, "This is a deserted place and it is already late; dismiss the crowds so that they can go to the villages and buy food for themselves." **16** [Jesus] said to them, "There is no need for them to go away; give them some food yourselves." **17** But they said to him, "Five loaves and two fish are all we have here." **18** Then he said, "Bring them here to me," **19** and he ordered the crowds to sit down on the grass. Taking the five loaves and the two fish, and looking up to heaven, he said the blessing, broke the loaves, and gave them to the disciples, who in turn gave them to the crowds. **20** They all ate and were satisfied, and they picked up the fragments left over—twelve wicker baskets full. **21** Those who ate were about five thousand men, not counting women and children.

Mk 6:33–44

33 People saw them leaving and many came to know about it. They hastened there on foot from all the towns and arrived at the place before them.

34 When he disembarked and saw the vast crowd, his heart was moved with pity for them, for they were like sheep without a shepherd; and he began to teach them many things. **35** By now it was already late and his disciples approached him and said, "This is a deserted place and it is already very late. **36** Dismiss them so that they can go to the surrounding farms and villages and buy themselves something to eat." **37** He said to them in reply, "Give them some food yourselves." But they said to him, "Are we to buy two hundred days' wages worth of food and give it to them to eat?" **38** He asked them, "How many loaves do you have? Go and see." And when they had found out they said, "Five loaves and two fish." **39** So he gave orders to have them sit down in groups on the green grass. **40** The people took their places in rows by hundreds and by fifties. **41** Then, taking the five loaves and the two fish and looking up to heaven, he said the blessing, broke the loaves, and gave them to [his] disciples to set before the people; he also divided the two fish among them all. **42** They all ate and were satisfied. **43** And they picked up twelve wicker baskets full of fragments and what was left of the fish. **44** Those who ate [of the loaves] were five thousand men.

Lk 9:11–17

11 The crowds, meanwhile, learned of this and followed him. He received them and spoke to them about the kingdom of God, and he healed those who needed to be cured. **12** As the day was drawing to a close, the Twelve approached him and said, "Dismiss the crowd so that they can go to the surrounding villages and farms and find lodging and provisions; for we are in a deserted place here." **13** He said to them, "Give them some food yourselves." They replied, "Five loaves and two fish are all we have, unless we ourselves go and buy food for all these people." **14** Now the men there numbered about five thousand. Then he said to his disciples, "Have them sit down in groups of [about] fifty." **15** They did so and made them all sit down. **16** Then taking the five loaves and the two fish, and looking up to heaven, he said the blessing over them, broke them, and gave them to the disciples to set before the crowd. **17** They all ate and were satisfied. And when the leftover fragments were picked up, they filled twelve wicker baskets.

Jn 6:1–15

1 After this, Jesus went across the Sea of Galilee [of Tiberias]. **2** A large crowd followed him, because they saw the signs he was performing on the sick. **3** Jesus went up on the mountain, and there he sat down with his disciples. **4** The Jewish feast of Passover was near. **5** When Jesus raised his eyes and saw that a large crowd was coming to him, he said to Philip, "Where can we buy enough food for them to eat?" **6** He said this to test him, because he himself knew what he was going to do. **7** Philip answered him, "Two hundred days' wages worth of food would not be enough for each of them to have a little [bit]." **8** One of his disciples, Andrew, the brother of Simon Peter, said to him, **9** "There is a boy here who has five barley loaves and two fish; but what good are these for so many?" **10** Jesus said, "Have the people recline." Now there was a great deal of grass in that place. So the men reclined, about five thousand in number. **11** Then Jesus took the loaves, gave thanks, and distributed them to those who were reclining, and also as much of the fish as they wanted. **12** When they had had their fill, he said to his disciples, "Gather the fragments left over, so that nothing will be wasted." **13** So they collected them, and filled twelve wicker baskets with fragments from the five barley loaves that had been more than they could eat. **14** When the people saw the sign he had done, they said, "This is truly the Prophet, the one who is to come into the world." **15** Since Jesus knew that they were going to come and carry him off to make him king, he withdrew again to the mountain alone.

This well-known miracle is described by all four evangelists. In Matthew, it occurs right after Jesus hears about John the Baptist's death. John places the miracle after much of the teaching material covered in Landmark 7. This provision of food is closely linked to Jesus' words to the Samaritan woman about providing "living water."

The feeding of this staggering number of followers was symbolic of Jesus providing for the needs of His people both then and now. This miracle was packed with rich symbolism. It was reminiscent of God providing manna for Israel during the long sojourn in the desert. It also gives us a glimpse into the future, when God will provide the heavenly banquet. The wording about the preparation when Jesus looked to heaven, said the blessing, broke the bread, and gave it to His disciples also anticipated the Lord's Supper in the not-too-distant future. By giving the bread to His disciples to distribute, Jesus showed how they would continue the work of nourishing God's people. The excessive amount of leftover fragments (twelve wicker baskets) was symbolic of how lavishly God provides for us. The twelve baskets were also a reference to God providing for His chosen people, the Twelve Tribes of Israel.

IT IS CLEAR THAT YOU will not be receiving the $5,000 refund for your golf bag and clubs. You decide to express your anger by demonstrating the inferior quality of the bag. With the salesperson watching, you proceed to pour a large container of **water** into it. Recall that what prompted you to return the bag was the bottom falling out. Without a bottom, the **water** pours through the bag and out onto the floor. The sight of **water** covering the floor of the shop is not pleasing to the salesperson. The customers walking in the **water** are not happy either. To further emphasize your point, you continue pouring **water** into the bottomless golf bag. As the **water** level on the floor rises, you feel confident that your demonstration is making a point. This unexpected **water** hazard in the golf shop helps you remember the unit when JESUS WALKS ON WATER.

JESUS WALKS ON WATER

Mt 14:22–33

22 Then he made the disciples get into the boat and precede him to the other side, while he dismissed the crowds. **23** After doing so, he went up on the mountain by himself to pray. When it was evening he was there alone. **24** Meanwhile the boat, already a few miles offshore, was being tossed about by the waves, for the wind was against it. **25** During the fourth watch of the night, he came toward them, walking on the sea. **26** When the disciples saw him walking on the sea they were terrified. "It is a ghost," they said, and they cried out in fear. **27** At once [Jesus] spoke to them, "Take courage, it is I; do not be afraid." **28** Peter said to him in reply, "Lord, if it is you, command me to come to you on the water." **29** He said, "Come." Peter got out of the boat and began to walk on the water toward Jesus. **30** But when he saw how [strong] the wind was he became frightened; and, beginning to sink, he cried out, "Lord, save me!" **31** Immediately Jesus stretched out his hand and caught him, and said to him, "O you of little faith, why did you doubt?" **32** After they got into the boat, the wind died down. **33** Those who were in the boat did him homage, saying, "Truly, you are the Son of God."

Mk 6:45–52

45 Then he made his disciples get into the boat and precede him to the other side toward Bethsaida, while he dismissed the crowd. **46** And when he had taken leave of them, he went off to the mountain to pray. **47** When it was evening, the boat was far out on the sea and he was alone on shore. **48** Then he saw that they were tossed about while rowing, for the wind was against them. About the fourth watch of the night, he came toward them walking on the sea. He meant to pass by them. **49** But when they saw him walking on the sea, they thought it was a ghost and cried out. **50** They had all seen him and were terrified. But at once he spoke with them, "Take courage, it is I, do not be afraid!" **51** He got into the boat with them and the wind died down. They were [completely] astounded. **52** They had not understood the incident of the loaves. On the contrary, their hearts were hardened.

Jn 6:16–21

16 When it was evening, his disciples went down to the sea, **17** embarked in a boat, and went across the sea to Capernaum. It had already grown dark, and Jesus had not yet come to them. **18** The sea was stirred up because a strong wind was blowing. **19** When they had rowed about three or four miles, they saw Jesus walking on the sea and coming near the boat, and they began to be afraid. **20** But he said to them, "It is I. Do not be afraid." **21** They wanted to take him into the boat, but the boat immediately arrived at the shore to which they were heading.

Jesus had planned a restful time alone with His disciples after their recent mission trip. Instead He had a very busy day of teaching, healing, and then providing food for the enormous crowd. Jesus now needed time alone in prayer to nourish Himself. He sent the disciples ahead while He retreated to pray, much like He had done at the outset of Landmark 5 following the busy day in Capernaum. By sending the disciples across the lake ahead of Him, the stage was set for another grand miracle and test of faith.

As Jesus approached the wind-tossed boat, the apostles became terrified. In their fear, they failed to recognize Jesus. Matthew, who often emphasizes the role of Peter, describes Peter's lack of faith in this stressful situation. Jesus exhorted the disciples to be brave since He was present. He demonstrated that there was no reason to fear, first by rescuing a sinking Peter and then by calming the storm.

The disciples' reaction to Jesus' control over nature is described quite differently by Mark. In his writing, they are portrayed somewhat negatively. The disciples were "completely astounded." A surprising reaction from a group who had witnessed previous amazing miracles, including the multiplication of fish and loaves a few hours earlier. Matthew describes the disciples positively. They reverently testified to Jesus' identity. They had discovered the answer to their question in Landmark 15 when they had asked themselves, "What sort of man is this?"

YOU DID NOT EXPECT YOUR water demonstration with the golf bag to result in a $5,000 refund. However, what happens next is shocking! As if to show indifference to your shenanigans, the salesperson begins to pour another clear liquid into the golf bag. The distinct odor indicates it is certainly not water. It smells like alcohol. The salesperson smugly says, "It is **gin**!" Your golf bag and the entire shop soon reek of **gin**. You are speechless at the sight of bottle after bottle of **gin** being poured into the bag and flowing out onto the floor. You had not expected a gentle or generous response to your previous demonstration, but this use of **gin** is shocking. The **gin** is a soundalike for the town of Gennesaret. The **gin** and its unusual use recall Jesus' HEALINGS AT GENNESARET.

‖‖

HEALINGS AT GENNESARET

‖‖

Mt 14:34–36

34 After making the crossing, they came to land at Gennesaret.
35 When the men of that place recognized him, they sent word to all the surrounding country. People brought to him all those who were

sick **36** and begged him that they might touch only the tassel on his cloak, and as many as touched it were healed.

Mk 6:53–56

53 After making the crossing, they came to land at Gennesaret and tied up there. **54** As they were leaving the boat, people immediately recognized him. **55** They scurried about the surrounding country and began to bring in the sick on mats to wherever they heard he was. **56** Whatever villages or towns or countryside he entered, they laid the sick in the marketplaces and begged him that they might touch only the tassel on his cloak; and as many as touched it were healed.

Gennesaret, like Capernaum, was a town on the western shore of the Sea of Galilee. It was about two miles south of Capernaum and six miles north of Tiberias, another seaside city. Here again, you see the popularity of Jesus and the faith of the people in His healing power. They sought only to touch the tassel of His prayer shawl for a cure, just as the hemorrhaging woman had done in Landmark 15.

Landmark 19:

THE GAME "GO"

Recall that the fifteenth Landmark was a pool table. As mentioned, it could be debated whether pool is a sport or game. The nineteenth Landmark is definitely a game. It is the nineteenth Landmark because it is a game played on a grid of nineteen horizontal and vertical lines. It is the **game of Go**. This very popular ancient Chinese game is played with small black-and-white discs called "stones." Now picture yourself walking along and coming upon a large **Go game** board lying on the ground. There are many discs lying at various intersections of the 19 x 19 lined game board. There does not appear to be anyone playing the game! This **Go game** is Landmark 19.

It is strange to find the seemingly abandoned game of Go. Yelling to see if either contestant is nearby yields no response. With careful footsteps, you approach the 19 x 19 grid. You do not want to disturb any of the carefully placed game pieces. To your surprise, the "stones" are not made of the typical shell or similar hard material used in the Go game. The game pieces are small pieces of **bread**! People are playing with small chunks of white and wheat **bread**! You reach down to make sure your eyes are not deceiving you. Sure enough, the game pieces feel and smell like **bread**. Soon you discover that they also taste like **bread**. These many small chunks of **bread** scattered about the Go board are a reminder of one of Jesus' most well-known blocks of teaching: THE BREAD OF LIFE DISCOURSE.

THE BREAD OF LIFE DISCOURSE

Jn 6:22–59

22 The next day, the crowd that remained across the sea saw that there had been only one boat there, and that Jesus had not gone along with his disciples in the boat, but only his disciples had left. **23** Other boats came from Tiberias near the place where they had eaten the bread when the Lord gave thanks. **24** When the crowd saw that neither Jesus nor his disciples were there, they themselves got into boats and came to Capernaum looking for Jesus. **25** And when they found him across the sea they said to him, "Rabbi, when did you get here?" **26** Jesus answered them and said, "Amen, amen, I say to you, you are looking for me not because you saw signs but because you ate the loaves and were filled. **27** Do not work for food that perishes but for the food that endures for eternal life, which the Son of Man will give you. For on him the Father, God, has set his seal." **28** So they said to him, "What can we do to accomplish the works of God?" **29** Jesus answered and said to them, "This is the work of God, that you believe in the one he sent." **30** So they said to him, "What sign can you do, that we may see and believe in you? What can you do? **31** Our ancestors ate manna in the desert, as it is written:

'He gave them bread from heaven to eat.'"

32 So Jesus said to them, "Amen, amen, I say to you, it was not Moses who gave the bread from heaven; my Father gives you the true bread from heaven. **33** For the bread of God is that which comes down from heaven and gives life to the world."

34 So they said to him, "Sir, give us this bread always." **35** Jesus said to them, "I am the bread of life; whoever comes to me will never hunger, and whoever believes in me will never thirst. **36** But I told you that although you have seen [me], you do not believe. **37** Everything that the Father gives me will come to me, and I will not reject anyone who comes to me, **38** because I came down from heaven not to do my own will but the will of the one who sent me. **39** And this is the will of the one who sent me that I should not lose anything of what he gave me, but that I should raise it [on] the last day. **40** For this is the will of my Father, that everyone who sees the Son and believes in him may have eternal life, and I shall raise him [on] the last day."

41 The Jews murmured about him because he said, "I am the bread that came down from heaven," **42** and they said, "Is this not Jesus, the son of Joseph? Do we not know his father and mother? Then how can he say, 'I have come down from heaven'?"**43** Jesus answered and said to them, "Stop murmuring among yourselves.

44 No one can come to me unless the Father who sent me draw him, and I will raise him on the last day. **45** It is written in the prophets:

'They shall all be taught by God.'

Everyone who listens to my Father and learns from him comes to me. **46** Not that anyone has seen the Father except the one who is from God; he has seen the Father. **47** Amen, amen, I say to you, whoever believes has eternal life. **48** I am the bread of life. **49** Your ancestors ate the manna in the desert, but they died; **50** this is the bread that comes down from heaven so that one may eat it and not die. **51** I am the living bread that came down from heaven; whoever eats this bread will live forever; and the bread that I will give is my flesh for the life of the world."

52 The Jews quarreled among themselves, saying, "How can this man give us [his] flesh to eat?" **53** Jesus said to them, "Amen, amen, I say to you, unless you eat the flesh of the Son of Man and drink his blood, you do not have life within you. **54** Whoever eat my flesh and drinks my blood has eternal life, and I will raise him on the last day. **55** For my flesh is true food, and my blood is true drink. **56** Whoever eats my flesh and drinks my blood remains in me and I in him. **57** Just as the living Father sent me and I have life because of the Father, so also the one who feeds on me will have life because of me. **58** This is the bread that came down from heaven. Unlike your ancestors who ate and still died, whoever eats this bread will live forever." **59** These things he said while teaching in the synagogue in Capernaum.

This unit, found only in John, contains some of Jesus' theological teachings. They were delivered to the large crowd that had been following Him. They had just been fed by the miracle of fish and loaves. They were now being fed by Jesus' words about "the Bread of Life." Jesus told the crowd that like the manna in the desert, He was also bread from heaven sent by the Father. Unlike manna, Jesus was the bread that when eaten leads to eternal life. This was reminiscent of Jesus' words to the Samaritan woman in Landmark 3 about living water. Jesus' teachings about having come down from heaven, being the Bread of Life, and eating His flesh understandably caused "murmuring" in the crowd. This was especially confusing for the people who knew Mary and Joseph.

Jesus wants people to believe His words, which are also the words of the Father. It is the will of the Father that people be drawn to Jesus, to believe in Him, and receive the bread of eternal life. The key to receiving the gift of Jesus, the Bread of Life, is faith that He is the one sent by God. Jesus is for everyone. No one who comes to Him will be rejected! These words were a foreshadowing of Jesus' words at the Lord's Supper. There, after taking, blessing, and breaking bread, Jesus said to the Twelve to "take and eat, this is My body."

YOU HAVE JUST EATEN A small chunk of bread from the Go board. You feel a bit guilty for eating one of the game pieces, though you are not guilty enough to stop your unexpected snack. The bread is tasty, and you are hungry. Unfortunately, the bread is cold. It would taste better if there was a way to warm it up. Looking around, you see a possible solution. Not far away is a flickering flame. It is not really a fire, but a constant flame that appears to be coming from the ground. You grab a handful of bread and walk over to inspect the curious flame. It is in fact coming from the ground! The flame has no visible source of fuel. You realize this is an **eternal** flame, like the one that burns constantly at the grave of President Kennedy. You wonder why there is an **eternal** flame in this location. A moment later, you are heating the bread over the **eternal** flame. The bread is now warm, crispy, and quite delicious thanks to the heat from the **eternal** flame. The **eternal** flame serves as a reminder of Jesus' WORDS OF ETERNAL LIFE.

WORDS OF ETERNAL LIFE

Jn 6:60–66

60 Then many of his disciples who were listening said, "This saying is hard; who can accept it?" **61** Since Jesus knew that his disciples were murmuring about this, he said to them, "Does this shock you? **62** What if you were to see the Son of Man ascending to where he was before? **63** It is the spirit that gives life, while the flesh is of no avail. The words I have spoken to you are spirit and life. **64** But there are some of you who do not believe." Jesus knew from the beginning the ones who would not believe and the one who would betray him. **65** And he said, "For this reason I have told you that no one can come to me unless it is granted him by my Father."

66 As a result of this, many [of] his disciples returned to their former way of life and no longer accompanied him.

The words Jesus had just spoken in the Bread of Life Discourse were very hard to believe. They became a source of division between Jesus and some of His followers. It is certainly easier to believe what one has seen, or in this case what the apostles would witness when Jesus ascended to the Father. The gift of the Spirit would allow Jesus' followers (including us) to have the faith to accept these teachings. Human reason alone is not enough.

Jesus again (recall Landmark 7) drew a connection between Himself and the Father. (This relationship will be further elaborated in Landmark 26.) Now many in the crowd have heard enough and parted ways with Jesus. May we not be among them!

YOU DECIDE TO RETURN TO the Go board and gather more pieces of bread to quiet your growling stomach. Approaching the board, you see two **elderly** men preparing to resume their game. The **elders** look puzzled. As you draw closer, the **elderly** men are wondering who has disrupted their game. Upon seeing you, they appear frightened. You calmly introduce yourself to the two **elderly** gentlemen and offer assurance that you mean no harm. Though you come in peace, you confess that you have been eating some pieces of bread from the game. The kind **elderly** men laugh and tell you to help yourself to more. You gladly accept the generosity of the **elders**. This encounter with the **elderly** men recalls the unit that discusses THE TRADITIONS OF THE ELDERS.

THE TRADITIONS OF THE ELDERS

Mt 15:1–20

1 Then Pharisees and scribes came to Jesus from Jerusalem and said, **2** "Why do your disciples break the tradition of the elders? They do not wash [their] hands when they eat a meal." **3** He said to them in reply, "And why do you break the commandment of God for the sake of your tradition? **4** For God said, 'Honor your father and your mother,' and 'Whoever curses father or mother shall die.' **5** But you say, 'Whoever says to father or mother, "Any support you might

have had from me is dedicated to God," **6** need not honor his father.'
You have nullified the word of God for the sake of your tradition.
7 Hypocrites, well did Isaiah prophesy about you when he said:

8 'This people honors me with their lips,
but their hearts are far from me;
9 in vain do they worship me,
teaching as doctrines human precepts.'"

10 He summoned the crowd and said to them, "Hear and
understand. **11** It is not what enters one's mouth that defiles that
person; but what comes out of the mouth is what defiles one."
12 Then his disciples approached and said to him, "Do you know that
the Pharisees took offense when they heard what you said?"**13** He
said in reply, "Every plant that my heavenly Father has not planted
will be uprooted. **14** Let them alone; they are blind guides [of the
blind]. If a blind person leads a blind person, both will fall into a pit."
15 Then Peter said to him in reply, "Explain [this] parable to us."
16 He said to them, "Are even you still without understanding? **17** Do
you not realize that everything that enters the mouth passes into the
stomach and is expelled into the latrine? **18** But the things that come
out of the mouth come from the heart, and they defile. **19** For from
the heart come evil thoughts, murder, adultery, unchastity, theft,
false witness, blasphemy. **20** These are what defile a person, but to eat
with unwashed hands does not defile."

Mk 7:1–23

1 Now when the Pharisees with some scribes who had come
from Jerusalem gathered around him, **2** they observed that some
of his disciples ate their meals with unclean, that is, unwashed,
hands. **3** (For the Pharisees and, in fact, all Jews, do not eat without
carefully washing their hands, keeping the tradition of the elders.
4 And on coming from the marketplace they do not eat without
purifying themselves. And there are many other things that they
have traditionally observed, the purification of cups and jugs and
kettles [and beds].) **5** So the Pharisees and scribes questioned him,
"Why do your disciples not follow the tradition of the elders but
instead eat a meal with unclean hands?" **6** He responded, "Well did
Isaiah prophesy about you hypocrites, as it is written:

'This people honors me with their lips,
but their hearts are far from me;
7 In vain do they worship me,
teaching as doctrines human precepts.'

8 You disregard God's commandment but cling to human
tradition." **9** He went on to say, "How well you have set aside the
commandment of God in order to uphold your tradition! **10** For
Moses said, 'Honor your father and your mother,' and 'Whoever
curses father or mother shall die.' **11** Yet you say, 'If a person says

to father or mother, "Any support you might have had from me
is *qorban*" (meaning, dedicated to God), **12** you allow him to do
nothing more for his father or mother. **13** You nullify the word of
God in favor of your tradition that you have handed on. And you do
many such things." **14** He summoned the crowd again and said to
them, "Hear me, all of you, and understand. **15** Nothing that enters
one from outside can defile that person; but the things that come
out from within are what defile." **[16]**

17 When he got home away from the crowd his disciples
questioned him about the parable. **18** He said to them, "Are even you
likewise without understanding? Do you not realize that everything
that goes into a person from outside cannot defile, **19** since it enters
not the heart but the stomach and passes out into the latrine?"
(Thus he declared all foods clean.) **20** "But what comes out of a
person, that is what defiles. **21** From within people, from their
hearts, come evil thoughts, unchastity, theft, murder, **22** adultery,
greed, malice, deceit, licentiousness, envy, blasphemy, arrogance,
folly. **23** All these evils come from within and they defile."

Lk 11:37–41

37 After he had spoken, a Pharisee invited him to dine at his
home. He entered and reclined at table to eat. **38** The Pharisee was
amazed to see that he did not observe the prescribed washing before
the meal. **39** The Lord said to him, "Oh you Pharisees! Although
you cleanse the outside of the cup and the dish, inside you are
filled with plunder and evil. **40** You fools! Did not the maker of the
outside also make the inside? **41** But as to what is within, give alms,
and behold, everything will be clean for you."

Lk 6:39–40

39 And he told them a parable, "Can a blind person guide
a blind person? Will not both fall into a pit? **40** No disciple is
superior to the teacher; but when fully trained, every disciple will
be like his teacher."

In this unit, the Pharisees were causing trouble once again. They
gave Jesus another opportunity to distinguish between traditional, legalistic thinking and viewing situations with understanding, compassion, and
love. There was controversy earlier in Landmark 7 regarding fasting, dining companions, and Sabbath behavior. At issue here were the purification
rituals. The traditions of the elders were not being strictly followed by Jesus' disciples. Jesus first countered by pointing out the Pharisees' hypocrisy
in their bending of the commandment to honor their parents to suit their

own needs. He then made the bold and controversial declaration that it is what comes out of a person, not what goes into a person, that defiles. This was an incredible twist on the traditional Jewish food laws.

Matthew and Luke also include the short parable about the blind leading the blind. This had the controversial implication that the Pharisees and their legalism were no longer in force. Jesus and His divine teachings were the new law. Jewish law was to be tempered with the new and radical teachings of Jesus.

EYE APPOINTMENT

O n your walk with Jesus, you have seen a number of strange, unbelievable people and places. What you have seen has made you question your vision. Perhaps an **eye** exam is in order. Your vision is probably not 20/20. Since the twentieth Landmark is next, it seems to be the perfect time to have your **eyesight** checked from the traditional distance of twenty feet. You decide to visit an **eye** doctor to see if your vision measures 20/20. For this reason, your **eye appointment** at the **eye** doctor's office building is Landmark 20.

Upon arrival at the eye doctor's office, you are greeted with a friendly "yasou." It sounds like the doctor has hired a Greek receptionist. It appears that way, too. She is an attractive woman with thick black hair, large dark eyes, an olive complexion, and a welcoming smile. This **Greek woman** begins speaking to you in Greek. You do not understand her words, but she seems to be indicating that you should sign in. You do so, but your name appears to have upset the **Greek woman**. She shakes her head in disapproval. She writes a few Greek letters on the paper. She motions for you to do the same. The **Greek woman** is asking you to write your name in Greek! Since you are unable to comply with this strange request, you point for her to do this for you. The **Greek woman** smiles and obliges with enthusiasm. This encounter with the **Greek woman** is a reminder of JESUS' ENCOUNTER WITH THE GREEK WOMAN.

JESUS' ENCOUNTER WITH THE GREEK WOMAN

Mt 15:21–28

21 Then Jesus went from that place and withdrew to the region of Tyre and Sidon. 22 And behold, a Canaanite woman of that district came and called out, "Have pity on me, Lord, Son of David! My daughter is tormented by a demon." 23 But he did not say a word in answer to her. His disciples came and asked him, "Send her away, for she keeps calling out after us." 24 He said in reply, "I was sent only to the lost sheep of the house of Israel." 25 But the woman came and did him homage, saying, "Lord, help me." 26 He said in reply, "It is not right to take the food of the children and throw it to the dogs." 27 She said, "Please, Lord, for even the dogs eat the scraps that fall from the table of their masters." 28 Then Jesus said to her in reply, "O woman, great is your faith! Let it be done for you as you wish." And her daughter was healed from that hour.

Mk 7:24–30

24 From that place he went off to the district of Tyre. He entered a house and wanted no one to know about it, but he could not escape notice. 25 Soon a woman whose daughter had an unclean spirit heard about him. She came and fell at his feet. 26 The woman was a Greek, a Syrophoenician by birth, and she begged him to drive the demon out of her daughter. 27 He said to her, "Let the children be fed first. For it is not right to take the food of the children and throw it to the dogs." 28 She replied and said to him, "Lord, even the dogs under the table eat the children's scraps." 29 Then he said to her, "For saying this, you may go. The demon has gone out of your daughter." 30 When the woman went home, she found the child lying in bed and the demon gone.

Jesus was again in Gentile territory. This time He was not in the Decapolis on the eastern side of the Sea of Galilee. He was some thirty to forty miles northwest of Capernaum in the area of Tyre and Sidon. This was a long walk for Jesus and the disciples. Matthew says Jesus "withdrew" to the region. Mark describes how He entered a house hoping to escape notice. Perhaps Jesus wanted some quiet time for rest and prayer.

When the Greek (Syrophoenician) woman approached Jesus, she did so with great respect. She came on behalf of someone else. We have seen similar scenes: the centurion/royal official in Landmark 6 and Jairus more recently in Landmark 15. Her request was initially met with rejection, which was somewhat surprising given previous descriptions of Jesus' ministry. Jesus said that His primary focus was on the people of Israel, "the children" or "the lost sheep." His concern was not the Gentiles or "the dogs." Jewish writers of the time often described Gentiles as "dogs." The woman's response showed both humility and great faith. As before, when faith is present, miracles can occur!

WHILE WAITING TO SEE THE eye doctor, you ponder why he would hire a receptionist who does not speak English! Within a few minutes, the Greek woman is leading you through a maze of hallways. At last, you are in an exam room where a doctor is waiting for you. You've never seen this doctor before. He neither introduces himself nor answers your questions as to the whereabouts of your regular eye doctor. In fact, he does not say a word. He seems to be **deaf**! Your suspicions are confirmed when he motions to his ears and shakes his head indicating that he is in fact **deaf**. How bizarre. First a non-English speaking receptionist, and now a **deaf** eye doctor. Fortunately, you are fluent in sign language. Recall that in Landmark 10 you were teaching using sign language. This scene with the **deaf** doctor helps recall the miracle of JESUS HEALING A DEAF MAN.

JESUS HEALING A DEAF MAN

Mt 15:29–31

29 Moving on from there Jesus walked by the Sea of Galilee, went up on the mountain, and sat down there. 30 Great crowds came to him, having with them the lame, the blind, the deformed, the mute, and many others. They placed them at his feet, and he cured them. 31 The crowds were amazed when they saw the mute speaking, the deformed made whole, the lame walking, and the blind able to see, and they glorified the God of Israel.

Mk 7:31–37

31 Again he left the district of Tyre and went by way of Sidon to the Sea of Galilee, into the district of the Decapolis. 32 And people

brought to him a deaf man who had a speech impediment and begged him to lay his hand on him. **33** He took him off by himself away from the crowd. He put his finger into the man's ears and, spitting, touched his tongue; **34** then he looked up to heaven and groaned, and said to him, *"Ephphatha!"* (that is, "Be opened!") **35** And [immediately] the man's ears were opened, his speech impediment was removed, and he spoke plainly. **36** He ordered them not to tell anyone. But the more he ordered them not to, the more they proclaimed it. **37** They were exceedingly astonished and they said, "He has done all things well. He makes the deaf hear and [the] mute speak."

———————————————

Jesus was now back by the Sea of Galilee, far from the region of Tyre and Sidon. He had again crossed the "sea" and was on the Gentile (eastern) side in the area of the Decapolis. Jesus did not simply say a few words or lay His hands on the deaf man. He healed the man by taking him aside and touching his ears and tongue. Then, as if to make a connection with the Father, He looked heavenward and commanded that the man's ears "be opened."

The crowd saw Jesus as an amazing healer. They proclaimed this by quoting Isaiah 35:5–6. Jesus was much more than a healer. In vain, He asked the crowd to keep this healing a secret. They were not yet aware of His full identity, which eventually would be made known by His death and resurrection.

Matthew provided another brief summary of Jesus' healing activity. He did not mention a deaf man being healed. Mark wrote specifically about the ritualistic healing of a deaf man with a speech impediment.

THIS APPOINTMENT TO SEE IF you need spectacles has become a spectacle. You wonder if you will be given an adequate exam. Your doubts are confirmed when the doctor pulls a **fork** from his pocket. A **fork**! How is he going to examine your eyes with a **fork**? The doctor walks across the room and holds the **fork** up with one hand. With the other hand, he indicates that you are to point to show which direction the tines of the **fork** are facing. You become indignant that you are paying good money only to have your vision tested with a **fork**. In this scene, you are to remember the **fork**, which represents the soundalike "**four-k**." As you know, **4K** is another way of saying **4,000**. Thus in a somewhat convoluted way **fork = 4K = 4,000**. This helps recall JESUS FEEDING THE FOUR THOUSAND.

JESUS FEEDING THE FOUR THOUSAND

Mt 15:32–39

32 Jesus summoned his disciples and said, "My heart is moved with pity for the crowd, for they have been with me now for three days and have nothing to eat. I do not want to send them away hungry, for fear they may collapse on the way." 33 The disciples said to him, "Where could we ever get enough bread in this deserted place to satisfy such a crowd?" 34 Jesus said to them, "How many loaves do you have?" "Seven," they replied, "and a few fish." 35 He ordered the crowd to sit down on the ground. 36 Then he took the seven loaves and the fish, gave thanks, broke the loaves, and gave them to the disciples, who in turn gave them to the crowds. 37 They all ate and were satisfied. They picked up the fragments left over—seven baskets full. 38 Those who ate were four thousand men, not counting women and children. 39 And when he had dismissed the crowds, he got into the boat and came to the district of Magadan.

Mk 8:1–10

1 In those days when there again was a great crowd without anything to eat, he summoned the disciples and said, 2 "My heart is moved with pity for the crowd, because they have been with me now for three days and have nothing to eat. 3 If I send them away hungry to their homes, they will collapse on the way, and some of them have come a great distance." 4 His disciples answered him, "Where can anyone get enough bread to satisfy them here in this deserted place?" 5 Still he asked them, "How many loaves do you have?" "Seven," they replied. 6 He ordered the crowd to sit down on the ground. Then, taking the seven loaves he gave thanks, broke them, and gave them to his disciples to distribute, and they distributed them to the crowd. 7 They also had a few fish. He said the blessing over them and ordered them distributed also. 8 They ate and were satisfied. They picked up the fragments left over—seven baskets. 9 There were about four thousand people.

He dismissed them 10 and got into the boat with his disciples and came to the region of Dalmanutha.

All four evangelists tell the story of Jesus feeding the five thousand back in Landmark 18. Only Matthew and Mark include this second multiplication miracle. This difference among the Gospels has prompted some to speculate that this second story is a retelling of the first with details changed for theological reasons. If there was a second feeding of a large magnitude starting with only a few loaves and fish, you would think the disciples would have remembered the first. If so, why would they have questioned Jesus' ability to feed the crowd?

The feeding of the five thousand took place on Jewish soil. Twelve baskets of leftovers corresponded to the Twelve Tribes of Israel. This miracle of feeding the four thousand took place in Gentile territory. It began with seven loaves and ended with seven baskets of leftovers. The number 7 corresponds to the seven Gentile nations of Canaan. Jesus had now abundantly fed both the Jews and the Gentiles. These miracles demonstrated that Jesus' mission is for all people. He wants everyone to partake in the heavenly banquet.

YOU HAVE HAD ENOUGH! BETWEEN the Greek woman, the difficulty communicating with the doctor, and the fork testing, it is time to leave. You remember having been led through a maze of hallways to get to the exam room. Hopefully, you can find the way out. Upon leaving the exam room, you immediately begin to **seek a sign** indicating an exit. Going down one hallway to **seek a sign**, you come to another hallway. Looking to the right, you do not see a **sign**. Taking a left, you continue looking for a **sign**. You begin to feel lost, but rather than ask for help, you continue to **seek a sign** showing the way out. Upon taking the next right, your persistence is rewarded. At the end of the hall is the exit **sign** you had been seeking. This effort to **seek a sign** is a reminder of THE PHARISEES SEEK A SIGN.

THE PHARISEES SEEK A SIGN

Mt 16:1–4

1 The Pharisees and Sadducees came and, to test him, asked him to show them a sign from heaven. 2 He said to them in reply, "[In the evening you say, 'Tomorrow will be fair, for the sky is red'; 3 and, in the morning, 'Today will be stormy, for the sky is red and threatening.' You know how to judge the appearance of the sky, but you cannot judge the signs of the times.] 4 An evil and unfaithful generation seeks a sign, but no sign will be given it except the sign of Jonah." Then he left them and went away.

Mk 8:11–13

11 The Pharisees came forward and began to argue with him, seeking from him a sign from heaven to test him. 12 He sighed from the depth of his spirit and said, "Why does this generation seek a sign? Amen, I say to you, no sign will be given to this generation." 13 Then he left them, got into the boat again, and went off to the other shore.

Lk 12:54–56

54 He also said to the crowds, "When you see [a] cloud rising in the west you say immediately that it is going to rain—and so it does; 55 and when you notice that the wind is blowing from the south you say that it is going to be hot—and so it is. 56 You hypocrites! You know how to interpret the appearance of the earth and the sky; why do you not know how to interpret the present time?"

This unit is similar to the unit "Against Seeking for Signs" associated with Landmark 10. There, Jesus refused the request for a sign and recalled "the sign of Jonah." Here Matthew repeats this statement by Jesus, with an additional saying similar to one found in Luke. Mark does not mention this new saying but does phrase the request of the Pharisees similarly to Satan's requests when testing Jesus in the desert following His Baptism (Landmark 2).

In Matthew and Luke, Jesus discussed the weather with those who came to test Him. This was not small talk. He pointed out that they were able to make certain conclusions by being aware of their surroundings— the sky, clouds, and wind. Unfortunately, they were not able to understand what is much more important. They were unable to draw conclusions from the words and works of Jesus, which also surrounded them.

YOU ARE RELIEVED TO BE back in the waiting room. The Greek woman is surprised to see you leaving so quickly. Without a word, you are soon outside. Feelings of guilt creep in. Perhaps leaving as you did was the wrong way to handle the awkward situation. You begin to **repent** for your behavior. You decide to call the office to explain. Taking out your phone, you think that maybe a **call to repent** is not necessary. However, the guilt persists and you decide to make the **call to repent**. After dialing the number, you hear a message in Greek. After the traditional "beep," you explain your behavior and end the call by asking for forgiveness. You hang up and feel better that you made the **call to repent**. Of course, you did not reschedule, but the **call to repent** has left you with a clear conscience. This admittedly strange phone call allows you to recall JESUS' CALL TO REPENTANCE.

JESUS' CALL TO REPENTANCE

Lk 13:1–5

1 At that time some people who were present there told him about the Galileans whose blood Pilate had mingled with the blood of their sacrifices. 2 He said to them in reply, "Do you think that because these Galileans suffered in this way they were greater sinners than all other Galileans? 3 By no means! But I tell you, if you do not repent, you will all perish as they did! 4 Or those eighteen people who were killed when the tower at Siloam fell on them—do you think they were more guilty than everyone else who lived in Jerusalem? 5 By no means! But I tell you, if you do not repent, you will all perish as they did!"

The killing of these Galileans by Pilate was thought to be due to their refusal to pay taxes to the Roman emperor. They were killed as they themselves had been killing their animals for sacrifice; hence, the mingling of blood. This bears some similarity to the death of the eighteen at Siloam (this event is not mentioned anywhere else in the Bible). They were killed during a spiritual, ritualistic practice (i.e., purifying themselves in the nearby pool of Siloam). An unfortunate end met both groups, though neither were doing wrong in the eyes of God. As is commonly said today, bad things can happen to good people. When bad things happen to you, it does not mean you are a bad person or are being punished for some misdeed. Jesus again spoke of repentance. This was a message He had preached since beginning His Galilean ministry. If one does not repent, then an unfortunate fate awaits, as it did for these two groups.

Landmark 21:

CASINO

L andmark 21 represents another game. More specifically, the Landmark is the place the game is played. You may already realize it is the card game Blackjack, also known as "21." Of course 21 can be played anywhere. However, since it is typically a gambling game played in a **casino**, we will use a **casino** as the twenty-first Landmark. Picture a grand, opulent, well-lit building. You are standing on the outside admiring the structure and watching the gamblers come and go. You are also debating whether to go inside the **casino** and try your luck at a game or two of 21.

The casino, with its lights, color, and glitter is a spectacular feast for the senses. However, the most memorable sight outside this lavish structure is the doorman. That's right, the doorman, but more accurately the doorbear! Yes, the casino has hired a **bear** to greet the guests and open the heavy doors. Of course the **bear** is well-trained and very friendly around people. The **bear** is also very effective at keeping misbehavior to a minimum. The **bear** is an imposing sight, though he is apparently quite modest. Below his waist, the **bear** is wearing a strategically placed **fig** leaf. Wearing the **fig** leaf, the doorbear is not self-conscious and can fully focus on his job. This **bear in the fig** leaf is not only a good worker, but somewhat of an attraction. Many people visit the casino just to see the **bear in the fig** leaf. The **bear in the fig** leaf frequently poses for pictures. This **bear in a fig** leaf working outside of the casino represents Jesus' PARABLE OF THE BARREN FIG (BEAR-IN-FIG) TREE.

PARABLE OF THE BARREN FIG TREE

Lk 13:6–9

6 And he told them this parable: "There once was a person who had a fig tree planted in his orchard, and when he came in search of fruit on it but found none, 7 he said to the gardener, 'For three years now I have come in search of fruit on this fig tree but have found none. [So] cut it down. Why should it exhaust the soil?' 8 He said to him in reply, 'Sir, leave it for this year also, and I shall cultivate the ground around it and fertilize it; 9 it may bear fruit in the future. If not, you can cut it down.'"

This parable reinforced Jesus' just-discussed message of repentance. In ancient writings, Israel was at times likened to a fig tree. We can also be likened to a fig tree that is planted to produce fruit. God is the owner of the orchard. He wants us to bear the fruit of faith and repentance. He sent His Son, Jesus, the Gardener, to cultivate the tree so it could be productive. It is no coincidence that the three-year period of Jesus' ministry is the same period of time it takes the fig tree to reach maturity. Through the intercession of Jesus, we are given the opportunity to repent and bear fruit. This parable should not be confused with an upcoming unit where Jesus curses the fig tree. As fig trees, we want to avoid that fate.

AS YOU WATCH THE BEAR work the front door of the casino, many people come and go. Most of the visitors arrive in expensive cars or limousines. There is one exception. A frail **crippled woman** rolls up in a wheelchair. When the **crippled woman** sees the large bear wearing the small fig leaf, her wheelchair screeches to a halt. She looks petrified. You ask the **crippled woman** if there is anything you can do. She begs you to quickly wheel her away from the bear. You try to calm the **crippled woman** by telling her the bear is quite gentle and harmless. She believes you, but to be sure, asks if you would be kind enough to roll her past the bear until she is safely inside the casino. You agree. Slowly, you proceed to push the **crippled woman** in her wheelchair toward the door and the waiting bear.

This encounter with the **crippled woman** is helpful in remembering Jesus HEALING THE CRIPPLED WOMAN ON THE SABBATH.

IIIIIIIIIIIIIIIIIIIIIIIIIIIIIIIIIIIIIIIIIIIIIIIIIIIIIIIIIIIIIIIIIIIIIIIIIIIIIIIIIIIIIIIIIIIIIIIIIIIIIIIIIIIIIIIIIIIIIIIIIIIIIIII

HEALING THE CRIPPLED WOMAN ON THE SABBATH

IIIIIIIIIIIIIIIIIIIIIIIIIIIIIIIIIIIIIIIIIIIIIIIIIIIIIIIIIIIIIIIIIIIIIIIIIIIIIIIIIIIIIIIIIIIIIIIIIIIIIIIIIIIIIIIIIIIIIIIIIIIIIIII

Lk 13:10–17

10 He was teaching in a synagogue on the sabbath. **11** And a woman was there who for eighteen years had been crippled by a spirit; she was bent over, completely incapable of standing erect. **12** When Jesus saw her, he called to her and said, "Woman, you are set free of your infirmity." **13** He laid his hands on her, and she at once stood up straight and glorified God. **14** But the leader of the synagogue, indignant that Jesus had cured on the sabbath, said to the crowd in reply, "There are six days when work should be done. Come on those days to be cured, not on the sabbath day." **15** The Lord said to him in reply, "Hypocrites! Does not each one of you on the sabbath untie his ox or his ass from the manger and lead it out for watering? **16** This daughter of Abraham, whom Satan has bound for eighteen years now, ought she not to have been set free on the sabbath day from this bondage?" **17** When he said this, all his adversaries were humiliated; and the whole crowd rejoiced at all the splendid deeds done by him.

This unit is found only in Luke. It is similar to the cure of a paralytic on the Sabbath in Landmark 7, although there are some differences. Here Jesus was in a synagogue in Galilee. The infirm was female, and Jesus laid His hands upon her. The righteous indignation of the legalistic leaders was the same. Jesus was criticized for His compassionate healing on the day of rest. His rebuttal to this hypocritical criticism was quite forceful and convincing. If they could unbind an animal from its feed box on the Sabbath, why was it that Jesus could not unbind a crippled woman from eighteen years of bondage? In the earlier Sabbath healing, Jesus' response left the Jews angry, wanting to kill Him for blasphemy. Here Jesus' response left the leaders of the synagogue humiliated.

AS YOU APPROACH THE BEAR pushing the crippled woman, your heart begins to race. The bear suddenly focuses his full attention on the woman in the wheelchair. When he raises his paw and points to the woman, she begins to tremble. The bear walks toward you and the woman while lifting a massive hairy arm above his head. Expecting the worst, you prepare to run, but your legs do not cooperate. Then a remarkable thing occurs. With the bear's arm raised directly over the woman, she begins to rise. Her legs and feet remain immobile, but her entire body **levitates** up out of the wheelchair. She slowly **levitates** upward until she hovers just beneath the bear's outstretched arm. You, she, and the crowd are rendered speechless by this **levitation**. The **levitated** woman slowly begins to move her long-motionless legs. The **levitation** seems to be a vehicle for healing. The bear breaks into a smile when the woman's legs begin to shake vigorously. He is thankful for the gift of **levitation**! This **levitation** is a soundalike for **leaven**. The thought of **leaven** reminds you of Jesus' warning about THE LEAVEN OF THE PHARISEES.

||||||||||||||||||||||||||||||||||||||||||||||||||||||||||||||||||||||||||||||||||||||||||||||||||||||||||||||||||||||

THE LEAVEN OF THE PHARISEES

||||||||||||||||||||||||||||||||||||||||||||||||||||||||||||||||||||||||||||||||||||||||||||||||||||||||||||||||||||||

Mt 16:5–12

5 In coming to the other side of the sea, the disciples had forgotten to bring bread. 6 Jesus said to them, "Look out, and beware of the leaven of the Pharisees and Sadducees." 7 They concluded among themselves, saying, "It is because we have brought no bread." 8 When Jesus became aware of this he said, "You of little faith, why do you conclude among yourselves that it is because you have no bread? 9 Do you not yet understand, and do you not remember the five loaves for the five thousand, and how many wicker baskets you took up? 10 Or the seven loaves for the four thousand, and how many baskets you took up? 11 How do you not comprehend that I was not speaking to you about bread? Beware of the leaven of the Pharisees and Sadducees." 12 Then they understood that he was not telling them to beware of the leaven of bread, but of the teaching of the Pharisees and Sadducees.

Mk 8:14–21

14 They had forgotten to bring bread, and they had only one loaf with them in the boat. 15 He enjoined them, "Watch out, guard

against the leaven of the Pharisees and the leaven of Herod."
16 They concluded among themselves that it was because they had
no bread. **17** When he became aware of this he said to them, "Why
do you conclude that it is because you have no bread? Do you not
yet understand or comprehend? Are your hearts hardened? **18** Do
you have eyes and not see, ears and not hear? And do you not
remember, **19** when I broke the five loaves for the five thousand,
how many wicker baskets full of fragments you picked up?" They
answered him, "Twelve." **20** "When I broke the seven loaves for the
four thousand, how many full baskets of fragments did you pick
up?" They answered [him], "Seven." **21** He said to them, "Do you
still not understand?"

Lk 12:1

1 Meanwhile, so many people were crowding together that they
were trampling one another underfoot. He began to speak, first to
his disciples, "Beware of the leaven—that is, the hypocrisy—of the
Pharisees."

———————————————

In Matthew, the disciples finally realized that leaven referred to the
false teaching of the Pharisees and Sadducees. However, Jesus was frustrated with the disciples for two reasons. He was disappointed that they
thought He was referring to actual bread. He was teaching on an ab-
stract, spiritual level while they were thinking in a concrete, material way.
Mark depicted Jesus as being a bit more perturbed with the disciples than
Matthew. Both, however, had Jesus express His disappointment in them.
Even if they were thinking materially, how could they doubt His ability
to provide bread? They had twice seen Him provide for vast crowds and
have enough leftovers to feed them (the disciples) many times over! The
disciples did not yet realize that Jesus was the "one loaf" they needed,
despite His recent teaching that He was the "bread of life."

WHEN THE BEAR LOWERS HIS arm, the levitated woman slowly descends.
When her feet contact the ground, she is able to stand erect for the first time
in years. She is clearly overjoyed as she takes several tentative, but steady
steps. After giving the bear a hug of gratitude, she makes what seems to be
a very strange request. She asks to take a **bath**! Her legs have come alive,
and she wants them to feel the warmth of a soothing **bath**. You decide
to help her find a **bathtub**. While you ponder where the closest **bathtub**

may be, the bear disappears inside the casino. He emerges moments later proudly pushing a big fancy **bathtub** full of warm soapy water. He grins and points to the tub's bear claw feet. Immediately, and fully clothed, the woman hops in. You have never seen anyone so happy to take a **bath**. Her legs, which have endured such a long hibernation, now come fully alive in the warm **bath** water. This unexpected **bath** helps recall the story about THE BLIND MAN IN BETH(BATH)SAIDA.

||||||||||||||||||||||||||||||||||||||||||||||||||||||||||||||||||||||||||||||||||||||||||||||||||||||||||||||||||||||||||||||||||||

THE BLIND MAN IN BETHSAIDA

||||||||||||||||||||||||||||||||||||||||||||||||||||||||||||||||||||||||||||||||||||||||||||||||||||||||||||||||||||||||||||||||||||

Mk 8:22–26

22 When they arrived at Bethsaida, they brought to him a blind man and begged him to touch him. **23** He took the blind man by the hand and led him outside the village. Putting spittle on his eyes he laid his hands on him and asked, "Do you see anything?" **24** Looking up he replied, "I see people looking like trees and walking." **25** Then he laid hands on his eyes a second time and he saw clearly; his sight was restored and he could see everything distinctly. **26** Then he sent him home and said, "Do not even go into the village."

Jesus and His disciples have again crossed the northern tip of the Sea of Galilee and arrived in Bethsaida. This small fishing town was about five miles from Capernaum. It is previously mentioned in Luke at the outset of Landmark 18. It is here that Jesus and His disciples retreated for some privacy after the apostles had returned from their missionary journey.

The scene is a familiar one. Upon arriving, the people brought Jesus someone in need of physical healing. Jesus took the blind man away from the crowd as He had done during his recent trip to the Decapolis. As before, He used spittle, but this time the healing was gradual rather than immediate. There was no reason to believe Jesus' healing powers were waning. This slow healing of sight is thought to be symbolic of the disciples' slowness to see and understand who Jesus truly was. This will become more evident in an upcoming unit when Jesus heals the blind Bartimaeus.

Landmark 22:

TUTU

L andmark 22 is straight ahead. It is something that will easily come to mind when thinking of the number 22. The Landmark is simply a **tutu**. You see a frilly blue **tutu** lying on the ground and wonder who must have left it in this unlikely location. You pick up the **tutu**. It appears to be brand new. There must be a ballerina nearby wondering where her new blue **tutu** has gone to. You decide that you will try to find her and return Landmark 22, the **tutu**, to her.

You are now walking along carrying the tutu. Hopefully, you will find the ballerina searching for her lost garment. Up ahead, someone appears to be searching, but it is not a ballerina. It is a rabbit! The rabbit looks frantic as his eyes quickly scan the area. You approach and introduce yourself. The rabbit extends a paw and replies, "Hello, my name is **Peter**." You are unable to stop yourself from laughing. The rabbit smiles and says, "Yes, I am **Peter** Rabbit!" You compose yourself and ask if he is *the* **Peter** Rabbit, the famous storybook **Peter** Rabbit. "I must **confess** that I am," says **Peter**. He emphasizes this by saying, "I do not **confess** this to everyone." **Peter** then shows you his official **Peter** Rabbit identification card. You are starstruck and ask **Peter** for an autograph. This unexpected meeting of **Peter confessing** his identity causes you to recall the pivotal unit describing PETER'S CONFESSION OF FAITH.

PETER'S CONFESSION OF FAITH

Mt 16:13–20

13 When Jesus went into the region of Caesarea Philippi he asked his disciples, "Who do people say that the Son of Man is?" 14 They replied, "Some say John the Baptist, others Elijah, still

others Jeremiah or one of the prophets." **15** He said to them, "But who do you say that I am?" **16** Simon Peter said in reply, "You are the Messiah, the Son of the living God." **17** Jesus said to him in reply, "Blessed are you, Simon son of Jonah. For flesh and blood has not revealed this to you, but my heavenly Father. **18** And so I say to you, you are Peter, and upon this rock I will build my church, and the gates of the netherworld shall not prevail against it. **19** I will give you the keys to the kingdom of heaven. Whatever you bind on earth shall be bound in heaven; and whatever you loose on earth shall be loosed in heaven." **20** Then he strictly ordered his disciples to tell no one that he was the Messiah.

Mk 8:27–30

27 Now Jesus and his disciples set out for the villages of Caesarea Philippi. Along the way he asked his disciples, "Who do people say that I am?" **28** They said in reply, "John the Baptist, others Elijah, still others one of the prophets." **29** And he asked them, "But who do you say that I am?" Peter said to him in reply, "You are the Messiah." **30** Then he warned them not to tell anyone about him.

Lk 9:18–21

18 Once when Jesus was praying in solitude, and the disciples were with him, he asked them, "Who do the crowds say that I am?" **19** They said in reply, "John the Baptist; others, Elijah; still others, 'One of the ancient prophets has arisen.'" **20** Then he said to them, "But who do you say that I am?" Peter said in reply, "The Messiah of God." **21** He rebuked them and directed them not to tell this to anyone.

Jn 6:67–69

67 Jesus then said to the Twelve, "Do you also want to leave?" **68** Simon Peter answered him, "Master, to whom shall we go? You have the words of eternal life. **69** We have come to believe and are convinced that you are the Holy One of God."

Jesus and the disciples traveled to Caesarea Philippi. It was a good day's walk, about twenty miles north of Bethsaida. Though they were currently walking away from Jerusalem, this unit is the turning point in Jesus' final journey to Jerusalem. Many people still saw Jesus as the return of a great prophet, perhaps John, Elijah, or Jeremiah.

Peter finally got it right when he confessed that Jesus was the Messiah, the Anointed One of God. Matthew took it one step further by emphasizing the Father-Son relationship Jesus had with the "living God." Peter and the other eleven now realized Jesus' special role, but they surely were not aware of how His purpose would be accomplished. They did not yet realize that Jesus' suffering and death were God's plan for His Son. He was not the long-awaited powerful, militaristic Messiah. The crowds were also not yet ready to hear or understand this.

In this unit, Matthew includes some key material not found in the other Gospels. He typically portrayed Peter much more positively than the other evangelists. Peter was declared the "rock," and the foundation of Jesus' future church. Peter subsequently became the first Pope.

From the mouth of Peter came the declaration: "You have the words of eternal life." Up to this point, the apostles were typically portrayed as not understanding the identity of Jesus. They were at times described as rather dense or "hard-hearted." Here John had Peter confess that Jesus was "the Holy One of God."

BEFORE PETER RABBIT SIGNS AN autograph for you, he catches sight of the tutu. He explains that his wife lost her tutu and that he had been sent to look for it. You express surprise that he knew where to search. Peter quickly looks around and then whispers in your ear, "I have a **crystal ball**." "A **crystal ball**?" you exclaim. "Shhh!" Peter says, placing his paw over your mouth. "I don't want anyone to know I have a **crystal ball**." Peter goes on to say that someone would surely want to steal the **crystal ball** if they knew it existed. You tell Peter you are sorry, but you do not believe **crystal balls** can provide information or predict the future. Peter then shows you a picture of his **crystal ball**. It is a beautiful transparent glass sphere. You tell Peter it is a nice picture, but you just don't believe it actually exists. This conversation and picture of the **crystal ball** helps to recall Jesus' FIRST PASSION PREDICTION. The **crystal ball** symbolizes the idea of prediction. Since in this story there is one crystal ball, it is THE FIRST PASSION PREDICTION. Soon there will be units with two and three **crystal balls**.

THE FIRST PASSION PREDICTION

Mt 16:21–23

21 From that time on, Jesus began to show his disciples that he must go to Jerusalem and suffer greatly from the elders, the chief priests, and the scribes, and be killed and on the third day be raised. 22 Then Peter took him aside and began to rebuke him, "God forbid, Lord! No such thing shall ever happen to you." 23 He turned and said to Peter, "Get behind me, Satan! You are an obstacle to me. You are thinking not as God does, but as human beings do."

Mk 8:31–33

31 He began to teach them that the Son of Man must suffer greatly and be rejected by the elders, the chief priests, and the scribes, and be killed, and rise after three days. 32 He spoke this openly. Then Peter took him aside and began to rebuke him. 33 At this he turned around and, looking at his disciples, rebuked Peter and said, "Get behind me, Satan. You are thinking not as God does, but as human beings do."

Lk 9:22

22 He said, "The Son of Man must suffer greatly and be rejected by the elders, the chief priests, and the scribes, and be killed and on the third day be raised."

How surprising this prediction must have been for the disciples! Peter had just correctly confessed that Jesus was the long-awaited Messiah. After agreeing that this was true, Jesus spoke about His upcoming suffering, rejection, and death! How could that happen? It made no sense! The prediction about being raised on the third day made it all too incredible. Peter's reaction showed that he and the other disciples did not yet understand what it meant for Jesus to be the Messiah. Peter, who had just been called a "rock," was now called an "obstacle." From this point on, as Jesus continued toward His fate in Jerusalem, He would teach the disciples what "Messiah" truly meant.

PETER RABBIT IS NOW UPSET. You have just told him you do not believe his crystal ball really exists. He defiantly reaffirms that it does. He will show it to you, but under one **condition**. You must beat him in a race! You are thankful that you have kept yourself in good physical **condition** (recall Landmark 16). However, outrunning a rabbit will be quite a challenge. The race will cover the one mile back to Peter's house. This distance requires one to be in good **condition**. Your hope is that Peter, undoubtedly a better sprinter, will not have sufficient **conditioning** to quickly cover this longer distance. When the race begins, Peter jumps ahead. However, as you hoped, toward the end you pass the pooped, panting Peter. He is in no **condition** to run a mile. By reaching the finish line first, superior **conditioning** has allowed you to fulfill the **condition** to see the crystal ball. This story of the **condition** and your **conditioning** helps to recall Jesus providing MORE CONDITIONS OF DISCIPLESHIP.

MORE CONDITIONS OF DISCIPLESHIP

Mt 16:24–28

24 Then Jesus said to his disciples, "Whoever wishes to come after me must deny himself, take up his cross, and follow me. 25 For whoever wishes to save his life will lose it, but whoever loses his life for my sake will find it. 26 What profit would there be for one to gain the whole world and forfeit his life? Or what can one give in exchange for his life? 27 For the Son of Man will come with his angels in his Father's glory, and then he will repay everyone according to his conduct. 28 Amen, I say to you, there are some standing here who will not taste death until they see the Son of Man coming in his kingdom."

Mk 8:34–9:1

34 He summoned the crowd with his disciples and said to them, "Whoever wishes to come after me must deny himself, take up his cross, and follow me. 35 For whoever wishes to save his life will lose it, but whoever loses his life for my sake and that of the gospel will save it. 36 What profit is there for one to gain the whole world and forfeit his life? 37 What could one give in exchange for his life? 38 Whoever is ashamed of me and of my words in this faithless and sinful generation, the Son of Man will be ashamed of when he comes in his Father's glory with the holy angels."

1 He also said to them, "Amen, I say to you, there are some standing here who will not taste death until they see that the kingdom of God has come in power."

Lk 9:23-27

23 Then he said to all, "If anyone wishes to come after me, he must deny himself and take up his cross daily and follow me. **24** For whoever wishes to save his life will lose it, but whoever loses his life for my sake will save it. **25** What profit is there for one to gain the whole world yet lose or forfeit himself? **26** Whoever is ashamed of me and of my words, the Son of Man will be ashamed of when he comes in his glory and in the glory of the Father and of the holy angels. **27** Truly I say to you, there are some standing here who will not taste death until they see the kingdom of God."

Jesus now reemphasized the conditions of discipleship He had set forth in Landmark 16. Then He was addressing His small group of twelve before sending them out for the first time. In these verses from Luke, Jesus provided similar information to the great crowd traveling with Him. Luke also told a parable about a tower and a king to describe the importance of disciples knowing what they are getting themselves into.

A half-finished tower and a decimated army are not our goal. When we make a commitment to follow Jesus, we need to know what it is we have decided to do. Once decided, we need to carry it through. Jesus has told us the cost is great, but the reward is beyond all understanding. No earthly relationship or material possession can compare to what awaits us in the kingdom of heaven.

A disciple must take up his cross and follow Jesus. In the process, we will lose our old life for Jesus' sake, but gain a new life with Him. This is the cost of discipleship. Jesus emphasizes that it is a good purchase, worth more than if one were to gain the whole world. It is through discipleship that one gains the riches of the kingdom of God. Denying oneself for Jesus' sake is how to become a true disciple. Jesus as the "Son of Man" will reward this discipleship when the kingdom of God comes in all of its power.

PETER RABBIT MUST NOW FULFILL his promise to show you his crystal ball. He returns from inside his little house carrying the transparent glass ball. When he hands you the ball, something unbelievable happens. When your fingers touch the glass, the crystal ball is **transfigured**! The clear glass is **transfigured** into a dazzling, glowing orb. Bright light shooting from the ball is painful to your eyes. This sudden change in the ball's appearance is frightening. In fact, the **transfiguration** causes Peter to hide his face. The **transfigured** ball soon becomes warm to the touch and shines even brighter. As you stand holding the **transfigured** crystal ball, you begin to think of the miraculous TRANSFIGURATION OF JESUS.

TRANSFIGURATION OF JESUS

Mt 17:1–8

1 After six days Jesus took Peter, James, and John his brother, and led them up a high mountain by themselves. 2 And he was transfigured before them; his face shone like the sun and his clothes became white as light. 3 And behold, Moses and Elijah appeared to them, conversing with him. 4 Then Peter said to Jesus in reply, "Lord, it is good that we are here. If you wish, I will make three tents here, one for you, one for Moses, and one for Elijah." 5 While he was still speaking, behold, a bright cloud cast a shadow over them, then from the cloud came a voice that said, "This is my beloved Son, with whom I am well pleased; listen to him." 6 When the disciples heard this, they fell prostrate and were very much afraid. 7 But Jesus came and touched them, saying, "Rise, and do not be afraid." 8 And when the disciples raised their eyes, they saw no one else but Jesus alone.

Mk 9:2–8

2 After six days Jesus took Peter, James, and John and led them up a high mountain apart by themselves. And he was transfigured before them, 3 and his clothes became dazzling white, such as no fuller on earth could bleach them. 4 Then Elijah appeared to them along with Moses, and they were conversing with Jesus. 5 Then Peter said to Jesus in reply, "Rabbi, it is good that we are here! Let us make three tents: one for you, one for Moses, and one for Elijah." 6 He hardly knew what to say, they were so terrified. 7 Then a cloud came, casting a shadow over them; then from the cloud came a voice, "This is my beloved Son. Listen to him." 8 Suddenly, looking around, they no longer saw anyone but Jesus alone with them.

Lk 9:28–36

28 About eight days after he said this, he took Peter, John, and James and went up the mountain to pray. 29 While he was praying his face changed in appearance and his clothing became dazzling white. 30 And behold, two men were conversing with him, Moses and Elijah, 31 who appeared in glory and spoke of his exodus

that he was going to accomplish in Jerusalem. **32** Peter and his companions had been overcome by sleep, but becoming fully awake, they saw his glory and the two men standing with him. **33** As they were about to part from him, Peter said to Jesus, "Master, it is good that we are here; let us make three tents, one for you, one for Moses, and one for Elijah." But he did not know what he was saying. **34** While he was still speaking, a cloud came and cast a shadow over them, and they became frightened when they entered the cloud. **35** Then from the cloud came a voice that said, "This is my chosen Son; listen to him." **36** After the voice had spoken, Jesus was found alone. They fell silent and did not at that time tell anyone what they had seen.

This spectacular event occurred six days after Jesus had taught more about discipleship. This corresponds to the six days the cloud of God covered Mount Sinai before God called to Moses (Ex 24:16). The transfiguration of Jesus witnessed by the three chosen apostles was a blindingly clear statement of Jesus' true identity. It provided a brief glimpse of Jesus' glory and the glory that awaits all of His disciples in the Kingdom.

To paraphrase Peter, it was good that Moses and Elijah were also there. These two men personified the "word" (Moses) and the "prophets" (Elijah) of the Hebrew Scriptures. They had been the most prominent "Seers of God." Peter's suggestion to build three tents initially seems strange. It was an allusion to the Feast of Tabernacles, the annual pilgrimage feast of thanksgiving. Perhaps Peter was thankful to be present. Perhaps he wanted to prolong the moment, since the feast lasted eight days.

Peter, James, and John were frightened. God's voice came from the cloud and echoed the words spoken at Jesus' Baptism. God again identified Jesus as His Son, but added the command "Listen to Him." Describing the disciples as "frightened" is an understatement. They had fallen prostrate, according to Matthew. Perhaps they were close to being paralyzed with fear. Then just as Jesus had healed the paralytics, He told them to "rise." He also told them not to be afraid. The disciples were then alone with Jesus. With Jesus, there is no reason to be afraid. As Jesus and His disciples descended the mountain (thought to be either Mount Tabor or Mount Hermon), He once again invoked the "Messianic Secret." Given what the disciples had just witnessed, that must have been a difficult request to obey.

THE TRANSFIGURED BALL CONTINUES TO grow warmer and warmer. Soon it is too hot for you to hold. Stooping down, you gently place the dazzling, radiant ball on the ground. Instantly, its brightness begins to fade. Soon the light is totally extinguished. The source of the blinding light is now revealed. Slowly, numerous tiny electric **eels** come slithering out of small holes in the ball! **Eels, eels**, and more **eels** wiggle out through the many small pores. Apparently, the **eels** lost their electric charge at the very moment you set the ball on the ground. Never would you have guessed that **eel**-power was the source of the dazzling light display. As you watch in amazement, the ongoing exit of the **eels** reminds you of a name. It is a name that sounds like **eel**. It is Elijah (**Eel**-lijah). This scene with the many **eels** recalls the next unit: THE COMING OF ELIJAH.

THE COMING OF ELIJAH

Mt 17:9–13

9 As they were coming down from the mountain, Jesus charged them, "Do not tell the vision to anyone until the Son of Man has been raised from the dead." 10 Then the disciples asked him, "Why do the scribes say that Elijah must come first?" 11 He said in reply, "Elijah will indeed come and restore all things; 12 but I tell you that Elijah has already come, and they did not recognize him but did to him whatever they pleased. So also will the Son of Man suffer at their hands." 13 Then the disciples understood that he was speaking to them of John the Baptist.

Mk 9:9–13

9 As they were coming down from the mountain, he charged them not to relate what they had seen to anyone, except when the Son of Man had risen from the dead. 10 So they kept the matter to themselves, questioning what rising from the dead meant. 11 Then they asked him, "Why do the scribes say that Elijah must come first?" 12 He told them, "Elijah will indeed come first and restore all things, yet how is it written regarding the Son of Man that he must suffer greatly and be treated with contempt? 13 But I tell you that Elijah has come and they did to him whatever they pleased, as it is written of him."

Jesus told Peter, James, and John that the prophecy of Malachi 3:1 had been fulfilled in the person and ministry of John the Baptist. Just as John was not recognized and was subsequently killed, Jesus would meet the same fate. Jesus still had not been recognized as the Messiah who must suffer greatly prior to rising from the dead. The disciples remained bewildered as to what this meant.

YOU AND PETER RABBIT ARE both in a speechless stupor watching the eels emerge from the once radiant transfigured ball. Soon you regain your composure. Peter has not. He begins **screaming** as loud as his rabbit lungs and vocal cords will allow. The **screaming** brings Peter's wife running from the house. Peter points to the eels, and she begins a high-pitched, hair-raising **scream**. With both parents screaming, their little bunnies slowly emerge from the house, fearful but curious. Soon they join in the **screaming**. Now the whole rabbit family is **screaming**. You decide to leave before you start **screaming** because of all the **screaming**. In another soundalike, the **screamin'(g)** rhymes with **demon**. Here is another healing story involving a **demon**. It is THE BOY WITH A DEMON.

THE BOY WITH A DEMON

Mt 17:14–20

14 When they came to the crowd a man approached, knelt down before him, **15** and said, "Lord, have pity on my son, for he is a lunatic and suffers severely; often he falls into fire, and often into water. **16** I brought him to your disciples, but they could not cure him." **17** Jesus said in reply, "O faithless and perverse generation, how long will I be with you? How long will I endure you? Bring him here to me." **18** Jesus rebuked him and the demon came out of him, and from that hour the boy was cured. **19** Then the disciples approached Jesus in private and said, "Why could we not drive it out?" **20** He said to them, "Because of your little faith. Amen, I say to you, if you have faith the size of a mustard seed, you will say to this mountain, 'Move from here to there,' and it will move. Nothing will be impossible for you."

Mk 9:14–29

14 When they came to the disciples, they saw a large crowd around them and scribes arguing with them. **15** Immediately on seeing him, the whole crowd was utterly amazed. They ran up to him and greeted him. **16** He asked them, "What are you arguing about with them?" **17** Someone from the crowd answered him, "Teacher, I have brought to you my son possessed by a mute spirit. **18** Wherever it seizes him, it throws him down; he foams at the mouth, grinds his teeth, and becomes rigid. I asked your disciples to drive it out, but they were unable to do so." **19** He said to them in reply, "O faithless generation, how long will I be with you? How long will I endure you? Bring him to me." **20** They brought the boy to him. And when he saw him, the spirit immediately threw the boy into convulsions. As he fell to the ground, he began to roll around and foam at the mouth. **21** Then he questioned his father, "How long has this been happening to him?" He replied, "Since childhood. **22** It has often thrown him into fire and into water to kill him. But if you can do anything, have compassion on us and help us." **23** Jesus said to him, "'If you can!' Everything is possible to one who has faith." **24** Then the boy's father cried out, "I do believe, help my unbelief!" **25** Jesus, on seeing a crowd rapidly gathering, rebuked the unclean spirit and said to it, "Mute and deaf spirit, I command you: come out of him and never enter him again!" **26** Shouting and throwing the boy into convulsions, it came out. He became like a corpse, which caused many to say, "He is dead!" **27** But Jesus took him by the hand, raised him, and he stood up. **28** When he entered the house, his disciples asked him in private, "Why could we not drive it out?" **29** He said to them, "This kind can only come out through prayer."

Lk 9:37–45; 17:5–6

37 On the next day, when they came down from the mountain, a large crowd met him. **38** There was a man in the crowd who cried out, "Teacher, I beg you, look at my son; he is my only child. **39** For a spirit seizes him and he suddenly screams and it convulses him until he foams at the mouth; it releases him only with difficulty, wearing him out. **40** I begged your disciples to cast it out but they could not." **41** Jesus said in reply, "O faithless and perverse generation, how long will I be with you and endure you? Bring your son here." **42** As he was coming forward, the demon threw him to the ground in a convulsion; but Jesus rebuked the unclean spirit, healed the boy, and returned him to his father. **43** And all were astonished by the majesty of God.

While they were all amazed at his every deed, he said to his disciples, **44** "Pay attention to what I am telling you. The Son of

Man is to be handed over to men." **45** But they did not understand this saying; its meaning was hidden from them so that they should not understand it, and they were afraid to ask him about this saying.

...

5 And the apostles said to the Lord, "Increase our faith." **6** The Lord replied, "If you have faith the size of a mustard seed, you would say to [this] mulberry tree, 'Be uprooted and planted in the sea,' and it would obey you."

———————

The three synoptic evangelists all tell the story about the healing of a boy with a demon. Mark's account is much longer and filled with many more details. It is a typical healing miracle where faith is needed by the person or the one who requests the healing. This miracle is unique in that the apostles had already attempted to heal the boy and failed. Mark did not have Jesus blame the apostles for their lack of faith. Instead, he used it as an opportunity to stress the importance of prayer, and to rely on the power of God.

Matthew tells a much briefer version of the healing. Jesus was hard on the apostles, blaming their lack of faith for their inability to heal the boy. This gave Him the opportunity to include a saying about faith not found in Mark. Jesus used the example of the tiny mustard seed to tell His disciples how powerful a true, trusting faith can be. The disciples displayed faith in the power of God, but not a faith with sufficient trust.

Luke's description of this miracle is also relatively brief. Jesus attributed the lack of faith to no one in particular, but rather the "faithless and perverse generation." Luke also has a faith saying similar to Matthew, but it was placed in a later teaching section. The saying is prefaced by the apostles asking Jesus to increase their faith. Here the mustard seed-sized faith is able to uproot a mulberry tree, though not a mountain. This is a large tree with an extensive root system. In either case, true faith and trust in God leads to great things.

Landmark 23:

PASTURE

andmark 23 will borrow imagery found in the most well-known psalm in the Book of Psalms. The Twenty-Third Psalm depicts God as a loving shepherd. He allows us, His sheep, to graze in green pastures. The twenty-third Landmark is thus a lush green **pasture**. Imagine a wide grassy **pasture** stretching out as far as your eyes can see. The thick green grass seems to be inviting you into the **pasture** to continue your walk with Jesus. See yourself standing at the **pasture** gate ready to walk through and enjoy the twenty-third Landmark.

As you open the pasture gate, you see **two crystal balls** sitting on the top rail. Unfortunately, in your haste to enter the beautiful pasture you do not notice the **two crystal balls** until it is too late. As the gate swings open, the shiny **crystal balls** fall from the rail. You dive to catch them. You miss! With a loud crash, the **two crystal balls** hit the ground just beyond your outstretched arms. They shatter into countless pieces. Slowly and with great care, you stand and manage to avoid cutting yourself on the sharp **crystal** shards. Recall from the most recent Landmark that a **crystal ball** represents a prediction. More specifically, a prediction that Jesus makes about His upcoming suffering and death. There are **two crystal balls** in this scene to represent the next unit: THE SECOND PASSION PREDICTION.

THE SECOND PASSION PREDICTION

Mt 17:22-23

22 As they were gathering in Galilee, Jesus said to them, "The Son of Man is to be handed over to men, **23** and they will kill him, and he will be raised on the third day." And they were overwhelmed with grief.

Mk 9:30–32

30 They left from there and began a journey through Galilee, but he did not wish anyone to know about it. 31 He was teaching his disciples and telling them, "The Son of Man is to be handed over to men and they will kill him, and three days after his death he will rise." 32 But they did not understand the saying, and they were afraid to question him.

Lk 9:44–45

44 "Pay attention to what I am telling you. The Son of Man is to be handed over to men." 45 But they did not understand this saying; its meaning was hidden from them so that they should not understand it, and they were afraid to ask him about this saying.

Jesus and the apostles were back in Galilee. In Mark, Jesus wanted His return to be kept a secret. That was easier said than done. Perhaps Jesus wanted to focus on instructing the disciples in the short time He had left with them. In making the second prediction of His death, Jesus referred to Himself as the "Son of Man." This title emphasized the human aspect of His nature and helps us appreciate the true pain and anguish He would endure. Though Jesus called Himself the "Son of Man" in this Passion prediction, He was vague as to who would be responsible for His death. In the first prediction, the various factions of the Sanhedrin were implicated. Here the anonymous term "men" was used. Neither Jews nor Gentiles were named.

In Matthew, the apostles were given some credit for understanding the fate that awaited Jesus. They were overwhelmed with grief. Mark portrays them as rather dense and fearful. Luke takes a middle position by excusing their lack of understanding because it was "hidden from them." For Luke, they would understand the meaning of the cross only after the resurrection.

NATURALLY, YOU FEEL REMORSEFUL ABOUT breaking the two crystal balls. You wonder why they were sitting atop the gate. Was there any way you could have prevented them from breaking? While pondering these questions, you are not paying attention to where you are walking. Suddenly, you feel sharp piercing pains in the soles of your feet. Though you successfully avoided the shards of crystal from the broken crystal balls, you have stepped on several long sharp **tacks**. Why in the world are these **tacks** in the pasture? You will never know, but you do know the **tacks** have penetrated your shoes and the soles of your feet. Yelling out in pain, you fall to the ground. Several more **tacks** pierce your backside. Ouch! You are now in significant pain and quite angry about this very unlucky encounter with the **tacks**. This situation with the **tacks** is a reminder of the unit about THE TEMPLE TAX.

THE TEMPLE TAX

Mt 17:24–27

24 When they came to Capernaum, the collectors of the temple tax approached Peter and said, "Doesn't your teacher pay the temple tax?" 25 "Yes," he said. When he came into the house, before he had time to speak, Jesus asked him, "What is your opinion, Simon? From whom do the kings of the earth take tolls or census tax? From their subjects or from foreigners?" 26 When he said, "From foreigners," Jesus said to him, "Then the subjects are exempt. 27 But that we may not offend them, go to the sea, drop in a hook, and take the first fish that comes up. Open its mouth and you will find a coin worth twice the temple tax. Give that to them for me and for you."

The temple tax was an annual obligation for every adult Jewish male. The half-shekel went toward the upkeep of the temple. Though Jesus paid the tax, in His mind He was exempt. The tax applied to members of an earthly kingdom, and He belonged to the heavenly kingdom. The word *subject* in this story can also be translated from the original Greek as "Son." Jesus, as the "Son of God," would certainly be exempt from the tax. Why should the child of the King have to pay a monetary tribute to His own Father? Jesus as a man and a Jew did not wish to be offensive, so He paid the tax and felt His disciples should do the same.

This unit is found in all three Synoptic Gospels. For Matthew, it was the beginning of the fourth of his five discourses. It is often called the "Community Discourse" and includes this and the next units. In this discourse, Jesus gave the disciples rules to live by until the coming of the Kingdom.

These included how to get along with one another, with members of their community (the early church), and with those outside of their community.

AFTER REMOVING THE SHARP TACKS, you begin to slowly hobble across the pasture. Off in the distance, you see something that appears to be a boxing ring. Could there actually be a boxing ring at the far end of this lush green pasture? As you draw closer, not only does the ring come into focus, but so does one of the most famous athletes of all time. It is Muhammad Ali, also known as **"The Greatest."** You instantly recognize him, but boxing shorts emblazoned with **"The Greatest"** verify his identity. His gloves and the heavy bag being pummeled are also labeled **"The Greatest."** You cautiously walk over and introduce yourself. **The Greatest** smiles and hands you something. It is a photograph that is appropriately signed **"The Greatest."** Muhammad Ali's self-proclaimed title, **"The Greatest,"** allows for easy recollection of the next unit: THE GREATEST IN THE KINGDOM.

THE GREATEST IN THE KINGDOM

Mt 18:1–5

1 At that time the disciples approached Jesus and said, "Who is the greatest in the kingdom of heaven?" **2** He called a child over, placed it in their midst, **3** and said, "Amen, I say to you, unless you turn and become like children, you will not enter the kingdom of heaven. **4** Whoever humbles himself like this child is the greatest in the kingdom of heaven. **5** And whoever receives one child such as this in my name receives me."

Mk 9:33–37

33 They came to Capernaum and, once inside the house, he began to ask them, "What were you arguing about on the way?" **34** But they remained silent. They had been discussing among themselves on the way who was the greatest. **35** Then he sat down, called the Twelve, and said to them, "If anyone wishes to be first, he shall be the last of all and the servant of all." **36** Taking a child he placed it in their midst, and putting his arms around it he said to them, **37** "Whoever receives one child such as this in my name, receives me; and whoever receives me, receives not me but the one who sent me."

Lk 9:46–48

46 An argument arose among the disciples about which of them was the greatest. 47 Jesus realized the intention of their hearts and took a child and placed it by his side 48 and said to them, "Whoever receives this child in my name receives me, and whoever receives me receives the one who sent me. For the one who is least among all of you is the one who is the greatest."

———

This lesson, like Jesus Himself, is a paradox. What could be more paradoxical than the Messiah, the mighty Savior, coming to be humbled by men and put to death? The Savior would not just be killed. He would be publicly humiliated and hung on a cross for all to see and ridicule. In their vanity and ignorance, the disciples were concerned with who among them was the greatest in the eyes of man, not in the eyes of God.

A young child is helpless and dependent on its parents for everything. In the time of Jesus, a child had no rights or legal status. Jesus taught that greatness comes in realizing that like a child, we are dependent on God our Father. We must be like Jesus, who humbled Himself like a child. From this, it follows that when we treat children and others who have little earthly standing with love and respect, it is as if we are "receiving" Jesus Himself. Thus we should be humble and treat those who are humbled with love.

AFTER WATCHING "THE GREATEST" WORK out for a few minutes, you begin to feel feverish. Your skin is cold and clammy, and you are shaking. Muhammad Ali notices and asks if you are feeling sick. After acknowledging that you do not feel well, he comes over with a small thermometer. The Greatest wants to take your **temperature**. He expresses concern as he slips the thermometer under your tongue. Someone with a high **temperature** needs help and should not be at his training camp. After several minutes, Muhammad Ali removes the thermometer and reads your **temperature**. You in fact do have a fever. He says, "I am sorry, but anyone with a high **temperature** must leave." Nodding in agreement, you continue to walk. How frustrating to have a high **temperature** and not be able to watch "The Greatest" in action. Having a high **temperature** ("a **temp**") does help you recall the next unit: THE TEMPTATION TO SIN.

THE TEMPTATION TO SIN

Mt 18:6–9

6 "Whoever causes one of these little ones who believe in me to sin, it would be better for him to have a great millstone hung around his neck and to be drowned in the depths of the sea. **7** Woe to the world because of things that cause sin! Such things must come, but woe to the one through whom they come! **8** If your hand or foot causes you to sin, cut it off and throw it away. It is better for you to enter into life maimed or crippled than with two hands or two feet to be thrown into eternal fire. **9** And if your eye causes you to sin, tear it out and throw it away. It is better for you to enter into life with one eye than with two eyes to be thrown into fiery Gehenna."

Mk 9:42–48

42 "Whoever causes one of these little ones who believe [in me] to sin, it would be better for him if a great millstone were put around his neck and he were thrown into the sea. **43** If your hand causes you to sin, cut it off. It is better for you to enter into life maimed than with two hands to go into Gehenna, into the unquenchable fire. **[44] 45** And if your foot causes you to sin, cut it off. It is better for you to enter into life crippled than with two feet to be thrown into Gehenna. **[46] 47** And if your eye causes you to sin, pluck it out. Better for you to enter into the kingdom of God with one eye than with two eyes to be thrown into Gehenna, **48** where 'their worm does not die, and the fire is not quenched.'"

Lk 17:1–2

1 He said to his disciples, "Things that cause sin will inevitably occur, but woe to the person through whom they occur. **2** It would be better for him if a millstone were put around his neck and he be thrown into the sea than for him to cause one of these little ones to sin."

Jesus told His disciples that there would be sin in the world. This is inevitable since we were created with free will. Some people will use this God-given freedom to sin and to cause sin. Jesus emphasized the gravity of causing others to sin, especially the young and malleable. We need to do all that we can to keep this from happening! We must also rid ourselves of all temptations to sin. Jesus used hyperbole to make His point by naming various body parts that should be parted with if they are temptations to sin. Avoid sin, and in so doing we will not lead others into sin.

Landmark 24:

CALENDAR SQUARE

U nlike previous Landmarks, which have been touchable, tangible people or objects, Landmark 24 is a concept. It is a concept that we use and think about each and every day. The twenty-fourth Landmark represents a day, which is of course made up of twenty-four hours. It is hard to think of a day without the many different things that happen in the course of a day coming to mind. Since **calendars** are used to keep track of days, a **calendar** will represent the concept of a day. More specifically, think of one **square on a calendar** to represent the concept of one day. Thus the twenty-fourth Landmark is simply a single **calendar square.**

Some people have the habit of crossing days off the calendar when they become yesterday. Each morning, their very first task is to draw a large **X** through the calendar square for the previous day. Take a pen and walk over to a large wall calendar. You see all of the **X**'s covering previous days. Now make another **X** through the calendar square for yesterday's date. You quickly draw the letter *X*, making first one diagonal line, then **another** to complete the **X**. You are now ready to begin a new day. This act of placing **another X** on the calendar is also a reminder of the first unit associated with this Landmark: ANOTHER EXORCIST.

ANOTHER EXORCIST

Mk 9:38–41

38 John said to him, "Teacher, we saw someone driving out demons in your name, and we tried to prevent him because he does not follow us." **39** Jesus replied, "Do not prevent him. There is no one who performs a mighty deed in my name who can at the same time speak ill of me. **40** For whoever is not against us is for us. **41** Anyone who gives you a cup of water to drink because you belong to Christ, amen, I say to you, will surely not lose his reward."

Lk 9:49–50

49 Then John said in reply, "Master, we saw someone casting out demons in your name and we tried to prevent him because he does not follow in our company." **50** Jesus said to him, "Do not prevent him, for whoever is not against you is for you."

This story is similar to events in Numbers 11:26–30. There, two men were prophesying without being "registered" to do so. Moses showed tolerance, just as Jesus did here with another exorcist. The disciples wrongly thought that their relationship with Jesus was exclusive. This prompted Jesus to utter the well-known phrase, "Whoever is not against us is for us." Jesus pointed out that doing a kindness in His name went both ways. In a recent unit ("The Greatest in the Kingdom"), Jesus had said receiving a child or another helpless individual in His name would be rewarded. Here, anyone who does a kindness to someone because they "belong to Christ" (a disciple) would also be rewarded.

YOU HAVE JUST PLACED ANOTHER X on the calendar with your pen. As you begin to think about the day ahead, you notice the pen has slipped. In your haste to place the X, you left a big mark on the wall next to the calendar. Upset with your carelessness, you begin to **scold** yourself. "How could you have been so sloppy?" you ask yourself in a harsh **scolding** fashion. The self-**scolding** continues as you grow angrier with yourself. You are now **scolding** yourself so loudly a crowd begins to gather. When they see what you have done, they, too, **scold** you for marking on the wall. Soon the **scolding** becomes so intense you must leave the room. All of this self-**scolding** and the **scolding** from others, though unpleasant, assists you in remembering the unit about SCOLDING ANOTHER BELIEVER.

SCOLDING ANOTHER BELIEVER

Mt 18:15–20

15 "If your brother sins [against you], go and tell him his fault between you and him alone. If he listens to you, you have won over your brother. **16** If he does not listen, take one or two others along with you, so that 'every fact may be established on the testimony of two or three witnesses.' **17** If he refuses to listen to them, tell the church. If he refuses to listen even to the church, then treat him as you would a Gentile or a tax collector. **18** Amen, I say to you, whatever you bind on earth shall be bound in heaven, and whatever you loose on earth shall be loosed in heaven. **19** Again, [amen,] I say to you, if two of you agree on earth about anything for which they are to pray, it shall be granted to them by my heavenly Father. **20** For where two or three are gathered together in my name, there am I in the midst of them."

Lk 17:3

3 "Be on your guard! If your brother sins, rebuke him; and if he repents, forgive him."

Jesus provided guidance about healing the wounds in relationships between fellow disciples before they become infected. Settling differences between people is usually best accomplished if the two parties can come to terms without others becoming involved. A private discussion may be sufficient. If not, involving two or three others as witnesses, as suggested in Deuteronomy 19:15, may be necessary. If this fails, the local community becomes involved. Jesus' hope was that reconciliation could take place so as to avoid the type of exclusion shown to a tax collector. Recall that Jesus welcomed Levi (Matthew), a tax collector, after his repentance. Jesus' entire life was about forgiveness. He came to free us from the sins that bind us. Jesus tells us that we must also be forgiving. The next unit will reinforce this teaching.

YOU ARE NO LONGER IN the room where a slip of your pen left a mark on the wall. More importantly, you have escaped to a quiet room where you are no longer being scolded by the crowd. Still, you feel a strong need to be

forgiven for your careless, though minor accident. You are in luck, for you have entered a room occupied by a priest. He senses your guilt and asks if there is something for which you need **forgiveness**. Of course there are many things, but you tell him of your recent "sin with a pen." The priest listens patiently. He then offers **forgiveness** through the power of Jesus. You leave the room feeling calm and at peace with a clear conscience. This desire for and reception of **forgiveness** represents the next unit that you will associate with Landmark 24. It is Jesus' TEACHING ON FORGIVENESS.

TEACHING ON FORGIVENESS

Mt 18:21–22

21 Then Peter approaching asked him, "Lord, if my brother sins against me, how often must I forgive him? As many as seven times?" 22 Jesus answered, "I say to you, not seven times but seventy-seven times."

Lk 17:4

4 "And if he wrongs you seven times in one day and returns to you seven times saying, 'I am sorry,' you should forgive him."

This brief saying on forgiveness complements the previous unit. There the emphasis was on an offending brother and seeking to mend the relationship caused by an offense. The instruction was to forgive if they repented. Now the emphasis is on the one who has been sinned against. Forgiveness is to be granted without limit, not just once but seventy-seven times. In other words, one must always be forgiving. This is in contrast to the boast of Lamech found in Genesis 4:23–24: "I have killed a man for wounding me, a boy for bruising me. If Cain is avenged sevenfold, then Lamech seventy-sevenfold."

UNFORTUNATELY, AFTER LEAVING THE ROOM where you received forgiveness, your feeling of peace is short-lived. Almost immediately, the sound of a shrill, high-pitched laugh pierces your ears. It sounds truly

wicked. Against your better judgment and with a racing heart, you summon the courage to investigate the source of the **wicked** laughter. Your worst fear is confirmed. Upon rounding a corner, you stand face to face with the **Wicked** Witch of the West (of Oz fame). Her black flowing dress, pointed hat, and equally pointed nose make her appear truly **wicked**. She greets you with another **wicked** laugh, making your hair stand on end. This encounter with the **wicked** witch, though frightening, serves as a reminder of THE PARABLE OF THE WICKED SERVANT.

THE PARABLE OF THE WICKED SERVANT

Mt 18:23–35

23 "That is why the kingdom of heaven may be likened to a king who decided to settle accounts with his servants. **24** When he began the accounting, a debtor was brought before him who owed him a huge amount. **25** Since he had no way of paying it back, his master ordered him to be sold, along with his wife, his children, and all his property, in payment of the debt. **26** At that, the servant fell down, did him homage, and said, 'Be patient with me, and I will pay you back in full.' **27** Moved with compassion the master of that servant let him go and forgave him the loan. **28** When that servant had left, he found one of his fellow servants who owed him a much smaller amount. He seized him and started to choke him, demanding, 'Pay back what you owe.' **29** Falling to his knees, his fellow servant begged him, 'Be patient with me, and I will pay you back.' **30** But he refused. Instead, he had him put in prison until he paid back the debt. **31** Now when his fellow servants saw what had happened, they were deeply disturbed, and went to their master and reported the whole affair. **32** His master summoned him and said to him, 'You wicked servant! I forgave you your entire debt because you begged me to. **33** Should you not have had pity on your fellow servant, as I had pity on you?' **34** Then in anger his master handed him over to the torturers until he should pay back the whole debt. **35** So will my heavenly Father do to you, unless each of you forgives his brother from his heart."

In this parable of divine forgiveness, Jesus explained why the forgiveness of our brothers discussed in the preceding units was so important. God our King has forgiven us an unpayable amount. The debt of our sins has been paid in full. The ultimate sacrifice of His Son has wiped away our debt. In return, we must do the same, be merciful to our brothers who may be in our debt. This key point will be emphasized in an upcoming unit when Jesus teaches His disciples to pray, "Forgive us our sins as we forgive those who sin against us."

AFTER STARING IN DISBELIEF AT the Wicked Witch, you make a speedy exit. As expected, the Wicked Witch quickly becomes hostile. She does not unleash a horde of flying monkeys upon you. Instead she sends a swarm of angry bees in your direction. However, they are made of wood! They are very capable of inflicting pain via splinters rather than stingers. These **wooden bees** instantly begin to circle your head. One of the **wooden bees** lands on your arm. Before you can brush it away, a painful splinter pierces your skin. You must escape these **wooden bees** before they all decide to attack. Screaming, you run for the door and are soon out of the house. After a moment, you turn to see if any **wooden bees** are in pursuit. Fortunately, they are not. You pray that you have seen and felt your last **wooden bee**. This painful experience with the **wooden bees** recalls the unit about the WOULD-BE FOLLOWERS OF JESUS.

WOULD-BE FOLLOWERS OF JESUS

Mt 8:19–22

19 A scribe approached and said to him, "Teacher, I will follow you wherever you go." 20 Jesus answered him, "Foxes have dens and birds of the sky have nests, but the Son of Man has nowhere to rest his head." 21 Another of [his] disciples said to him, "Lord, let me go first and bury my father." 22 But Jesus answered him, "Follow me, and let the dead bury their dead."

Lk 9:57-62

57 As they were proceeding on their journey someone said to him, "I will follow you wherever you go." **58** Jesus answered him, "Foxes have dens and birds of the sky have nests, but the Son of Man has nowhere to rest his head." **59** And to another he said, "Follow me." But he replied, "[Lord,] let me go first and bury my father." **60** But he answered him, "Let the dead bury their dead. But you, go and proclaim the kingdom of God." **61** And another said, "I will follow you, Lord, but first let me say farewell to my family at home." **62** [To him] Jesus said, "No one who sets a hand to the plow and looks to what was left behind is fit for the kingdom of God."

Jesus made it very clear that following Him, being a disciple, is not easy or comfortable. The educated scribe likely did not know what he was committing to. Jesus explained that being a disciple would require a risky, itinerant lifestyle. Detachment from creature comforts would be necessary. One's view of what is important has to change. This is illustrated by the use of hyperbole in the proverbs about burying one's father and bidding farewell to family. The latter is reminiscent of Elisha wanting to say good-bye when called by Elijah (1 Kg 19:19–21). Jesus was not advocating abdicating relationship responsibilities. He wanted His would-be followers to know what they were getting into. Discipleship and all that it entails comes first. One needs to commit to discipleship and plow straight ahead. In Jesus' time, the primitive plow required coordination and concentration. The farmer needed to be committed to plowing. Distraction resulted in a crooked path.

Landmark 25:

U.S. QUARTER

The last Landmark and its associated units were not particularly pleasant. It is definitely time to find Landmark 25. This Landmark is actually close by and has been all along. It is in your pocket! You reach into your pocket and pull out a shiny new United States **quarter**. This coin, worth 25 American cents, is Landmark 25. Carefully examine the **quarter**. Observe the details of George Washington's profile. Read the familiar words "In God We Trust." You trust that this **quarter** will lead to good and memorable experiences.

Immediately, you see that your quarter may lead to a very good and memorable experience. Just a few steps away is a kissing **booth**. A sign on the front of the **booth** reads "Kisses for a Quarter." You walk over to the **booth** and place the quarter on the counter. Standing in the **booth** is the person who will give you the kiss. It is up to you to imagine who is standing in the **booth**. However, it is the **booth** itself you need to keep in mind. The **booth** is a reminder of the unit describing events at THE FEAST OF BOOTHS.

THE FEAST OF BOOTHS

Jn 7:1–13

1 After this, Jesus moved about within Galilee; but he did not wish to travel in Judea, because the Jews were trying to kill him. 2 But the Jewish feast of Tabernacles was near. 3 So his brothers said to him, "Leave here and go to Judea, so that your disciples also may see the works you are doing. 4 No one works in secret if he wants to be known publicly. If you do these things, manifest yourself to the world." 5 For his brothers did not believe in him. 6 So Jesus said to them, "My time is not yet here, but the time is always right for you. 7 The world cannot hate you, but it hates

me, because I testify to it that its works are evil. **8** You go up to the feast. I am not going up to this feast, because my time has not yet been fulfilled." **9** After he had said this, he stayed on in Galilee.

10 But when his brothers had gone up to the feast, he himself also went up, not openly but [as it were] in secret. **11** The Jews were looking for him at the feast and saying, "Where is he?" **12** And there was considerable murmuring about him in the crowds. Some said, "He is a good man," [while] others said, "No; on the contrary, he misleads the crowd." **13** Still, no one spoke openly about him because they were afraid of the Jews.

This unit and the next four consist of material found only in the Gospel of John. This group of units make up John's seventh chapter. Jesus initially explained His reluctance to attend the Feast of Tabernacles (Booths) to His disciples. He knew His earthly time would soon come to an end, but there was still much to do. Jesus' time had not yet come. The Feast of Booths was a time of thanksgiving for the gift of the harvest. Ironically, the Messiah, God's greatest gift for which no amount of thanks would be sufficient, feared for His life. In spite of Jesus' life being in danger, He was challenged to go to Jerusalem and "manifest yourself to the world." How reminiscent of the temptations of Satan in the wilderness, "Come on, Jesus, prove Yourself!"

Jesus did attend the Feast. He entered the city alone. His triumphant entry with disciples and other followers would come later. As Jesus slipped in unrecognized, people were expressing very different opinions of Him. Still today He is in our midst and controversy about Him continues.

In the Hebrew Scriptures, the tabernacle (or booth) was a tent-like portable structure constructed as a dwelling place for the presence of God. It was a holy place where the ark of the covenant was kept when the Israelites traveled through the desert on their way to the Promised Land. The people also constructed portable tents (booths) for themselves during their sojourn in the desert. These smaller booths were constructed in Jesus' time during the weeklong Feast of Tabernacles (Booths) each year. These structures were a reminder of the Jews' itinerant history while they celebrated and gave thanks for that year's harvest.

STANDING AT THE KISSING BOOTH, you are now looking forward to the 25 cent kiss. With eyes closed and lips puckered, you lean over the counter. After feeling a little peck on the side of your head, you open your eyes. You have been kissed on the **temple.** That's right, you only got a **temple** kiss! Expecting a nice kiss on the kisser, you are quite disappointed with a kiss on the **temple.** When asked if you want a kiss on the other **temple**, you politely decline. One **temple** kiss is quite enough. This less-than-thrilling kiss on the **temple** causes you to remember the next unit: JESUS' TEACHING IN THE TEMPLE.

JESUS' TEACHING IN THE TEMPLE

Jn 7:14–31

14 When the feast was already half over, Jesus went up into the temple area and began to teach. **15** The Jews were amazed and said, "How does he know scripture without having studied?" **16** Jesus answered them and said, "My teaching is not my own but is from the one who sent me. **17** Whoever chooses to do his will shall know whether my teaching is from God or whether I speak on my own. **18** Whoever speaks on his own seeks his own glory, but whoever seeks the glory of the one who sent him is truthful, and there is no wrong in him. **19** Did not Moses give you the law? Yet none of you keeps the law. Why are you trying to kill me?" **20** The crowd answered, "You are possessed! Who is trying to kill you?" **21** Jesus answered and said to them, "I performed one work and all of you are amazed **22** because of it. Moses gave you circumcision—not that it came from Moses but rather from the patriarchs—and you circumcise a man on the sabbath. **23** If a man can receive circumcision on a sabbath so that the law of Moses may not be broken, are you angry with me because I made a whole person well on a sabbath? **24** Stop judging by appearances, but judge justly."

25 So some of the inhabitants of Jerusalem said, "Is he not the one they are trying to kill? **26** And look, he is speaking openly and they say nothing to him. Could the authorities have realized that he is the Messiah? **27** But we know where he is from. When the Messiah comes, no one will know where he is from." **28** So Jesus cried out in the temple area as he was teaching and said, "You know me and also know where I am from. Yet I did not come on my own, but the one who sent me, whom you do not know, is true. **29** I know him, because I am from him, and he sent me." **30** So they tried to arrest him, but no one laid a hand upon him, because his hour had

not yet come. 31 But many of the crowd began to believe in him, and said, "When the Messiah comes, will he perform more signs than this man has done?"

Jesus was not speaking on His own behalf or for His own self-satisfaction. He did not seek praise for His learned teaching. He was speaking for the glory of God.

Earlier John told the story of Jesus healing a paralytic on the Sabbath. This apparent breaking of Sabbath law had greatly provoked some of the Jews. They had wanted to kill Jesus for an obvious breach of Mosaic Law. Jesus now points out that the practice of circumcision, which was part of the Mosaic Covenant (Lev 12:3), is allowed to trump Sabbath observance. Jesus reasoned that if the foreskin can be attended to on the Sabbath, why not the whole body?

Again people were wondering if Jesus could possibly be the Messiah. Previously, they argued He was not since they knew His family. Now it was because they knew He was from Nazareth. These Jews who questioned Jesus did not believe in His divine origin. They did not know that He would return to the Father who sent Him. Jesus would not be found among the Greeks or back in Nazareth. He would be in the Kingdom, where we hope to eventually "find" Him.

YOU ARE NOW WALKING AWAY from the booth without your quarter, but with some anger. Several local police **officers** are even angrier. You have just unknowingly broken a local law against public displays of affection. The **officers** approach, explain what you have done, and try to **arrest** you. You are dumbfounded that **officers** have been sent to **arrest** you for a pitiful peck on the temple. You start to argue with the **arresting officers**. It does not go well. When one of the **officers** pulls out handcuffs, you decide to run. Perhaps not a good decision, but you do not want to be **arrested** for such an innocent kiss. You begin running, with the **arresting officers** in hot pursuit. This scene with the **arresting officers** recalls the unit after the temple teaching when OFFICERS ARE SENT TO ARREST JESUS.

OFFICERS ARE SENT TO ARREST JESUS

Jn 7:32–36

32 The Pharisees heard the crowd murmuring about him to this effect, and the chief priests and the Pharisees sent guards to arrest him. **33** So Jesus said, "I will be with you only a little while longer, and then I will go to the one who sent me. **34** You will look for me but not find [me], and where I am you cannot come." **35** So the Jews said to one another, "Where is he going that we will not find him? Surely he is not going to the dispersion among the Greeks to teach the Greeks, is he? **36** What is the meaning of his saying, 'You will look for me and not find [me], and where I am you cannot come'?"

Jesus continued to stir up the crowds. He was a source of dissension and unrest. The religious officials were nervous, especially with so many people gathered for the feast. A riot would not only be embarrassing, but a cause for a show of Roman force.

Jesus again foreshadowed His death and resurrection, but this was not one of the three Passion predictions. It was also not a plan to evangelize the Greeks, as the unknowing crowd suggests. It was a positive anticipation of being reunited with the Father after Jesus' hour had come and gone and His purpose had been fulfilled.

THE OFFICERS TRYING TO ARREST you are slowly closing in. You need to devise a better escape plan, and quickly. Just then a **river** comes into view. This **river** is just what you need to avoid being arrested. Whether or not the officers will follow you into the **river** remains to be seen. You decide to take the plunge. Jumping from the bank, you are soon swiftly moving downstream and away from the officers. You are reminded of another **river** experience, but this **river** is quite different from the one in Landmark 2. This **river** feels **alive**! All about you are the many creatures that **live** in the river. Several dolphins leap from the **water** a few feet away. Fish brush against your legs. Other animals **living in the water** include turtles, frogs, crabs, and snakes. This **river** is teeming with life. You quickly forget the officers, who have now given up the chase. As you continue to swim amidst the menagerie of **living** creatures, you remember the next unit: RIVERS OF LIVING WATER.

RIVERS OF LIVING WATER

Jn 7:37–39

37 On the last and greatest day of the feast, Jesus stood up and exclaimed, "Let anyone who thirsts come to me and drink. **38** Whoever believes in me, as scripture says:

'Rivers of living water will flow from within him.'"

39 He said this in reference to the Spirit that those who came to believe in him were to receive. There was, of course, no Spirit yet, because Jesus had not yet been glorified.

———

The weeklong festival was coming to an end. On this day, the priests used water from the spring of Siloam for a ritual ceremony. This was when Jesus proclaimed that He is the source of living water. Earlier, in private, to the Samaritan woman at the well (Landmark 3), Jesus had said that He was the source of living water. He told her that after drinking of it she would never thirst again. Now, at the climax of a great feast, amongst a large crowd in Jerusalem, Jesus repeated this astounding claim. Belief in Him creates an internal river of living water. The source of this gift is the Holy Spirit, the guiding presence of God that will come after Jesus' death and resurrection.

SLOWLY, YOU SWIM TO THE other side of the river. Many of the creatures in this "living river" are now following you. In fact, as you clamber up the bank, several are tugging on your pants leg. When you finally get both feet back on dry land, a predictable sight awaits. Since the river is so alive with all varieties of fish and aquatic life, there is no shortage of **bait** shops to serve the local fishermen. There are **bait** shops lined up along the river as far as the eye can see. Every imaginable variety of **bait** is available at these **bait** shops. With so many **bait** shops, you wonder how they can all stay afloat.

However, each of the **bait** shops appears to be doing a brisk business. There are lines of people outside each shop waiting to purchase **bait**. You walk to the nearest **bait** shop and join the back of the line. **The bait** is a soundalike for "debate." This is the unit describing THE DEBATE ABOUT JESUS.

THE DEBATE ABOUT JESUS

Jn 7:40–52

40 Some in the crowd who heard these words said, "This is truly the Prophet."**41** Others said, "This is the Messiah." But others said, "The Messiah will not come from Galilee, will he? **42** Does not scripture say that the Messiah will be of David's family and come from Bethlehem, the village where David lived?" **43** So a division occurred in the crowd because of him. **44** Some of them even wanted to arrest him, but no one laid hands on him.

45 So the guards went to the chief priests and Pharisees, who asked them, "Why did you not bring him?" **46** The guards answered, "Never before has anyone spoken like this one." **47** So the Pharisees answered them, "Have you also been deceived? **48** Have any of the authorities or the Pharisees believed in him? **49** But this crowd, which does not know the law, is accursed." **50** Nicodemus, one of their members who had come to him earlier, said to them, **51** "Does our law condemn a person before it first hears him and finds out what he is doing?" **52** They answered and said to him, "You are not from Galilee also, are you? Look and see that no prophet arises from Galilee."

Jesus had created disagreement and division since the early days of His Galilean ministry. In Jerusalem, as the Feast of Tabernacles (Booths) was coming to an end, the controversy and division reached a new level. It would soon result in Jesus' death. Fellow Jews in the crowd at the festival were divided. The Pharisees, as well as the guards sent to arrest Jesus, were also divided. The seemingly awestruck guards were ridiculed. The Pharisees deemed the crowd to be "accursed." Nicodemus, a fellow Pharisee, was not exempt. He was also ridiculed for suggesting that Jesus deserved legal due process. Sadly, to this day the identity and purpose of Jesus continues to cause much division and debate.

Landmark 26:

MARATHON

Landmark 26 is the longest Landmark. It stretches for twenty-six tiring miles. You will cover this distance primarily by running. You will not be alone. You and a number of others will be covering the twenty-six miles together. You will be running a **marathon**! As you cover the twenty-six miles that represent this Landmark, several objects and encounters will enable you to recall specific units. You are on the starting line of the **marathon**. It is early morning and still dark outside. You feel anxious, but also confident, thinking of the many miles of training you have completed. On your mark, get set, go! The twenty-six-mile **marathon** has begun!

When the race begins, you reach up and turn on your head**light**. It is an early morning start, so the first few miles will be run before sunrise. When your **light** comes on, so do hundreds more around you. The **light** from so many head**lights** casts bouncing shadows on the pavement below. This **light** is sufficient, but you look forward to the bright **light** and warmth of the sun. This early morning artificial **light** beaming down from your forehead is a reminder of the unit when Jesus speaks about THE LIGHT OF THE WORLD. This unit and all of the units associated with Landmark 26 are found exclusively in the Gospel of John.

THE LIGHT OF THE WORLD

Jn 8:12–20

12 Jesus spoke to them again, saying, "I am the light of the world. Whoever follows me will not walk in darkness, but will have the light of life." **13** So the Pharisees said to him, "You testify on your own behalf, so your testimony cannot be verified." **14** Jesus answered and said to them, "Even if I do testify on my own behalf, my testimony can be verified, because I know where I came from and where I am going. But you do not know where I come from or where I am going. **15** You judge by appearances, but I do not judge anyone. **16** And even if I should judge, my judgment is valid, because I am not alone, but it is I and the Father who sent me. **17** Even in your law it is written that the testimony of two men can be verified. **18** I testify on my behalf and so does the Father who sent me." **19** So they said to him, "Where is your father?" Jesus answered, "You know neither me nor my Father. If you knew me, you would know my Father also." **20** He spoke these words while teaching in the treasury in the temple area. But no one arrested him, because his hour had not yet come.

Jesus was still in Jerusalem at the Feast of Tabernacles (Booths) and continued to teach in the temple area. John mentioned that Jesus was near the treasury. This was adjacent to the Court of Women, with its four large golden candelabras. They were lit each night during the festival. Perhaps it was soon after their lighting that Jesus proclaimed that He was "the light of the world." Jesus was not just the light in the temple or in Jerusalem or in Israel. He is the light of the entire world. He is illumination for all. Though Jesus seemed to speak on His own, without another person for verification, He knew the truth. His Father, who sent Him to earth for salvation, not for judgment, testified on His behalf. This was the same Father who testified at His Baptism and the transfiguration. This was the truth, and Jesus spoke the truth. It is the "truth which gives light to the world."

In the three Synoptic Gospels, Jesus intermittently spoke of His relationship with the Father who sent Him. Here John focused on the closeness, even the unity of the relationship.

YOU HAVE BEEN RUNNING LONG enough to have settled into a steady, relaxed pace. Your muscles are warm and the sun has risen. There is no more need for the headlight. Prior to the race, you and your **father** had calculated the general area where you would no longer need the light. Your **father** was to meet you there and take the light so you would not have to carry it any farther. Looking ahead, you see your **father** waiting beside the road. He is a proud **father**, smiling with his arms outstretched as you pass. Your **father** takes the light and wishes you good luck. You thank your **father** and continue running toward the next water station. This encounter with your **father** early in the race helps recall the unit about JESUS AND THE FATHER.

|||||||||||||||||||||||||||||||||||||||||||||||||||||||||||||||||||||||||||||||||||||||||||||||||||||||||||||||||||||||||||||||||||||||||||||||||||||||||||||||||

JESUS AND THE FATHER

|||||||||||||||||||||||||||||||||||||||||||||||||||||||||||||||||||||||||||||||||||||||||||||||||||||||||||||||||||||||||||||||||||||||||||||||||||||||||||||||||

Jn 8:21–30

21 He said to them again, "I am going away and you will look for me, but you will die in your sin. Where I am going you cannot come." **22** So the Jews said, "He is not going to kill himself, is he, because he said, 'Where I am going you cannot come'?" **23** He said to them, "You belong to what is below, I belong to what is above. You belong to this world, but I do not belong to this world. **24** That is why I told you that you will die in your sins. For if you do not believe that I AM, you will die in your sins." **25** So they said to him, "Who are you?" Jesus said to them, "What I told you from the beginning. **26** I have much to say about you in condemnation. But the one who sent me is true, and what I heard from him I tell the world." **27** They did not realize that he was speaking to them of the Father. **28** So Jesus said [to them], "When you lift up the Son of Man, then you will realize that I AM, and that I do nothing on my own, but I say only what the Father taught me. **29** The one who sent me is with me. He has not left me alone, because I always do what is pleasing to him." **30** Because he spoke this way, many came to believe in him.

Jesus would soon be returning to His Father, though in many ways He had never left the Father. What He spoke was from the Father, and all of His actions were guided by the Father. The Father was always with Him. But until this point, this unity has not been apparent to the disciples. However, by alluding to His crucifixion, Jesus revealed that an event was coming that would allow them to understand this unity between Father and Son.

THE WATER STATION IS NOW coming into view. It looks like it is being managed by just one man. The man is tall and lean with a long beard. He looks like he may also be a runner, but he is not dressed like a runner. He is busy providing water in a black suit. The way he is handing out the water is even stranger. People are drinking from his black top hat! Arriving at the aid station, you immediately recognize the man as **Abraham** Lincoln. Wow, **Abraham** Lincoln has volunteered to work an aid station! The runners ahead of you quickly drink from the top hat and thank **Abraham**. It is finally your turn. You take a drink, shake **Abraham's** hand, and express your appreciation. This unlikely but memorable encounter with **Abraham** Lincoln represents the unit about JESUS AND ABRAHAM.

JESUS AND ABRAHAM

Jn 8:31–59

31 Jesus then said to those Jews who believed in him, "If you remain in my word, you will truly be my disciples, 32 and you will know the truth, and the truth will set you free." 33 They answered him, "We are descendants of Abraham and have never been enslaved to anyone. How can you say, 'You will become free'?" 34 Jesus answered them, "Amen, amen, I say to you, everyone who commits sin is a slave of sin. 35 A slave does not remain in a household forever, but a son always remains. 36 So if a son frees you, then you will truly be free. 37 I know that you are descendants of Abraham. But you are trying to kill me, because my word has no room among you. 38 I tell you what I have seen in the Father's presence; then do what you have heard from the Father."

39 They answered and said to him, "Our father is Abraham." Jesus said to them, "If you were Abraham's children, you would be doing the works of Abraham. 40 But now you are trying to kill me, a man who has told you the truth that I heard from God; Abraham did not do this. 41 You are doing the works of your father!" [So] they said to him, "We are not illegitimate. We have one Father, God." 42 Jesus said to them, "If God were your Father, you would love me, for I came from God and am here; I did not come on my own, but he sent me. 43 Why do you not understand what I am saying? Because you cannot bear to hear my word. 44 You belong to your father the devil and you willingly carry out your father's desires. He was a murderer from the beginning and does not stand in truth, because there is no truth in him. When he tells a lie, he speaks in character, because he is a liar and the father of lies. 45 But because I speak the truth, you do not believe me. 46 Can any of you charge me with sin? If I am telling the truth, why do you not believe me? 47 Whoever

belongs to God hears the words of God; for this reason you do not listen, because you do not belong to God."

48 The Jews answered and said to him, "Are we not right in saying that you are a Samaritan and are possessed?" **49** Jesus answered, "I am not possessed; I honor my Father, but you dishonor me. **50** I do not seek my own glory; there is one who seeks it and he is the one who judges. **51** Amen, amen, I say to you, whoever keeps my word will never see death." **52** [So] the Jews said to him, "Now we are sure that you are possessed. Abraham died, as did the prophets, yet you say, 'Whoever keeps my word will never taste death.' **53** Are you greater than our father Abraham, who died? Or the prophets, who died? Who do you make yourself out to be?" **54** Jesus answered, "If I glorify myself, my glory is worth nothing; but it is my Father who glorifies me, of whom you say, 'He is our God.' **55** You do not know him, but I know him. And if I should say that I do not know him, I would be like you a liar. But I do know him and I keep his word. **56** Abraham your father rejoiced to see my day; he saw it and was glad." **57** So the Jews said to him, "You are not yet fifty years old and you have seen Abraham?" **58** Jesus said to them, "Amen, amen, I say to you, before Abraham came to be, I AM." **59** So they picked up stones to throw at him; but Jesus hid and went out of the temple area.

Abraham was the first great patriarch of the Hebrew people. God's covenant with Abraham made him the "Father of Judaism." He maintained a close relationship with God and, at the time of Jesus, was still a revered figure for all Jews. Jews who did not believe in Jesus would certainly have found it offensive to hear that they were not acting as children of Abraham. Hearing that they were also slaves to sin would not have gone over well either.

To change these feelings, people needed to recognize that Jesus spoke and acted for God. They must love Jesus, who is from God, in order to be children of God (and Abraham). Many could not accept this. The final straw came when Jesus intimated that He was greater than Abraham by invoking the divine name "I Am" for Himself. This led to the attempted stoning, the punishment for blasphemy. Given the words of John the Baptist (in Landmark 2), "And do not presume to say to yourselves, we have Abraham as our Father, for I tell you, God can raise up children to Abraham from these stones," it is ironic that the people attempted to stone Jesus for this reason.

YOU FEEL REFRESHED AFTER DRINKING from Abraham's hat. Striding along smoothly, you begin to wonder if you will run into any other celebrities or former presidents. Unfortunately, at that moment someone runs into you. Coming up quickly from behind, a young man almost knocks you down. He instantly apologizes and adds that he did not see you. Before you can respond, you notice his red-tipped cane and realize the **man is blind**. You are amazed and ask how he is able to do so well running while **blind** in such a crowd. He explains that he was **born blind** and has had years of practice. Sensing your disbelief, the **blind** man produces his birth certificate from a pocket in his running shorts. Sure enough, stamped in the bottom righthand corner are the words "**born blind**." You hand the document back to the **man born blind** and wish him luck as he runs ahead. Not surprisingly, this inspirational exchange with the **man born blind** represents the next unit about THE MAN BORN BLIND.

||||||||||||||||||||||||||||||||||||||||||||||||||||||||||||||||||||||||||||||||||||||||||||||||||||||||||||||||||||||||||

THE MAN BORN BLIND

||||||||||||||||||||||||||||||||||||||||||||||||||||||||||||||||||||||||||||||||||||||||||||||||||||||||||||||||||||||||||

Jn 9:1–41

1 As he passed by he saw a man blind from birth. **2** His disciples asked him, "Rabbi, who sinned, this man or his parents, that he was born blind?" **3** Jesus answered, "Neither he nor his parents sinned; it is so that the works of God might be made visible through him. **4** We have to do the works of the one who sent me while it is day. Night is coming when no one can work. **5** While I am in the world, I am the light of the world." **6** When he had said this, he spat on the ground and made clay with the saliva, and smeared the clay on his eyes, **7** and said to him, "Go wash in the Pool of Siloam" (which means Sent). So he went and washed, and came back able to see.

8 His neighbors and those who had seen him earlier as a beggar said, "Isn't this the one who used to sit and beg?" **9** Some said, "It is," but others said, "No, he just looks like him." He said, "I am." **10** So they said to him, "[So] how were your eyes opened?" **11** He replied, "The man called Jesus made clay and anointed my eyes and told me, 'Go to Siloam and wash.' So I went there and washed and was able to see." **12** And they said to him, "Where is he?" He said, "I don't know."

13 They brought the one who was once blind to the Pharisees. **14** Now Jesus had made clay and opened his eyes on a sabbath. **15** So then the Pharisees also asked him how he was able to see. He said to them, "He put clay on my eyes, and I washed, and now I can see." 16 So some of the Pharisees said, "This man is not from God, because he does not keep the sabbath." [But] others said, "How can a sinful man do such signs?" And there was a division among them. 17 So they said to the blind man again, "What do you have to say about him, since he opened your eyes?" He said, "He is a prophet."

18 Now the Jews did not believe that he had been blind and gained his sight until they summoned the parents of the one who had gained his sight. 19 They asked them, "Is this your son, who you say was born blind? How does he now see?" 20 His parents answered and said, "We know that this is our son and that he was born blind. 21 We do not know how he sees now, nor do we know who opened his eyes. Ask him, he is of age; he can speak for himself." 22 His parents said this because they were afraid of the Jews, for the Jews had already agreed that if anyone acknowledged him as the Messiah, he would be expelled from the synagogue. 23 For this reason his parents said, "He is of age; question him."

24 So a second time they called the man who had been blind and said to him, "Give God the praise! We know that this man is a sinner." 25 He replied, "If he is a sinner, I do not know. One thing I do know is that I was blind and now I see." 26 So they said to him, "What did he do to you? How did he open your eyes?" 27 He answered them, "I told you already and you did not listen. Why do you want to hear it again? Do you want to become his disciples, too?" 28 They ridiculed him and said, "You are that man's disciple; we are disciples of Moses! 29 We know that God spoke to Moses, but we do not know where this one is from." 30 The man answered and said to them, "This is what is so amazing, that you do not know where he is from, yet he opened my eyes. 31 We know that God does not listen to sinners, but if one is devout and does his will, he listens to him. 32 It is unheard of that anyone ever opened the eyes of a person born blind. 33 If this man were not from God, he would not be able to do anything." 34 They answered and said to him, "You were born totally in sin, and are you trying to teach us?" Then they threw him out.

35 When Jesus heard that they had thrown him out, he found him and said, "Do you believe in the Son of Man?" 36 He answered and said, "Who is he, sir, that I may believe in him?" 37 Jesus said to him, "You have seen him and the one speaking with you is he." 38 He said, "I do believe, Lord," and he worshiped him. 39 Then Jesus said, "I came into this world for judgment, so that those who do not see might see, and those who do see might become blind."

40 Some of the Pharisees who were with him heard this and said to him, "Surely we are not also blind, are we?" 41 Jesus said to them, "If you were blind, you would have no sin; but now you are saying, 'We see,' so your sin remains."

Once again there was conflict between Jesus and the Jewish authorities over Sabbath activity. John repeated the same pattern from the story about the healing of the paralytic in Landmark 7. A healing occurred. Hostility from those with authority followed. Then the Jews and the person healed had another encounter with Jesus.

Before healing the blind man, Jesus dispelled the belief that he was handicapped due to personal or parental sin. Jesus reaffirmed that He is the light of the world by bringing light to the man's eyes. Rather than touching the man's eyes or simply saying a few words, Jesus symbolically used elements of Himself (saliva) and the earth (dirt) for the healing. In this miracle, the man's sight did not return until he washed in the water of Siloam, though he was just healed by "Living Water."

Nonetheless, at the end of the story blindness still remained. It was the blindness of the Pharisees. They were blind due to their disbelief in Jesus.

YOU HAVE BEEN RUNNING FOR several hours. Fatigue is now your constant companion, but you push on. Soon you decide to walk. As you slow your pace, you are again hit from behind. This time it is not by a blind man, or by any person for that matter. It is sheep! You are being jostled as a herd of sheep pass by. Soon their **shepherd**, with his long wooden staff, is walking beside you. The **shepherd** says hello and invites you to run along with him and his herd. The **shepherd** offers to lead you to the finish line to make sure you complete the race. You accept the **shepherd's** offer. Soon you are again running, but now surrounded by a herd of sheep. You move along confidently as the **shepherd** offers words of encouragement. This meeting of the **shepherd** signifies the unit describing Jesus as THE GOOD SHEPHERD.

THE GOOD SHEPHERD

Jn 10:1–21

1 "Amen, amen, I say to you, whoever does not enter a sheepfold through the gate but climbs over elsewhere is a thief and a robber. **2** But whoever enters through the gate is the shepherd of the sheep. **3** The gatekeeper opens it for him, and the sheep hear his voice, as he calls his own sheep by name and leads them out. **4** When he has driven out all his own, he walks ahead of them, and the sheep follow him, because they recognize his voice. **5** But they will not follow a stranger; they will run away from him, because they do not recognize the voice of strangers." **6** Although Jesus used this figure of speech, they did not realize what he was trying to tell them.

7 So Jesus said again, "Amen, amen, I say to you, I am the gate for the sheep. **8** All who came [before me] are thieves and robbers, but the sheep did not listen to them. **9** I am the gate. Whoever enters through me will be saved, and will come in and go out and find pasture. **10** A thief comes only to steal and slaughter and destroy; I came so that they might have life and have it more abundantly. **11** I am the good shepherd. A good shepherd lays down his life for the sheep. **12** A hired man, who is not a shepherd and whose sheep are not his own, sees a wolf coming and leaves the sheep and runs away, and the wolf catches and scatters them. **13** This is because he works for pay and has no concern for the sheep. **14** I am the good shepherd, and I know mine and mine know me, **15** just as the Father knows me and I know the Father; and I will lay down my life for the sheep. **16** I have other sheep that do not belong to this fold. These also I must lead, and they will hear my voice, and there will be one flock, one shepherd. **17** This is why the Father loves me, because I lay down my life in order to take it up again. **18** No one takes it from me, but I lay it down on my own. I have power to lay it down, and power to take it up again. This command I have received from my Father."

19 Again there was a division among the Jews because of these words. **20** Many of them said, "He is possessed and out of his mind; why listen to him?" **21** Others said, "These are not the words of one possessed; surely a demon cannot open the eyes of the blind, can he?"

The Good Shepherd is perhaps the most popular and beloved image of Jesus. For many, it is the most comforting. A helpless sheep being cared for and protected by a devoted, loving shepherd is reassuring, especially in difficult times. Though this parable is found only in John, the other Gospels also make use of shepherd imagery. Mark talks of the crowd being like sheep without a shepherd in Landmark 18. Luke tells the "Parable of the Lost Sheep" in upcoming Landmark 29. In Matthew, believers are sheep that must be on guard against the wolves who are false prophets (Mt 7:15).

This parable describes many qualities we sheep are blessed to have in our Shepherd. He loves us individually, calling us each by name. He loves us as a flock, willing to lay down His life for the benefit of all. In times of trouble when the wolf comes calling, He does not abandon us. Jesus went so far as to compare our relationship with Him to the one He has with His Father. That is truly incredible!

Though this unit is not one of the three formal Passion predictions, Jesus foreshadowed His coming death as well as His resurrection. These words caused division amongst the Jews, just as they did in the previous unit about the man born blind. It was the nonbelievers who were truly blind. The sheep were able to see and recognize their Shepherd.

FINALLY, AND MERCIFULLY, THE FINISH line is in sight. You and the ewes have been running together for several miles. Not only are you physically exhausted, you are famished. It will be great to cross the finish line. It will be wonderful to partake in the post-race **feast** provided for all of the **dedicated** runners. You smile with satisfaction as you finish the race. Immediately, you ask, "Where is the **feast**?" You are pointed in the direction of loud music and laughter. Walking briskly, you arrive at a large field where the **dedicated** runners who finished before you are already **feasting**. What a **feast** it is! Tables are piled high with a wide variety of fruits, meats, and treats. You fill your plate and commence **feasting** at a table of familiar faces. Yes, your father, Abraham, the blind man, and the shepherd have saved you a seat. They each commend you for the **dedication** required to train for the race. They also discuss your **dedication** to finish the race. Never did a **feast** taste so good. This post-race **feast** and talk of your **dedication** recalls the unit about THE FEAST OF THE DEDICATION.

THE FEAST OF THE DEDICATION

Jn 10:22–42

22 The feast of the Dedication was then taking place in Jerusalem. It was winter. **23** And Jesus walked about in the temple area on the Portico of Solomon. **24** So the Jews gathered around him and said to him, "How long are you going to keep us in suspense? If you are the Messiah, tell us plainly." **25** Jesus answered them, "I told you and you do not believe. The works I do in my Father's name testify to me. **26** But you do not believe, because you are not among my sheep. **27** My sheep hear my voice; I know them, and they follow me. **28** I give them eternal life, and they shall never perish. No one can take them out of my hand. **29** My Father, who has given them to me, is greater than all, and no one can take them out of the Father's hand. **30** The Father and I are one."

31 The Jews again picked up rocks to stone him. **32** Jesus answered them, "I have shown you many good works from my Father. For which of these are you trying to stone me?" **33** The Jews answered him, "We are not stoning you for a good work but for blasphemy. You, a man, are making yourself God." **34** Jesus answered them, "Is it not written in your law, 'I said "You are gods"'? **35** If it calls them gods to whom the word of God came, and scripture cannot be set aside, **36** can you say that the one whom the Father has consecrated and sent into the world blasphemes because I said, 'I am the Son of God'? **37** If I do not perform my Father's works, do not believe me; **38** but if I perform them, even if you do not believe me, believe the works, so that you may realize [and understand] that the Father is in me and I am in the Father." **39** [Then] they tried again to arrest him; but he escaped from their power.

40 He went back across the Jordan to the place where John first baptized, and there he remained. **41** Many came to him and said, "John performed no sign, but everything John said about this man was true." **42** And many there began to believe in him.

Jesus was back in Jerusalem for another extended celebration. The eight-day winter festival referred to then as the Feast of Dedication is today more familiarly called Hanukkah. This feast commemorates the purification and rededication of the Jerusalem Temple in 164 BC. This occurred three years after Antiochus Epiphanes (a Hellenistic king of the Seleucid Empire) desecrated the holy temple altar with pagan sacrifices.

Jesus continued the imagery from the parable of the Good Shepherd. If the crowd had faith, as did His sheep, they would know the answer to their question. Jesus had already identified Himself to the Samaritan woman (Landmark 3). Very recently, He told the man born blind that He was "The Son of Man." In this Landmark, when talking about His relationship with His Father, He invoked the sacred title "I Am." In addition, Jesus told the crowd that all of His great works should make His identity clear. He then took things one step further by saying something the crowd was not able to tolerate: "The Father and I are one."

The crowd was outraged that Jesus had made Himself God. Jesus used a verse from the Scriptures (Ps 82:6) as partial justification. The judges of ancient Israel were called "gods" because they had been given divine authority to lead God's people. If these rulers who often abused their power could be referred to as "gods," how much more deserving of the title was the true Son of God sent into the world by the Father!

It was at this feast that the temple was consecrated. It is no coincidence that Jesus identified Himself as the one whom the Father had "consecrated," one who is set apart as holy.

Landmark 27:

THREE CUBES

The next Landmark involves a bit of mathematics. The math function of multiplying a number by itself is known as "squaring" a number. Thus 3 "squared" (3 x 3) equals 9. Extending this idea by multiplying a number by itself again is "cubing" a number. That is to say 3 "cubed" (3 x 3 x 3) equals 27. It is no coincidence that we have arrived at the twenty-seventh Landmark. We have just established that the number 27 is "3 cubed." With that in mind, it is easy to imagine that the twenty-seventh Landmark is **three cubes**. Imagine the **cubes** are made of wood and are the size of the wooden blocks that a young child would typically play with. To sum up, the twenty-seventh Landmark is **three cubes** (3 x 3 x 3 = 33 = 27).

Upon seeing the three cubes, you reach down and pick them up. They are small enough that you can hold all three in one hand. You begin to toss them back and forth from one hand to the other. Soon you are juggling them like a skilled entertainer. People begin to gather to watch your juggling performance. As you toss the three cubes higher and higher, more and more people crowd around you. A total of **seventy-two people** are now loudly cheering. A helpful coincidence is that each of the **seventy-two people** is wearing a jersey emblazoned with the **number** 72. The **crowd of seventy-two** remains constant. No one else joins in, but none of the **seventy-two** in your audience leave. When you finally stop juggling the three wooden cubes, the **crowd of seventy-two** goes wild. The enthusiastic screams of appreciation are deafening. It is amazing how loud **seventy-two people** can be. This juggling act performed for the **seventy-two people** corresponds to the unit describing THE MISSION OF THE SEVENTY-TWO.

THE MISSION OF THE SEVENTY-TWO

Lk 10:1–12

1 After this the Lord appointed seventy [-two] others whom he sent ahead of him in pairs to every town and place he intended to visit. 2 He said to them, "The harvest is abundant but the laborers are few; so ask the master of the harvest to send out laborers for his harvest. 3 Go on your way; behold, I am sending you like lambs among wolves. 4 Carry no money bag, no sack, no sandals; and greet no one along the way. 5 Into whatever house you enter, first say, 'Peace to this household.' 6 If a peaceful person lives there, your peace will rest on him; but if not, it will return to you. 7 Stay in the same house and eat and drink what is offered to you, for the laborer deserves his payment. Do not move about from one house to another. 8 Whatever town you enter and they welcome you, eat what is set before you, 9 cure the sick in it and say to them, 'The kingdom of God is at hand for you.' 10 Whatever town you enter and they do not receive you, go out into the streets and say, 11 'The dust of your town that clings to our feet, even that we shake off against you.' Yet know this: the kingdom of God is at hand. 12 I tell you, it will be more tolerable for Sodom on that day than for that town."

This unit shares some of the same instructions given to the twelve apostles prior to their initial missionary journey in Landmark 16. Just as the number of apostles—twelve—was not arbitrary, neither was the number 72. In the tenth chapter of Genesis, the number of the nations of the world mentioned was seventy-two. This current group of seventy-two people can be seen as representing the entire world. This includes us! We are all to be missionaries for Jesus, "laborers for the harvest." We are instructed to tend to the needs of others. Our own personal needs will be taken care of. We are to go forth like faithful lambs. We will be protected from the wolves by our Good Shepherd. This does not exempt us from using common sense. There will be difficulties and rejections, just as Jesus Himself endured difficulty and rejection. In the end, Jesus and His Word will triumph.

THE CROWD OF SEVENTY-TWO IS so enthralled with your juggling exhibition that they all want to learn the skill. You decide to teach them, but not here. Nearby is an old, abandoned, dilapidated town. The town is in such a state of disrepair that it has been **condemned**. It is in the privacy of the **condemned town** where you will teach the seventy-two how to juggle. They all agree to follow you to the **condemned town**. It is quite a sight to see. You are juggling the three cubes. The crowd of seventy-two is following behind as you walk toward the **condemned town**. Finally, you all arrive at the **condemned town**. It is in even worse shape than you imagined. Walls have crumbled, paint is faded, and windows are broken. No wonder the old town has been **condemned**. The sight of the town is a vivid reminder of when JESUS CONDEMNS UNREPENTANT TOWNS.

JESUS CONDEMNS UNREPENTANT TOWNS

Mt 11:20–24

20 Then he began to reproach the towns where most of his mighty deeds had been done, since they had not repented. 21 "Woe to you, Chorazin! Woe to you, Bethsaida! For if the mighty deeds done in your midst had been done in Tyre and Sidon, they would long ago have repented in sackcloth and ashes. 22 But I tell you, it will be more tolerable for Tyre and Sidon on the day of judgment than for you. 23 And as for you, Capernaum:

'Will you be exalted to heaven?
You will go down to the netherworld.'

For if the mighty deeds done in your midst had been done in Sodom, it would have remained until this day. 24 But I tell you, it will be more tolerable for the land of Sodom on the day of judgment than for you."

Lk 10:13–16

13 "Woe to you, Chorazin! Woe to you, Bethsaida! For if the mighty deeds done in your midst had been done in Tyre and Sidon, they would long ago have repented, sitting in sackcloth and ashes. 14 But it will be more tolerable for Tyre and Sidon at the judgment than for you. 15 And as for you, Capernaum, 'Will you be exalted to heaven? You will go down to the netherworld.' 16 Whoever listens to you listens to me. Whoever rejects you rejects me. And whoever rejects me rejects the one who sent me."

In spite of Jesus' amazing words and deeds, a large number of people did not accept Him. You have already witnessed the rejection in His hometown of Nazareth. You now see that many in Capernaum, His adopted home during the Galilean ministry, treated him similarly. Many in the nearby towns of Chorazin and Bethsaida (where the blind man was healed in Landmark 21) also rejected Jesus. These were some of the people who had the most exposure to Jesus. They had ample opportunity to repent and believe in the good news. Tyre and Sidon (the area where the Greek woman lived in Landmark 20) were faraway Gentile towns that had very little direct contact with Jesus. Their citizens had long ago been doomed by Isaiah (23:1–18) and Ezekiel (26–28). However, they and the people of the infamous town of Sodom had more to look forward to. These were frightening words! In what town do we live?

YOU AND THE SEVENTY-TWO ASPIRING jugglers are now in the condemned town. As you begin to teach them some basic juggling skills, it is quite evident that they have something else in mind. They want to have a party! More specifically, they want to **revel** in the streets of the condemned and abandoned town. These **revelers** seem to have no interest whatsoever in juggling. You have never seen such joyful, carefree **reveling**. You are unsure why they are so happy. You finally ask one of the seventy-two the reason for such extreme **reveling**. You are told that all seventy-two people previously lived in this town before it was condemned. Upon hearing this, you join in the **revelry**. All of the **revelry** is a reminder of the next unit: THE REVELATION OF THE FATHER.

THE REVELATION OF THE FATHER

Mt 11:25–27

25 At that time Jesus said in reply, "I give praise to you, Father, Lord of heaven and earth, for although you have hidden these things from the wise and the learned you have revealed them to the

childlike. **26** Yes, Father, such has been your gracious will. **27** All things have been handed over to me by my Father. No one knows the Son except the Father, and no one knows the Father except the Son and anyone to whom the Son wishes to reveal him."

Lk 10:21–22

21 At that very moment he rejoiced [in] the holy Spirit and said, "I give you praise, Father, Lord of heaven and earth, for although you have hidden these things from the wise and the learned you have revealed them to the childlike. Yes, Father, such has been your gracious will. **22** All things have been handed over to me by my Father. No one knows who the Son is except the Father, and who the Father is except the Son and anyone to whom the Son wishes to reveal him."

———————

Jesus expressed several ideas in this brief unit. Just as He and the Father were interconnected, so, too, were Jesus and the revelation of the Father. Jesus praised the Father for the gift of revelation. He then stated that this gift comes through Jesus Himself. Jesus, the Father's Son, was not only the gift of salvation, but also the source of revelation about His generous gift-giving Father. Revelation does not come through study and learning. It is given to us by the Father through His Son. Revelation is thus divine communication initiated by the Father. Jesus is "the way" it occurs.

YOU ENJOY THE REVELRY, BUT feel some disappointment that the seventy-two did not really want to learn how to juggle. Sensing your disappointment, the seventy-two stop celebrating. They ask what is bothering you. After you explain, they all begin to smile. You soon find out why. They are all **master** jugglers! Each of them had **mastered** the skill as children. Picking up all sorts of random objects, the seventy-two begin to demonstrate their **mastery**. They are amazing. Juggling alone and in groups, their incredible skill and **mastery** of juggling is something you could only dream of achieving. They had kept their **mastery** a secret so you would lead them to the condemned town where they had once lived. You are no longer disappointed as you watch all of the **mastery** on display. This demonstration of **mastery** causes you to remember the unit about THE GENTLE MASTERY OF JESUS.

THE GENTLE MASTERY OF JESUS

Mt 11:28–30

28 "Come to me, all you who labor and are burdened, and I will give you rest. 29 Take my yoke upon you and learn from me, for I am meek and humble of heart; and you will find rest for your selves. 30 For my yoke is easy, and my burden light."

In the previous unit, Jesus instructed the crowd about revelation and its source. We learned that Jesus Himself is the revelation. Jesus now invites everyone to that revelation, which is Himself. If we answer His call, we will still shoulder a yoke. The demands of following Jesus, the demands of love, are not easy. Those in Jesus' time who labored under the burden of religious legalism and Roman oppression could find rest by following Him. In our busy, stressful world, we can do the same.

THE REVELING IS OVER. IT is now time to leave the condemned town and **return** home. The **return** trip is different from the departure. The seventy-two are out in front showing off their juggling skills. This **return of the seventy-two** is met with much fanfare. People along the way are cheering, excited to see so much entertainment. You are thankful that everyone **returned** home safely. This exciting **return home of the seventy-two** is a reminder of THE RETURN OF THE SEVENTY-TWO.

THE RETURN OF THE SEVENTY-TWO

Lk 10:17–20

17 The seventy [-two] returned rejoicing, and said, "Lord, even the demons are subject to us because of your name." 18 Jesus said, "I have observed Satan fall like lightning from the sky. 19 Behold, I have given you the power 'to tread upon serpents' and scorpions and upon the full force of the enemy and nothing will harm you.

20 Nevertheless, do not rejoice because the spirits are subject to you, but rejoice because your names are written in heaven."

———

Doing the work of Jesus brings joy! One can accomplish much if it is done in the name of Jesus. The seventy-two were successful, just as the Twelve had been back in Landmark 18. The power of evil can be overcome as long as Jesus is with us. Christians today can be just as effective as these two groups. We are all called by Jesus to fight the evil that He used serpents and scorpions to symbolize. However, true joy comes not with missionary success, but in the gift (not reward) of heaven that awaits.

Landmark 28:

DOMINOES

L andmark 28 is another game. If you are not a game player, do not despair. This is the last game you will play on the journey. Get ready to play a game of **dominoes**. This game is typically played with twenty-eight rectangular pieces or tiles. As you may know, each of the twenty-eight **dominoes** is blank on one side. The other side of the **domino** (the face) is painted or embossed with varying numbers of spots. Now picture these twenty-eight **dominoes** lying on a table. The table is located in a small room. You walk up to the table and sit down to play a rousing game of **dominoes**.

You typically play dominoes with the same person, though he was not available today. He sent two substitutes to fill in for him: his wife, **Martha** Washington, and his mother, **Mary** Washington. Yes, George was busy, but he sent his regrets via **Martha and Mary**. You are a bit intimidated by **Martha and Mary**, both of whom are renowned domino players. **Martha and Mary** greet you rather formally and then sit down for a serious game of dominoes. **Martha** turns over the dominoes and mixes them up. **Mary** readies the score sheet and asks if you would like to play for money. You tell **Martha and Mary** you would prefer not to gamble. They give you a rather indignant glare, and reluctantly agree. This preparation for a game of dominoes with **Martha and Mary** Washington represents the unit when Jesus is with His friends MARTHA AND MARY.

MARTHA AND MARY

Lk 10:38–42

38 As they continued their journey he entered a village where a woman whose name was Martha welcomed him. **39** She had a sister named Mary [who] sat beside the Lord at his feet listening to him

261

speak. **40** Martha, burdened with much serving, came to him and said, "Lord, do you not care that my sister has left me by myself to do the serving? Tell her to help me." **41** The Lord said to her in reply, "Martha, Martha, you are anxious and worried about many things. **42** There is need of only one thing. Mary has chosen the better part and it will not be taken from her."

———————————————

This unit takes place in Bethany, a small town about three miles southeast of Jerusalem. Jesus was traveling with His disciples, though it seems that He was the only guest of Martha and Mary. Both women showed their care and love for Jesus. Martha's style is probably easier to relate to for most people. Her busyness and worry were burdensome. Her activity got in the way of really hearing what Jesus had to say. Mary realized that spending time with Jesus and carefully listening to His words was the "better part." She sat at His feet as a disciple, unusual behavior for a woman in Jesus' time. Though good works and its associated activity are important in the Christian life, they should not get in the way of spending quiet time with Jesus.

YOU, MARTHA, AND MARY ARE now ready to begin a friendly game of dominoes. You begin to draw your tiles from the center of the table. Suddenly, a loud crashing sound comes from the direction of the door. Looking up, you see a very unwelcome intruder. It is a very large bearded **samurai** warrior wielding a razor-sharp sword. This is definitely not the friendly **samurai** who released you from the handcuffs back in Landmark 3. It does not appear that he has come to join the game. The **samurai's inhospitable** glare indicates his mission is to destroy the game. You try to be friendly and **hospitable** to the **samurai**. He responds with a loud blood-curdling scream. The **samurai** has no intention of accepting your **hospitality**. He raises the sword above his head and brings it crashing down, slicing the table in half. Dominoes go flying. This **inhospitable** behavior of the **samurai** helps recall another unit regarding the **Samaritans**. It is the story about THE SAMARITANS' INHOSPITALITY.

THE SAMARITANS' INHOSPITALITY

Lk 9:51–56

51 When the days for his being taken up were fulfilled, he resolutely determined to journey to Jerusalem, **52** and he sent messengers ahead of him. On the way they entered a Samaritan village to prepare for his reception there, **53** but they would not welcome him because the destination of his journey was Jerusalem. **54** when the disciples James and John saw this they asked, "Lord do you want us to call down fire from heaven to consume them?" **55** Jesus turned and rebuked them, **56** and they journeyed to another village.

This unit represents the beginning of the end of Jesus' earthly ministry. He now begins His final journey to Jerusalem, where His Passion will be played out during the Passover Festival. Once there, Jesus will fulfill the will of the Father and be "taken up" to rejoin Him.

At the outset of this final journey, Jesus was rejected by the Samaritans. These people of central Palestine had long been enemies of the Jews. When Jews traveled north or south between Galilee and Jerusalem, they would typically avoid Samaria. They considered Samaritans unclean due to their history of intermarrying with foreigners and worshiping foreign gods. Jesus rejected this notion. Rather than rebuking the Samaritans, He rebuked two of His closest disciples. They had wanted to destroy the Samaritans in a way reminiscent of Elijah destroying the men sent by the Samaritan king (2 Kg 1:10–12). The disciples had become ardent followers of Jesus, but did not yet understand His mercy.

THE GAME OF DOMINOES WITH Martha and Mary has come to an abrupt end. Not wanting to meet the same fate as the table, you must quickly escape. The large inhospitable samurai stands between you and the door. Fortunately, a **narrow gate** on the other side of the room is open. Hopefully, all three of you can squeeze through the **narrow gate** before the deadly sword falls again. You point to the **narrow gate** and yell to Martha and Mary, "Run!" As they squeeze through the **gate**, you reach down and scoop up a handful of dominoes. When you arrive at the **narrow gate** with a few dominoes, you glance back and see the sword raised high. Just a couple more steps and you, too, will be safely through the **narrow gate**. As you turn sideways to pass through, you feel the sword graze the back of your head. You manage to escape in one piece. This dramatic exit through the **narrow gate** represents Jesus' teaching about THE NARROW GATE.

THE NARROW GATE

Lk 13:22–30

> **22** He passed through towns and villages, teaching as he went and making his way to Jerusalem. **23** Someone asked him, "Lord, will only a few people be saved?" He answered them, **24** "Strive to enter through the narrow gate, for many, I tell you, will attempt to enter but will not be strong enough. **25** After the master of the house has arisen and locked the door, then will you stand outside knocking and saying, 'Lord, open the door for us.' He will say to you in reply, 'I do not know where you are from.' **26** And you will say, 'We ate and drank in your company and you taught in our streets.' **27** Then he will say to you, 'I do not know where [you] are from. Depart from me, all you evildoers!' **28** And there will be wailing and grinding of teeth when you see Abraham, Isaac, and Jacob and all the prophets in the kingdom of God and you yourselves cast out. **29** And people will come from the east and the west and from the north and the south and will recline at table in the kingdom of God. **30** For behold, some are last who will be first, and some are first who will be last."

On His way to Jerusalem, Jesus continued to teach His disciples and others along the way. The material in this unit is found only in Luke's Gospel. Luke places it after Jesus' telling of the mustard seed and yeast parables about the kingdom of God. Though the kingdom of God is available to all because of God's grace, Jesus taught that effort on our part is expected. The narrow opening is small, but it is open to all.

Jesus continued to use the imagery of passing through an opening by shifting to a door. The door is locked. People who have no more than a casual relationship with Jesus will find themselves on the outside. We are to share deeply in Jesus' life in order to share the heavenly banquet with Him and the patriarchs. There is room for all at the table.

YOU ESCAPED THE SAMURAI, BUT were not totally unscathed. Martha and Mary gasp and point to the back of your head. You reach back and touch tender skin where just a few seconds earlier had been thick, healthy **hair**. The two women also gently touch the large **hairless** area. Looking back toward the narrow gate, you see a small pile of **hair**. You miss the **hair,** but are thankful to be alive. Most of your **hair** is intact, and the **hair** you so quickly lost will slowly grow back. This loss of **hair** triggers thoughts about Herod (**Hair**-od). Since the samurai wanted to kill you, it recalls the unit about HEROD'S DESIRE TO KILL JESUS.

||||||||||||||||||||||||||||||||||||||||||||||||||||||||||||||||||||||||||||||||||||||||||||||||||||||||||||||||||||||||

HEROD'S DESIRE TO KILL JESUS

||||||||||||||||||||||||||||||||||||||||||||||||||||||||||||||||||||||||||||||||||||||||||||||||||||||||||||||||||||||||

Lk 13:31–33

31 At that time some Pharisees came to him and said, "Go away, leave this area because Herod wants to kill you." 32 He replied, "Go and tell that fox, 'Behold, I cast out demons and I perform healings today and tomorrow, and on the third day I accomplish my purpose. 33 Yet I must continue on my way today, tomorrow, and the following day, for it is impossible that a prophet should die outside of Jerusalem.'"

―――――――――――

Here Luke casts the Pharisees in a positive light. They warned Jesus of Herod's deadly intentions. This was Herod Antipas, the killer of John the Baptist. He was the Jewish ruler of Galilee and Perea. The latter was a strip of land on the eastern side of the Jordan River, adjacent to the Decapolis. Jesus may have been in Perea at the time of this warning. Though warned, Jesus said that things would be business as usual as He journeyed onward to Jerusalem. Jesus again alluded to His coming fate. A third, more explicit prediction would be made soon.

AFTER QUICKLY COMING TO TERMS with your missing hair, you turn to tell Martha and Mary goodbye. Surprisingly, they begin to walk back toward the narrow gate. They say you have **dropped** something. They giggle and say you must have a case of "the **dropsies**." You do not recall **dropping** anything. Your mind was on escaping the sword. You wonder what you could have **dropped** during all of the excitement. While still laughing about the "**dropsies**," the two ladies bend down to pick up the **dropped** items. They soon return with the handful of dominoes that you had taken from the table prior to the escape. As they **drop** them in your hand, you thank them and bid them farewell. This talk of **dropping** dominoes and having the "**dropsies**" is a reference to Jesus HEALING A MAN WITH DROPSY.

|||||||||||||||||||||||||||||||||||||||||||||||||||||||||||||||||||||||||||||||||||||||||||||||||||||||||||||||||||||||||||||||||||||||||||||||||

HEALING A MAN WITH DROPSY

|||||||||||||||||||||||||||||||||||||||||||||||||||||||||||||||||||||||||||||||||||||||||||||||||||||||||||||||||||||||||||||||||||||||||||||||||

Lk 14:1–6

1 On a sabbath he went to dine at the home of one of the leading Pharisees, and the people there were observing him carefully. 2 In front of him there was a man suffering from dropsy. 3 Jesus spoke to the scholars of the law and Pharisees in reply, asking, "Is it lawful to cure on the sabbath or not?" 4 But they kept silent; so he took the man and, after he had healed him, dismissed him. 5 Then he said to them, "Who among you, if your son or ox falls into a cistern, would not immediately pull him out on the sabbath day?" 6 But they were unable to answer his question.

This healing story takes place on the Sabbath and is controversial, as were the three previous Sabbath healings. They involved the demoniac (Landmark 4), the paralytic (Landmark 7), and most recently the crippled woman (Landmark 21). Here Jesus heals a man with dropsy, now more commonly referred to as edema. In this condition, the body retains excess fluid, which can cause a variety of problems.

Jesus had been invited to dine with a Pharisee. Jesus asked a legal question to the legal experts. For fear of embarrassment or appearing uncaring, they declined to answer. Jesus again affirmed that it is lawful to be compassionate every day of the week. If an unfortunate animal can be attended to, then how much more an unfortunate brother? In an upcoming unit, Jesus will go one step further, implying that the sick man should have also been a dinner guest.

WINTER PARTY

In the northern hemisphere, winter extends through the month of February. When February rolls around, most people are weary of **winter** weather. It is still cold and snowy, but the promise of spring is just around the corner. We just have to get through the four weeks of February. Every four years, there is an extra day of **winter** when February has a twenty-ninth day. Only February has exactly twenty-nine days, and it does not happen often. It seems fitting that this twenty-ninth day be a day of celebration. A **party** to mark **winter** coming to a close. This **winter party** on the twenty-ninth would also celebrate those whose true birthdate comes around so rarely. Thus we have good reasons to have a **party** on the twenty-ninth. With this in mind, our twenty-ninth Landmark will be a festive outdoor **winter party** with snow on the ground and a chill in the air.

Approaching the cold outdoor winter party, you are somewhat surprised by the large number of **guests**. The **guests** appear to be enjoying themselves. They are laughing and chatting, all seeming to know one another. Though you, too, are an invited **guest**, you do not recognize any of the other **guests**. You do not even know the **host** who invited you! You are anxious to meet the **host** who is throwing such a lavish party. A **host** who would invite **guests** such as yourself who he does not even know must be an unusual person! Soon several of the other **guests** come over and speak to you. Strangely, they do not tell you their names. They simply say, "Hello, I am a **guest**!" You ask them who is **hosting** the party. They remain consistently strange by saying, "**Host is hosting**!" You ask if they would be kind enough to introduce you to the **host**. They agree and lead you through a crowd of other **guests**. Soon you come to a very large table where a sad-looking elderly man sits alone. He looks up and without a smile says in a monotone, "Hello, I am the **host**." This strange meeting of **guests and host** helps to recall Jesus' parable about THE CONDUCT OF INVITED GUESTS AND HOST.

THE CONDUCT OF INVITED GUESTS AND HOST

Lk 14:7–14

7 He told a parable to those who had been invited, noticing how they were choosing the places of honor at the table. **8** "When you are invited by someone to a wedding banquet, do not recline at table in the place of honor. A more distinguished guest than you may have been invited by him, **9** and the host who invited both of you may approach you and say, 'Give your place to this man,' and then you would proceed with embarrassment to take the lowest place. **10** Rather, when you are invited, go and take the lowest place so that when the host comes to you he may say, 'My friend, move up to a higher position.' Then you will enjoy the esteem of your companions at the table. **11** For everyone who exalts himself will be humbled, but the one who humbles himself will be exalted." **12** Then he said to the host who invited him, "When you hold a lunch or a dinner, do not invite your friends or your brothers or your relatives or your wealthy neighbors, in case they may invite you back and you have repayment. **13** Rather, when you hold a banquet, invite the poor, the crippled, the lame, the blind; **14** blessed indeed will you be because of their inability to repay you. For you will be repaid at the resurrection of the righteous."

This parable about humility and hospitality is found only in Luke. Matthew also tells a parable centered around a wedding banquet, but it is the parallel to Luke's upcoming parable of the great feast. Those will be discussed together in the next unit. For now, we will focus on Luke's unique parable, which takes place at a wedding banquet.

Jesus told this parable to His fellow guests at a Pharisee's home, the home where the man with dropsy had been cured. The first part of the parable concerns the behavior of guests. It bears a strong resemblance to the advice offered in Proverbs 25:6–7: behave in a humble fashion and conduct yourself with humility toward others. This behavior will help avoid future embarrassment. One's status in society does not equate with one's "status" in the eyes of God. The Host at the heavenly banquet has ultimate control of the seating chart.

Like the guests, the host should also behave in a certain fashion. Conduct aimed at receiving earthly reward is shortsighted. Focusing on the less fortunate, those truly in need of hospitality, is correct behavior. Merciful behavior will ultimately be met with mercy from the heavenly Host.

AFTER YOU MEET THE HOST, all the other guests gather around the long table where the host is seated. He invites everyone to sit down. A seemingly endless line of servants begins to lay out a **great feast**. You have never seen such an elaborate **feast**. What you thought was going to be a small winter party has become a **feast** of epic proportions. The host has provided every imaginable food for the **great feast**. You and all the other guests are overwhelmed by the quantity and quality of the **feast**. The servants have finished bringing out the food. The table appears to be on the verge of collapsing under the weight of the **great feast**. The host then stands. He looks out over the vast table and the drooling guests. Finally, he proclaims, "Let the **great feast** begin!" This **great feast** helps recall Jesus' PARABLE OF THE GREAT FEAST.

PARABLE OF THE GREAT FEAST

Mt 22:1–14

1 Jesus again in reply spoke to them in parables, saying, 2 "The kingdom of heaven may be likened to a king who gave a wedding feast for his son. 3 He dispatched his servants to summon the invited guests to the feast, but they refused to come. 4 A second time he sent other servants, saying, 'Tell those invited: "Behold, I have prepared my banquet, my calves and fattened cattle are killed, and everything is ready; come to the feast."' 5 Some ignored the invitation and went away, one to his farm, another to his business. 6 The rest laid hold of his servants, mistreated them, and killed them. 7 The king was enraged and sent his troops, destroyed those murderers, and burned their city. 8 Then he said to his servants, 'The feast is ready, but those who were invited were not worthy to come. 9 Go out, therefore, into the main roads and invite to the feast

whomever you find.' **10** The servants went out into the streets and gathered all they found, bad and good alike, and the hall was filled with guests. **11** But when the king came in to meet the guests he saw a man there not dressed in a wedding garment. **12** He said to him, 'My friend, how is it that you came in here without a wedding garment?' But he was reduced to silence. **13** Then the king said to his attendants, 'Bind his hands and feet, and cast him into the darkness outside, where there will be wailing and grinding of teeth.' **14** Many are invited, but few are chosen."

Lk 14:15–24

15 One of his fellow guests on hearing this said to him, "Blessed is the one who will dine in the kingdom of God." **16** He replied to him, "A man gave a great dinner to which he invited many. **17** When the time for the dinner came, he dispatched his servant to say to those invited, 'Come, everything is now ready.' **18** But one by one, they all began to excuse themselves. The first said to him, 'I have purchased a field and must go to examine it; I ask you, consider me excused.' **19** And another said, 'I have purchased five yoke of oxen and am on my way to evaluate them; I ask you, consider me excused.' **20** And another said, 'I have just married a woman, and therefore I cannot come.' **21** The servant went and reported this to his master. Then the master of the house in a rage commanded his servant, 'Go out quickly into the streets and alleys of the town and bring in here the poor and the crippled, the blind and the lame.' **22** The servant reported, 'Sir, your orders have been carried out and still there is room.' **23** The master then ordered the servant, 'Go out to the highways and hedgerows and make people come in that my home may be filled. **24** For, I tell you, none of those men who were invited will taste my dinner.'"

This is another parable about the kingdom of God. Matthew says so directly, while Luke has one of Jesus' fellow dinner guests make the reference. The kingdom of God depicted as a banquet would have been familiar imagery to those aware of Isaiah 25:6:

> **6 On this mountain the LORD of Hosts**
> **will provide for all peoples**
> **A feast of rich food and choice wines,**
> **juicy rich food and pure, choice wines.**

In Matthew, the details of the parable are more extreme and harsh. The host was a king who twice sent out his servants to retrieve the invited guests. The second time the servants were murdered. The host then had the invited guests killed and their city destroyed. This last detail is thought to be a reference to the Roman destruction of Jerusalem in AD 70. The king emphasized the readiness of the feast several times. The urgency of the Kingdom is underscored just as it had been at the outset of Jesus' Galilean ministry, "Repent for the kingdom of heaven is at hand."

In Luke, the host is a man who sends out his single servant. He is sent out once and does manage to come back alive. In Matthew and Luke, the invited guests are said to prefer mundane, earthly pursuits to participation in the great feast.

In Matthew, the king then sent out other servants to invite anyone they could find, the "bad and good alike." Sinners were also invited. Luke has his servant invite those with handicaps, not the "bad." These are the same "poor, crippled, blind, and lame" mentioned in Luke in the previous parable. Perhaps some of Jesus' listeners inferred that these people were sinners, and thus handicapped as a result. In Luke, the host was determined to fill his house, and dispatched his servant a second time.

Only Matthew has the additional material about the wedding garment. It appears to be more harsh behavior from the king, who had earlier lethally retaliated against the invited guests. Jesus often used hyperbole to make His point. Here He was warning His listeners against complacency. Jesus recognized that those invited to the heavenly feast were sinners, but they were expected to repent for their behavior, which was symbolized by the wedding garment.

AS YOU BEGIN TO ENJOY the great feast, neither you nor any of the guests know that an even greater surprise is about to occur. On the command of the host, a herd of **sheep** rushes up to the table. In unison, all of the **sheep** leap upon the table. Food goes flying. You, the guests, and the intrusive **sheep** are now covered in feast food. Surprising? Yes, but the real surprise happens next. The **sheep** begin to loudly bleat, "Baaah, baaah." **Coins** then flow forth from their open mouths. Valuable gold and silver **coins** begin to pile up on the table and in the food. With each "baaah," more **coins** are expelled by the **sheep**. Chaos ensues as the food-splattered guests clamor for the **coins**. You step back from the table in disbelief. This scene of **sheep and coins** allows for easy recollection of two more of Jesus' parables: THE PARABLE OF THE LOST SHEEP and THE PARABLE OF THE LOST COIN. These are the first of four parables depicting the loving and merciful nature of God.

THE PARABLES OF THE LOST SHEEP
AND COIN

Mt 18:10–14

10 "See that you do not despise one of these little ones, for I say to you that their angels in heaven always look upon the face of my heavenly Father. **[11] 12** What is your opinion? If a man has a hundred sheep and one of them goes astray, will he not leave the ninety-nine in the hills and go in search of the stray? **13** And if he finds it, amen, I say to you, he rejoices more over it than over the ninety-nine that did not stray. **14** In just the same way, it is not the will of your heavenly Father that one of these little ones be lost."

Lk 15:1–10

1 The tax collectors and sinners were all drawing near to listen to him, **2** but the Pharisees and scribes began to complain, saying, "This man welcomes sinners and eats with them." **3** So to them he addressed this parable. **4** "What man among you having a hundred sheep and losing one of them would not leave the ninety-nine in the desert and go after the lost one until he finds it? **5** And when he does find it, he sets it on his shoulders with great joy **6** and, upon his arrival home, he calls together his friends and neighbors and says to them, 'Rejoice with me because I have found my lost sheep.' **7** I tell you, in just the same way there will be more joy in heaven over one sinner who repents than over ninety-nine righteous people who have no need of repentance.

8 "Or what woman having ten coins and losing one would not light a lamp and sweep the house, searching carefully until she finds it? **9** And when she does find it, she calls together her friends and neighbors and says to them, 'Rejoice with me because I have found the coin that I lost.' **10** In just the same way, I tell you, there will be rejoicing among the angels of God over one sinner who repents."

You have already seen Jesus as the Good Shepherd in Landmark 26. The Hebrew Scriptures depict God as a loving Shepherd several times (Ps 23:1; Is 40:11; Ez 34:11–31). Ezekiel specifically describes God as a Shepherd who seeks out the lost and brings back the strayed (34:16). Our sins often cause us to stray from the flock. Fortunately, we have a Shepherd who is always ready to seek us out and carry us back. At times, we may run from the Shepherd's outstretched arms. However, He will continue to pursue us.

This powerful story was a perfect response to the question of why Jesus would not only welcome, but seek out and share a meal with sinners.

The short parable of the lost coin reinforces the message of the lost sheep. To carefully search the entire house for a single coin and then call the neighbors to rejoice seems extreme. It is equally extreme to leave ninety-nine sheep to focus on finding one. We are much more valuable to God than a sheep or a coin. Imagine His extreme love and concern for us when we are lost!

THE HOST HAS SEEN ALL that he can tolerate. His great feast has deteriorated into an out-of-control food fight. The specially prepared food seems to be everywhere but on plates. Sheep are on the table. Guests are groveling for regurgitated coins. The host decides to summon his **son** for assistance. His **son** is a very large, intimidating man. The mere sight of the host's **son** usually causes people to flee in fear. For this reason, he had not invited his **son** to the great feast, but now he is needed. The host yells loudly for his **son**. Soon a giant of a man appears. His broad shoulders, massive chest, bulging biceps, and thick thighs await his father's bidding. The host asks his **son** to restore order to the chaotic feast. This helps recall one of Jesus' parables about a man's **son**. Since we have just been reminded of the parables of the lost sheep and lost coin, the **son** now reminds us of THE PARABLE OF THE LOST (PRODIGAL) SON.

THE PARABLE OF THE LOST (PRODIGAL) SON

Lk 15:11–32

11 Then he said, "A man had two sons, 12 and the younger son said to his father, 'Father, give me the share of your estate that should come to me.' So the father divided the property between them. 13 After a few days, the younger son collected all his belongings and set off to a distant country where he squandered his inheritance on a life of dissipation. 14 When he had freely spent everything, a severe famine struck that country, and he found himself in dire need. 15 So he hired himself out to one of the local

citizens who sent him to his farm to tend the swine. **16** And he longed to eat his fill of the pods on which the swine fed, but nobody gave him any. **17** Coming to his senses he thought, 'How many of my father's hired workers have more than enough food to eat, but here am I, dying from hunger. **18** I shall get up and go to my father and I shall say to him, "Father, I have sinned against heaven and against you. **19** I no longer deserve to be called your son; treat me as you would treat one of your hired workers."' **20** So he got up and went back to his father. While he was still a long way off, his father caught sight of him, and was filled with compassion. He ran to his son, embraced him and kissed him. **21** His son said to him, 'Father, I have sinned against heaven and against you; I no longer deserve to be called your son.' **22** But his father ordered his servants, 'Quickly bring the finest robe and put it on him; put a ring on his finger and sandals on his feet. **23** Take the fattened calf and slaughter it. Then let us celebrate with a feast, **24** because this son of mine was dead, and has come to life again; he was lost, and has been found.' Then the celebration began. **25** Now the older son had been out in the field and, on his way back, as he neared the house, he heard the sound of music and dancing. **26** He called one of the servants and asked what this might mean. **27** The servant said to him, 'Your brother has returned and your father has slaughtered the fattened calf because he has him back safe and sound.' **28** He became angry, and when he refused to enter the house, his father came out and pleaded with him. **29** He said to his father in reply, 'Look, all these years I served you and not once did I disobey your orders; yet you never gave me even a young goat to feast on with my friends. **30** But when your son returns who swallowed up your property with prostitutes, for him you slaughter the fattened calf.' **31** He said to him, 'My son, you are here with me always; everything I have is yours. **32** But now we must celebrate and rejoice, because your brother was dead and has come to life again; he was lost and has been found.'"

This parable in Luke is perhaps the best known and most loved of Jesus' parables. It continues the theme of something lost being found, but on a more personal level. Rather than a sheep or a coin, it is a beloved son who is found. In a very profound way, this story reveals how infinitely merciful the Father can be, when we, His children, are repentant.

The parable continues the familiar theme of younger brother versus older brother (Cain and Abel, Jacob and Esau, Joseph and his brothers). Here, the younger brother seemed to go out of his way to create as much distance as possible from his father. The presumptuous and shameful demand for his inheritance was like telling his father that he was already dead in his eyes. Then he squandered his father's hard-earned money. Finally, working for a Gentile amongst unclean swine would not have made any Jewish father proud. Remarkably, actually unbelievably, sincere repentance made it all go away! The merciful, compassionate father forgave his son. He was once again an esteemed member of the family. The father lovingly welcomed him with an embrace and a kiss. He bestowed upon his repentant son a robe of honor, a ring of authority, and the sandals of a free man. His son was no longer a slave to sin.

The older son became the "slave." He was a slave to his anger and envy, perhaps like the scribes and Pharisees to whom the story was being addressed. The father tried to counter the elder son's self-righteous behavior with reassurance of his love and an invitation to join in the feast. Did he accept the father's invitation? Will we?

AT HIS FATHER'S REQUEST, THE son takes action. He quickly surmises that the sheep are at the root of the problem. He formulates a plan to restore order and to feed the guests. Since the food has been ruined, he will prepare some sheep **stew**! The son proceeds to round up the main ingredient. With all of the sheep piled in his arms, he disappears into the nearby kitchen. He quickly commences **stew** preparations. He first readies the sheep. Vegetables and seasonings are then added. The **stew** begins to simmer. Soon the appetizing aroma of the **stew** fills the air. The guests, eager for the **stew**, sit and wait patiently for it to cook. The son returns carrying an overflowing cauldron of **stew**. The host and son watch with satisfaction as the guests partake of the rich savory **stew**. This description of **stew** preparation and consumption represents the final parable associated with Landmark 29: THE PARABLE OF THE UNJUST (STEW)ARD.

THE PARABLE OF THE UNJUST
STEWARD

Lk 16:1–13

1 Then he also said to his disciples, "A rich man had a steward who was reported to him for squandering his property. **2** He summoned him and said, 'What is this I hear about you? Prepare a full account of your stewardship, because you can no longer be my steward.' **3** The steward said to himself, 'What shall I do, now that my master is taking the position of steward away from me? I am not strong enough to dig and I am ashamed to beg. **4** I know what I shall do so that, when I am removed from the stewardship, they may welcome me into their homes.' **5** He called in his master's debtors one by one. To the first he said, 'How much do you owe my master?' **6** He replied, 'One hundred measures of olive oil.' He said to him, 'Here is your promissory note. Sit down and quickly write one for fifty.' **7** Then to another he said, 'And you, how much do you owe?' He replied, 'One hundred kors of wheat.' He said to him, 'Here is your promissory note; write one for eighty.' **8** And the master commended that dishonest steward for acting prudently.

"For the children of this world are more prudent in dealing with their own generation than are the children of light. **9** I tell you, make friends for yourselves with dishonest wealth, so that when it fails, you will be welcomed into eternal dwellings. **10** The person who is trustworthy in very small matters is also trustworthy in great ones; and the person who is dishonest in very small matters is also dishonest in great ones. **11** If, therefore, you are not trustworthy with dishonest wealth, who will trust you with true wealth? **12** If you are not trustworthy with what belongs to another, who will give you what is yours? **13** No servant can serve two masters. He will either hate one and love the other, or be devoted to one and despise the other. You cannot serve God and mammon."

This parable is also found only in Luke. It also has a main character skilled at squandering property. Here the squanderer was not a wanderer, but a steward. A wealthy man would often have a steward, a head servant that he could trust to handle his business decisions. After being confronted by the master for his mismanagement, the steward proceeded to do more of the same. He quickly and selfishly prepared for his future by trying to endear himself to his master's debtors. He promptly squandered a large amount of wealth, behavior reminiscent of the lost son. Again we see an unexpected reaction. The rich man did not get angry. He actually commended the shrewdness of the steward! Preparing for the future is prudent.

We all have possessions. What we possess comes in various amounts and varieties: material wealth, physical skills, intellectual abilities, health, family, and friends. Most of what we have we take for granted. Some is earned through hard work; some is given to us by others. Ultimately, however, all we possess—including our life itself—is from God. Jesus instructs us to be good stewards of our possessions, but we are to act quickly. The short time we are given to prepare for the Kingdom makes it urgent. We are to use our "mammon" shrewdly to benefit others. In so doing, we benefit ourselves in our quest for lasting wealth, rather than temporal riches. Our possessions are a temporary loan to be invested in our eternal future.

Landmark 30:

BAG OF SILVER COINS

C ontinuing the journey, you see a plain-looking cloth bag lying in the road. You approach the **bag** with caution. It appears to be stuffed full of something. Curiously, you pull open the drawstring and peek inside. Wow! Someone has dropped a **bag** of **silver coins**. You spill the **silver coins** out onto the road and begin to count. One, two, three ... thirty. The **bag** is filled with **thirty silver coins**. You notice a coincidence. It was for **thirty silver coins** that Judas betrayed Jesus. There is another coincidence. You are in need of a thirtieth Landmark. This **bag of thirty silver coins** will be Landmark 30.

Who does the bag of silver coins belong to? Who could have dropped this small treasure? You decide to find out. You try to pick up the bag of coins and immediately realize it is much heavier than anticipated. Carrying them for any distance is out of the question. Luckily, a means of transport approaches. It is a **hippopotamus**! Yes, a large **hippo** quite capable of carrying the bag of silver coins happens to wander by. You struggle again to lift the coins. With a mighty heave, you sling the bag on the **hippo's** back. The slow lumbering **hippo** does not seem to notice the added burden. You and the coin-laden **hippo** proceed down the road in search of their owner. *Hippo* sounds like "hypocrisy," which helps recall the unit about THE HYPOCRISY OF THE PHARISEES.

THE HYPOCRISY OF THE PHARISEES

Lk 16:14–15

14 The Pharisees, who loved money, heard all these things and sneered at him. 15 And he said to them, "You justify yourselves

in the sight of others, but God knows your hearts; for what is of human esteem is an abomination in the sight of God."

―――――――

The Pharisees were again an example of how not to behave. Their misplaced values were a parable come to life. They saw money as an end in itself, something to be loved. The idea that it is God's gift to be shared with others was foreign and unacceptable to them. God knew their public displays were not heartfelt. This type of behavior will be addressed again by Jesus in an upcoming parable.

YOU AND THE COIN-CARRYING HIPPO have not gotten far. A police officer drives up and demands that you pull your hippo over. The officer says you are breaking **the law**. Actually, you are violating a number of **laws!** You cannot believe that your effort with the hippo to return the thirty coins is against **the law**. The **law** enforcement officer reiterates that **laws** have been broken. She then tells you about these hippo violations of **the law**:

Law 1: "No hippo shall be made to carry heavy coins."

Law 2: "Hippos are not allowed on paved roads."

Law 3: "Hippos must be walked on a leash."

Law 4: "Hippos—"

"Stop!" you scream.

You have heard enough hippo **laws**. The officer says there are more **laws**. You repeat that hearing more hippo violations is more than you can tolerate. This discussion about hippo **laws** and the officer reciting each **law** represents the unit, JESUS' SAYINGS ABOUT THE LAW.

JESUS' SAYINGS ABOUT THE LAW

Lk 16:16–17

16 "The law and the prophets lasted until John; but from then on the kingdom of God is proclaimed, and everyone who enters does so with violence. **17** It is easier for heaven and earth to pass away than for the smallest part of a letter of the law to become invalid."

This is a brief, but powerful unit. John the Baptist, whose time on the Gospel stage was brief but important, was again mentioned by Jesus. John was described as the bridge between the old and the new, between the Jewish prophesies of the coming Messiah and their fulfillment in Jesus. Those who choose to follow this path to the kingdom of God should expect difficulty along the way. Perhaps not the ultimate sacrifice John and Jesus made, but some degree of persecution nonetheless. Jesus reemphasized the importance of the Scriptures, as He had in the Sermon on the Mount. Jesus is the fulfillment of the law, but all that came before is still of great importance.

JUST AS THE OFFICER FINISHES her recitation of all the broken laws, a man approaches. He appears to be a very **rich man**! He is lavishly dressed and wearing an excessive amount of jewelry. He is definitely a **rich man**. Perhaps he is the man who dropped the bag of thirty silver coins. Soon the **rich man** spots the bag of coins atop the hippo. He begins to run toward you. While running, the **rich man** reaches into his pocket and pulls out a **laser**. That's right, a **laser**! It appears that the **rich man** is going to use the **laser** as a weapon. He must think you will not return his thirty silver coins. He begins to aim the piercing **laser** beam into your eyes. The **laser** is blinding. The officer orders the **rich man** to stop and put down the **laser**. He refuses. This scenario of the **rich man** with the **laser** helps to recall the story Jesus tells about THE RICH MAN AND LAZARUS.

THE RICH MAN AND LAZARUS

Lk 16:19–31

19 "There was a rich man who dressed in purple garments and fine linen and dined sumptuously each day. 20 And lying at his door was a poor man named Lazarus, covered with sores, 21 who would gladly have eaten his fill of the scraps that fell from the rich man's table. Dogs even used to come and lick his sores. 22 When the poor man died, he was carried away by angels to the bosom of Abraham. The rich man also died and was buried, 23 and from the netherworld, where he was in torment, he raised his eyes and saw Abraham far off and Lazarus at his side. 24 And he cried out, 'Father Abraham, have pity on me. Send Lazarus to dip the tip of his finger in water and cool my tongue, for I am suffering torment in these flames.' 25 Abraham replied, 'My child, remember that you received what was good during your lifetime while Lazarus likewise received what was bad; but now he is comforted here, whereas you are tormented. 26 Moreover, between us and you a great chasm is established to prevent anyone from crossing who might wish to go from our side to yours or from your side to ours.' 27 He said, 'Then I beg you, father, send him to my father's house, 28 for I have five brothers, so that he may warn them, lest they too come to this place of torment.' 29 But Abraham replied, 'They have Moses and the prophets. Let them listen to them.' 30 He said, 'Oh no, father Abraham, but if someone from the dead goes to them, they will repent.' 31 Then Abraham said, 'If they will not listen to Moses and the prophets, neither will they be persuaded if someone should rise from the dead.'"

This is more material found only in Luke. Jesus told another parable to His disciples and the Pharisees. This parable about the large-living rich man who ignored the sore-infested Lazarus was quite a reversal of fortunes. The rich man squandered the gift of his wealth on himself, disregarding the needy who were as close as his own front door. Unlike the prodigal son, he never repented and changed his ways. He was dogged by flames. Lazarus has left behind a life of misery and rests in the bosom of Abraham. It is Abraham who tells the once rich man that he has experienced all the good he will receive. Being blessed with material possessions was a gift. There was nothing inherently wrong with his wealth. What matters is the kind of steward you are with your wealth. Caring for the needy when able is very important in reaching the kingdom of God. Remember, there are many like Lazarus in our midst sorely in need of help.

MANY RICH MEN HAVE **servants**. This particular rich man with the laser was no exception, but he is currently angry with his **servant**. The rich man had blamed the **servant** for losing his bag of thirty silver coins. As punishment, he has made the **servant** follow far behind. He does not want to see the **servant's** face. As the rich man with the laser is running toward you and the police officer, he has forgotten about his **servant** trailing behind. While you are considering your options regarding the fast-approaching rich man, the **servant** also begins to run toward you. Now you have two attackers! But no! When the fleet-footed **servant** pulls even with the rich man, something quite unexpected occurs. The **servant** tackles the rich man! The laser goes flying. The **servant** has subdued his master and protected you from harm. You are grateful for this brave gesture. You are also grateful to recall the unit about THE ATTITUDE OF A SERVANT.

THE ATTITUDE OF A SERVANT

Lk 17:7–10

7 "Who among you would say to your servant who has just come in from plowing or tending sheep in the field, 'Come here immediately and take your place at table'? 8 Would he not rather say to him, 'Prepare something for me to eat. Put on your apron and wait on me while I eat and drink. You may eat and drink when I am finished'? 9 Is he grateful to that servant because he did what was commanded? 10 So should it be with you. When you have done all you have been commanded, say, 'We are unprofitable servants; we have done what we were obliged to do.'"

On the surface, this unit seems quite harsh. However, this is not about a relationship between two human beings. Jesus was making a point about our relationship with God. When we take on the role of disciple, we are accepting certain conditions that this relationship requires. Service to others is part of the bargain. It is part of our Christian duty. We should not expect a pat on the back or some form of material reward. All we have is due to the love and generosity of God. By doing our duty as disciples, we cannot repay or deem ourselves worthy of God's favor toward us. Certainly the good works we do as Christians are important, but there is nothing we can do that could equal what God has done for us.

Landmark 31:

NEW YEAR'S EVE PARTY

Recall that just two Landmarks ago you attended a festive outdoor party. Landmark 31 will be a special indoor party. What is the occasion? The majority of months have 31 days, so a month-ending party as was held for leap year in February would not be very special. However, there is one exception: December! The thirty-first of December is also the last day of the year. It is **New Year's Eve**. This particular thirty-first of the month is a celebration of anticipation of the year to come. It is a **New Year's Eve** party. The thirty-first Landmark will be a **New Year's Eve party**, but there will be a big difference from the recent party. You will not be a guest. You are hosting the **New Year's Eve party!**

You are hoping to make the New Year's Eve party special and memorable. For the decorations, no expense will be spared. You begin by illuminating the exterior of the house with a variety of colorful **laser** beams. Red **lasers** shine on the roof. Orange and yellow **lasers** light up the front of the house, while the back is lit with green and blue **laser** beams. A violet **laser** is focused on the garage. A spectacular **laser** light show will entertain your guests as they arrive for the party. You have some concern that the **laser** display will be so captivating that the guests will not want to come inside! All of the brightly shining **lasers** are another reminder of **Lazarus**. It is the story of when JESUS RAISES LAZARUS FROM THE DEAD.

JESUS RAISES LAZARUS FROM THE DEAD

Jn 11:1–44

1 Now a man was ill, Lazarus from Bethany, the village of Mary and her sister Martha. **2** Mary was the one who had anointed the Lord with perfumed oil and dried his feet with her hair; it was her brother Lazarus who was ill. **3** So the sisters sent word to him, saying, "Master, the one you love is ill." **4** When Jesus heard this he said, "This illness is not to end in death, but is for the glory of God, that the Son of God may be glorified through it." **5** Now Jesus loved Martha and her sister and Lazarus. **6** So when he heard that he was ill, he remained for two days in the place where he was. **7** Then after this he said to his disciples, "Let us go back to Judea." **8** The disciples said to him, "Rabbi, the Jews were just trying to stone you, and you want to go back there?" **9** Jesus answered, "Are there not twelve hours in a day? If one walks during the day, he does not stumble, because he sees the light of this world. **10** But if one walks at night, he stumbles, because the light is not in him." **11** He said this, and then told them, "Our friend Lazarus is asleep, but I am going to awaken him." **12** So the disciples said to him, "Master, if he is asleep, he will be saved." **13** But Jesus was talking about his death, while they thought that he meant ordinary sleep. **14** So then Jesus said to them clearly, "Lazarus has died. **15** And I am glad for you that I was not there, that you may believe. Let us go to him." **16** So Thomas, called Didymus, said to his fellow disciples, "Let us also go to die with him."

17 When Jesus arrived, he found that Lazarus had already been in the tomb for four days. **18** Now Bethany was near Jerusalem, only about two miles away. **19** And many of the Jews had come to Martha and Mary to comfort them about their brother. **20** When Martha heard that Jesus was coming, she went to meet him; but Mary sat at home. **21** Martha said to Jesus, "Lord, if you had been here, my brother would not have died. **22** [But] even now I know that whatever you ask of God, God will give you." **23** Jesus said to her, "Your brother will rise." **24** Martha said to him, "I know he will rise, in the resurrection on the last day." **25** Jesus told her, "I am the resurrection and the life; whoever believes in me, even if he dies, will live, **26** and everyone who lives and believes in me will never die. Do you believe this?" **27** She said to him, "Yes, Lord. I have come to believe that you are the Messiah, the Son of God, the one who is coming into the world."

28 When she had said this, she went and called her sister Mary secretly, saying, "The teacher is here and is asking for you." **29** As soon as she heard this, she rose quickly and went to him. **30** For Jesus had not yet come into the village, but was still where Martha had met him. **31** So when the Jews who were with her in the house comforting her saw Mary get up quickly and go out, they followed her, presuming that she was going to the tomb to weep there.

32 When Mary came to where Jesus was and saw him, she fell at his feet and said to him, "Lord, if you had been here, my brother would not have died." **33** When Jesus saw her weeping and the Jews who had come with her weeping, he became perturbed and deeply troubled, **34** and said, "Where have you laid him?" They said to him, "Sir, come and see." **35** And Jesus wept. **36** So the Jews said, "See how he loved him." **37** But some of them said, "Could not the one who opened the eyes of the blind man have done something so that this man would not have died?"

38 So Jesus, perturbed again, came to the tomb. It was a cave, and a stone lay across it. **39** Jesus said, "Take away the stone." Martha, the dead man's sister, said to him, "Lord, by now there will be a stench; he has been dead for four days." **40** Jesus said to her, "Did I not tell you that if you believe you will see the glory of God?" **41** So they took away the stone. And Jesus raised his eyes and said, "Father, I thank you for hearing me. **42** I know that you always hear me; but because of the crowd here I have said this, that they may believe that you sent me." **43** And when he had said this, he cried out in a loud voice, "Lazarus, come out!" **44** The dead man came out, tied hand and foot with burial bands, and his face was wrapped in a cloth. So Jesus said to them, "Untie him and let him go."

Again Jesus showed His union with the Father by performing the ultimate miracle or sign. Jesus had twice before restored life to the dead. Recall the widow's son (Landmark 11) and Jairus's daughter (Landmark 15). This resurrection miracle, found only in John, comes across as more powerful than the previous two. It seems as if Jesus waited several extra days so there would be no doubt that Lazarus was dead. This resulted in the dramatic emergence from the tomb of the cloth-covered Lazarus.

Jesus' miracles of restoring sight to the blind showed that He was the light of the world. With this miracle, there could be no doubt that He was also the life of the world. With His words of thanksgiving to the Father prior to the miracle, Jesus again showed that He was sent by and does the will of the Father. It was through the Father that Jesus was the life of the world. In Landmark 7 ("The Work of the Son" unit), Jesus spoke of the hour when all of the dead would hear His voice and come out from the tomb. This description of the Final Judgment is now played out in the story of Lazarus, by the work of the Son.

IT IS TIME TO DO some interior decorating for the New Year's Eve party. In keeping with the goal of making the party memorable, you have obtained several hundred bags of **sand**. No, you are not expecting a flood! You begin the heavy and tedious job of emptying the bags and spreading the **sand** throughout the house. It is a long process, but finally **sand** is spread a foot or so deep in every room. There is one exception; you did not spread **sand** in the kitchen. Wading through deep **sand** would significantly slow down party food preparation. It will be a challenge for the party guests to negotiate the **sand**. The **sand** will also get into their shoes and perhaps soil some party garb. However, the **sand** will help the guests have pleasant memories of the beach. Certainly slogging through the deep **sand** will also make it a memorable party! The **sand** will also help you remember "San(d)hedrin and more specifically a SESSION OF THE SANHEDRIN.

SESSION OF THE SANHEDRIN

Jn 11:45–54

45 Now many of the Jews who had come to Mary and seen what he had done began to believe in him. **46** But some of them went to the Pharisees and told them what Jesus had done. **47** So the chief priests and the Pharisees convened the Sanhedrin and said, "What are we going to do? This man is performing many signs. **48** If we leave him alone, all will believe in him, and the Romans will come and take away both our land and our nation." **49** But one of them, Caiaphas, who was high priest that year, said to them, "You know nothing, **50** nor do you consider that it is better for you that one man should die instead of the people, so that the whole nation may not perish." **51** He did not say this on his own, but since he was high priest for that year, he prophesied that Jesus was going to die for the nation, **52** and not only for the nation, but also to gather into one the dispersed children of God. **53** So from that day on they planned to kill him.

54 So Jesus no longer walked about in public among the Jews, but he left for the region near the desert, to a town called Ephraim, and there he remained with his disciples.

The chief priests and Pharisees were again fearful of Jesus and His influence. Recently (in Landmark 25), we saw them send guards to arrest Jesus. Now, as members of the Sanhedrin (the Jewish High Court), they made plans to kill Jesus. They planned something they did not have the authority to carry out. It is ironic that Jesus' action of restoring life triggered the planning of His death. The act of raising Lazarus from the dead was probably particularly offensive to one portion of the Sanhedrin. The Sadducees did not believe in resurrection. Other members of the Sanhedrin were more concerned with the political ramifications of Jesus' actions. Caiaphas, the high priest, (from AD 18–36) was accurate in saying that Jesus came for all people, Israelites and Gentiles everywhere.

WHEN ALL OF THE SAND has been spread, it is time to focus on the food. Since many people will be attending your New Year's Eve party, you have purchased a massive amount of food. You have hired **ten lepers** to prepare the food, and they are busy working in the sand-free kitchen. Though **ten lepers** were not your first choice to prepare the food, they seemed like nice people. The **lepers** were also available and in need of work. Entering the kitchen, you find the **ten lepers** hard at work. They are functioning like a well-oiled machine. Several **lepers** are preparing appetizers. More **lepers** are busy at the stove. The remaining **lepers** are creating elaborate desserts. You realize now that hiring the **ten lepers** was a stroke of genius. Watching the **ten lepers** prepare all of the party food also reminds you of when JESUS HEALS THE TEN LEPERS.

JESUS HEALS THE TEN LEPERS

Lk 17:11–19

11 As he continued his journey to Jerusalem, he traveled through Samaria and Galilee. 12 As he was entering a village, ten lepers met [him]. They stood at a distance from him 13 and raised their voice, saying, "Jesus, Master! Have pity on us!" 14 And when

he saw them, he said, "Go show yourselves to the priests." As they were going they were cleansed. **15** And one of them, realizing he had been healed, returned, glorifying God in a loud voice; **16** and he fell at the feet of Jesus and thanked him. He was a Samaritan. **17** Jesus said in reply, "Ten were cleansed, were they not? Where are the other nine? **18** Has none but this foreigner returned to give thanks to God?" **19** Then he said to him, "Stand up and go; your faith has saved you."

As Jesus continued the walk toward His death in Jerusalem, He also continued to restore life. As in Landmark 6, Jesus again encountered the dreaded disease of leprosy. The previous leper had approached Jesus, but these ten begged for healing from a distance. Here the healing itself was brief. The focus of the unit is on the encounter between Jesus and the one grateful leper who returned to give thanks. The healed leper's return to Jesus signified an inner conversion. He received more than an outward healing. Jesus indicated a greater reward with His closing words, "Your faith has saved you." The salvation of this Samaritan man was another proclamation that God's salvation is for all people. It was also an indication that the future work of the church would be to minister to everyone. We are all diseased in some way and in need of Jesus' healing.

THERE IS ONE LAST CHORE to do before the New Year's Eve party begins. The windows need to be washed. Even though it is a nighttime party, you must clean the filthy **windows**. Some of the **windows** are so caked with dirt that you cannot see through them. There are even a few cobwebs on some of the **windows**. Washing **windows** is not your favorite activity, but it must be done. You gather all of your **window**-cleaning supplies and a ladder. As you begin washing the **windows**, you are filled with excitement and anticipation waiting for the first guests to arrive. *Window* sounds like "widow." The **window** washing is a reminder of THE PARABLE OF THE PERSISTENT WIDOW.

THE PARABLE OF THE PERSISTENT
WIDOW

Lk 18:1–8

1 Then he told them a parable about the necessity for them to pray always without becoming weary. He said, 2 "There was a judge in a certain town who neither feared God nor respected any human being. 3 And a widow in that town used to come to him and say, 'Render a just decision for me against my adversary.' 4 For a long time the judge was unwilling, but eventually he thought, 'While it is true that I neither fear God nor respect any human being, 5 because this widow keeps bothering me I shall deliver a just decision for her lest she finally come and strike me.'" 6 The Lord said, "Pay attention to what the dishonest judge says. 7 Will not God then secure the rights of his chosen ones who call out to him day and night? Will he be slow to answer them? 8 I tell you, he will see to it that justice is done for them speedily. But when the Son of Man comes, will he find faith on earth?"

As Jesus' disciples continue to follow Him toward the cross, we continue to learn what it means to truly be one of His disciples. In the healing of the lepers, we saw the importance of faith and thanksgiving. In this parable found in Luke, we learn about faith and the need for prayer. Not just prayer, but persistent prayer. To emphasize this point, Jesus chose characters at the opposite ends of the power spectrum: a powerful and apparently unjust judge who rendered legal decisions and a widow with no legal standing in Jewish society. The widow's continued pestering for justice finally wore the judge down. She obtained the decision she had relentlessly sought. If an unjust judge could be persuaded to deliver justice, then surely a loving and gracious God will hear our prayer and do the same, though our prayer is of course not always answered as we would like. Furthermore, we are not powerless widows. We are so loved by God that He sacrificed His Son for us!

This parable goes beyond persistence. We are told of the necessity to "pray always." This is a tall order in a busy, distracting life. However, our lives can be led so that our daily actions themselves are a form of prayer. Others have taken a more literal approach to these instructions with the "Jesus Prayer." In their minds, and eventually in their hearts, are the words "Lord Jesus Christ, Son of God, have mercy on me, a sinner." These words encapsulate the meaning of the parable. A strong faith drives a desire to always be in contact with our God through prayer. Hopefully, this is the faith the Son of Man will find in our hearts when He returns.

YOU ARE NOW LOOKING THROUGH a clean window and waiting for the arrival of the first guests. Here comes someone! It is a woman you had concerns about inviting. Your concerns are now justified. She is dressed in a **fairy** outfit! It is not a costume party, yet here she is dressed as a **fairy**. She has little wings on her back. Sequined tights and a wand complete the outfit. There is no doubt she is trying to be a **fairy**. You can tolerate her appearance, but what she is doing is another matter. The **fairy** is dropping **tacks** on your lawn, driveway, and sidewalk. Yes, sharp, pointy **tacks**! Other guests are sure to step on or even fall on the **tacks**. You must act quickly. You run outside and yell to the **fairy** to stop spreading the **tacks**. Then you begin to **collect** the **tacks** as fast as you can. You **collect** them from the sidewalk and driveway first. Then comes the more tedious job of **tack collecting** from the grass. Thankfully, the **fairy** has stopped scattering the **tacks**. Finally, all of the **tacks** have been **collected**! You are relieved and pleased that you were such an efficient **tack collector**. This last scene of preparation for the New Year's Eve party signifies THE PARABLE OF THE PHARISEE (FAIRY) AND THE TAX (TACK) COLLECTOR.

THE PARABLE OF THE PHARISEE AND THE TAX COLLECTOR

Lk 18:9–14

9 He then addressed this parable to those who were convinced of their own righteousness and despised everyone else. **10** "Two people went up to the temple area to pray; one was a Pharisee and the other was a tax collector. **11** The Pharisee took up his position and spoke this prayer to himself, 'O God, I thank you that I am not like the rest of humanity—greedy, dishonest, adulterous—or even like this tax collector. **12** I fast twice a week, and I pay tithes on my whole income.' **13** But the tax collector stood off at a distance and would not even raise his eyes to heaven but beat his breast and prayed, 'O God, be merciful to me a sinner.' **14** I tell you, the latter went home justified, not the former; for everyone who exalts himself will be humbled, and the one who humbles himself will be exalted."

————————————

In this parable, Jesus contrasts two styles of prayer. He compares a Pharisee, who should be a role model in the religious community, to the universally despised tax collector. The Pharisee proudly recited his actions to God. An all-knowing God was already fully aware of his behavior. The Pharisee's practice of traditional forms of piety were a good thing, but what of his self-righteous attitude? The tax collector rightly took a more humble approach and posture. He knew he was a sinner in need of God's mercy. His prayer was actually a portion of the "Jesus Prayer" mentioned previously. It was this tax collector, rejected by men, who found favor in the eyes of God.

Landmark 32:

ICE

You are in need of a thirty-second Landmark. While looking for the Landmark, you begin to slip and slide. It is impossible to keep your balance. You ungracefully fall and land on your backside. Fortunately, you are unharmed. Looking about, you realize you are sitting on a cold, wet, slick sheet of **ice**. No wonder walking had been such a challenge. You were searching for the Landmark while walking on **ice**! You now realize that Landmark 32 is the **ice**, since at 32 degrees Fahrenheit water freezes and becomes **ice**. Thus, Landmark 32 is now making your backside a bit chilly!

This sheet of ice is in a very unusual place. Typically, a sheet of ice is outside or indoors at a skating rink. Imagine that it is indoors, but inside a church! The center aisle of the church is a thick, slick sheet of ice. This is unfortunate, since a wedding is about to begin in this very church. The **bride,** radiant in her wedding dress, is understandably worried about sliding down the icy aisle. Fortunately, a sure-footed white **horse** is standing nearby. The brave **bride** quickly jumps up on the surprised **horse,** gown and all. The **bride** then slowly coaxes the **horse** down the ice-covered aisle. The pair make quite a sight as they cautiously approach the altar. This memorable scene of **bride** and **horse** represent the first unit to be associated with the ice. The **bride** represents marriage. Recall from Landmark 5 that **horse** stands for divorce. This unit is JESUS' TEACHING ON MARRIAGE AND DIVORCE.

JESUS' TEACHING ON MARRIAGE AND DIVORCE

Mt 19:1–12

1 When Jesus finished these words, he left Galilee and went to the district of Judea across the Jordan. **2** Great crowds followed him, and he cured them there. **3** Some Pharisees approached him, and tested him, saying, "Is it lawful for a man to divorce his wife for any cause whatever?" **4** He said in reply, "Have you not read that from the beginning the Creator 'made them male and female' **5** and said, 'For this reason a man shall leave his father and mother and be joined to his wife, and the two shall become one flesh'? **6** So they are no longer two, but one flesh. Therefore, what God has joined together, no human being must separate." **7** They said to him, "Then why did Moses command that the man give the woman a bill of divorce and dismiss [her]?" **8** He said to them, "Because of the hardness of your hearts Moses allowed you to divorce your wives, but from the beginning it was not so. **9** I say to you, whoever divorces his wife (unless the marriage is unlawful) and marries another commits adultery." **10** [His] disciples said to him, "If that is the case of a man with his wife, it is better not to marry." **11** He answered, "Not all can accept [this] word, but only those to whom that is granted. **12** Some are incapable of marriage because they were born so; some, because they were made so by others; some, because they have renounced marriage for the sake of the kingdom of heaven. Whoever can accept this ought to accept it."

Mk 10:1–12

1 He set out from there and went into the district of Judea [and] across the Jordan. Again crowds gathered around him and, as was his custom, he again taught them. **2** The Pharisees approached and asked, "Is it lawful for a husband to divorce his wife?" They were testing him. **3** He said to them in reply, "What did Moses command you?" **4** They replied, "Moses permitted him to write a bill of divorce and dismiss her." **5** But Jesus told them, "Because of the hardness of your hearts he wrote you this commandment. **6** But from the beginning of creation, 'God made them male and female. **7** For this reason a man shall leave his father and mother [and be joined to his wife], **8** and the two shall become one flesh.' So they are no longer two but one flesh. **9** Therefore what God has joined together no human being must separate." **10** In the house the disciples again questioned him about this. **11** He said to them, "Whoever divorces his wife and marries another commits adultery against her; **12** and if she divorces her husband and marries another, she commits adultery."

18 "Everyone who divorces his wife and marries another commits adultery, and the one who marries a woman divorced from her husband commits adultery."

———————————

We heard Jesus speak briefly about marriage and divorce in the Sermon on the Mount in Landmark 5. Jesus essentially did away with all but one of the grounds for divorce that had been granted under Mosaic Law (Deut 24:1–4). Here Jesus repeated the message that divorce and remarriage is akin to adultery unless the marriage was "unlawful." Here He expounded on those words. The teaching was prompted by the Pharisees posing a trick question. Their hope was that Jesus would answer in such a way as to anger Herod Antipas, who had divorced and remarried under very questionable circumstances.

John the Baptist's opinion about Herod's marital activity had cost him his head. Perhaps Jesus' words would lead to a similar fate. Jesus asked the supposedly learned Pharisees the same type of question He posed back in Landmark 7. The question began: "Have you not read ..." It was a little jab at their intellectual pride. Jesus referred to the Book of Genesis and the creation of man and woman who would join to become "one flesh" (Gen 2:21–24). Marriage was established by the Creator, so what authority does man have to break the bond? Here Jesus restored God's original intent. It had been weakened by Moses, who had allowed for the "hardness" of men's hearts. Jesus conceded this was a difficult, challenging teaching and that some are just not capable of marriage.

Controversy still exists today as to the meaning of "unlawful" marriage and the allowing of divorce. Suffice it to say that marriage is of the utmost importance in the eyes of God. It should be cherished and nurtured and not be entered into lightly.

WHEN THE HORSE REACHES THE front of the church, the bride carefully dismounts. She thanks the horse for the ride. The bride is then greeted by two **children**, the ring bearer and the flower girl. The **children** had not ventured down the aisle due to the precarious conditions. The **children** had entered from the side carrying the flowers and rings. Both of the **chil-**

dren are beaming with excitement, happy to be part of the wedding. You marvel at how well-behaved the **children** are. The presence of the **children** serves as a reminder of JESUS' BLESSING OF THE CHILDREN.

JESUS' BLESSSING OF THE CHILDREN

Mt 19:13–15

13 Then children were brought to him that he might lay his hands on them and pray. The disciples rebuked them, 14 but Jesus said, "Let the children come to me, and do not prevent them; for the kingdom of heaven belongs to such as these." 15 After he placed his hands on them, he went away.

Mk 10:13–16

13 And people were bringing children to him that he might touch them, but the disciples rebuked them. 14 When Jesus saw this he became indignant and said to them, "Let the children come to me; do not prevent them, for the kingdom of God belongs to such as these. 15 Amen, I say to you, whoever does not accept the kingdom of God like a child will not enter it." 16 Then he embraced them and blessed them, placing his hands on them.

Lk 18:15–17

15 People were bringing even infants to him that he might touch them, and when the disciples saw this, they rebuked them. 16 Jesus, however, called the children to himself and said, "Let the children come to me and do not prevent them; for the kingdom of God belongs to such as these. 17 Amen, I say to you, whoever does not accept the kingdom of God like a child will not enter it."

A favorite image for many people is of Jesus sitting and surrounded by children. Parents showed their faith in Jesus by bringing their children to Him for a blessing. Jesus' concern and respect for children was unusual for His time. However, this unit is more about the kingdom of God than about Jesus and His interactions with children. Our attitude toward the Kingdom should be like many of the traits seen in children. We need to be open and receptive. Like children, we have no claim to the Kingdom based on our status or power. We are dependent on God and His loving mercy. The kingdom of God is not something to be earned. It is a gift.

YOU HAVE SEEN A BRIDE on a horse ride down an ice-covered church aisle. You have just seen the children with the flowers and rings. Where is the groom? You wonder if the groom has gotten cold feet. Just then the children run over and open the church's side door. In walks a lavishly dressed **young man**! This **young man** must be the groom. Judging by his fine clothing and jewelry, he must be a **rich young man**. He also looks familiar. He very much resembles the rich older man you encountered in Landmark 30. In fact, this **rich young man** is his son. With jewels shimmering, the **rich young man** strolls over and joins hands with his bride. The groom represents the unit when JESUS SPEAKS WITH THE RICH YOUNG MAN.

JESUS SPEAKS WITH THE RICH YOUNG MAN

Mt 19:16–30

16 Now someone approached him and said, "Teacher, what good must I do to gain eternal life?" **17** He answered him, "Why do you ask me about the good? There is only One who is good. If you wish to enter into life, keep the commandments." **18** He asked him, "Which ones?" And Jesus replied, "'You shall not kill; you shall not commit adultery; you shall not steal; you shall not bear false witness; **19** honor your father and your mother'; and 'you shall love your neighbor as yourself.'" **20** The young man said to him, "All of these I have observed. What do I still lack?" **21** Jesus said to him, "If you wish to be perfect, go, sell what you have and give to [the] poor, and you will have treasure in heaven. Then come, follow me." **22** When the young man heard this statement, he went away sad, for he had many possessions. **23** Then Jesus said to his disciples, "Amen, I say to you, it will be hard for one who is rich to enter the kingdom of heaven. **24** Again I say to you, it is easier for a camel to pass through the eye of a needle than for one who is rich to enter the kingdom of God." **25** When the disciples heard this, they were greatly astonished and said, "Who then can be saved?" **26** Jesus looked at them and said, "For human beings this is impossible, but for God all things are possible." **27** Then Peter said to him in reply, "We have given up everything and followed you. What will there be for us?" **28** Jesus said to them, "Amen, I say to you that you who have followed me, in the new age, when the Son of Man is seated on his throne of glory, will yourselves sit on twelve thrones, judging the twelve tribes of Israel. **29** And everyone who has given up houses or brothers or sisters or father or mother or children or lands for the sake of my name will receive a hundred times more, and will inherit eternal life. **30** But many who are first will be last, and the last will be first."

Mk 10:17–31

17 As he was setting out on a journey, a man ran up, knelt down before him, and asked him, "Good teacher, what must I do to inherit eternal life?" **18** Jesus answered him, "Why do you call me good? No one is good but God alone. **19** You know the commandments: 'You shall not kill; you shall not commit adultery; you shall not steal; you shall not bear false witness; you shall not defraud; honor your father and your mother.'" **20** He replied and said to him, "Teacher, all of these I have observed from my youth." **21** Jesus, looking at him, loved him and said to him, "You are lacking in one thing. Go, sell what you have, and give to [the] poor and you will have treasure in heaven; then come, follow me." **22** At that statement his face fell, and he went away sad, for he had many possessions.

23 Jesus looked around and said to his disciples, "How hard it is for those who have wealth to enter the kingdom of God!" **24** The disciples were amazed at his words. So Jesus again said to them in reply, "Children, how hard it is to enter the kingdom of God! **25** It is easier for a camel to pass through [the] eye of [a] needle than for one who is rich to enter the kingdom of God." **26** They were exceedingly astonished and said among themselves, "Then who can be saved?" **27** Jesus looked at them and said, "For human beings it is impossible, but not for God. All things are possible for God." **28** Peter began to say to him, "We have given up everything and followed you." **29** Jesus said, "Amen, I say to you, there is no one who has given up house or brothers or sisters or mother or father or children or lands for my sake and for the sake of the gospel **30** who will not receive a hundred times more now in this present age: houses and brothers and sisters and mothers and children and lands, with persecutions, and eternal life in the age to come. **31** But many that are first will be last, and [the] last will be first."

Lk 18:18–30

18 An official asked him this question, "Good teacher, what must I do to inherit eternal life?" **19** Jesus answered him, "Why do you call me good? No one is good but God alone. **20** You know the commandments, 'You shall not commit adultery; you shall not kill; you shall not steal; you shall not bear false witness; honor your father and your mother.'" **21** And he replied, "All of these I have observed from my youth." **22** When Jesus heard this he said to him, "There is still one thing left for you: sell all that you have and distribute it to the poor, and you will have a treasure in heaven. Then come, follow me." **23** But when he heard this he became quite sad, for he was very rich.

24 Jesus looked at him [now sad] and said, "How hard it is for those who have wealth to enter the kingdom of God! **25** For it is easier for a camel to pass through the eye of a needle than for a rich person to enter the kingdom of God." **26** Those who heard this said, "Then who can be saved?" **27** And he said, "What is impossible for human beings is possible for God." **28** Then Peter said, "We have given up our possessions and followed you." **29** He said to them, "Amen, I say to you, there is no one who has given up house or wife or brothers or parents or children for the sake of the kingdom of God **30** who will not receive [back] an overabundant return in this present age and eternal life in the age to come."

The rich young man asked Jesus a question we would all like the answer to. The first part of Jesus' response was challenging and not unexpected. The second part was surprising and also quite challenging if you are fortunate (or perhaps unfortunate) enough to have possessions or wealth. Parting with possessions is very difficult. With the camel comment, Jesus indicated that without God's assistance it is impossible for a rich man to enter the Kingdom.

In Jesus' time, people believed that wealth was a sign of God's favor. Jesus reversed this idea. Wealth can be a stumbling block that separates us from others. It can be a distraction that places our focus on earthly things rather than on God. God can free us from our attachment to possessions. Wealth itself is not the problem. It is our attitude toward money and what we do with it that causes trouble. If we are true disciples of Christ and put the transitory nature of material riches in perspective, we realize the reward of eternal life is infinitely more important. In doing so, our happiness in this present life will likely be greater.

YOU, THE WEDDING PARTY, AND all of the invited guests are now ready for the wedding to begin. There is one important person still missing. The minister has not yet arrived. Everyone is getting restless, especially the many guests. Looking out over the congregation, you are surprised at what you see. All of the guests appear to be **laborers**. Everyone is wearing dirty, soiled clothing indicating recent physical **labor**. Each guest also has **vines** draped over their shoulders. How unusual for **laborers** to attend a wedding in their work clothes while draped with **vines**. Closer inspection reveals the **vines** to be grape **vines**. The guests are all **laborers** in the nearby **vineyard**. These **laborers in the vineyard** must be friends and relatives of the bride and groom. The church full of **laborers in the vineyard** represents Jesus' PARABLE OF LABORERS IN THE VINEYARD.

|||||||||||||||||||||||||||||||||||||||||||||||||||||||||||||||||||||||||||||||||||||||||||||||||||||||||||||||||||||||||||||||||||||||||||||||||

PARABLE OF LABORERS IN THE VINEYARD

|||||||||||||||||||||||||||||||||||||||||||||||||||||||||||||||||||||||||||||||||||||||||||||||||||||||||||||||||||||||||||||||||||||||||||||||||

Mt 20:1–16

1 "The kingdom of heaven is like a landowner who went out at dawn to hire laborers for his vineyard. 2 After agreeing with them for the usual daily wage, he sent them into his vineyard. 3 Going out about nine o'clock, he saw others standing idle in the marketplace, 4 and he said to them, 'You too go into my vineyard, and I will give you what is just.' 5 So they went off. [And] he went out again around noon, and around three o'clock, and did likewise. 6 Going out about five o'clock, he found others standing around, and said to them, 'Why do you stand here idle all day?' 7 They answered, 'Because no one has hired us.' He said to them, 'You too go into my vineyard.' 8 When it was evening the owner of the vineyard said to his foreman, 'Summon the laborers and give them their pay, beginning with the last and ending with the first.' 9 When those who had started about five o'clock came, each received the usual daily wage. 10 So when the first came, they thought that they would receive more, but each of them also got the usual wage. 11 And on receiving it they grumbled against the landowner, 12 saying, 'These last ones worked only one hour, and you have made them equal to us, who bore the day's burden and the heat.' 13 He said to one of them in reply, 'My friend, I am not cheating you. Did you not agree with me for the usual daily wage? 14 Take what is yours and go. What if I wish to give this last one the same as you? 15 [Or] am I not free to do as I wish with my own money? Are you envious because I am generous?' 16 Thus, the last will be first, and the first will be last."

In the previous unit, Jesus urged people to be generous with their God-given wealth and possessions. Here He told a parable about the Kingdom and described the generosity of God. All of the workers were given the same daily wage, much to the surprise and dismay of the workers called earlier in the day. They had understandably expected more compensation. Human expectations are not the same as God's. The "all-generous" love of God provided not only for the long-suffering Jews who came to believe in Jesus, but for everyone else, too!

Those hired late in the day were not lazy. They had been looking for work, but were not given the opportunity. This is akin to Jesus' teaching that the Gentiles, like the Jews, are welcome in the Kingdom. This must have been a surprise to many Jews, since they had been called to be God's chosen people some two thousand years earlier.

People come to know and believe in Jesus at different times in their lives. Many come to know Him in the dawn of childhood. Others develop a relationship with Jesus in the midday of middle age. Others come to Jesus in the afternoon and evening of life. God generously always welcomes all into the Kingdom.

RECORD ALBUM

Recent advances in technology have provided new ways to listen to our favorite music. For many years, and not too many years ago, music was served up on a vinyl platter. The vinyl **record** with its long spiral groove was music to our ears. The **record album**, a long-playing (LP) vinyl disc, was placed on a turntable. The **record** would then spin thirty-three times each minute as a needle tracked along the **record's** groove. The **record** was sometimes simply referred to as a 33, referring to its RPMs (revolutions per minute). Since we are now in need of a thirty-third Landmark, a vinyl record, which spun at 33 RPMs, will work just fine. Imagine yourself holding an old vinyl **record album**. Since these records have made a comeback, the **record** you hold may even be new. Either way, the thirty-third Landmark is a vinyl **record album**.

Holding the vinyl record album, you notice it is warped. It cannot be played unless it is flattened back into its original shape. You begin to search for something to place on the record to flatten it out. Nearby, you spot three bright spherical objects. They look heavy enough to do the job. The three spheres are also quite familiar. They are **crystal balls** identical to the ones encountered back in Landmarks 22 and 23. You walk over to the **three crystal balls**. After inspecting them, you decide that they will be perfect. You give each of the **three crystal balls** a nudge with your foot. They begin to roll toward the warped record you left lying on the ground. One, two, **three**, each **crystal ball** slowly comes to rest on a portion of the record. You now stand and wait for the weight of the **three crystal balls** to make the record playable. As before, a **crystal ball** represents a prediction, specifically a Passion prediction. The **three crystal balls** are thus the unit when Jesus makes THE THIRD PASSION PREDICTION.

THE THIRD PASSION PREDICTION

Mt 20:17–19

17 As Jesus was going up to Jerusalem, he took the twelve [disciples] aside by themselves, and said to them on the way, **18** "Behold, we are going up to Jerusalem, and the Son of Man will be handed over to the chief priests and the scribes, and they will condemn him to death, **19** and hand him over to the Gentiles to be mocked and scourged and crucified, and he will be raised on the third day."

Mk 10:32–34

32 They were on the way, going up to Jerusalem, and Jesus went ahead of them. They were amazed, and those who followed were afraid. Taking the Twelve aside again, he began to tell them what was going to happen to him. **33** "Behold, we are going up to Jerusalem, and the Son of Man will be handed over to the chief priests and the scribes, and they will condemn him to death and hand him over to the Gentiles **34** who will mock him, spit upon him, scourge him, and put him to death, but after three days he will rise."

Lk 18:31–34

31 Then he took the Twelve aside and said to them, "Behold, we are going up to Jerusalem and everything written by the prophets about the Son of Man will be fulfilled. **32** He will be handed over to the Gentiles and he will be mocked and insulted and spat upon; **33** and after they have scourged him they will kill him, but on the third day he will rise." **34** But they understood nothing of this; the word remained hidden from them and they failed to comprehend what he said.

There are some differences in the three accounts of Jesus' prediction of His impending death. We will focus on the similarities. With the crucifixion drawing closer, Jesus' prediction became more specific and detailed. He described how God's plan would be carried out through a collaborative effort of the Jewish leaders and Roman authorities. The Jews would condemn Jesus on false charges. The Romans would then take care of the dirty (and bloody) work. Jesus clearly understood and accepted His destiny. He did not demand more from His disciples (or from us) than He did from Himself. There will be suffering in following Jesus, but He taught repeatedly that it pales in comparison to the reward. In Luke, the disciples did not understand this Passion prediction or its implications. Matthew and Mark make the disciples' ignorance evident in the next unit.

YOU ARE GETTING MORE EXCITED to listen to the record, even though you do not know what music it contains. You have not yet looked to see the name of the artist. The three crystal balls cover the label, so you will just have to wait a bit longer. Finally, you can no longer contain your curiosity. Pushing aside the crystal balls reveals the name **James** Taylor. Great! You love **James**'s music. You assume the flip side contains additional **James** Taylor songs. You turn the record over to find that you were mistaken. Recordings by **John** Lennon are on the flip side. You are surprised and pleased. **John's** music is great. This record is quite a find. The music of **James and John** on the same album. Perhaps some of the songs have **James and John** performing together! The discovery of these two music legends on the same record stands for our next unit: THE REQUEST OF JAMES AND JOHN.

THE REQUEST OF JAMES AND JOHN

Mt 20:20–28

20 Then the mother of the sons of Zebedee approached him with her sons and did him homage, wishing to ask him for something. **21** He said to her, "What do you wish?" She answered him, "Command that these two sons of mine sit, one at your right and the other at your left, in your kingdom." **22** Jesus said in reply, "You do not know what you are asking. Can you drink the cup that I am going to drink?" They said to him, "We can." **23** He replied, "My cup you will indeed drink, but to sit at my right and at my left [, this] is not mine to give but is for those for whom it has been prepared by my Father." **24** When the ten heard this, they became indignant at the two brothers. **25** But Jesus summoned them and said, "You know that the rulers of the Gentiles lord it over them, and the great ones make their authority over them felt. **26** But it shall not be so among you. Rather, whoever wishes to be great among you shall be your servant; **27** whoever wishes to be first among you shall be your slave. **28** Just so, the Son of Man did not come to be served but to serve and to give his life as a ransom for many."

Mk 10:35–45

35 Then James and John, the sons of Zebedee, came to him and said to him, "Teacher, we want you to do for us whatever we ask of you." 36 He replied, "What do you wish [me] to do for you?" 37 They answered him, "Grant that in your glory we may sit one at your right and the other at your left." 38 Jesus said to them, "You do not know what you are asking. Can you drink the cup that I drink or be baptized with the baptism with which I am baptized?" 39 They said to him, "We can." Jesus said to them, "The cup that I drink, you will drink, and with the baptism with which I am baptized, you will be baptized; 40 but to sit at my right or at my left is not mine to give but is for those for whom it has been prepared." 41 When the ten heard this, they became indignant at James and John. 42 Jesus summoned them and said to them, "You know that those who are recognized as rulers over the Gentiles lord it over them, and their great ones make their authority over them felt. 43 But it shall not be so among you. Rather, whoever wishes to be great among you will be your servant; 44 whoever wishes to be first among you will be the slave of all. 45 For the Son of Man did not come to be served but to serve and to give his life as a ransom for many."

Of the twelve apostles, Peter, James, and John are considered to have had the closest relationship with Jesus. They were the so-called "inner circle." That makes it all the more surprising that James and John would make such a bold request. This request indicated that even then they did not grasp the true meaning of Jesus' teachings and purpose. Matthew lessened their presumptuous, status-seeking request by having their mother pose the question, not even mentioning James and John by name. Jesus did not scold them for the bold request. Instead He explained that a place in the Kingdom would require suffering.

To "drink of the cup" was a reference to Jesus' upcoming suffering. It was a phrase used in the Hebrew Scriptures (Isaiah, Jeremiah) to represent suffering. James and John did suffer for Christ. In later years, they were martyred and exiled, respectively.

In this unit, Jesus also commented on what it means to be a Christian leader. Power and authority are not to be used to bully others. Just the opposite is suggested. The behavior of a humble servant, one without any legal rights or authority, should be adopted. Again Jesus' radical teaching turned traditional teaching and practice upside down. Jesus Himself provided the perfect example of this behavior. The Son of God willingly gave His life to free us from the slavery of sin.

IT IS NOW TIME TO listen to the record with songs from both James and John. While placing the record on the turntable, you feel a touch on your shoulder. Then a strangely familiar voice says, "You might like this one, too." You turn around and cannot believe your eyes. To say you are met with a wonderful surprise would be appropriate. It is Stevie Wonder! Though **blind**, he was able to find you. Stevie smiles and hands you an autographed album entitled, *The Best of Stevie Wonder.* You are overwhelmed, but manage to thank Mr. Wonder for his gift. Stevie Wonder has always been one of your favorite artists. You greatly admire his music and how he has succeeded in spite of his **blindness**. This encounter serves as a reminder of JESUS' HEALING OF THE BLIND.

JESUS' HEALING OF THE BLIND

Mt 20:29–34

29 As they left Jericho, a great crowd followed him. 30 Two blind men were sitting by the roadside, and when they heard that Jesus was passing by, they cried out, "[Lord,] Son of David, have pity on us!" 31 The crowd warned them to be silent, but they called out all the more, "Lord, Son of David, have pity on us!" 32 Jesus stopped and called them and said, "What do you want me to do for you?" 33 They answered him, "Lord, let our eyes be opened." 34 Moved with pity, Jesus touched their eyes. Immediately they received their sight, and followed him.

Mk 10:46–52

46 They came to Jericho. And as he was leaving Jericho with his disciples and a sizable crowd, Bartimaeus, a blind man, the son of Timaeus, sat by the roadside begging. 47 On hearing that it was Jesus of Nazareth, he began to cry out and say, "Jesus, son of David, have pity on me." 48 And many rebuked him, telling him to be silent. But he kept calling out all the more, "Son of David, have pity on me." 49 Jesus stopped and said, "Call him." So they called the blind man, saying to him, "Take courage; get up, he is calling you." 50 He threw aside his cloak, sprang up, and came to Jesus.

51 Jesus said to him in reply, "What do you want me to do for you?" The blind man replied to him, "Master, I want to see." **52** Jesus told him, "Go your way; your faith has saved you." Immediately he received his sight and followed him on the way.

Lk 18:35–43

35 Now as he approached Jericho a blind man was sitting by the roadside begging, **36** and hearing a crowd going by, he inquired what was happening. **37** They told him, "Jesus of Nazareth is passing by." **38** He shouted, "Jesus, Son of David, have pity on me!" **39** The people walking in front rebuked him, telling him to be silent, but he kept calling out all the more, "Son of David, have pity on me!" **40** Then Jesus stopped and ordered that he be brought to him; and when he came near, Jesus asked him, **41** "What do you want me to do for you?" He replied, "Lord, please let me see." **42** Jesus told him, "Have sight; your faith has saved you." **43** He immediately received his sight and followed him, giving glory to God. When they saw this, all the people gave praise to God.

You have seen Jesus restore sight to the blind on several occasions. The unit in Landmark 15 recorded only by Matthew is similar to the current healing described by Matthew, Mark, and Luke. In both stories, the blind men expressed their faith. Jesus touched their eyes, and their sight was restored. In all three of the current healings, the blind referred to Jesus as the "Son of David." This reflected the common belief that the Messiah would be a descendent of the great king. It was perhaps also a reference to Solomon, who was literally the Son of David and who also had healing power.

In this unit, Mark and Luke describe Jesus healing one rather than two blind men. In Mark, the blind man who came to Jesus was named Bartimaeus. This is different from Mark's last story of Jesus' healing of the blind man in Bethesda (Landmark 21). There the man was unnamed and brought to Jesus. His sight was restored gradually, and he was told to keep the healing a secret. Here, Bartimaeus is healed instantly and then follows Jesus. If blindness is a metaphor for a lack of faith and understanding, these different healings in Mark mirror the disciples' development of faith and understanding. Back in Caesarea Philippi, when they began the journey toward Jerusalem, their faith was shaky. Now in Jericho, only fifteen miles northeast of Jerusalem, they saw Jesus more clearly. Hopefully as we walk through life with Jesus, our faith will also grow stronger and we will see Him more clearly.

STEVIE WONDER HAS GIVEN YOU a gift. It would certainly be nice to give him a small token of your appreciation. Looking around, there does not seem to be anything appropriate. You then remember that you do have something he might like. Reaching into your pocket, you pull out a small **zucchini**. It is your special "good luck" **zucchini**. You are so accustomed to carrying the **zucchini**, you almost forgot about it. It is a beautiful, yellow, homegrown **zucchini**. You ask Mr. Wonder if he likes **zucchini**. He responds, "Of course I like **zucchini**; it is my favorite vegetable." He goes on to tell you he likes everything about **zucchini**. He likes the smell, the texture, and especially the taste of **zucchini**. You then hand Mr. Wonder your "good luck" **zucchini**. The **zucchini** is a soundalike for the name Zacchaeus. Your good luck **zucchini**, which becomes a gift, helps to recall the story of ZACCHAEUS THE TAX COLLECTOR.

ZACCHAEUS THE TAX COLLECTOR

Lk 19:1–10

1 He came to Jericho and intended to pass through the town.
2 Now a man there named Zacchaeus, who was a chief tax collector and also a wealthy man, 3 was seeking to see who Jesus was; but he could not see him because of the crowd, for he was short in stature.
4 So he ran ahead and climbed a sycamore tree in order to see Jesus, who was about to pass that way. 5 When he reached the place, Jesus looked up and said to him, "Zacchaeus, come down quickly, for today I must stay at your house." 6 And he came down quickly and received him with joy. 7 When they all saw this, they began to grumble, saying, "He has gone to stay at the house of a sinner."
8 But Zacchaeus stood there and said to the Lord, "Behold, half of my possessions, Lord, I shall give to the poor, and if I have extorted anything from anyone I shall repay it four times over." 9 And Jesus said to him, "Today salvation has come to this house because this man too is a descendant of Abraham. 10 For the Son of Man has come to seek and to save what was lost."

Once again Jesus had a surprising interaction with a tax collector, someone who was routinely despised in Jewish society. Recall back in Landmark 7 when Jesus called Levi to follow Him and then ate at his house. Here Zacchaeus was seeking Jesus before he was called down from the tree. In response to Jesus, Zacchaeus pledged to give half of what he owned to the poor and to repay quadruple any of his ill-gotten wealth. This latter offer coincided with the stringent demands of restitution found in Exodus 22. Zacchaeus's acts of faith and repentance show that with Jesus' help a wealthy man can indeed fit "through the eye of a needle." Again, just prior to reaching His Jerusalem destination, Jesus reiterated His purpose: "to seek and to save what was lost."

Landmark 34:

INFERNO

R ecall that recently there was a very cold Landmark. It was the slippery sheet of ice. The next Landmark is just the opposite. It is extremely hot. It is a fire, but we will call it an **inferno.**

The *Inferno* is the first book in Dante's great masterpiece, *The Divine Comedy. The Inferno* is about his sojourn through hell. *The Inferno* is divided into thirty-four parts, or cantos. Since we are in need of a thirty-fourth Landmark, *The Inferno* and its thirty-four cantos will be helpful. However, the Landmark is not the book itself. The Landmark is a hot, scorching **inferno,** or fire. Imagine slowly approaching a blazing **inferno.** Feel the heat of the flames and the sweat dripping from your forehead. Though the **inferno** is a blast of scorching heat, you continue to draw closer to this very hot Landmark.

To continue your journey, you must somehow pass through the inferno. You certainly need some powerful protection from the intense flames. There is no fireproof clothing available, but you see a large jar that may be helpful. The jar contains thick, gooey ointment. Perhaps a self-**anointing** with the ointment will provide adequate fire protection. You begin to slather the ointment on your skin and clothing. You essentially **anoint** yourself from head to toe. The entire ointment **anointing** takes several hours! You need as much ointment as possible between skin and fire. Finally, the **anointing** is complete. The jar is empty. You move closer to the inferno to test your thick layer of protection. It feels like the **anointing** was successful. The ointment seems to be effectively blocking the inferno's heat. Covered with the thick layer of protective ointment, it is time to pass through the inferno. With confidence, you walk through unscathed. This extensive **anointing** with ointment refers to the first unit you will associate with the inferno. It is JESUS' ANOINTING AT BETHANY.

JESUS' ANOINTING AT BETHANY

Mt 26:6–13

6 Now when Jesus was in Bethany in the house of Simon the leper 7 a woman came up to him with an alabaster jar of costly perfumed oil, and poured it on his head while he was reclining at table. 8 When the disciples saw this, they were indignant and said, "Why this waste? 9 It could have been sold for much, and the money given to the poor." 10 Since Jesus knew this, he said to them, "Why do you make trouble for the woman? She has done a good thing for me. 11 The poor you will always have with you; but you will not always have me. 12 In pouring this perfumed oil upon my body, she did it to prepare me for burial. 13 Amen, I say to you, wherever this gospel is proclaimed in the whole world, what she has done will be spoken of, in memory of her."

Mk 14:3–9

3 When he was in Bethany reclining at table in the house of Simon the leper, a woman came with an alabaster jar of perfumed oil, costly genuine spikenard. She broke the alabaster jar and poured it on his head. 4 There were some who were indignant. "Why has there been this waste of perfumed oil? 5 It could have been sold for more than three hundred days' wages and the money given to the poor." They were infuriated with her. 6 Jesus said, "Let her alone. Why do you make trouble for her? She has done a good thing for me. 7 The poor you will always have with you, and whenever you wish you can do good for them, but you will not always have me. 8 She has done what she could. She has anticipated anointing my body for burial. 9 Amen, I say to you, wherever the gospel is proclaimed in the whole world, what she has done will be told in memory of her."

Jn 12:1–11

1 Six days before Passover Jesus came to Bethany, where Lazarus was, whom Jesus had raised from the dead. 2 They gave a dinner for him there, and Martha served, while Lazarus was one of those reclining at table with him. 3 Mary took a liter of costly perfumed oil made from genuine aromatic nard and anointed the feet of Jesus and dried them with her hair; the house was filled with the fragrance of the oil. 4 Then Judas the Iscariot, one [of] his disciples, and the one who would betray him, said, 5 "Why was this oil not sold for three hundred days' wages and given to the poor?" 6 He said this not because he cared about the poor but because he was a thief and held the money bag and used to steal the contributions. 7 So Jesus said, "Leave her alone. Let her keep this for the day of

my burial. **8** You always have the poor with you, but you do not always have me."

9 [The] large crowd of the Jews found out that he was there and came, not only because of Jesus, but also to see Lazarus, whom he had raised from the dead. **10** And the chief priests plotted to kill Lazarus too, **11** because many of the Jews were turning away and believing in Jesus because of him.

This pivotal Landmark begins with a unit very similar to one we saw before in Landmark 11. Again, while Jesus was a dinner guest, a woman anointed Him with expensive oil (ointment). Could this have been a single event told in two different ways? Perhaps, but the two stories convey two different messages. The show of love and repentance by the woman during Jesus' Galilean ministry was quite different from the meaning of the anointing in Bethany. This second show of love and reverence was interpreted as an anticipation of Jesus' death. It was an anointing of His body prior to burial. There would be no time for this after the crucifixion. The woman, either Mary (the sister of Lazarus) or an unnamed woman, showed an understanding of Jesus' identity and mission. The Messiah, the royal descendant of King David, was worthy of this extravagant and costly anointing. This was a powerful contrast to the ignorance of the protestors, including Judas.

In this anointing scene, unlike the one from Landmark 11, Jesus defended the woman's action by pointing out that the poor would always be present. His physical presence, however, was coming to an end. Jesus was not in any way snubbing the poor or making light of their needs. A key aspect of His preaching and teaching was always to care for the poor. Showing Jesus hospitality was good; giving money to the poor was also good. But showing love for Jesus and anointing His body for burial was priceless!

EMERGING FROM THE INFERNO, YOU find yourself in a courtroom. You are standing before a surprised group of men and women. They are seated in two rows of chairs. The back row is slightly higher than the front. Both rows of chairs and their surprised occupants are surrounded by a low wooden enclosure. You are standing before a **jury**! You immediately wonder if you are on trial and if this **jury** is to decide your fate. Each member of the **jury** is now glaring at you. Apparently your entry into the courtroom has disrupted the concentration of the entire **jury**. In unison, the **jury** motions for you to step aside. You are blocking their view of the defendant who is testifying at that moment. You are relieved that the **jury** is not there to decide your fate. You gladly step aside so the **jury** can continue their civic duty. This unexpected **entry** before the **jury** helps you recall another **entry**. The **jury** is a soundalike for Jerusalem. Your **entry** before the **jury** thus represents JESUS' ENTRY INTO JERUSALEM.

JESUS' ENTRY INTO JERUSALEM

Mt 21:1–11

1 When they drew near Jerusalem and came to Bethpage on the Mount of Olives, Jesus sent two disciples, 2 saying to them, "Go into the village opposite you, and immediately you will find an ass tethered, and a colt with her. Untie them and bring them here to me. 3 And if anyone should say anything to you, reply, 'The master has need of them.' Then he will send them at once." 4 This happened so that what had been spoken through the prophet might be fulfilled:

5 "Say to daughter Zion,
'Behold, your king comes to you,
meek and riding on an ass,
and on a colt, the foal of a beast of burden.'"

6 The disciples went and did as Jesus had ordered them. 7 They brought the ass and the colt and laid their cloaks over them, and he sat upon them. 8 The very large crowd spread their cloaks on the road, while others cut branches from the trees and strewed them on the road. 9 The crowds preceding him and those following kept crying out and saying:

"Hosanna to the Son of David;
blessed is he who comes in the name of the Lord;
hosanna in the highest."

10 And when he entered Jerusalem the whole city was shaken and asked, "Who is this?" 11 And the crowds replied, "This is Jesus the prophet, from Nazareth in Galilee."

Mk 11:1–10

1 When they drew near to Jerusalem, to Bethpage and Bethany at the Mount of Olives, he sent two of his disciples 2 and said to them,

"Go into the village opposite you, and immediately on entering it, you will find a colt tethered on which no one has ever sat. Untie it and bring it here. 3 If anyone should say to you, 'Why are you doing this?' reply, 'The Master has need of it and will send it back here at once.'"4 So they went off and found a colt tethered at a gate outside on the street, and they untied it. 5 Some of the bystanders said to them, "What are you doing, untying the colt?" 6 They answered them just as Jesus had told them to, and they permitted them to do it. 7 So they brought the colt to Jesus and put their cloaks over it. And he sat on it. 8 Many people spread their cloaks on the road, and others spread leafy branches that they had cut from the fields. 9 Those preceding him as well as those following kept crying out:

"Hosanna!
Blessed is he who comes in the name of the Lord!
10 Blessed is the kingdom of our father David that is to come!
Hosanna in the highest!"

Lk 19:28–38

28 After he had said this, he proceeded on his journey up to Jerusalem. 29 As he drew near to Bethpage and Bethany at the place called the Mount of Olives, he sent two of his disciples. 30 He said, "Go into the village opposite you, and as you enter it you will find a colt tethered on which no one has ever sat. Untie it and bring it here. 31 And if anyone should ask you, 'Why are you untying it?' you will answer, 'The Master has need of it.'" 32 So those who had been sent went off and found everything just as he had told them. 33 And as they were untying the colt, its owners said to them, "Why are you untying this colt?" 34 They answered, "The Master has need of it." 35 So they brought it to Jesus, threw their cloaks over the colt, and helped Jesus to mount. 36 As he rode along, the people were spreading their cloaks on the road; 37 and now as he was approaching the slope of the Mount of Olives, the whole multitude of his disciples began to praise God aloud with joy for all the mighty deeds they had seen. 38 They proclaimed:

"Blessed is the king who comes
in the name of the Lord.
Peace in heaven
and glory in the highest."

Jn 12:12–18

12 On the next day, when the great crowd that had come to the feast heard that Jesus was coming to Jerusalem, 13 they took palm branches and went out to meet him, and cried out:

"Hosanna!
Blessed is he who comes in the name of the Lord,
[even] the king of Israel."

14 Jesus found an ass and sat upon it, as is written:

15 "Fear no more, O daughter Zion;
see, your king comes, seated upon an ass's colt."

16 His disciples did not understand this at first, but when Jesus had been glorified they remembered that these things were written about him and that they had done this for him. **17** So the crowd that was with him when he called Lazarus from the tomb and raised him from death continued to testify. **18** This was [also] why the crowd went to meet him, because they heard that he had done this sign.

Jesus has finally reached His destination and His destiny. In the preceding Landmarks, He has been slowly but surely walking toward Jerusalem. He has arrived. Jesus has begun the final week of His life on earth.

Jesus had been to Jerusalem many times in His life. Previously, He had entered the holy city as a visitor or pilgrim. Not so with this final arrival, which corresponded with the Passover celebration. Amid great fanfare, the long-awaited Messiah rode into the city on a humble donkey, a sign He had come in peace. His painful, public, humiliating death on a cross awaited Him. Ironic, paradoxical, confusing, wonderful? Words alone cannot convey the unfolding of God's plan for His Son!

Jesus' ride into Jerusalem recalled Solomon upon his father's mule (1 Kg 1:38–40). That original Son of David had traveled to his coronation on the lowly beast before he sat upon the throne of Israel. Though on a lowly donkey, Jesus was ushered into Jerusalem in a kingly fashion by His disciples and the crowd. With cloaks strewn upon the ground and branches waving in the air, Jesus was greeted with enthusiastic shouts of "Hosanna" ("save please"). These shouts of welcoming praise and blessing are from Psalm 118. They were prayers typically recited by pilgrims on their way to Jerusalem for the great Passover Feast. These were the words Jesus heard as He, the Passover Lamb, entered Jerusalem prior to the slaughter.

YOU ARE STILL RELIEVED THAT the jury is not deliberating your fate. You look to see who is the unfortunate person testifying. It is a **fairy**! Well, not a real **fairy**. It is the same woman who came to your New Year's Eve party dressed as a **fairy**. There she is, still wearing the **fairy** outfit while on trial.

Surely, going around dressed like a **fairy** is not a crime. You soon learn of the charges against her. Sitting there beside her chair is what appears to be a small nuclear **reactor**. Wow! The **reactor** belongs to the **fairy**. The **fairy's reactor** looks to be in need of repair. The **reactor** belonging to the **fairy** may be hazardous to all of those in the courtroom, yourself included! Recall from a recent Landmark (31) that the **fairy** represents the Pharisees. The **reactor** stands for "reaction." This scene with the **fairy's reactor** helps to recall the unit about THE PHARISEES' REACTION (after Jesus entered Jerusalem).

THE PHARISEES' REACTION

Lk 19:39–40

39 Some of the Pharisees in the crowd said to him, "Teacher, rebuke your disciples." 40 He said in reply, "I tell you, if they keep silent, the stones will cry out!"

Jn 12:19

19 So the Pharisees said to one another, "You see that you are gaining nothing. Look, the whole world has gone after him."

Over the course of Jesus' ministry, the Pharisees had become increasingly hostile. They were threatened by His radical new teachings and popularity among fellow Jews. Their authority, their very identity, had been called into question. They wanted Jesus dead. The Pharisees now witnessed Jesus' humble yet triumphant entry into their city. This sight, combined with the crowd's adoring and enthusiastic welcome, brought their anger to a boil. They insisted that Jesus not just silence His followers, but also scold them. Jesus' response indicated that He knew full well the significance of His arrival and of the events that were to follow. Jesus' arrival must be heralded, for He had come to atone for generations of injustice. His sacrifice would be God's ultimate act of love and forgiveness. Though silent, the stones bore witness to generations of sin. We are not stones, so hopefully when we are witness to sin and injustice we will not remain silent. Hopefully, we will "cry out" with words, or better yet, actions.

YOU CONTINUE TO STARE ANXIOUSLY at the fairy and her reactor. There is great concern from all in the courtroom that they are in danger. Sensing this, the fairy takes action to defuse the tense situation. She reaches both arms down into the reactor! Slowly, she pulls something out. To everyone's relief, she is holding several **lemons**! Yes, **lemons**. The fairy has pulled harmless **lemons** from the reactor. She then walks over to the **jury** to distribute the **lemons**. The **lemons** are for the jury. Perhaps she thinks this will convince the **jury** that the reactor is harmless. Providing **lemons** for the **jury** appears to be a good strategy. After receiving their **lemons**, the members of the **jury** appear relieved. The fairy's gesture helps recall Jesus' feelings upon entering Jerusalem. The **jury** again stands for Jerusalem. The "**lemons**" sound like "lament." Thus **lemons** for the **jury** is Jesus' LAMENT FOR JERUSALEM.

LAMENT FOR JERUSALEM

Mt 23:37–39

37 "Jerusalem, Jerusalem, you who kill the prophets and stone those sent to you, how many times I yearned to gather your children together, as a hen gathers her young under her wings, but you were unwilling! 38 Behold, your house will be abandoned, desolate. 39 I tell you, you will not see me again until you say, 'Blessed is he who comes in the name of the Lord.'"

Lk 13:34–35; 19:41–44

34 "Jerusalem, Jerusalem, you who kill the prophets and stone those sent to you, how many times I yearned to gather your children together as a hen gathers her brood under her wings, but you were unwilling! 35 Behold, your house will be abandoned. [But] I tell you, you will not see me until [the time comes when] you say, 'Blessed is he who comes in the name of the Lord.'"

...

41 As he drew near, he saw the city and wept over it, 42 saying, "If this day you only knew what makes for peace—but now it is hidden from your eyes. 43 For the days are coming upon you when your enemies will raise a palisade against you; they will encircle you and hem you in on all sides. 44 They will smash you to the ground and your children within you, and they will not leave one

stone upon another within you because you did not recognize the time of your visitation."

The name *Jerusalem* means "peace." Jerusalem was anything but peaceful for many of the prophets who came before Jesus. Though He would also be killed there, Jesus spoke with love and compassion toward Jerusalem and its "children." Jesus was undoubtedly familiar with the city and many of its people. Over the preceding thirty-plus years, He had been within its walls for many religious festivals and other occasions. In echoing the prophet Jeremiah (Jer 12:7), Jesus lamented the eventual destruction of the great temple that would occur thirty plus years later. In Luke, Jesus also spoke of the coming destruction of the entire city. This would be the second fall of Jerusalem. The first was at the hands of the Babylonians more than six centuries earlier. The city whose name means "peace" would not have peace because it did not recognize the one who brings peace!

Landmark 35:

CAMERA

In our high-tech world, many people carry a device in their pocket that previously had to be toted by hand or over the shoulder. Not only is this item now much smaller, in many cases it also performs better. Can you picture this item? It is a camera, which many people now have built into their phones. Landmark 35 is a **camera**, but one of the "old-fashioned variety." It is a 35 mm **camera**. A 35 mm **camera** can still be purchased and can be quite sophisticated. The 35 mm **camera** has improved considerably since it was first invented over one hundred years ago. Today, as throughout the past century, it still uses 35 mm film. So imagine holding the next Landmark, a 35 mm **camera**.

With the camera in hand, you begin to survey the landscape. You would like to take a unique, memorable picture. Off in the distance, you spot a strange-looking tree. Looking through the camera's viewfinder, you can see that the tree is even stranger than you thought. It is a **fig tree**, but not just any **fig tree**. This tree has not produced **figs**. It has grown **fig** cookies! Each branch is loaded with sweet, chewy, brown rectangular cookies. If you told anyone about seeing a **fig tree** that produced **fig** cookies, they would question your sanity. Fortunately, you have the camera to capture this special **fig tree** on film. You carefully bring the **fig tree** into focus. One, two, three, click. You now have a picture of the **fig tree** to show the skeptics. This one-of-a-kind **fig tree** represents the first unit associated with the camera: THE CURSING OF THE FIG TREE.

THE CURSING OF THE FIG TREE

Mt 21:18–19

18 When he was going back to the city in the morning, he was hungry. **19** Seeing a fig tree by the road, he went over to it, but found nothing on it except leaves. And he said to it, "May no fruit ever come from you again." And immediately the fig tree withered.

Mk 11:12–14

12 The next day as they were leaving Bethany he was hungry. **13** Seeing from a distance a fig tree in leaf, he went over to see if he could find anything on it. When he reached it he found nothing but leaves; it was not the time for figs. **14** And he said to it in reply, "May no one ever eat of your fruit again!" And his disciples heard it.

After Jesus' prophecy-fulfilling entry into Jerusalem the previous day, He and His disciples returned to Bethany for the night. The next morning Jesus was hungry. He needed to eat in preparation for the busy day ahead. Though Jesus was hungry, the encounter with the fig tree was more of a symbolic action than a search for breakfast. Jesus knew that figs could not be found until June, not in the month of Passover. If the story was not symbolic, then Jesus' behavior was irrational and an act of destruction based on anger!

Back in Landmark 21, we discussed how Jewish prophets used the fig tree as a symbol for Israel. Jesus also told the parable of the barren fig tree. In that parable, the tree was given another chance. Not here! As the events of the coming week would show, there were still many unfaithful in Israel. They did not see Jesus as the Messiah. The withered fig was symbolic of their lack of faith and repentance.

AFTER PHOTOGRAPHING THE FIG TREE, you decide to walk over for a closer look, and perhaps taste a cookie! Beginning the short stroll, you reach down to place the camera in your pocket. The side of the camera feels sticky. Closer inspection reveals a gooey black substance stuck to the camera. You feel the side of your head. Sure enough, while taking the picture some of the black goo became stuck to your **temple** area. What a mess! The hair over your **temple** is matted and stiff. You must **clean your temple** before going over to the fig tree. **Cleansing your temple** is no easy task. You have no cloth or cleaning solution. You begin to rub your **temple** with saliva-moistened fingers. This seems to help, though the black substance from your **temple** is now on your fingers. After several more minutes of rubbing, your **temple** is sore but finally clean. This **cleaning of your temple** is a reference to Jesus' CLEANSING OF THE TEMPLE.

CLEANSING OF THE TEMPLE

Mt 21:12–17

12 Jesus entered the temple area and drove out all those engaged in selling and buying there. He overturned the tables of the money changers and the seats of those who were selling doves. 13 And he said to them, "It is written:

'My house shall be a house of prayer,
but you are making it a den of thieves."

14 The blind and the lame approached him in the temple area, and he cured them. 15 When the chief priests and the scribes saw the wondrous things he was doing, and the children crying out in the temple area, "Hosanna to the Son of David," they were indignant 16 and said to him, "Do you hear what they are saying?" Jesus said to them, "Yes; and have you never read the text, 'Out of the mouths of infants and nurslings you have brought forth praise'?" 17 And leaving them, he went out of the city to Bethany, and there he spent the night.

Mk 11:15–19

15 They came to Jerusalem, and on entering the temple area he began to drive out those selling and buying there. He overturned the tables of the money changers and the seats of those who were selling doves. 16 He did not permit anyone to carry anything through the temple area. 17 Then he taught them saying, "Is it not written:

'My house shall be called a house of prayer for all peoples'?
But you have made it a den of thieves."

18 The chief priests and the scribes came to hear of it and were seeking a way to put him to death, yet they feared him because the whole crowd was astonished at his teaching. 19 When evening came, they went out of the city.

Lk 19:45–46

45 Then Jesus entered the temple area and proceeded to drive out those who were selling things, 46 saying to them, "It is written, 'My house shall be a house of prayer, but you have made it a den of thieves.'"

Jn 2:13–25

13 Since the Passover of the Jews was near, Jesus went up to Jerusalem. 14 He found in the temple area those who sold oxen, sheep, and doves, as well as the money-changers seated there. 15 He made a whip out of cords and drove them all out of the temple area, with the sheep and oxen, and spilled the coins of the money-changers and overturned their tables, 16 and to those who sold doves he said, "Take these out of here, and stop making my Father's house a marketplace." 17 His disciples recalled the words of scripture, "Zeal for your house will consume me." 18 At this the Jews answered and said to him, "What sign can you show us for doing this?" 19 Jesus answered and said to them, "Destroy this temple and in three days I will raise it up." 20 The Jews said, "This temple has been under construction for forty-six years, and you will raise it up in three days?" 21 But he was speaking about the temple of his body. 22 Therefore, when he was raised from the dead, his disciples remembered that he had said this, and they came to believe the scripture and the word Jesus had spoken.

23 While he was in Jerusalem for the feast of Passover, many began to believe in his name when they saw the signs he was doing. 24 But Jesus would not trust himself to them because he knew them all, 25 and did not need anyone to testify about human nature. He himself understood it well.

In Jerusalem at Passover, the great and holy temple was the place to be. It was the destination of the many pilgrims who often traveled long distances. The temple was also where profiteers gathered to take advantage of the faithful. The money changers were quite willing to oblige those who needed the correct currency to pay the annual temple tax or to purchase animals for sacrifice. Those selling the animals would often prey on the pilgrims by taking extra money for themselves. All of this activity made for a less than prayerful atmosphere. This scene made Jesus very angry. To see Him overturn tables and chairs, and drive out the businessmen and scoundrels with a whip while quoting Isaiah and Jeremiah, must have been quite a shock for His disciples. This event is interpreted by many to be a foreshadowing of the temple's destruction almost four decades later.

In John, the temple cleansing occurs at the outset, rather than the end of Jesus' ministry. The indignant leaders asked Jesus for a sign to justify His authority to behave so boldly. His response was a foreshadowing of His own death and resurrection. They mistakenly saw it as a prediction of the destruction of the temple itself.

For Matthew, Mark, and Luke, this event is the last straw for the Jewish leaders. Fear, anger, and lack of faith increased their desire to put Jesus to death, a death that gives us the possibility of eternal life.

THOUGH YOU NOW HAVE A headache, it is time to examine the tree bearing fig cookies. As you approach the tree, it seems to look different than it did through the viewfinder of the camera. The closer you get, the more **withered** and sickly the tree appears. You are just a few feet away, and not only is the **tree withered**, the fig cookies also have a **withered** look. How could a tree that not long ago appeared healthy and robust be so droopy and **withered**? Perhaps the camera had distorted its appearance, making the **withered** old tree look young and healthy. You reach out and touch the worn bark and sagging limbs. The old **withered** tree has seen better days. This **withered fig** easily reminds you of the next unit about THE WITHERED FIG TREE.

THE WITHERED FIG TREE

Mt 21:20–22

20 When the disciples saw this, they were amazed and said, "How was it that the fig tree withered immediately?" **21** Jesus said to them in reply, "Amen, I say to you, if you have faith and do not waver, not only will you do what has been done to the fig tree, but even if you say to this mountain, 'Be lifted up and thrown into the sea,' it will be done. **22** Whatever you ask for in prayer with faith, you will receive."

Mk 11:20–25

20 Early in the morning, as they were walking along, they saw the fig tree withered to its roots. **21** Peter remembered and said to him, "Rabbi, look! The fig tree that you cursed has withered."

22 Jesus said to them in reply, "Have faith in God. **23** Amen, I say to you, whoever says to this mountain, 'Be lifted up and thrown into the sea,' and does not doubt in his heart but believes that what he says will happen, it shall be done for him. **24** Therefore I tell you, all that you ask for in prayer, believe that you will receive it and it shall be yours. **25** When you stand to pray, forgive anyone against whom you have a grievance, so that your heavenly Father may in turn forgive you your transgressions."

In Matthew, the fig tree withers immediately after Jesus finds it barren and declares that it will never again bear fruit. This dramatic statement likely made His subsequent words about prayer and faith more powerful. Mark chooses to separate the cursing and the withering of the fig tree, "sandwiching" the cleansing of the temple in between. This "sandwiching" technique allowed Mark to emphasize different events with similar themes. Both the fig tree without fruit and the temple as a place of business represent Israel's loss of direction and lack of faith. Jesus then taught His disciples about prayer and faith and how they are connected. Faith in God is most important. God is the source of all power; the power that allows Jesus to wither the fig and for us to "move mountains." It is faith that leads us to prayer, which in turn will strengthen our faith.

YOU SEE THE FIG TREE is withered, but not dead. Perhaps there is something you can do to restore it to health. While considering your options, someone with very different intentions approaches the tree. It is **Thor**, the Norse god of thunder! **Thor** is very upset. He appears to be on a mission to destroy the fig tree! When **Thor** starts to swing his mighty hammer, your suspicion is confirmed. **Thor** lets out a mighty roar and releases the hammer. As the hammer of **Thor** flies toward the helpless tree, you cover your ears. Wham! The tree is split wide open. A smile now covers the face of mighty **Thor**. This rather bizarre assault on the fig tree by **Thor** helps recall "au**thor**ity," a soundalike for **Thor**. This is the unit where THE AUTHORITY OF JESUS IS QUESTIONED.

THE AUTHORITY OF JESUS IS
QUESTIONED

Mt 21:23–27

23 When he had come into the temple area, the chief priests and the elders of the people approached him as he was teaching and said, "By what authority are you doing these things? And who gave you this authority?" **24** Jesus said to them in reply, "I shall ask you one question, and if you answer it for me, then I shall tell you by what authority I do these things. **25** Where was John's baptism from? Was it of heavenly or of human origin?" They discussed this among themselves and said, "If we say 'Of heavenly origin,' he will say to us, 'Then why did you not believe him?' **26** But if we say, 'Of human origin,' we fear the crowd, for they all regard John as a prophet." **27** So they said to Jesus in reply, "We do not know." He himself said to them, "Neither shall I tell you by what authority I do these things."

Mk 11:27–33

27 They returned once more to Jerusalem. As he was walking in the temple area, the chief priests, the scribes, and the elders approached him **28** and said to him, "By what authority are you doing these things? Or who gave you this authority to do them?" **29** Jesus said to them, "I shall ask you one question. Answer me, and I will tell you by what authority I do these things. **30** Was John's baptism of heavenly or of human origin? Answer me." **31** They discussed this among themselves and said, "If we say, 'Of heavenly origin,' he will say, '[Then] why did you not believe him?' **32** But shall we say, 'Of human origin'?"—they feared the crowd, for they all thought John really was a prophet. **33** So they said to Jesus in reply, "We do not know." Then Jesus said to them, "Neither shall I tell you by what authority I do these things."

Lk 20:1–8

1 One day as he was teaching the people in the temple area and proclaiming the good news, the chief priests and scribes, together with the elders, approached him **2** and said to him, "Tell us, by what authority are you doing these things? Or who is the one who gave you this authority?" **3** He said to them in reply, "I shall ask you a question. Tell me, **4** was John's baptism of heavenly or of human origin?" **5** They discussed this among themselves, and said, "If we say, 'Of heavenly origin,' he will say, 'Why did you not believe him?' **6** But if we say, 'Of human origin,' then all the people will stone us, for they are convinced that John was a prophet." **7** So they answered that they did not know from where it came. **8** Then Jesus said to them, "Neither shall I tell you by what authority I do these things."

Both religious and civic leaders (the elders) were concerned by what they deemed to be outrageous behavior by Jesus. His healing powers were amazing and His teaching was radical. However, His zealous, disruptive behavior at the temple was more than they could tolerate. We have previously seen Jesus being asked to justify His behavior with a sign. Here He was asked directly about the source of His authority and power. After all, He was not even from the Tribe of Levi, which provided the Jewish priests. He was just a poor man from Galilee!

Jesus responded to their question with a question of His own. His question was brilliant! The chief priests, scribes, and elders were trying to trap Jesus. They were hoping He would respond with the blasphemous claim that His authority was from God. Then they could charge Him with the capital crime of blasphemy and be done with Him. This would be the eventual charge against Jesus, but He avoided it here and caught the leaders in their own trap. They were unwilling to answer His counter question, knowing either response about John would rile the crowd. In this way, Jesus proclaimed that His authority was from God without being arrested. This was the beginning of a week of controversy that would culminate in perhaps the most controversial event in history.

THOR'S MOTIVE FOR SPLITTING OPEN the withered fig tree is now apparent. Standing there amidst the broken limbs and shattered trunk are his **two sons**. The **two sons** had been hiding from their father inside the withered fig. Thor is clearly pleased to have found his **two sons**. He orders his **two sons** to come to him. With downcast eyes, the **two sons** approach their father. Thor demands that his **sons** explain their childish behavior. The **two sons** are speechless, not with fear, but with guilt at having disappointed their father. This story about the **two sons** of Thor hiding within the fig tree represents Jesus' PARABLE OF THE TWO SONS.

PARABLE OF THE TWO SONS

Mt 21:28–32

> **28** "What is your opinion? A man had two sons. He came to the first and said, 'Son, go out and work in the vineyard today.' **29** He said in reply, 'I will not,' but afterwards he changed his mind and went. **30** The man came to the other son and gave the same order. He said in reply, 'Yes, sir,' but did not go. **31** Which of the two did his father's will?" They answered, "The first." Jesus said to them, "Amen, I say to you, tax collectors and prostitutes are entering the kingdom of God before you. **32** When John came to you in the way of righteousness, you did not believe him; but tax collectors and prostitutes did. Yet even when you saw that, you did not later change your minds and believe him."

Jesus continued His discussion with the chief priests and elders by explaining His question about John's authority. He did this in the form of a parable that had a conclusion that surely did not endear Him to them. As in earlier parables, the vineyard was symbolic of the nation of Israel. The two sons represented two groups within the nation. The deceitful leaders plotting to do away with Jesus were represented by the son who does not follow through on his word to work in the vineyard. The outcasts of society were represented by the other son, who changed his mind and did his father's will. To be publicly judged as less deserving of the Kingdom than tax collectors and prostitutes must have made the chief priests and elders want to be rid of Jesus more than ever. Sinners had heard John and now they heard Jesus. They recognized the need to repent and work in the vineyard. The self-righteous heard the message, but felt no need to repent.

THOR IS NOW GLARING AT his sons. He is waiting for them to explain why they had been inside the withered fig tree. With his voice shaking, one son says they had been searching for **ants**. The other son adds, "We needed **ten ants**." Thor shakes his head in disbelief. "Why do you need **ants**, and why specifically **ten ants**?" The sons are hesitant to explain, knowing that **ants** are one of mighty Thor's favorite snacks. Again he demands an explanation of their need for **ten ants**. Together they tell Thor that their mother had sent them to find the **ten ants**. She was planning a special surprise for Thor. It is a new recipe that requires **ten ants** as a secret ingredient. Thor's irritation quickly turns to delight. He can now hardly wait to taste the **ten ant** dish his wife will prepare! This questioning and explaining of the **ten ants** represents another parable: THE PARABLE OF THE TENANTS.

THE PARABLE OF THE TENANTS

Mt 21:33–46

33 "Hear another parable. There was a landowner who planted a vineyard, put a hedge around it, dug a wine press in it, and built a tower. Then he leased it to tenants and went on a journey. **34** When vintage time drew near, he sent his servants to the tenants to obtain his produce. **35** But the tenants seized the servants and one they beat, another they killed, and a third they stoned. **36** Again he sent other servants, more numerous than the first ones, but they treated them in the same way. **37** Finally, he sent his son to them, thinking, 'They will respect my son.' **38** But when the tenants saw the son, they said to one another, 'This is the heir. Come, let us kill him and acquire his inheritance.' **39** They seized him, threw him out of the vineyard, and killed him. **40** What will the owner of the vineyard do to those tenants when he comes?" **41** They answered him, "He will put those wretched men to a wretched death and lease his vineyard to other tenants who will give him the produce at the proper times." **42** Jesus said to them, "Did you never read in the scriptures:

'The stone that the builders rejected
has become the cornerstone;
by the Lord has this been done,
and it is wonderful in our eyes'?

43 Therefore, I say to you, the kingdom of God will be taken away from you and given to a people that will produce its fruit. **44** [The one who falls on this stone will be dashed to pieces; and it will crush anyone on whom it falls.]" **45** When the chief priests and the Pharisees heard his parables, they knew that he was speaking about them. **46** And although they were attempting to arrest him, they feared the crowds, for they regarded him as a prophet.

Mk 12:1–12

1 He began to speak to them in parables. "A man planted a vineyard, put a hedge around it, dug a wine press, and built a tower. Then he leased it to tenant farmers and left on a journey.

2 At the proper time he sent a servant to the tenants to obtain from them some of the produce of the vineyard. 3 But they seized him, beat him, and sent him away empty-handed. 4 Again he sent them another servant. And that one they beat over the head and treated shamefully. 5 He sent yet another whom they killed. So, too, many others; some they beat, others they killed. 6 He had one other to send, a beloved son. He sent him to them last of all, thinking, 'They will respect my son.' 7 But those tenants said to one another, 'This is the heir. Come, let us kill him, and the inheritance will be ours.' 8 So they seized him and killed him, and threw him out of the vineyard. 9 What [then] will the owner of the vineyard do? He will come, put the tenants to death, and give the vineyard to others. 10 Have you not read this scripture passage:

'The stone that the builders rejected
has become the cornerstone;
11 by the Lord has this been done,
and it is wonderful in our eyes'?"

12 They were seeking to arrest him, but they feared the crowd, for they realized that he had addressed the parable to them. So they left him and went away.

Lk 20:9–19

9 Then he proceeded to tell the people this parable. "[A] man planted a vineyard, leased it to tenant farmers, and then went on a journey for a long time. 10 At harvest time he sent a servant to the tenant farmers to receive some of the produce of the vineyard. But they beat the servant and sent him away empty-handed. 11 So he proceeded to send another servant, but him also they beat and insulted and sent away empty-handed. 12 Then he proceeded to send a third, but this one too they wounded and threw out. 13 The owner of the vineyard said, 'What shall I do? I shall send my beloved son; maybe they will respect him.' 14 But when the tenant farmers saw him they said to one another, 'This is the heir. Let us kill him that the inheritance may become ours.' 15 So they threw him out of the vineyard and killed him. What will the owner of the vineyard do to them? 16 He will come and put those tenant farmers to death and turn over the vineyard to others." When the people heard this, they exclaimed, "Let it not be so!" 17 But he looked at them and asked, "What then does this scripture passage mean:

'The stone which the builders rejected
has become the cornerstone'?

18 Everyone who falls on that stone will be dashed to pieces; and it will crush anyone on whom it falls." 19 The scribes and chief priests sought to lay their hands on him at that very hour, but they feared the people, for they knew that he had addressed this parable to them.

This parable addressed to Jesus' critics is packed with meaning and uses extensive symbolism. Elements of the parable and what they represent include landlord/God, vineyard/Israel, tenants/Israel's leaders, servants/Jewish prophets, tower/temple, son/Jesus, tenants' death/destruction of Jerusalem, "other tenants"/the church.

In the Hebrew Scriptures, the Psalms, Jeremiah, and Hosea all used the image of a vineyard to represent God's chosen people, Israel. Isaiah's description of Israel as God's vineyard is perhaps the most well-known (Is 5:1–7). Isaiah not only described a vineyard, but also a watchtower and wine press. As Jesus' parable about the vineyard and its tenants unfolds, the reader can see it is a retelling of salvation history. Jesus' opponents, to whom He told the story, unknowingly condemn themselves. In Matthew, the chief priests and elders responded that the wretched tenants should suffer a wretched death. However, when Jesus quoted Psalm 118 it became apparent to the leaders that Jesus Himself was the stone rejected by the builders and the parable was a condemnation of them. Jesus had outsmarted them again, as He had regarding the question of John's Baptism.

In Jesus, there is a transition in God's relationship with His people. There is a shift from the Old Covenant represented by the temple and Jewish leaders to the New Covenant church of which Jesus is the cornerstone.

THOR'S WIFE NOW APPEARS CARRYING a large bowl. Thor rushes over and peers into the bowl. Seeing a fresh **Caesar** salad, he instinctively licks his lips. **Caesar** salad is his favorite! The thought of sprinkling his favorite snack on a delicious Caesar salad sends mighty Thor into a frenzy. He motions for his sons to come quickly with the ten ants. Thor watches with glee as they sprinkle the ants onto the **Caesar** salad. His wife tosses the salad to evenly distribute the crunchy ants. At this point, you are hoping Thor does not offer you a portion of the **Caesar** salad. Fortunately, he does not. His family stands back and watches Thor devour the entire **Caesar** salad himself. This less-than-appetizing scene causes you to remember Jesus' words about PAYING TAXES TO CAESAR.

PAYING TAXES TO CAESAR

Mt 22:15–22

15 Then the Pharisees went off and plotted how they might entrap him in speech. 16 They sent their disciples to him, with the Herodians, saying, "Teacher, we know that you are a truthful man and that you teach the way of God in accordance with the truth. And you are not concerned with anyone's opinion, for you do not regard a person's status. 17 Tell us, then, what is your opinion: Is it lawful to pay the census tax to Caesar or not?" 18 Knowing their malice, Jesus said, "Why are you testing me, you hypocrites? 19 Show me the coin that pays the census tax." Then they handed him the Roman coin. 20 He said to them, "Whose image is this and whose inscription?" 21 They replied, "Caesar's." At that he said to them, "Then repay to Caesar what belongs to Caesar and to God what belongs to God." 22 When they heard this they were amazed, and leaving him they went away.

Mk 12:13–17

13 They sent some Pharisees and Herodians to him to ensnare him in his speech. 14 They came and said to him, "Teacher, we know that you are a truthful man and that you are not concerned with anyone's opinion. You do not regard a person's status but teach the way of God in accordance with the truth. Is it lawful to pay the census tax to Caesar or not? Should we pay or should we not pay?" 15 Knowing their hypocrisy he said to them, "Why are you testing me? Bring me a denarius to look at." 16 They brought one to him and he said to them, "Whose image and inscription is this?" They replied to him, "Caesar's." 17 So Jesus said to them, "Repay to Caesar what belongs to Caesar and to God what belongs to God." They were utterly amazed at him.

Lk 20:20–26

20 They watched him closely and sent agents pretending to be righteous who were to trap him in speech, in order to hand him over to the authority and power of the governor. 21 They posed this question to him, "Teacher, we know that what you say and teach is correct, and you show no partiality, but teach the way of God in accordance with the truth. 22 Is it lawful for us to pay tribute to Caesar or not?" 23 Recognizing their craftiness he said to them, 24 "Show me a denarius; whose image and name does it bear?" They replied, "Caesar's." 25 So he said to them, "Then repay to Caesar what belongs to Caesar and to God what belongs to God." 26 They were unable to trap him by something he might say before the people, and so amazed were they at his reply that they fell silent.

The old adage about the certainty of death and taxes appears to have applied in Jesus' time. The Pharisees and Herodians, groups typically at odds with each other, combined forces to see how Jesus felt about the matter of taxes. It appeared that wolves and lions were working together to trap a Lamb. Their question about paying taxes to Caesar was an attempt to put Jesus in a "no-win" situation. Depending on His response, Jesus would either anger His fellow tax-paying Jews or the harsh Roman rulers.

When Jesus' enemies correctly responded that the image on the coin was Caesar, He again answered a question with a question. Jesus replied that it was acceptable to give the coin back to the one whose likeness it bears. More importantly, we need to give back to God that which bears God's image. That is us! Our lives should be given over to serving God. Serving Caesar by paying the tax was permitted, but serving God is necessary. Spiritual matters are more important than political correctness. Jesus wanted to effect social change, but in a nonviolent fashion. He was not the warrior or political Messiah many had been praying for.

Landmark 36:

YARDSTICK

The thirty-sixth Landmark is poking up from the ground straight ahead. It needs to be one that "sticks" with you. To help ensure this, the Landmark will actually be a stick. Since it is Landmark 36, it is a wooden **yardstick**, which is thirty-six inches long. Currently, only several inches of the **yardstick** are visible above the ground. Someone has gone to great lengths to bury most of the **yardstick**. With this in mind, you will watch more of the **yardstick** come into view.

As you approach the yardstick, it begins to slowly rise from the ground. The flat wooden stick is somehow being **resurrected** from the earth several feet from where you are standing. In stunned silence, you watch as inch by inch the **resurrection** of the yardstick takes place. You **question** what could be causing this **resurrection**. Never before have you witnessed an inanimate object like a yardstick rise from the ground. As more of the yardstick becomes visible, you **question** whether anyone will believe your story about this particular **resurrection**. Watching the thirty-sixth Landmark's **resurrection** from the ground recalls the unit when the Sadducees ask THE QUESTION ABOUT THE RESURRECTION.

THE QUESTION ABOUT THE RESURRECTION

Mt 22:23–33

23 On that day Sadducees approached him, saying that there is no resurrection. They put this question to him, 24 saying, "Teacher, Moses said, 'If a man dies without children, his brother shall marry his wife and raise up descendants for his brother.' 25 Now there were seven brothers among us. The first married

and died and, having no descendants, left his wife to his brother.
26 The same happened with the second and the third, through all
seven. **27** Finally the woman died. **28** Now at the resurrection, of
the seven, whose wife will she be? For they all had been married to
her." **29** Jesus said to them in reply, "You are misled because you do
not know the scriptures or the power of God. **30** At the resurrection
they neither marry nor are given in marriage but are like the
angels in heaven. **31** And concerning the resurrection of the dead,
have you not read what was said to you by God, **32** 'I am the God of
Abraham, the God of Isaac, and the God of Jacob'? He is not the God
of the dead but of the living." **33** When the crowds heard this, they
were astonished at his teaching.

Mk 12:18–27

18 Some Sadducees, who say there is no resurrection, came
to him and put this question to him, **19** saying, "Teacher, Moses
wrote for us, 'If someone's brother dies, leaving a wife but no child,
his brother must take the wife and raise up descendants for his
brother.' **20** Now there were seven brothers. The first married a
woman and died, leaving no descendants. **21** So the second married
her and died, leaving no descendants, and the third likewise.
22 And the seven left no descendants. Last of all the woman also
died. **23** At the resurrection [when they arise] whose wife will she
be? For all seven had been married to her." **24** Jesus said to them,
"Are you not misled because you do not know the scriptures or the
power of God? **25** When they rise from the dead, they neither marry
nor are given in marriage, but they are like the angels in heaven.
26 As for the dead being raised, have you not read in the Book of
Moses, in the passage about the bush, how God told him, 'I am the
God of Abraham, [the] God of Isaac, and [the] God of Jacob'? **27** He
is not God of the dead but of the living. You are greatly misled."

Lk 20:27–40

27 Some Sadducees, those who deny that there is a resurrection,
came forward and put this question to him, **28** saying, "Teacher,
Moses wrote for us, 'If someone's brother dies leaving a wife but no
child, his brother must take the wife and raise up descendants for
his brother.' **29** Now there were seven brothers; the first married
a woman but died childless. **30** Then the second **31** and the third
married her, and likewise all the seven died childless. **32** Finally the
woman also died. **33** Now at the resurrection whose wife will that
woman be? For all seven had been married to her." **34** Jesus said to
them, "The children of this age marry and are given in marriage;
35 but those who are deemed worthy to attain to the coming age
and to the resurrection of the dead neither marry nor are given in
marriage. **36** They can no longer die, for they are like angels; and
they are the children of God because they are the ones who will rise.
37 That the dead will rise even Moses made known in the passage

about the bush, when he called 'Lord' the God of Abraham, the God of Isaac, and the God of Jacob; **38** and he is not God of the dead, but of the living, for to him all are alive." **39** Some of the scribes said in reply, "Teacher, you have answered well." **40** And they no longer dared to ask him anything.

The Pharisees and Herodians had their chance to trick and trap Jesus. Now it was the Sadducees' turn. This group of aristocratic Jewish conservatives questioned Jesus about resurrection. They did not believe in the afterlife. In fact, they did not believe in anything that was not specifically discussed in the Torah.

The Sadducees cited the directive in Deuteronomy 25 that a man should marry the childless widow of his deceased brother. This would allow the family name to be perpetuated and keep property within the family. Jesus' teachings about resurrection make this an absurd question. Jesus said there is no need for marriage in the afterlife. Having offspring and supporting a spouse are not necessary for the "angels in heaven."

Jesus deftly refuted the Sadducees' nonbelief in resurrection. He quoted from Exodus, the second book of the Torah, and their source of truth. Moses wrote that God declared Himself to continue to be the God of the long-deceased patriarchs, Abraham, Isaac, and Jacob. If that was so, then God still maintained a close relationship after their earthly bodies were long gone. They had thus been resurrected in another form or state. Jesus taught that the power of God can overcome anything, even death. In just a few short days, Jesus Himself would show this to be true.

YOU CONTINUE TO WATCH THE yardstick rise from the ground. Walking closer, you try to determine what is powering this strange phenomenon. You decide to test your own power (or lack thereof). You loudly **command** the yardstick to stop. You do not truly expect your **command** to have any effect. However, soon after yelling the **command** "stop," the yardstick ceases inching its way out of the ground. Is this just a coincidence or has your **command** really been obeyed? Either way, the yardstick has stopped with only two or three inches remaining underground. Do you dare issue another **command** for this resurrection to resume? You decide against issuing a second **command**, fearful of what might happen.

Your **command**, though certainly not **great**, represents the next unit: THE GREATEST COMMANDMENT.

THE GREATEST COMMANDMENT

Mt 22:34–40

34 When the Pharisees heard that he had silenced the Sadducees, they gathered together, **35** and one of them [a scholar of the law] tested him by asking, **36** "Teacher, which commandment in the law is the greatest?" **37** He said to him, "You shall love the Lord, your God, with all your heart, with all your soul, and with all your mind. **38** This is the greatest and the first commandment. **39** The second is like it: You shall love your neighbor as yourself. **40** The whole law and the prophets depend on these two commandments."

Mk 12:28–34

28 One of the scribes, when he came forward and heard them disputing and saw how well he had answered them, asked him, "Which is the first of all the commandments?" **29** Jesus replied, "The first is this: 'Hear, O Israel! The Lord our God is Lord alone! **30** You shall love the Lord your God with all your heart, with all your soul, with all your mind, and with all your strength.' **31** The second is this: 'You shall love your neighbor as yourself.' There is no other commandment greater than these." **32** The scribe said to him, "Well said, teacher. You are right in saying, 'He is One and there is no other than he.' **33** And 'to love him with all your heart, with all your understanding, with all your strength, and to love your neighbor as yourself' is worth more than all burnt offerings and sacrifices." **34** And when Jesus saw that [he] answered with understanding, he said to him, "You are not far from the kingdom of God." And no one dared to ask him any more questions.

Lk 10:25–28

25 There was a scholar of the law who stood up to test him and said, "Teacher, what must I do to inherit eternal life?" **26** Jesus said to him, "What is written in the law? How do you read it?" **27** He said in reply, "You shall love the Lord, your God, with all your heart, with all your being, with all your strength, and with all your mind, and your neighbor as yourself." **28** He replied to him, "You have answered correctly; do this and you will live."

Jesus was again tested by the Pharisees. One of their scribes, an expert in Jewish Law, posed what seemed like a difficult question. Asking which of the 613 commands of the Jewish Law is the greatest sounded like a setup for controversy. Jesus' elegant response was a beautiful summary of His entire message. He cited Deuteronomy 6:4–5, which instructs us to love God with all of the gifts we have been given. This is the first of the Ten Commandments that says there is but one God to whom all of our love should be directed. This command focuses on having a personal relationship with God, not on the many external precepts of the Jewish Law which had become so burdensome.

Jesus then added a second commandment, which stemmed from the first. It emphasized that loving others goes hand in hand with loving God. Again the focus was on love. Jesus quoted Leviticus 19:18, reminding us to love others as we love ourselves. Hopefully we have a healthy form of self-love and realize that the all-loving God is our Father. This all-loving Father made us in His image and then sacrificed His only Son for us. We certainly must be special and lovable!

A YARDSTICK IS OF LITTLE use in the ground. You walk over and give it a tug. A firm yank on the end of the stick does nothing. It feels as if the yardstick is anchored in cement. A stronger pull has the same results. While planning your next effort, up walks a smiling **samurai** with a sharp, shiny sword. This **samurai** is a welcome sight. You recognize him as the same **samurai** who cut off your handcuffs back in Landmark 3. This **good samurai** has seen you struggle to free the yardstick and offers to help. The **good samurai** grabs the thin wood with both hands and pulls mightily. No luck. The yardstick does not move an inch. Quickly, the **good samurai** grabs his sword. With a smooth turn of his shoulder, the sword flashes through the air. It easily slices through the yardstick at ground level. The **good samurai** picks up the not-quite-a-yard stick and hands it to you with a smile. This encounter with the **good samurai** helps you recall THE PARABLE OF THE GOOD SAMARITAN.

THE PARABLE OF THE GOOD
SAMARITAN

Lk 10:29–37

> 29 But because he wished to justify himself, he said to Jesus, "And who is my neighbor?" 30 Jesus replied, "A man fell victim to robbers as he went down from Jerusalem to Jericho. They stripped and beat him and went off leaving him half-dead. 31 A priest happened to be going down that road, but when he saw him, he passed by on the opposite side. 32 Likewise a Levite came to the place, and when he saw him, he passed by on the opposite side. 33 But a Samaritan traveler who came upon him was moved with compassion at the sight. 34 He approached the victim, poured oil and wine over his wounds and bandaged them. Then he lifted him up on his own animal, took him to an inn and cared for him. 35 The next day he took out two silver coins and gave them to the innkeeper with the instruction, 'Take care of him. If you spend more than what I have given you, I shall repay you on my way back.' 36 Which of these three, in your opinion, was neighbor to the robbers' victim?" 37 He answered, "The one who treated him with mercy." Jesus said to him, "Go and do likewise."

In this often told, but less often followed parable, Jesus clarified what He meant by "neighbor." The Samaritans were geographic neighbors of the Jews. Surely Jesus did not mean the Jews should love these nearby, but long-despised people. A Jew was considered to become "unclean" by having contact with one of these "foreigners." Similarly, coming into contact with a corpse would also make a Jew unclean. For this latter reason, the priest and the Levite avoided the man on the road who appeared to be dead. However, the Samaritan treated the man with love and compassion, as if he were a brother. How it must have stung to hear that the hated Samaritan, but not the Jewish leaders, did the right thing. He treated the stranger as a neighbor. He demonstrated that we are all neighbors to each other. We are all God's people, even those we may consider to be our "Samaritans." The Samaritan demonstrates Jesus' new standard of holiness.

YOU ARE NOW IN POSSESSION of a short yardstick. Though missing a few inches, it can still be used for measuring. You decide to do just that. Looking around, you spot what appears to be a large marble statue in the distance. You walk over to take a few measurements. As you approach the statue, you cannot believe your eyes. Standing before you, bigger than life, is perhaps the most famous sculpture in all the world. It is *David*, the masterpiece created by Michelangelo over five hundred years ago. You must be seeing things! Standing beside **David**, you feel dwarfed by this towering treasure. Running your hands over **David's** feet and ankles verifies that you are not hallucinating. It is actually **David**. You climb up onto the pedestal with the yardstick and begin measuring. First to be measured are **David's** legs and his right arm extended by his side. Next is **David's** muscled torso, followed by his flexed left arm, which holds a slingshot draped over his shoulder. Last to be measured is **David's** head and its chiseled features. This close encounter with **David** signifies the unit regarding THE QUESTION ABOUT DAVID'S SON.

THE QUESTION ABOUT DAVID'S SON

Mt 22:41–46

41 While the Pharisees were gathered together, Jesus questioned them, **42** saying, "What is your opinion about the Messiah? Whose son is he?" They replied, "David's." **43** He said to them, "How, then, does David, inspired by the Spirit, call him 'lord,' saying:

44 'The Lord said to my lord,
"Sit at my right hand
until I place your enemies under your feet"'?

45 If David calls him 'lord,' how can he be his son?" **46** No one was able to answer him a word, nor from that day on did anyone dare to ask him any more questions.

Mk 12:35–37

35 As Jesus was teaching in the temple area he said, "How do the scribes claim that the Messiah is the son of David? **36** David himself, inspired by the holy Spirit, said:

'The Lord said to my lord,
"Sit at my right hand

until I place your enemies under your feet.'"

37 David himself calls him 'lord'; so how is he his son?" [The] great crowd heard this with delight.

Lk 20:41–44

41 Then he said to them, "How do they claim that the Messiah is the Son of David? 42 For David himself in the Book of Psalms says:

'The Lord said to my lord,
"Sit at my right hand
43 till I make your enemies your footstool."'

44 Now if David calls him 'lord,' how can he be his son?"

———————————

Jesus continued to clarify His identity. To those without faith, all of His previous words and deeds were still not enough. The Pharisees certainly believed in the greatness and power of their revered King David. Many believed that the Messiah, the expected "Son of David," would be great, yet inferior to David himself. Jesus cited Psalm 110:1 written by David, to show that this was incorrect. "Inspired" by the Holy Spirit, David referred to God as "Lord" and to the Messiah as "my Lord." David knew the Messiah would be greater than himself. Jesus descended from the Davidic line. He was part of the family tree. However, He was much more than another branch. He was the Son of David in His humanity, but the Son of God in His divinity.

YOU ARE FINISHING THE FINAL Davidic measurements when loud yelling begins. "Get down, get down, get down" is the stern order you hear from a number of voices below. You look down and see that you are surrounded by a large group of concerned **nuns** dressed in their black-and-white habits. When you try to speak, the shouting of the **nuns** drowns out your words. The **nuns'** current attitude toward you is worrisome. You quickly climb down the statue. The **nuns** back away, forming a circle with you and David in the center. You feel relieved that the **nuns** are now smiling. The **nun** who appears to be in charge begins to speak. She explains that this specially chosen group of **nuns** has temporarily been tasked with guarding David. You apologize, telling the **nuns** you certainly meant no harm. The **nuns** remind you of the word "deNUNciation." This encounter with the **nuns** is a reminder of the next unit: JESUS' DENUNCIATION OF THE SCRIBES.

||||||||||||||||||||||||||||||||||||||||||||||||||||||||||||||||||||||||||||||||||||||||||||||||||||||||||||||||||||||||||||

JESUS' DENUNCIATION OF THE SCRIBES

||||||||||||||||||||||||||||||||||||||||||||||||||||||||||||||||||||||||||||||||||||||||||||||||||||||||||||||||||||||||||||

Mt 23:1–36

1 Then Jesus spoke to the crowds and to his disciples, **2** saying, "The scribes and the Pharisees have taken their seat on the chair of Moses. **3** Therefore, do and observe all things whatsoever they tell you, but do not follow their example. For they preach but they do not practice. **4** They tie up heavy burdens [hard to carry] and lay them on people's shoulders, but they will not lift a finger to move them. **5** All their works are performed to be seen. They widen their phylacteries and lengthen their tassels. **6** They love places of honor at banquets, seats of honor in synagogues, **7** greetings in marketplaces, and the salutation 'Rabbi.' **8** As for you, do not be called 'Rabbi.' You have but one teacher, and you are all brothers. **9** Call no one on earth your father; you have but one Father in heaven. **10** Do not be called 'Master'; you have but one master, the Messiah. **11** The greatest among you must be your servant. **12** Whoever exalts himself will be humbled; but whoever humbles himself will be exalted.

13 "Woe to you, scribes and Pharisees, you hypocrites. You lock the kingdom of heaven before human beings. You do not enter yourselves, nor do you allow entrance to those trying to enter. **[14]**

15 "Woe to you, scribes and Pharisees, you hypocrites. You traverse sea and land to make one convert, and when that happens you make him a child of Gehenna twice as much as yourselves.

16 "Woe to you, blind guides, who say, 'If one swears by the temple, it means nothing, but if one swears by the gold of the temple, one is obligated.' **17** Blind fools, which is greater, the gold, or the temple that made the gold sacred? **18** And you say, 'If one swears by the altar, it means nothing, but if one swears by the gift on the altar, one is obligated.' **19** You blind ones, which is greater, the gift, or the altar that makes the gift sacred? **20** One who swears by the altar swears by it and all that is upon it; **21** one who swears by the temple swears by it and by him who dwells in it; **22** one who swears by heaven swears by the throne of God and by him who is seated on it.

23 "Woe to you, scribes and Pharisees, you hypocrites. You pay tithes of mint and dill and cummin, and have neglected the weightier things of the law: judgment and mercy and fidelity. [But] these you should have done, without neglecting the others. **24** Blind guides, who strain out the gnat and swallow the camel!

25 "Woe to you, scribes and Pharisees, you hypocrites. You cleanse the outside of cup and dish, but inside they are full of plunder and self-indulgence. **26** Blind Pharisee, cleanse first the inside of the cup, so that the outside also may be clean.

27 "Woe to you, scribes and Pharisees, you hypocrites. You are like whitewashed tombs, which appear beautiful on the outside, but inside are full of dead men's bones and every kind of filth. **28** Even so, on the outside you appear righteous, but inside you are filled with hypocrisy and evildoing.

29 "Woe to you, scribes and Pharisees, you hypocrites. You build the tombs of the prophets and adorn the memorials of the righteous, **30** and you say, 'If we had lived in the days of our ancestors, we would not have joined them in shedding the prophets' blood.' **31** Thus you bear witness against yourselves that you are the children of those who murdered the prophets; **32** now fill up what your ancestors measured out! **33** You serpents, you brood of vipers, how can you flee from the judgment of Gehenna? **34** Therefore, behold, I send to you prophets and wise men and scribes; some of them you will kill and crucify, some of them you will scourge in your synagogues and pursue from town to town, **35** so that there may come upon you all the righteous blood shed upon earth, from the righteous blood of Abel to the blood of Zechariah, the son of Barachiah, whom you murdered between the sanctuary and the altar. **36** Amen, I say to you, all these things will come upon this generation."

Mk 12:38–40

38 In the course of his teaching he said, "Beware of the scribes, who like to go around in long robes and accept greetings in the marketplaces, **39** seats of honor in synagogues, and places of honor at banquets. **40** They devour the houses of widows and, as a pretext, recite lengthy prayers. They will receive a very severe condemnation."

Lk 11:37–54

37 After he had spoken, a Pharisee invited him to dine at his home. He entered and reclined at table to eat. **38** The Pharisee was amazed to see that he did not observe the prescribed washing before the meal. **39** The Lord said to him, "Oh you Pharisees! Although you cleanse the outside of the cup and the dish, inside you are filled with plunder and evil. **40** You fools! Did not the maker of the outside also make the inside? **41** But as to what is within, give alms, and behold, everything will be clean for you. **42** Woe to you Pharisees! You pay tithes of mint and of rue and of every garden herb, but you pay no attention to judgment and to love for God. These you should have done, without overlooking the others.

43 Woe to you Pharisees! You love the seat of honor in synagogues and greetings in marketplaces. **44** Woe to you! You are like unseen graves over which people unknowingly walk."

45 Then one of the scholars of the law said to him in reply, "Teacher, by saying this you are insulting us too." **46** And he said, "Woe also to you scholars of the law! You impose on people burdens hard to carry, but you yourselves do not lift one finger to touch them. **47** Woe to you! You build the memorials of the prophets whom your ancestors killed. **48** Consequently, you bear witness and give consent to the deeds of your ancestors, for they killed them and you do the building. **49** Therefore, the wisdom of God said, 'I will send to them prophets and apostles; some of them they will kill and persecute' **50** in order that this generation might be charged with the blood of all the prophets shed since the foundation of the world, **51** from the blood of Abel to the blood of Zechariah who died between the altar and the temple building. Yes, I tell you, this generation will be charged with their blood! **52** Woe to you, scholars of the law! You have taken away the key of knowledge. You yourselves did not enter and you stopped those trying to enter." **53** When he left, the scribes and Pharisees began to act with hostility toward him and to interrogate him about many things, **54** for they were plotting to catch him at something he might say.

Jesus' controversy with the Pharisees has now reached its climax. His harsh words toward them should also be taken as a warning to us. It is a warning against certain attitudes and behaviors. In contrast to the Beatitudes and their encouragement of an attitude, the woes warn us of what to avoid. In Matthew and Mark, Jesus spoke to His disciples and the crowd. In Luke, Jesus' harsh words provided food for thought after He had eaten at the home of a Pharisee.

The Pharisees were not devoid of good qualities. Jesus did acknowledge that much of their teaching had merit. However, they were still hypocrites. They did not practice what they preached. Their demands were more about strict adherence to many minor "laws" than about following the principles described by Jesus in "The Greatest Commandment" several units back. Their burdensome demands demonstrated misplaced values. The Pharisees imposed a burden, while Jesus calls us to Himself, where we will find rest and a burden that is light.

Jesus often preached the importance of humility. Previously, He had scolded the vanity of the Pharisees (and perhaps us) by comparing the praying styles of a Pharisee and a tax collector (Landmark 31). Now He strongly discouraged the seeking of public recognition in other forms.

The series of "woes" (seven in Matthew, six in Luke) are a reminder to us of what is important. Hair-splitting distinctions between trivial matters is not. What comes from inside should be the focus of our efforts. Cultivating the inner self will be made manifest in our love of God and neighbor.

These scathing words directed at the Pharisees must have stung. Jesus had exposed their efforts to conceal their inner corruption with outwardly pious behaviors. He was not quite finished. Comparing them to their ancestors who killed the prophets and the righteous was the final blow. It was also an observation that would be replayed in a few short days.

AFTER HEARING YOUR APOLOGY, THE nuns resume the guarding of David. Coming toward the nuns is another group of women that look familiar to you. They are all dressed in black, looking quite similar to the nuns in their habits. Now you remember! They are the **widows** who played soccer with you back in Landmark 11. They now have a different agenda. Each of the **widows** gives some money to the nuns. You hear the **widows** say that they are making a **contribution**. The surprised nuns ask what their **contribution** is for. The **widows** explain that they are **contributing** money so the nuns can hire a security officer to guard the statue of David. The nuns express their gratitude to the **widows** for their thoughtful **contribution**. It has been quite stressful bearing the responsibility of guarding the priceless masterpiece. This **contribution** from the **widows** recalls the final unit to be associated with the yardstick Landmark: THE POOR WIDOW'S CONTRIBUTION.

THE POOR WIDOW'S CONTRIBUTION

Mk 12:41–44

41 He sat down opposite the treasury and observed how the crowd put money into the treasury. Many rich people put in large sums. 42 A poor widow also came and put in two small coins worth a few cents. 43 Calling his disciples to himself, he said to them,

"Amen, I say to you, this poor widow put in more than all the other contributors to the treasury. 44 For they have all contributed from their surplus wealth, but she, from her poverty, has contributed all she had, her whole livelihood."

Lk 21:1–4

1 When he looked up he saw some wealthy people putting their offerings into the treasury 2 and he noticed a poor widow putting in two small coins. 3 He said, "I tell you truly, this poor widow put in more than all the rest; 4 for those others have all made offerings from their surplus wealth, but she, from her poverty, has offered her whole livelihood."

Mark and Luke describe a dramatic contrast in the behavior of some of the scribes and Pharisees. Scribes at times were guilty of padding their wallets at the expense of widows. Functioning as trustees of the deceased husband's estate provided the opportunity to help themselves to a portion. Compare that to the poor widow's contribution to the temple treasury. She makes a true sacrifice by giving from what she needed to live on. Not only that, it was given with humility, without any desire for prestige or honor. Her gift of love was reward enough.

THERMOMETER

The thirty-seventh Landmark is quite different from the last one, though they do have something in common. Both are used for measuring. It is a **thermometer**. The type of **thermometer** used to measure body rather than air temperature. It is a medical **thermometer**. Why is it Landmark 37? "Normal" body temperature is considered to be 37 degrees Celsius (also 98.6 degrees F). So imagine yourself feeling a bit feverish. You happen to have a temporal **thermometer**, not the type that goes under the tongue. It is called a temporal **thermometer** because it records the temperature of the temporal artery. You are now holding the **thermometer** in your hand. As you prepare to take your temperature, you hope the reading will be a "normal" 37 degrees Celsius.

Your thermometer is properly used by swiping it across the forehead. However, since it is called a temporal thermometer you mistakenly press it against your **temple** area. This is the same **temple** area where you received the disappointing kiss back in Landmark 25. Though it feels odd, you continue to press the thermometer to your **temple** for several minutes. The thermometer is getting tangled in the hair covering your **temple**. Even worse, your **temple** is getting sore from the applied pressure. Finally, it seems like you have held the thermometer against your **temple** long enough. You begin to wonder if you should hold it against your other **temple**. You decide against this and remove the thermometer from your **temple** to check the result. This improper placement of the thermometer against your **temple** helps recall another unit concerning the temple in Jerusalem. It is Jesus' FORETELLING THE TEMPLE'S DESTRUCTION.

FORETELLING THE TEMPLE'S DESTRUCTION

Mt 24:1–2

1 Jesus left the temple area and was going away, when his disciples approached him to point out the temple buildings. 2 He said to them in reply, "You see all these things, do you not? Amen, I say to you, there will not be left here a stone upon another stone that will not be thrown down."

Mk 13:1–2

1 As he was making his way out of the temple area one of his disciples said to him, "Look, teacher, what stones and what buildings!" 2 Jesus said to him, "Do you see these great buildings? There will not be one stone left upon another that will not be thrown down."

Lk 21:5–6

5 While some people were speaking about how the temple was adorned with costly stones and votive offerings, he said, 6 "All that you see here—the days will come when there will not be left a stone upon another stone that will not be thrown down."

The great Jerusalem Temple and its adjacent buildings must have been a spectacular sight. The temple's grandeur and massive size made it the largest structure that the vast majority of its visitors would ever see. Herod the Great had begun the ambitious project of renovating the temple some fifty years earlier. With its great walls and massive stones, the temple probably looked as if it would last forever. Jesus' prediction of the temple's destruction must have seemed incredible and frightening. The literal meaning of this prophecy was fulfilled close to forty years later. The Roman army did "throw down the stones" when the temple, as well as the city of Jerusalem, were destroyed in AD 70.

The temple was the most important place in the world for the Jewish people. It was their center of worship. The Jews gathered from everywhere to praise their God at the great holy temple. It symbolized the presence of their God among them. It symbolized their world. Jesus' prophetic words about the end of the temple were words of warning, but also much more.

Foretelling the destruction of the great temple was also symbolic in several ways. This unit is the beginning of Matthew's "Apocalyptic Discourse," in which Jesus teaches about future events and the end times. The temple's destruction symbolically marked the end of the Old Covenant, to make room for Jesus' New Covenant Church. It was also a foreshadowing of the end of the world and the coming of the kingdom of God. This included Jesus' second coming and the Final Judgment. Upcoming units will address these apocalyptic events.

YOU ARE ALARMED BY THE reading on the thermometer. It indicates that your body temperature is critically elevated. It is so high the thermometer flashes the words "**the end** is near." Can this be accurate? Just then, as if to reinforce the warning, a woman walks by carrying two **signs**. One **sign** reads "**The End** Is Coming." The other **sign** warns "**The End** Is Closer Than You Think." These **signs** about "**the end**" are extremely frightening. You ask the woman with the **signs** what you should do. She asks if you have any other symptoms that may be a **sign** that your **end** is near. You respond, "No." She decides to put her **signs** of "**the end**" face down to lessen your anxiety. These worrisome **signs of the end** refer to the next unit when Jesus discusses SIGNS OF THE END.

SIGNS OF THE END

Mt 24:3–8

3 As he was sitting on the Mount of Olives, the disciples approached him privately and said, "Tell us, when will this happen, and what sign will there be of your coming, and of the end of the age?" **4** Jesus said to them in reply, "See that no one deceives you. **5** For many will come in my name, saying, 'I am the Messiah,' and they will deceive many. **6** You will hear of wars and reports of wars; see that you are not alarmed, for these things must happen, but it will not yet be the end. **7** Nation will rise against nation, and kingdom against kingdom; there will be famines and earthquakes from place to place. **8** All these are the beginning of the labor pains."

Mk 13:3-8

3 As he was sitting on the Mount of Olives opposite the temple area, Peter, James, John, and Andrew asked him privately, 4 "Tell us, when will this happen, and what sign will there be when all these things are about to come to an end?" 5 Jesus began to say to them, "See that no one deceives you. 6 Many will come in my name saying, 'I am he,' and they will deceive many. 7 When you hear of wars and reports of wars do not be alarmed; such things must happen, but it will not yet be the end. 8 Nation will rise against nation and kingdom against kingdom. There will be earthquakes from place to place and there will be famines. These are the beginnings of the labor pains."

Lk 21:7-11

7 Then they asked him, "Teacher, when will this happen? And what sign will there be when all these things are about to happen?" 8 He answered, "See that you not be deceived, for many will come in my name, saying, 'I am he,' and 'The time has come.' Do not follow them! 9 When you hear of wars and insurrections, do not be terrified; for such things must happen first, but it will not immediately be the end." 10 Then he said to them, "Nation will rise against nation, and kingdom against kingdom. 11 There will be powerful earthquakes, famines, and plagues from place to place; and awesome sights and mighty signs will come from the sky."

People like to feel a sense of control in their lives. Few want to be taken by complete surprise by anything, especially when it comes to major life events. Here Jesus provided His disciples, both past and present, with information about future occurrences. Not just major occurrences, but cataclysmic and literally earth-shaking events. It is ironic that He delivered this apocalyptic information on the very mountain where Zechariah prophesied that the Great Battle at the end of time would occur (Zech 14:4).

Jesus' prediction about the destruction of the temple did come true relatively soon (about forty years) after He delivered this discourse. What of the other dire predictions? Many look at our chaotic world today and say the "labor pains" have begun. This is an appropriate description. The pain and suffering at the end of time will occur before the delivery of the Kingdom. Though we might like to know the specific time, it is beyond our control. We do have control over what kind of condition our individual God-given temple is in when our personal time comes to an end.

YOU WERE SO FOCUSED ON the woman's signs of "The End" that you failed to notice the small **purse** she had on her arm. This **purse** is very different from the large heavy **purse** that struck you in the chest back in Landmark 16. After putting down her signs, the woman stands before you holding the small, seemingly harmless **purse**. You are struck by the elegance and beauty of the **purse**. It appears to be made from some exotic hide. It is the **purse's** glittering jewels that catch your eyes. The woman notices you admiring the **purse**. She now clutches it a bit tighter, as if she is hiding something inside. You ask her where she got the **purse**. She refuses to answer. Your curiosity about the **purse** grows. You ask her what is inside the **purse**. The woman is now clearly upset and moves toward you. You recall from Landmark 16 that "**purse**" stands for persecution. This rather unpleasant scenario about the woman's **purse** refers to Jesus' description of THE COMING PERSECUTION.

THE COMING PERSECUTION

Mt 10:17–22; 24:9–14

17 "But beware of people, for they will hand you over to courts and scourge you in their synagogues, **18** and you will be led before governors and kings for my sake as a witness before them and the pagans. **19** When they hand you over, do not worry about how you are to speak or what you are to say. You will be given at that moment what you are to say. **20** For it will not be you who speak but the Spirit of your Father speaking through you. **21** Brother will hand over brother to death, and the father his child; children will rise up against parents and have them put to death. **22** You will be hated by all because of my name, but whoever endures to the end will be saved.

...

9 "Then they will hand you over to persecution, and they will kill you. You will be hated by all nations because of my name. **10** And then many will be led into sin; they will betray and hate one another. **11** Many false prophets will arise and deceive many; **12** and because of the increase of evildoing, the love of many will grow cold. **13** But the one who perseveres to the end will be saved. **14** And this gospel of the kingdom will be preached throughout the world as a witness to all nations, and then the end will come."

Mk 13:9–13

9 "Watch out for yourselves. They will hand you over to the courts. You will be beaten in synagogues. You will be arraigned before governors and kings because of me, as a witness before them. 10 But the gospel must first be preached to all nations. 11 When they lead you away and hand you over, do not worry beforehand about what you are to say. But say whatever will be given to you at that hour. For it will not be you who are speaking but the holy Spirit. 12 Brother will hand over brother to death, and the father his child; children will rise up against parents and have them put to death. 13 You will be hated by all because of my name. But the one who perseveres to the end will be saved."

Lk 12:10–12; 21:12–19

10 "Everyone who speaks a word against the Son of Man will be forgiven, but the one who blasphemes against the holy Spirit will not be forgiven. 11 When they take you before synagogues and before rulers and authorities, do not worry about how or what your defense will be or about what you are to say. 12 For the holy Spirit will teach you at that moment what you should say.

...

12 "Before all this happens, however, they will seize and persecute you, they will hand you over to the synagogues and to prisons, and they will have you led before kings and governors because of my name. 13 It will lead to your giving testimony. 14 Remember, you are not to prepare your defense beforehand, 15 for I myself shall give you a wisdom in speaking that all your adversaries will be powerless to resist or refute. 16 You will even be handed over by parents, brothers, relatives, and friends, and they will put some of you to death. 17 You will be hated by all because of my name, 18 but not a hair on your head will be destroyed. 19 By your perseverance you will secure your lives."

Jesus had warned His disciples that following Him and preaching the Gospel would involve persecution. He now tells us all that witnessing for His sake and in His name will involve persecution. Jesus would soon be handed over to a court, beaten, and scourged. We, too, will endure hardship for our beliefs and behavior. In His suffering, Jesus knew He was doing the will of the Father and had His support. We also know that in our Christian lives we do the will of the Father. To assist us, we are given the gift of the Spirit to guide our words and deeds. Matthew, Mark, and Luke all record these words of reassurance in the face of future persecution. In Luke, there is an additional warning. Speaking against Jesus can be forgiven. Blasphemy against the Spirit is another matter. That is to say that refusing to even consider the Christian message inspired by the Spirit will not be forgiven.

YOU AND THE WOMAN HOLDING the purse are now standing toe to toe. This confrontation is quite uncomfortable. If your temperature was not elevated before, it certainly is now. The woman angrily opens her purse saying, "Well you wanted to know, so take a look inside." You are shocked to see that she is carrying a **bomb!** The **bomb** has several wires and buttons. Most concerning is the **bomb's** ticking sound! The woman says it will explode very soon. She further explains that her signs were a warning about the **bomb**. You are frozen with fear and stare wide-eyed at the **bomb** inside her purse. You want to run, but you would also like to do something to prevent the **bomb** from detonating. As if reading your mind, the woman says, "The **bomb** will go off and there is nothing you can do about it!" This life-threatening turn of events with the **bomb** will certainly cause you to think of the next unit: THE GREAT ABOMINATION.

THE GREAT ABOMINATION

Mt 24:15–28

15 "When you see the desolating abomination spoken of through Daniel the prophet standing in the holy place (let the reader understand), **16** then those in Judea must flee to the mountains, **17** a person on the housetop must not go down to get things out of his house, **18** a person in the field must not return to get his cloak. **19** Woe to pregnant women and nursing mothers in those days. **20** Pray that your flight not be in winter or on the sabbath, **21** for at that time there will be great tribulation, such as has not been since the beginning of the world until now, nor ever will be. **22** And if those days had not been shortened, no one would be saved; but for the sake of the elect they will be shortened. **23** If anyone says to you then, 'Look, here is the Messiah!' or, 'There he is!' do not believe it. **24** False messiahs and false prophets will arise, and they will perform signs and wonders so great as to deceive, if that were possible, even the elect. **25** Behold, I have told it to you beforehand. **26** So if they say to you, 'He is in the desert,' do not go out there; if they say, 'He is in the inner rooms,' do not believe it. **27** For just as lightning comes from the east and is seen as far as the west, so will the coming of the Son of Man be. **28** Wherever the corpse is, there the vultures will gather."

Mk 13:14–23

14 "When you see the desolating abomination standing where he should not (let the reader understand), then those in Judea must flee to the mountains, **15** [and] a person on a housetop must not go down or enter to get anything out of his house, **16** and a person in a field must not return to get his cloak. **17** Woe to pregnant women and nursing mothers in those days. **18** Pray that this does not happen in winter. **19** For those times will have tribulation such as has not been since the beginning of God's creation until now, nor ever will be. **20** If the Lord had not shortened those days, no one would be saved; but for the sake of the elect whom he chose, he did shorten the days. **21** If anyone says to you then, 'Look, here is the Messiah! Look, there he is!' do not believe it. **22** False messiahs and false prophets will arise and will perform signs and wonders in order to mislead, if that were possible, the elect. **23** Be watchful! I have told it all to you beforehand."

Lk 17:31–37; 21:20–24

31 "On that day, a person who is on the housetop and whose belongings are in the house must not go down to get them, and likewise a person in the field must not return to what was left behind. **32** Remember the wife of Lot. **33** Whoever seeks to preserve his life will lose it, but whoever loses it will save it. **34** I tell you, on that night there will be two people in one bed; one will be taken, the other left. **35** And there will be two women grinding meal together; one will be taken, the other left." **[36]** **37** They said to him in reply, "Where, Lord?" He said to them, "Where the body is, there also the vultures will gather."

...

20 "When you see Jerusalem surrounded by armies, know that its desolation is at hand. **21** Then those in Judea must flee to the mountains. Let those within the city escape from it, and let those in the countryside not enter the city, **22** for these days are the time of punishment when all the scriptures are fulfilled. **23** Woe to pregnant women and nursing mothers in those days, for a terrible calamity will come upon the earth and a wrathful judgment upon this people. **24** They will fall by the edge of the sword and be taken as captives to all the Gentiles; and Jerusalem will be trampled underfoot by the Gentiles until the times of the Gentiles are fulfilled."

Jesus' audience and the early readers of the Gospels were painfully aware of Jewish history, particularly several of the darker moments. These included the destruction of the original temple by the Babylonians in 586 BC and the more recent "abomination" in the temple in 167 BC. It is this latter event, the construction of a pagan altar of sacrifice in the temple by Antiochus Epiphanes IV, which Jesus recalled and Daniel had prophesied. Jesus now predicted the coming second destruction of the temple and the great suffering the people of Jerusalem would endure. It would be a time for which people must be prepared. Priorities must be in order. One must be able to leave behind earthly possessions, which will not last. Gentiles would cause this tribulation and be the source of abominable actions, but God was in control. Those who were faithful would be spared in the end. The righteous would be saved. Jesus' words also referred to the end times, which would also be a time of great tribulation, for which we all must be prepared.

FEELING FRANTIC INSIDE, YOU ARE trying your best to maintain the appearance of being in control. Calmly, you ask the woman why she wants to explode a bomb. She responds with a vague and worrisome answer. "I want to blow everything to **kingdom come**." You press her for more details, and she again says, "I want to blow everything to **kingdom come**." You are making no progress, and the bomb continues to tick. You are looking forward to the **coming of the Kingdom**, but this is not what you had in mind. If you don't do something fast, certainly everything in the vicinity, including yourself, is going to be blown to **kingdom come**. The woman then mutters something about being angry with her son. Perhaps her relationship with him is at the root of her statement of "blowing everything to **kingdom come**." The response and behavior of the woman and your concerns are a reminder of Jesus' PREACHING ABOUT THE COMING OF THE KINGDOM.

PREACHING ABOUT THE COMING OF
THE KINGDOM

Lk 17:20–21

20 Asked by the Pharisees when the kingdom of God would come, he said in reply, "The coming of the kingdom of God cannot be observed, 21 and no one will announce, 'Look, here it is,' or, 'There it is.' For behold the kingdom of God is among you."

Recall that Jesus began His Galilean ministry by making several declarations. "The Kingdom is at hand" and entry into the Kingdom requires a change in heart and behavior. Throughout His ministry, Jesus provided the instruction and example for making these changes. The Pharisees, who had been a thorn in Jesus' side (and soon His head) from the outset, now questioned when this kingdom of God would come. They did not realize that it was already present in Jesus Himself. Jesus responded to their question by telling them that indeed the Kingdom was among them. But they were too deaf to hear. Let us pray that we recognize that the Kingdom is present in Jesus. Hopefully, we will change our lives and follow Jesus so that the Kingdom is not only among us, but within us.

AS YOU CONTINUE SPEAKING WITH the woman, her calm demeanor in the face of imminent death suddenly changes to uncertainty. She sees someone **coming**. Turning around, you see a man **coming** toward you and the woman. The woman yells, "That's my **son coming**!" This **coming of her son** has certainly changed her mood. You now hope that the **coming of the son** will keep her from exploding the bomb. The woman appears to have mixed feelings about **the coming of her son**. She seems at once to be angry, but also relieved by his **coming**. The **son** arrives and gives his mother a caring, yet frustrated look. He says, "I hope I have **come** in time." The **son** quickly reaches into his mother's purse and yanks on several wires. The ticking stops. You breathe a sigh of relief. The **coming of the son** has saved you and the woman. This close call is a reminder of Jesus' words about THE COMING OF THE SON OF MAN.

THE COMING OF THE SON OF MAN

Mt 24:29–31, 37–42

29 Immediately after the tribulation of those days,

the sun will be darkened,
and the moon will not give its light,
and the stars will fall from the sky,
and the powers of the heavens will be shaken.

30 And then the sign of the Son of Man will appear in heaven, and all the tribes of the earth will mourn, and they will see the Son of Man coming upon the clouds of heaven with power and great glory. **31** And he will send out his angels with a trumpet blast, and they will gather his elect from the four winds, from one end of the heavens to the other.

...

37 "For as it was in the days of Noah, so it will be at the coming of the Son of Man. **38** In [those] days before the flood, they were eating and drinking, marrying and giving in marriage, up to the day that Noah entered the ark. **39** They did not know until the flood came and carried them all away. So will it be [also] at the coming of the Son of Man. **40** Two men will be out in the field; one will be taken, and one will be left. **41** Two women will be grinding at the mill; one will be taken and one will be left. **42** Therefore, stay awake! For you do not know on which day your Lord will come."

Mk 13:24–27

24 "But in those days after that tribulation

the sun will be darkened,
and the moon will not give its light,
25 and the stars will be falling from the sky,
and the powers in the heavens will be shaken.

26 And then they will see 'the Son of Man coming in the clouds' with great power and glory, **27** and then he will send out the angels and gather [his] elect from the four winds, from the end of the earth to the end of the sky."

Lk 17:22–30; 21:25–28

22 Then he said to his disciples, "The days will come when you will long to see one of the days of the Son of Man, but you will not see it. **23** There will be those who will say to you, 'Look, there he is,' [or] 'Look, here he is.' Do not go off, do not run in pursuit. **24** For just as lightning flashes and lights up the sky from one side to the other, so will the Son of Man be [in his day]. **25** But first he must suffer greatly and be rejected by this generation. **26** As it was in the days of Noah, so it will be in the days of the Son of Man; **27** they were eating and drinking, marrying and giving in marriage up to the day that Noah entered the ark, and the flood came and destroyed them all. **28** Similarly, as it was in the days of Lot: they were eating, drinking, buying, selling, planting, building: **29** on the day when Lot left Sodom, fire and brimstone rained from the sky to destroy them all. **30** So it will be on the day the Son of Man is revealed."

...

25 "There will be signs in the sun, the moon, and the stars, and on earth nations will be in dismay, perplexed by the roaring of the sea and the waves. **26** People will die of fright in anticipation of what is coming upon the world, for the powers of the heavens will be shaken. **27** And then they will see the Son of Man coming in a cloud with power and great glory. **28** But when these signs begin to happen, stand erect and raise your heads because your redemption is at hand."

Jesus has told His disciples of many things to come: the destruction of Jerusalem and the holy temple, warning signs, persecution, and the Kingdom. There is just one coming attraction to mention, and ironically He has already come! It is the Son of Man, Jesus Himself.

The title "Son of Man" is often used in the Hebrew Scriptures and frequently used by Jesus Himself. In both circumstances, the title had different meanings. The most obvious was to indicate humanity. We are all a "son of man." We were all born by a woman and have human parents. In using this term, Jesus indicated that He was one of us. He knew firsthand how we think, feel, and behave. The other meaning of this title was rooted in the Book of Daniel (Dan 7:13). It has a powerful Messianic meaning. Jesus, who was now sitting on the Mount of Olives with His disciples, would be this figure. He would be the one sitting upon the clouds, accompanied by the angels. He would come with great power and glory and victory. It would be quite the contrast to the apparent terrible defeat the apostles would witness in a few short days.

When will this occur? It is a question Jesus was asked and one we all ask ourselves. Jesus was not specific, though He warned it would be "after the tribulation." Jesus also used apocalyptic imagery similar to several Jewish prophets. Scenes of cosmic catastrophe were described to depict the downfall of pagan nations by Amos, Joel, Ezekiel, and Isaiah. Jesus talked of a dark sun, falling stars, and shaking heavens to emphasize the significance and magnificence of His second coming. We should not fear! Jesus also offered words of hope for His followers. Their reward would be at hand.

Landmark 38:

REVOLVER

Y our heart is still racing from the recent close call with the bomb. Fortunately, that encounter is behind you. It is time to move on to the
next Landmark, 38. Just ahead, you spot an object lying on the ground.
It appears to be some type of gun. It is fairly small, so if it is a gun it is
probably a pistol. Approaching the object, you see that in fact it is a .38
revolver. After the recent bomb scare, the gun causes a bit of anxiety.
Your first thoughts are whether the .38 **revolver** is loaded and who the
revolver may belong to. Cautiously, you bend over and pick it up. While
contemplating what to do next, you realize you are now holding the thir-
ty-eighth Landmark, a .38 **revolver**.

 While holding the revolver, you first check to see if it is loaded. The
bullet chambers are empty. You feel relieved since you do not know how
to properly handle this revolver. You have never taken any **lessons** on
gun safety or proper usage. This seems to be the perfect opportunity to
take some **lessons**. Unfortunately, you do not know of any place where
you could go for **lessons**. Walking along carrying the unloaded revolver,
you begin to hear gunfire. If you follow the sound, it may lead you to
the much-needed **lessons**. Indeed, it does. You soon arrive at a shooting
range. A large sign reads "**Lessons** Available for All Types of Guns." You
are relieved that you can take the necessary **lessons** to properly handle the
revolver. All of this talk about **lessons** is a reminder of a lesson that Jesus
taught: THE LESSON OF THE FIG TREE.

THE LESSON OF THE FIG TREE

Mt 24:32–35

32 "Learn a lesson from the fig tree. When its branch becomes tender and sprouts leaves, you know that summer is near. **33** In the same way, when you see all these things, know that he is near, at the gates. **34** Amen, I say to you, this generation will not pass away until all these things have taken place. **35** Heaven and earth will pass away, but my words will not pass away."

Mk 13:28–31

28 "Learn a lesson from the fig tree. When its branch becomes tender and sprouts leaves, you know that summer is near. **29** In the same way, when you see these things happening, know that he is near, at the gates. **30** Amen, I say to you, this generation will not pass away until all these things have taken place. **31** Heaven and earth will pass away, but my words will not pass away."

Lk 21:29–33

29 He taught them a lesson. "Consider the fig tree and all the other trees. **30** When their buds burst open, you see for yourselves and know that summer is now near; **31** in the same way, when you see these things happening, know that the kingdom of God is near. **32** Amen, I say to you, this generation will not pass away until all these things have taken place. **33** Heaven and earth will pass away, but my words will not pass away."

While preaching the Apocalyptic Discourse to His disciples, Jesus told a short parable. Again the fig tree made an appearance. This time it was not cursed or found withered. Jesus used its familiar growth cycle to further discuss the coming sequence of earth-shaking events. Jesus told the disciples that these events would occur within a generation. In the first century, a generation was considered to be forty years. The destruction of Jerusalem and the temple, events symbolizing the end of Old Covenant times, did in fact occur within a generation. Of course, Jesus' death and resurrection both occurred within a matter of days.

Some consider Jesus' resurrection a "second coming." Though it is not the final coming, it makes the ultimate coming of the Son of Man at the end of time possible. Perhaps Jesus did not mean that this final apocalyptic event would occur by the end of His current generation. In the next unit, we will see Jesus stress the need for watchfulness. He also said that only the Father knows the time of the final hour. Although the time is uncertain, Jesus does assure us of the authority and certainty of His words.

YOU ARE EXCITED TO LEARN the proper way to handle the revolver. The excitement soon gives way to disappointment when you look inside your wallet. It is empty. You have no money to pay for the lessons! The man collecting the fee senses your disappointment. He also notices the expensive **watch** on your wrist. He then offers lessons in exchange for the **watch**. You have to think about this for a moment. The **watch** is a family heirloom. You have worn the **watch** for many years and become quite attached to it. Perhaps it is time to give someone else the opportunity to enjoy the **watch**. You surprise yourself and agree to use the **watch** as payment for the lessons. Setting the gun down, you remove the **watch** from your wrist and hand it to the man. This parting with your **watch** in exchange for lessons signifies the next unit: THE NEED FOR WATCHFULNESS.

THE NEED FOR WATCHFULNESS

Mt 24:36–44

36 "But of that day and hour no one knows, neither the angels of heaven, nor the Son, but the Father alone. **37** For as it was in the days of Noah, so it will be at the coming of the Son of Man. **38** In [those] days before the flood, they were eating and drinking, marrying and giving in marriage, up to the day that Noah entered the ark. **39** They did not know until the flood came and carried them all away. So will it be [also] at the coming of the Son of Man. **40** Two men will be out in the field; one will be taken, and one will be left. **41** Two women will be grinding at the mill; one will be taken, and one will be left. **42** Therefore, stay awake! For you do not know on which day your Lord will come. **43** Be sure of this: if the master of the house had known the hour of night when the thief was coming, he would have stayed awake and not let his house be broken into. **44** So too, you also must be prepared, for at an hour you do not expect, the Son of Man will come."

Mk 13:32–37

32 "But of that day or hour, no one knows, neither the angels in heaven, nor the Son, but only the Father. **33** Be watchful! Be alert! You do not know when the time will come. **34** It is like a man traveling abroad. He leaves home and places his servants in charge, each with his work, and orders the gatekeeper to be on the watch. **35** Watch, therefore; you do not know when the lord of the house is coming, whether in the evening, or at midnight, or at cockcrow, or in the morning. **36** May he not come suddenly and find you sleeping. **37** What I say to you, I say to all: 'Watch!'"

Lk 17:26–30; 21:34–38; 12:35–40

26 "As it was in the days of Noah, so it will be in the days of the Son of Man; **27** they were eating and drinking, marrying and giving in marriage up to the day that Noah entered the ark, and the flood came and destroyed them all. **28** Similarly, as it was in the days of Lot: they were eating, drinking, buying, selling, planting, building; **29** on the day when Lot left Sodom, fire and brimstone rained from the sky to destroy them all. **30** So it will be on the day the Son of Man is revealed."

...

34 "Beware that your hearts do not become drowsy from carousing and drunkenness and the anxieties of daily life, and that day catch you by surprise **35** like a trap. For that day will assault everyone who lives on the face of the earth. **36** Be vigilant at all times and pray that you have the strength to escape the tribulations that are imminent and to stand before the Son of Man."

37 During the day, Jesus was teaching in the temple area, but at night he would leave and stay at the place called the Mount of Olives. **38** And all the people would get up early each morning to listen to him in the temple area.

...

35 "Gird your loins and light your lamps **36** and be like servants who await their master's return from a wedding, ready to open immediately when he comes and knocks. **37** Blessed are those servants whom the master finds vigilant on his arrival. Amen, I say to you, he will gird himself, have them recline at table, and proceed to wait on them. **38** And should he come in the second or third watch and find them prepared in this way, blessed are those servants. **39** Be sure of this: if the master of the house had known the hour when the thief was coming, he would not have let his house be broken into. **40** You also must be prepared, for at an hour you do not expect, the Son of Man will come."

What are we to make of Jesus' statement that He, the Son of the Father, did not know "the day or hour"? In Landmark 26, Jesus spoke of His inseparable relationship with the Father and all that the Father had revealed to Him. Was it possible that the Father had held back what would seem like important information? Since Jesus did share our human condition, perhaps He, like us, was not privy to this. Or perhaps Jesus was using hyperbole to emphasize a point that we need to live our lives with expectant watchfulness. This does not mean living in a constant state of anxiety, never knowing when the "flood" may come or if we will be "taken." Rather, we should live in a state of preparedness knowing that our loving Master will return one day and reward us for our vigilance. Luke made this point with the master who unexpectedly returned from the wedding. Upon his arrival, the master waited upon the servants. They were rewarded for their vigilance.

To the people of Jesus' time, these words also had a more immediate meaning. They were a warning of the imminent destruction of Jerusalem and the slaughter of those who did not flee. Like Sodom, Jerusalem would not escape the fire and brimstone of the Romans.

AFTER YOUR WATCH CHANGES HANDS, you are directed to the shooting range. Walking to the range, you see a woman working on her shooting skills. There is something about her that really stands out. It is not her excellent marksmanship or appearance. It is what she is wearing. Emblazoned on her shirt is a large scarlet letter. It is a scarlet *A*. You recall from Nathaniel Hawthorne's book, *The Scarlet Letter,* that the scarlet *A* designated an **adulterer**. Surely this woman is not advertising that she has committed **adultery**. Perhaps the *A* stands for her name rather than for "**adultery**." The woman notices you looking at the *A* and stops shooting. She does not take aim at you, but does seem to know what you are thinking. "Yes," she says, "it does stand for **adultery**." You are taken aback by her forthright admission. You are then reminded of the story of THE WOMAN CAUGHT IN ADULTERY.

THE WOMAN CAUGHT IN ADULTERY

Jn 8:1–11

1 Jesus went to the Mount of Olives. 2 But early in the morning he arrived again in the temple area, and all the people started coming to him, and he sat down and taught them. 3 Then the scribes and the Pharisees brought a woman who had been caught in adultery and made her stand in the middle. 4 They said to him, "Teacher, this woman was caught in the very act of committing adultery. 5 Now in the law, Moses commanded us to stone such women. So what do you say?" 6 They said this to test him, so that they could have some charge to bring against him. Jesus bent down and began to write on the ground with his finger. 7 But when they continued asking him, he straightened up and said to them, "Let the one among you who is without sin be the first to throw a stone at her." 8 Again he bent down and wrote on the ground. 9 And in response, they went away one by one, beginning with the elders. So he was left alone with the woman before him. 10 Then Jesus straightened up and said to her, "Woman, where are they? Has no one condemned you?" 11 She replied, "No one, sir." Then Jesus said, "Neither do I condemn you. Go, [and] from now on do not sin any more."

Jesus' teaching in the temple area in the days prior to His death continues with a well-known display of compassion. This story, found only in the Gospel of John, bears a strong resemblance to a scene you encountered back in Landmark 35. There the Pharisees tried to trap Jesus by asking Him if it was lawful to pay the census tax. Here they tried to force Jesus to either go against Roman Law or the Law of Moses. If Jesus followed the Mosaic Law in Deuteronomy 22, He would condone the stoning of a woman who had committed adultery. However, Rome had decreed that the Jews could not execute the death penalty. Conversely, following this Roman law would go against the Law of Moses. Jesus' brilliant reply turned the tables on the scheming Pharisees. If they stoned the woman, they would incur Rome's wrath. Jesus was not condoning this, because He knew that they were not without sin. When they realized they could not carry out the death penalty and dropped their stones, they appeared to be acknowledging that they were sinners. The story concluded with Jesus' words of compassion to the woman, and to us. He offers forgiveness and understanding, but with it the challenge to do better.

BIRTHDAY CAKE

Most people under a certain age enjoy their birthday each year. As we age, reminders of our fading youth and mortality grow stronger. For this reason, many people adopt a custom of having a "thirty-ninth birthday" every year. They never quite want to admit they have reached or passed "the big 4–0." Since you are now in need of a thirty-ninth Landmark, it seems fitting that it is a **birthday cake**. Picture a **birthday cake**, glowing brightly with thirty-nine candles. It must be a large cake to accommodate all thirty-nine flickering candles. Perhaps several of the candles are dripping wax on the icing that spells out your name. Thus, the thirty-ninth Landmark is a large, brightly lit **birthday cake**.

You are in a room seated at a large table, waiting for your birthday cake to arrive. An extra-large cake has been ordered this year, so you anticipate it being delivered by a number of **servants**. You actually employ a great many **servants**. Most of the servants are loyal and **faithful** to you. However, you have several **servants** who are rumored to be dishonest and **unfaithful**. You think you have discovered how to tell the **faithful** from the **unfaithful** servants. The **faithful servants** dress in white and walk about with their hands folded in prayer. The **unfaithful servants** are garbed in gray. They typically keep their hands in their pockets to conceal items they have stolen from you.

The gigantic birthday cake finally arrives. As expected, the **servants** carrying the cake are dressed in white from head to toe. The rest are in gray. After placing the cake before you, the **servants** circle the table to await your guests. The **servants** in white stand with folded hands. The others place their hands in their gray pants pockets. These **faithful** and **unfaithful** servants bring to mind the parable of THE FAITHFUL AND UN-FAITHFUL SERVANTS.

THE FAITHFUL AND UNFAITHFUL
SERVANTS

Mt 24:45–51

45 "Who, then, is the faithful and prudent servant, whom the master has put in charge of his household to distribute to them their food at the proper time? **46** Blessed is that servant whom his master on his arrival finds doing so. **47** Amen, I say to you, he will put him in charge of all his property. **48** But if that wicked servant says to himself, 'My master is long delayed,' **49** and begins to beat his fellow servants, and eat and drink with drunkards, **50** the servant's master will come on an unexpected day and at an unknown hour **51** and will punish him severely and assign him a place with the hypocrites, where there will be wailing and grinding of teeth."

Lk 12:41–48

41 Then Peter said, "Lord, is this parable meant for us or for everyone?" **42** And the Lord replied, "Who, then, is the faithful and prudent steward whom the master will put in charge of his servants to distribute [the] food allowance at the proper time? **43** Blessed is that servant whom his master on arrival finds doing so. **44** Truly, I say to you, he will put him in charge of all his property. **45** But if that servant says to himself, 'My master is delayed in coming,' and begins to beat the menservants and the maidservants, to eat and drink and get drunk, **46** then that servant's master will come on an unexpected day and at an unknown hour and will punish him severely and assign him a place with the unfaithful. **47** That servant who knew his master's will but did not make preparations nor act in accord with his will shall be beaten severely; **48** and the servant who was ignorant of his master's will but acted in a way deserving of a severe beating shall be beaten only lightly. Much will be required of the person entrusted with much, and still more will be demanded of the person entrusted with more."

Jesus discussed the importance of vigilance and preparedness for those awaiting His return. This period of expectation also required action, not only from the apostles, but from everyone. Like servants, we are given responsibilities. These tasks include caring for our fellow servants. We are given a period of time to tend to these responsibilities. Perhaps a few years or perhaps a hundred, we do not know. What we do know is that during our lives of uncertain duration we care for ourselves, but Jesus charged us with the task of caring for others.

EACH YEAR YOU INVITE A number of strangers to your birthday party. Admittedly, this is an odd practice. However, it is your way of rewarding moral behavior. This year the invited guests are **ten** unmarried women who have remained **virgins**. You and your servants now await the arrival of the **ten virgins**. Soon you hear the approaching guests. The **ten virgins** quietly enter the room. Like your faithful servants, the **ten virgins** are dressed all in white. Each of them is carrying a white purse, as well. After greeting the **ten virgins**, you invite them to join you at the table where the cake awaits. The **ten virgins** approach the table and take their seats. Each of the **ten** then places their small white purse on the table. The birthday party is now ready to begin! The inviting and arrival of the **ten virgins** is an obvious reference to Jesus' PARABLE OF THE TEN VIRGINS.

PARABLE OF THE TEN VIRGINS

Mt 25:1–13

1 "Then the kingdom of heaven will be like ten virgins who took their lamps and went out to meet the bridegroom. 2 Five of them were foolish and five were wise. 3 The foolish ones, when taking their lamps, brought no oil with them, 4 but the wise brought flasks of oil with their lamps. 5 Since the bridegroom was long delayed, they all became drowsy and fell asleep. 6 At midnight, there was a cry, 'Behold, the bridegroom! Come out to meet him!' 7 Then all those virgins got up and trimmed their lamps. 8 The foolish ones said to the wise, 'Give us some of your oil, for our lamps are going out.' 9 But the wise ones replied, 'No, for there may not be enough for us and you. Go instead to the merchants and buy some for yourselves.' 10 While they went off to buy it, the bridegroom came and those who were ready went into the wedding feast with him. Then the door was locked. 11 Afterwards the other virgins came and said, 'Lord, Lord, open the door for us!' 12 But he said in reply, 'Amen, I say to you, I do not know you.' 13 Therefore, stay awake, for you know neither the day nor the hour."

This parable in Matthew contains additional teaching about the uncertain time of the coming of the Kingdom. Not only do we need to be watchful, ready, and vigilant, we must be prepared. The virgins awaiting the bridegroom would have been a scene familiar to Jesus' listeners. Jewish custom of the day called for the bridegroom to lead a procession to the home that he would share with his new bride. Upon arrival, there would be celebrating and feasting with the invited guests. Five of the virgins were not prepared. They found themselves on the wrong side of a locked door after they tried to make up for their lack of preparedness.

The symbolism of the lamp and the oil are important in understanding the meaning of this parable. Without oil, the unprepared women were left in the dark. If the "oil" is taken literally, the five women who were prepared seem quite selfish. Why not give their fellow virgins enough oil to see them through? The oil represents "good works." While we await the coming of Christ, the bridegroom, we are expected to become prepared by performing good works. If we do not, we cannot borrow them from someone else. Jesus invites us all to the heavenly feast; we must be prepared to meet Him through our actions toward others.

THE FAITHFUL AND UNFAITHFUL SERVANTS are still standing around the table. The ten virgins are comfortably seated at the table with you. The servants and virgins now begin to sing a rousing rendition of "Happy Birthday." Everyone claps after you successfully blow out all thirty-nine candles. The ten virgins reach for their small white purses in unison. Each of them has brought you an identical birthday gift. They each place a large shiny **gold coin** on the table in front of you. Looking at the small pile of **gold coins**, you are overcome with gratitude. Each **gold coin** is very valuable and represents a significant sacrifice. You are hesitant to accept the **gold coins**, but refusing them would be seen as an insult. This generous gift of the **gold coins** helps you recall THE PARABLE OF THE GOLD COINS.

THE PARABLE OF THE GOLD COINS (TALENTS)

Mt 25:14–30

14 "It will be as when a man who was going on a journey called in his servants and entrusted his possessions to them. **15** To one he gave five talents; to another, two; to a third, one—to each according to his ability. Then he went away. Immediately **16** the one who received five talents went and traded with them, and made another five. **17** Likewise, the one who received two made another two. **18** But the man who received one went off and dug a hole in the ground and buried his master's money. **19** After a long time the master of those servants came back and settled accounts with them. **20** The one who had received five talents came forward bringing the additional five. He said, 'Master, you gave me five talents. See, I have made five more.' **21** His master said to him, 'Well done, my good and faithful servant. Since you were faithful in small matters, I will give you great responsibilities. Come, share your master's joy.' **22** [Then] the one who had received two talents also came forward and said, 'Master, you gave me two talents. See, I have made two more.' **23** His master said to him, 'Well done, my good and faithful servant. Since you were faithful in small matters, I will give you great responsibilities. Come, share your master's joy.' **24** Then the one who had received the one talent came forward and said, 'Master, I knew you were a demanding person, harvesting where you did not plant and gathering where you did not scatter; **25** so out of fear I went off and buried your talent in the ground. Here it is back.' **26** His master said to him in reply, 'You wicked, lazy servant! So you knew that I harvest where I did not plant and gather where I did not scatter? **27** Should you not then have put my money in the bank so that I could have got it back with interest on my return? **28** Now then! Take the talent from him and give it to the one with ten. **29** For to everyone who has, more will be given and he will grow rich; but from the one who has not, even what he has will be taken away. **30** And throw this useless servant into the darkness outside, where there will be wailing and grinding of teeth.'"

Lk 19:11–27

11 While they were listening to him speak, he proceeded to tell a parable because he was near Jerusalem and they thought that the kingdom of God would appear there immediately. **12** So he said, "A nobleman went off to a distant country to obtain the kingship for himself and then to return. **13** He called ten of his servants and gave them ten gold coins and told them, 'Engage in trade with these until I return.' **14** His fellow citizens, however, despised him and sent a delegation after him to announce, 'We do not want this man to be our king.' **15** But when he returned after obtaining the kingship, he had the servants called, to whom he had given the money, to learn what they had gained by trading. **16** The first came forward and said, 'Sir, your gold coin has earned ten additional ones.' **17** He replied, 'Well done, good servant! You have been faithful in this very small matter; take charge of ten cities.' **18** Then the second came and reported, 'Your gold coin, sir, has earned five more.' **19** And to this servant too he said, 'You, take charge of five cities.' **20** Then the other servant came and said, 'Sir, here is your gold coin; I kept it stored away in a handkerchief, **21** for I was afraid of you, because you are a demanding person; you take up what you did not lay down and you harvest what you did not plant.' **22** He said to him, 'With your own words I shall condemn you, you wicked servant. You knew I was a demanding person, taking up what I did not lay down and harvesting what I did not plant; **23** why did you not put my money in a bank? Then on my return I would have collected it with interest.' **24** And to those standing by he said, 'Take the gold coin from him and give it to the servant who has ten.' **25** But they said to him, 'Sir, he has ten gold coins.' **26** 'I tell you, to everyone who has, more will be given, but from the one who has not, even what he has will be taken away. **27** Now as for those enemies of mine who did not want me as their king, bring them here and slay them before me.'"

It is no coincidence that the name of the coin (talent) in this parable is the same as the word for our various skills and abilities. God gives us each talents, some more than others. We are also given the ability to improve these talents and to develop others. Just as the servants in the parable, we have choices as to what we do with our talents.

In the previous unit, Jesus taught about the importance of good works. Here He made the point that we are each given talents in order to carry out these good works. If we are good stewards of what we have been given, we will be rewarded. Our selfish nature often makes the investment of our talents in others very difficult. It seems much too risky. What if using what we have for the good of others turns out to be a foolish waste? Jesus assured us that this will not be the case. We need to have faith that the giving of the talents that we have been blessed with is our responsibility. This requires living with a spirit of detachment from earthly, material things and attachment to a life of good stewardship. We do not want to be like the servant who was afraid to take risks for his master. This servant shows us that "If you don't use it, you will lose it!"

THE GOLD COINS PILED ON the table are making you a bit uneasy. You are concerned about the temptation they present to your unfaithful servants. The coins need to be put away in a safe place. You know just the person for the job. You call for a close friend who is also a **judge**. She arrives quickly, wearing her unique robe. It is not the traditional black robe of a **judge**. She is a scholar of international law, so her robe bears the likeness of flags from many **nations**. An image of the flag of virtually every **nation** is printed on her very colorful robe. Your friend the **judge** wishes you a happy birthday as she scoops up the gold coins. She places them in the pocket of her "robe of all **nations**." The **judge** then says goodbye and quickly departs. The appearance of the **judge** wearing her robe bearing the flags of many **nations** helps recall Jesus' words about THE JUDGMENT OF THE NATIONS.

THE JUDGMENT OF THE NATIONS

Mt 25:31–46

31 "When the Son of Man comes in his glory, and all the angels with him, he will sit upon his glorious throne, **32** and all the nations will be assembled before him. And he will separate them one from another, as a shepherd separates the sheep from the goats. **33** He will place the sheep on his right and the goats on his left. **34** Then the king will say to those on his right, 'Come, you who are blessed by my Father. Inherit the kingdom prepared for you from the foundation of the world. **35** For I was hungry and you gave me food, I was thirsty and you gave me drink, a stranger and you welcomed me, **36** naked and you clothed me, ill and you cared for me, in prison and you visited me.' **37** Then the righteous will answer him and say, 'Lord, when did we see you hungry and feed you, or thirsty and give you drink? **38** When did we see you a stranger and welcome you, or naked and clothe you? **39** When did we see you ill or in prison, and visit you?' **40** And the king will say to them in reply, 'Amen, I say to you, whatever you did for one of these least brothers of mine, you did for me.' **41** Then he will say to those on his left, 'Depart from me, you accursed, into the eternal fire prepared for the devil and his angels. **42** For I was hungry and you gave me no food, I was thirsty and you gave me no drink, **43** a stranger and you gave me no welcome, naked and you gave me no clothing, ill and in prison, and you did not care for me.' **44** Then they will answer and say, 'Lord, when did we see you hungry or thirsty or a stranger or naked or ill or in prison, and not minister to your needs?' **45** He will answer them, 'Amen, I say to you, what you did not do for one of these least ones, you did not do for me.' **46** And these will go off to eternal punishment, but the righteous to eternal life."

While Jesus sat with His disciples on the Mount of Olives overlooking Jerusalem, He spoke of many events that would occur before the destruction of the city below. He described difficult times before the Son of Man would return and how to be prepared. Now at the end of the Apocalyptic Discourse, Jesus discussed the end of time. It is a sobering prophecy that demands our attention. Will we find ourselves among the sheep or the goats? Jesus told us the choice is ours. We must decide now! When the Son of Man is sitting upon the throne of judgment, it will be too late to wander over and graze with the sheep.

Jesus said to be prepared to enter the Kingdom we must tend to the needs of the needy. We must be a servant to others. Jesus' ministry to the poor and disadvantaged provided the example. We will not heal crippling diseases with a touch, or feed thousands with a loaf of bread. We can do the simpler things Jesus mentioned. In so doing, we serve our brothers and our Savior and become faithful sheep in the process.

Landmark 40:

BED

So far, it has been an exciting, but tiring journey. However, the most challenging and difficult section lies ahead. For Jesus, this is certainly true! Your body is tired. A short nap, sometimes referred to as "forty winks," seems like a great idea. It is also the perfect time, since you have now arrived at Landmark 40, which is your **bed**. Imagine yourself standing next to your **bed** (or any **bed** you choose). The **bed** looks very comfortable and inviting. The mattress has the firmness that is just right for your tired back. The **bed** has clean, soft sheets. A quick forty winks in this **bed** should be just enough sleep to revive you for the rest of your journey with Jesus.

Before getting into bed for a nap, you decide to sleep for one **hour**. You do not want to sleep too long, for there is much more to experience with Jesus. An **hour** seems to be just right. Being tired, you are concerned that you may not wake up after an **hour**. You decide to set an alarm. Unfortunately, you no longer have your watch since you exchanged it for shooting lessons (Landmark 38). Fortunately, on the bedside table is an alarm clock. You quickly set it to go off in one **hour**. You then jump into bed hoping to get a restful one-**hour** nap. This decision and preparation to sleep for an **hour** will help you remember the unit about THE COMING OF JESUS' HOUR.

THE COMING OF JESUS' HOUR

Jn 12:20–36

20 Now there were some Greeks among those who had come up to worship at the feast. 21 They came to Philip, who was from Bethsaida in Galilee, and asked him, "Sir, we would like to see Jesus." 22 Philip went and told Andrew; then Andrew and Philip went and told Jesus. 23 Jesus answered them, "The hour has come

for the Son of Man to be glorified. **24** Amen, amen, I say to you, unless a grain of wheat falls to the ground and dies, it remains just a grain of wheat; but if it dies, it produces much fruit. **25** Whoever loves his life loses it, and whoever hates his life in this world will preserve it for eternal life. **26** Whoever serves me must follow me, and where I am, there also will my servant be. The Father will honor whoever serves me.

27 "I am troubled now. Yet what should I say? 'Father, save me from this hour'? But it was for this purpose that I came to this hour. **28** Father, glorify your name." Then a voice came from heaven, "I have glorified it and will glorify it again." **29** The crowd there heard it and said it was thunder; but others said, "An angel has spoken to him." **30** Jesus answered and said, "This voice did not come for my sake but for yours. **31** Now is the time of judgment on this world; now the ruler of this world will be driven out. **32** And when I am lifted up from the earth, I will draw everyone to myself." **33** He said this indicating the kind of death he would die. **34** So the crowd answered him, "We have heard from the law that the Messiah remains forever. Then how can you say that the Son of Man must be lifted up? Who is this Son of Man?" **35** Jesus said to them, "The light will be among you only a little while. Walk while you have the light, so that darkness may not overcome you. Whoever walks in the dark does not know where he is going. **36** While you have the light, believe in the light, so that you may become children of the light."

After he had said this, Jesus left and hid from them.

Jesus predicted His Passion three different times (Landmarks 22, 23, 33). In John, Jesus now announced that the time had come. His earthly ministry was coming to an end. His death would bring about new life when He was glorified by the Father. This would make new and eternal life possible for us. We, too, must die to the material and impermanent things of this life. Jesus again emphasized what is truly important for us.

Facing the end of His ministry and the agony of His death was not easy for Jesus. He was "troubled," just as He would be later in the week while awaiting His arrest in the garden. In spite of this, Jesus was resolved to be obedient to His purpose.

Jesus heard words of encouragement and approval from His Father. These words recalled the Father's previous proclamations at His Baptism (Landmark 2) and when His glory was manifest in the transfiguration (Landmark 22).

When Jesus told the disciples that His death was approaching, He also provided words of encouragement. At the time, they were not able to understand, but we can. Jesus' death would be followed by a new life. He would be "lifted up from the earth." This would allow everyone to be raised with Him, Jews and Gentiles alike. Jesus calls us all to "the light."

THE ALARM IS GOING OFF. It feels as though you just closed your eyes. The hour is over. Slowly, you open your eyes and see that you are not alone. A crowd of **Jewish** men has gathered on either side of your bed! No, you are not dreaming! The **Jewish** men are all wearing yarmulkes. It is a wonder their head coverings stay in place, since each man is violently shaking his head. The **Jews** on one side of the bed are shaking their heads from side to side. It is as if they are disagreeing or in **disbelief** about something (recall that you were shaking your head back and forth in **disbelief** back in Landmark 7). Their **disbelief** is in contrast to the **Jewish** men on the other side of the bed. They are vigorously nodding their heads up and down. They appear to **believe** what the other **Jews** do not. This show of **belief and disbelief** is so strong you fear a fight may break out. You are also reminded of the next unit, which describes BELIEF AND DISBELIEF AMONG THE JEWS.

BELIEF AND DISBELIEF AMONG THE JEWS

Jn 12:37–43

37 Although he had performed so many signs in their presence they did not believe in him, **38** in order that the word which Isaiah the prophet spoke might be fulfilled:

"Lord, who has believed our preaching,
to whom has the might of the Lord been revealed?"

39 For this reason they could not believe, because again Isaiah said:

40 "He blinded their eyes
and hardened their heart,
so that they might not see with their eyes
and understand with their heart and be converted,
and I would heal them."

41 Isaiah said this because he saw his glory and spoke about him. **42** Nevertheless, many, even among the authorities, believed in him, but because of the Pharisees they did not acknowledge it openly in order not to be expelled from the synagogue. **43** For they preferred human praise to the glory of God.

In this unit, Jesus recalls the words spoken by Isaiah nearly eight hundred years earlier. At that time, the Israelites were a rebellious, sinful, and unbelieving people. Many had rejected Yahweh and the warnings of earlier prophets. Isaiah preached of the harsh judgment that would come down on Israel. It eventually took place with the Babylonian invasion and exile from the Promised Land. Now, many years later, the words of Isaiah rang true with the Jews' rejection of Jesus in spite of His many miraculous signs. Remember that you heard similar words regarding the purpose of the parables—about "eyes being blinded" and "hearts being hardened"—in Landmark 12. However, in Jesus' time, just as in the time of Isaiah, there was not a total rejection of God. John pointed out that even some of the Jewish authorities believed in Jesus. Notable among them were Nicodemus (Landmark 3) and Joseph of Arimathea, whom you will meet soon in Landmark 46. These two men were like bookends. Nicodemus came at the outset of Jesus' ministry and heard about the concept of being "born again." Joseph of Arimathea will be involved with Jesus' burial prior to His rebirth as the risen Lord. Let us pray that neither will our hearts be hardened nor our minds be filled with disbelief. Let us see the many signs Jesus continues to perform in our lives and believe in His undying love for us.

IT IS TIME TO GET out of bed and continue the journey. Immediately after rising, you notice how warm the room has become. Certainly the presence of the Jewish men is a factor. However, the primary reason for the heat is the sweltering **summer** sun. The **summer** day has filled the room with bright light and oppressive heat. You are sweating after taking only a few short steps toward the door. You long for a refreshing **mint** to help deal with the **summer** heat. As luck would have it, you feel something underfoot. You have stepped on several **mints**. The Jewish men must have been unaware that the **mints** fell from their pockets. Anticipating relief from the **summer** heat, you quickly unwrap the **mints**. Soon the **mints** are rolling around on your tongue, and the **summer** heat begins to feel tolerable. You have previously experienced **summer** in Landmark 5 when it represented the concept of "summary." Even earlier, the **mints** in Landmark 4 stood for "ministry." Now combing the two, these **summer mints** represent this unit, which gives a broad SUMMARY OF JESUS' MINISTRY.

SUMMARY OF JESUS' MINISTRY

Jn 12:44–50

44 Jesus cried out and said, "Whoever believes in me believes not only in me but also in the one who sent me, **45** and whoever sees me sees the one who sent me. **46** I came into the world as light, so that everyone who believes in me might not remain in darkness. **47** And if anyone hears my words and does not observe them, I do not condemn him, for I did not come to condemn the world but to save the world. **48** Whoever rejects me and does not accept my words has something to judge him: the word that I spoke, it will condemn him on the last day, **49** because I did not speak on my own, but the Father who sent me commanded me what to say and speak. **50** And I know that his commandment is eternal life. So what I say, I say as the Father told me."

Jesus concluded His public ministry by reinforcing His identity and purpose. It was a reiteration of the famous words He spoke to Nicodemus. He was the Son of God. He was the light of the world. His teachings, healings, and eventual death illuminated and reflected the love the Father has for all of us, His children. In accepting Jesus, we accept the love of God our Father and the invitation of eternal life. With these words, Jesus now boldly faced His suffering, crucifixion, and resurrection.

Landmark 41:

PEARL HARBOR

Y ou have now arrived at Landmark 41. It can be remembered by thinking of *41* as part of the larger number *1941*. This number is easily remembered as a significant year in history, particularly American history. In 1941, the United States entered WWII after the Japanese attack on **Pearl Harbor** in Hawaii. The number *41* will thus trigger thoughts of **Pearl Harbor**. After visiting and paying your respects at **Pearl Harbor**, imagine being out on a beautiful Hawaiian beach. It is clear and sunny, with a gentle breeze blowing in from the ocean. You are slowly strolling along the beach, thoroughly relaxed and enjoying the day. This peaceful Hawaiian beach scene near **Pearl Harbor** is Landmark 41.

Walking along the Hawaiian beach, you are watching the waves and not focusing on your feet. Ouch! Your bare toes strike a heavy object half-buried in the sand. It is smooth, round, and quite bright. It is definitely not a seashell. Reaching down, you push aside sand and uncover a **crystal ball**. It is very similar to the **crystal balls** previously seen in Landmarks 22, 23, and 33, which represented Jesus' three Passion predictions. There is a significant difference with this **crystal ball**. Through the glass, you can see something inside. It is a **crucifix**. Inside the **crystal ball** is a cross bearing the body of Jesus. You pick up this beautiful treasure and carefully wipe off the remaining sand. You stare in awe and reverence at the **crystal ball containing the crucifix**. Like the other **crystal balls**, this one also signifies a prediction, but more specifically it represents JESUS PREDICTS THE DAY OF HIS CRUCIFIXION.

JESUS PREDICTS THE DAY OF HIS CRUCIFIXION

Mt 26:1–2

1 When Jesus finished all these words, he said to his disciples,
2 "You know that in two days' time it will be Passover, and the Son of Man will be handed over to be crucified."

———

Only Matthew recorded this very specific prediction by Jesus of His impending death by crucifixion. Imagine the horror and sadness Jesus' disciples must have felt. Their Messiah, the one they loved and trusted, would be put to death like a common criminal!

What had begun with the proclamation, "Repent, for the kingdom of heaven is at hand," was to conclude with an agonizing death by crucifixion. It made no sense to the disciples that the true Lamb of God would be sacrificed at this Passover. However, Jesus knew that the feast commemorating the delivery of the Jewish people from the bonds of slavery would be different this year. Jesus knew His destiny was to fulfill the Father's plan by obediently proceeding forward toward the cross. In doing so, He would make the kingdom of heaven a possibility for all of His disciples.

YOU FEEL VERY FORTUNATE TO have uncovered the crystal ball containing the crucifix. It is not only beautiful, but gazing upon it is a moving spiritual experience. You have a strong desire to share it with others. You would like to carry it high above your head to make it more visible. You begin to comb the beach for something that will allow you to hold the crystal ball aloft. Lying in the sand not far down the beach is an old wooden **spear**. Perhaps the **spear** was once used to catch fish or for protection. You will use the **spear** for an entirely different purpose. First you remove the sharp tip from the end of the **spear**. Next you pull a small piece of rope from your pocket and carefully secure the crystal ball containing the crucifix to the end of the **spear**. You begin your walk down the beach with the crystal ball held high. Your wish is that people will appear and draw near to peer at the sphere on the **spear**. The **spear** is another soundalike and stands for "conspiracy." This scene with the **spear** represents the next unit: THE CONSPIRACY AGAINST JESUS.

THE CONSPIRACY AGAINST JESUS

Mt 26:3–5

3 Then the chief priests and the elders of the people assembled in the palace of the high priest, who was called Caiaphas, 4 and they consulted together to arrest Jesus by treachery and put him to death. 5 But they said, "Not during the festival, that there may not be a riot among the people."

Mk 14:1–2

1 The Passover and the Feast of Unleavened Bread were to take place in two days' time. So the chief priests and the scribes were seeking a way to arrest him by treachery and put him to death. 2 They said, "Not during the festival, for fear that there may be a riot among the people."

Lk 22:1–2

1 Now the feast of Unleavened Bread, called the Passover, was drawing near, 2 and the chief priests and the scribes were seeking a way to put him to death, for they were afraid of the people.

———————————

In Jesus' time, more than 100,000 pilgrims were typically in Jerusalem for the Passover. With so many visitors, any action against Jesus in order to put Him to death could cause Rome to respond unfavorably. Waiting until the festival was over would require eight more days of patience. The Jewish leaders would have to wait until Passover was over. They could not kill the Lamb of God until after the Passover lamb was sacrificed and eaten at the Seder meal. Then they would have to wait seven days for the Feast of Unleavened Bread to end. During this time, leaven (or yeast), which was symbolic of sin, could not be consumed. Could they wait that long before committing their sin?

The Jewish leaders had heard and seen all that they could tolerate from Jesus. They had been plotting against Him in earnest since the cleansing of the temple and the parable of the tenants (Landmark 35). Something had to be done. He was not in Galilee, Samaria, the Decapolis, or elsewhere. Jesus was right there with them in Jerusalem.

YOUR WISH IS SOON FULFILLED. Many people gather and follow you down the Hawaiian beach. They are quite moved by the sphere containing the crucifix. They also seem appreciative of your effort. It has truly been an effort! Your arms are tired and sore from holding the sphere high above your head. A woman in the crowd senses your fatigue. She comes forward carrying an intricately carved wooden **tray**. The **tray** is quite old, but well preserved. She suggests that you place the sphere on the **tray** to give your aching arms a rest. You are very grateful for her kind offer. After lowering the spear, you remove the crystal ball and gently place it on the wooden **tray**. In the center of the **tray** is a slight depression allowing the sphere to rest securely. The wooden **tray** is a reminder of THE BETRAYAL BY JUDAS.

THE BETRAYAL BY JUDAS

Mt 26:14–16

14 Then one of the Twelve, who was called Judas Iscariot, went to the chief priests 15 and said, "What are you willing to give me if I hand him over to you?" They paid him thirty pieces of silver, 16 and from that time on he looked for an opportunity to hand him over.

Mk 14:10–11

10 Then Judas Iscariot, one of the Twelve, went off to the chief priests to hand him over to them. 11 When they heard him they were pleased and promised to pay him money. Then he looked for an opportunity to hand him over.

Lk 22:3–6

3 Then Satan entered into Judas, the one surnamed Iscariot, who was counted among the Twelve, 4 and he went to the chief priests and temple guards to discuss a plan for handing him over to them. 5 They were pleased and agreed to pay him money. 6 He accepted their offer and sought a favorable opportunity to hand him over to them in the absence of a crowd.

This brief unit succinctly describes one of the most infamous acts in all of history. A member of the special handpicked Twelve betrays the Son of God. We may wonder how someone who had traveled with Jesus throughout His ministry could conspire with His enemies to have Him put to death. How could someone who had heard Jesus' teachings and witnessed His miracles betray Him for the mere price of a slave (Ex 21:32)? Perhaps we should ask ourselves how, knowing what He did for us, we can repeatedly betray Jesus (on a lesser scale) with our actions.

Luke softened the culpability of Judas by having Satan enter the picture. However, Judas was not able to fend off temptation as Jesus had done in the desert at the outset of His ministry. Judas's greed for a paltry thirty pieces of silver stands in stark contrast to the lavish display of love shown by the woman who anointed Jesus with costly oil (Landmark 34).

42ND STREET

The next Landmark along the road with Jesus is itself a road. More specifically, it is a well-known street. It is the famous **42nd Street** in New York City. On **42nd Street**, you can work in the Chrysler building, find a book in the public library, or be entertained in Times Square. For now, just imagine a very busy street. It can certainly be the actual **42nd Street** in New York. However, any busy street that you would like to imagine is just fine. Thus, for Landmark 42, picture yourself standing in the middle of **42nd Street** in New York City or a busy street somewhere else.

Recall that at Landmark 29 you were an invited guest at a great winter feast. You also hosted a New Year's Eve party in Landmark 31. It is now time to throw a dinner party! It will be a dinner party held on a city street. This ambitious undertaking will require a significant amount of **preparation**. The big challenge is that you will take care of all the **preparations** yourself! The first thing to **prepare** is the street itself. After all of the people, vehicles, and trash have been removed, you begin the daunting task of food **preparation**. It is a large dinner, so purchasing and **preparing** the extensive menu is expensive and time-consuming. The last phase of **preparation** is decorating and setting the tables. When you finally finish all of the **preparations**, you are exhausted. However, it is almost time for the supper to begin. There is no time to rest. All of these **preparations**, though tiring, allow you to recall the unit about PREPARATIONS FOR PASSOVER.

PREPARATIONS FOR PASSOVER

Mt 26:17–20

17 On the first day of the Feast of Unleavened Bread, the disciples approached Jesus and said, "Where do you want us to prepare for you to eat the Passover?" **18** He said, "Go into the city to a certain man and tell him, 'The teacher says, "My appointed time draws near; in your house I shall celebrate the Passover with my disciples."'" **19** The disciples then did as Jesus had ordered, and prepared the Passover.

20 When it was evening, he reclined at table with the Twelve.

Mk 14:12–17

12 On the first day of the Feast of Unleavened Bread, when they sacrificed the Passover lamb, his disciples said to him, "Where do you want us to go and prepare for you to eat the Passover?" **13** He sent two of his disciples and said to them, "Go into the city and a man will meet you, carrying a jar of water. Follow him. **14** Wherever he enters, say to the master of the house, 'The Teacher says, "Where is my guest room where I may eat the Passover with my disciples?"' **15** Then he will show you a large upper room furnished and ready. Make the preparations for us there." **16** The disciples then went off, entered the city, and found it just as he had told them; and they prepared the Passover.

17 When it was evening, he came with the Twelve.

Lk 22:7–14

7 When the day of the Feast of Unleavened Bread arrived, the day for sacrificing the Passover lamb, **8** he sent out Peter and John, instructing them, "Go and make preparations for us to eat the Passover." **9** They asked him, "Where do you want us to make the preparations?" **10** And he answered them, "When you go into the city, a man will meet you carrying a jar of water. Follow him into the house that he enters **11** and say to the master of the house, 'The teacher says to you, "Where is the guest room where I may eat the Passover with my disciples?"' **12** He will show you a large upper room that is furnished. Make the preparations there." **13** Then they went off and found everything exactly as he had told them, and there they prepared the Passover.

14 When the hour came, he took his place at table with the apostles.

Sharing a meal with others was an important recurring event in Jesus' ministry. This Passover meal would be the most important. In fact, it was the most important meal in all of history. Several important events occurred here, although the institution of the Eucharist stood far above the others.

Passover was the great Jewish celebration occurring on the first of the eight days of the Feast of Unleavened Bread. The Passover lamb was sacrificed and eaten as the Jewish nation commemorated its freedom from Egyptian slavery. Christians now recall this as Jesus' last meal before His ultimate sacrifice to free us from the slavery of sin. Jesus had sent disciples into Jerusalem a few days earlier to secure a colt for His entry into the city. He now sent disciples to secure what seemed like a prearranged room in order to prepare their Passover meal. With a large crowd of pilgrims coming to Jerusalem for Passover, it would have been important to arrange a room in advance. According to Matthew, Mark, and Luke, the preparation of the prearranged room would have occurred during the day on Thursday the 14th of Nisan. Passover itself would begin later that day after sundown.

BEFORE YOUR GUESTS ARRIVE, YOU notice that the street has again become messy. During your preparations, some trash and dirt have accumulated here and there on the street. The street needs one final **washing**. You decide it will be a thorough **washing**. After obtaining a fire hose, you attach it to a nearby hydrant. Even though the water from the hydrant comes bursting from the hose under high pressure, you manage to **wash** the street without spraying any of the food, tables, or decorations. **Washing** the street is actually relaxing. You get a sense of accomplishment seeing the debris being **washed** away. Once the street is clean, you turn off the water and await your guests. This **washing** of the street helps recall the unit when Jesus does some washing: JESUS WASHES THE DISCIPLES' FEET.

JESUS WASHES THE DISCIPLES' FEET

Jn 13:1–20

1 Before the feast of Passover, Jesus knew that his hour had come to pass from this world to the Father. He loved his own in the world and he loved them to the end. **2** The devil had already induced Judas, son of Simon the Iscariot, to hand him over. So, during supper,

3 fully aware that the Father had put everything into his power and that he had come from God and was returning to God, **4** he rose from supper and took off his outer garments. He took a towel and tied it around his waist. **5** Then he poured water into a basin and began to wash the disciples' feet and dry them with the towel around his waist. **6** He came to Simon Peter, who said to him, "Master, are you going to wash my feet?" **7** Jesus answered and said to him, "What I am doing, you do not understand now, but you will understand later." **8** Peter said to him, "You will never wash my feet." Jesus answered him, "Unless I wash you, you will have no inheritance with me." **9** Simon Peter said to him, "Master, then not only my feet, but my hands and head as well." **10** Jesus said to him, "Whoever has bathed has no need except to have his feet washed, for he is clean all over; so you are clean, but not all." **11** For he knew who would betray him; for this reason, he said, "Not all of you are clean."

12 So when he had washed their feet [and] put his garments back on and reclined at table again, he said to them, "Do you realize what I have done for you? **13** You call me 'teacher' and 'master,' and rightly so, for indeed I am. **14** If I, therefore, the master and teacher, have washed your feet, you ought to wash one another's feet. **15** I have given you a model to follow, so that as I have done for you, you should also do. **16** Amen, amen, I say to you, no slave is greater than his master nor any messenger greater than the one who sent him. **17** If you understand this, blessed are you if you do it. **18** I am not speaking of all of you. I know those whom I have chosen. But so that the scripture might be fulfilled, 'The one who ate my food has raised his heel against me.' **19** From now on I am telling you before it happens, so that when it happens you may believe that I AM. **20** Amen, amen, I say to you, whoever receives the one I send receives me, and whoever receives me receives the one who sent me."

This profound display of humility has only been recorded in the Gospel of John. In Jesus' time, washing the feet of a guest was a display of hospitality. A slave of the host would typically wash the feet of the guests. The host himself would not do the washing. Jesus' action was not a display of hospitality. It was a vivid example of how to be a disciple. A follower of Jesus must be a humble servant to others. We must do as Jesus did. Peter's misunderstanding of the gesture was akin to our frequent misunderstanding of true discipleship. It must be on Jesus' terms, not ours. This act of humility and self-sacrifice was a prelude to the ultimate sacrifice that would occur the next day.

It must have been difficult for Jesus to share this last meal with His disciples knowing that one of His trusted Twelve would betray Him. In predicting this to the disciples, Jesus' words fulfill Psalm 41:10 ("Even the friend who had my trust, who shared my table, has scorned me"). The next unit will more specifically deal with Judas.

SINCE YOU ARE HOSTING AN outdoor party and will be serving alcohol, the city has requested that you check the **identification** of each guest. Hopefully, your guests will not mind showing **identification** bearing their date of birth. Finally, people begin to arrive. When you request to see a form of **identification**, the guests seem surprised, but comply with a smile. Some younger guests with **identification** receive a hand stamp **identifying** them as ones not to be served alcohol. In general, the **identification** process goes smoothly without strong objections. You are now reminded of the unit about THE IDENTIFICATION OF THE BETRAYER.

THE IDENTIFICATION OF THE BETRAYER

Mt 26:21–25

21 And while they were eating, he said, "Amen, I say to you, one of you will betray me." 22 Deeply distressed at this, they began to say to him one after another, "Surely it is not I, Lord?" 23 He said in reply, "He who has dipped his hand into the dish with me is the one who will betray me. 24 The Son of Man indeed goes, as it is written of him, but woe to that man by whom the Son of Man is betrayed. It would be better for that man if he had never been born." 25 Then Judas, his betrayer, said in reply, "Surely it is not I, Rabbi?" He answered, "You have said so."

Mk 14:18–21

18 And as they reclined at table and were eating, Jesus said, "Amen, I say to you, one of you will betray me, one who is eating with me." 19 They began to be distressed and to say to him, one by one, "Surely it is not I?" 20 He said to them, "One of the Twelve, the one who dips with me into the dish. 21 For the Son of Man indeed goes, as it is written of him, but woe to that man by whom the Son of Man is betrayed. It would be better for that man if he had never been born."

Lk 22:21–23

21 "And yet behold, the hand of the one who is to betray me is with me on the table; **22** for the Son of Man indeed goes as it has been determined; but woe to that man by whom he is betrayed." **23** And they began to debate among themselves who among them would do such a deed.

Jn 6:70–71; 13:21–30

70 Jesus answered them, "Did I not choose you twelve? Yet is not one of you a devil?" **71** He was referring to Judas, son of Simon the Iscariot; it was he who would betray him, one of the Twelve.

...

21 When he had said this, Jesus was deeply troubled and testified, "Amen, amen, I say to you, one of you will betray me." **22** The disciples looked at one another, at a loss as to whom he meant. **23** One of his disciples, the one whom Jesus loved, was reclining at Jesus' side. **24** So Simon Peter nodded to him to find out whom he meant. **25** He leaned back against Jesus' chest and said to him, "Master, who is it?" **26** Jesus answered, "It is the one to whom I hand the morsel after I have dipped it." So he dipped the morsel and [took it and] handed it to Judas, son of Simon the Iscariot. **27** After he took the morsel, Satan entered him. So Jesus said to him, "What you are going to do, do quickly." **28** [Now] none of those reclining at table realized why he said this to him. **29** Some thought that since Judas kept the money bag, Jesus had told him, "Buy what we need for the feast," or to give something to the poor. **30** So he took the morsel and left at once. And it was night.

We knew that Jesus was going to be betrayed by Judas. In Landmark 41, we saw him do the deed for a mere thirty pieces of silver. The other eleven were unaware of the unthinkable, that there was a traitor among them. Here, in varying degrees, depending on the evangelist, Jesus revealed that one of them would betray Him. Mark and Luke were fairly vague. In Matthew, there was a direct confrontation with Judas. In the Gospel of John, the identity of the betrayer was made clear to the disciple, John ("the one whom Jesus loved").

Though Jesus knew in advance that one of His chosen Twelve would betray Him, when the time came, He was still "deeply troubled." It is no small thing to share and then prepare to give your life for someone only to find that they place a higher value on trivial material gain. It was part of God's plan that Judas would betray Jesus, but it was still Judas's choice.

Judas had free will to choose to betray the Messiah. We do as well, on a daily basis.

EVERYONE HAS ARRIVED. ALL OF the identification has been checked. It is time to mingle with your guests and be a welcoming host. You are at once struck by how well people seem to be getting along with **one another**. All the guests are exchanging warm embraces and kind words. It is as if people truly **love one another**. You join in on several conversations and are struck by the **love** the guests are showing **one another**. You ask several people about this. They simply explain that, "We all **love one another**." People you thought were unlikely to even know one another actually seem to **love one another**! You have no explanation as to why these people **love one another**, but as the host you are pleased. This represents JESUS' COMMAND TO LOVE ONE ANOTHER.

JESUS' COMMAND TO LOVE ONE ANOTHER

Jn 13:31–35

31 When he had left, Jesus said, "Now is the Son of Man glorified, and God is glorified in him. 32 [If God is glorified in him,] God will also glorify him in himself, and he will glorify him at once. 33 My children, I will be with you only a little while longer. You will look for me, and as I told the Jews, 'Where I go you cannot come,' so now I say it to you. 34 I give you a new commandment: love one another. As I have loved you, so you also should love one another. 35 This is how all will know that you are my disciples, if you have love for one another."

Jesus again alluded to His death before telling His disciples the key to Christian identity. It would be the love they show for one another. Jesus' preaching about love for fellow man was not new. He had been teaching and living out that lifestyle from the beginning of His ministry. Here He added a significant twist to the directive: "as I have loved you." He was commanding that we, His disciples, should love our fellow man with a "Jesus love," "a divine love," "a perfect love!" How in the world are we, with all of our imperfections, to do this? The way to do so is not of this world. It will occur with the help of the Holy Spirit, who will be our Advocate. Jesus will explain this in an upcoming discourse. Jesus wants us, His disciples, to preach the good news of His saving love. However, by actually loving one another, our actions will speak much louder than our words.

IT IS NOW TIME TO eat. You are eager for your guests to enjoy the large **supper** you have worked so hard to prepare. Everyone seems to be enjoying themselves. You have been asked by several hungry guests, "When is **supper**?" You announce to the guests to take their seats, for **supper** is about to be served. Everyone sits down and you begin to serve the **supper** yourself. As the guests begin to eat, you are pleased to hear so many positive comments about the food. Then you serve the dessert, and the **supper** comes to an end. The guests are full and satisfied. You are also satisfied that you have provided such an excellent **supper**. This lavish **supper** reminds you of a much simpler, but infinitely more important **supper**: THE LORD'S SUPPER.

|||||||||||||||||||||||||||||||||||||||||||||||||||||||||||||||||||||||||||||||||||||||||||||||||||||||||||||||||||||||||||||||||||||||||||||||||

THE LORD'S SUPPER

|||||||||||||||||||||||||||||||||||||||||||||||||||||||||||||||||||||||||||||||||||||||||||||||||||||||||||||||||||||||||||||||||||||||||||||||||

Mt 26:26–30

26 While they were eating, Jesus took bread, said the blessing, broke it, and giving it to his disciples said, "Take and eat; this is my body." 27 Then he took a cup, gave thanks, and gave it to them, saying, "Drink from it, all of you, 28 for this is my blood of the covenant, which will be shed on behalf of many for the forgiveness of sins. 29 I tell you, from now on I shall not drink this fruit of the vine until the day when I drink it with you new in the kingdom of my Father." 30 Then, after singing a hymn, they went out to the Mount of Olives.

Mk 14:22–26

22 While they were eating, he took bread, said the blessing, broke it, and gave it to them, and said, "Take it; this is my body." 23 Then he took a cup, gave thanks, and gave it to them, and they all drank

from it. **24** He said to them, "This is my blood of the covenant, which will be shed for many. **25** Amen, I say to you, I shall not drink again the fruit of the vine until the day when I drink it new in the kingdom of God." **26** Then, after singing a hymn, they went out to the Mount of Olives.

Lk 22:14–30

14 When the hour came, he took his place at table with the apostles. **15** He said to them, "I have eagerly desired to eat this Passover with you before I suffer, **16** for, I tell you, I shall not eat it [again] until there is fulfillment in the kingdom of God." **17** Then he took a cup, gave thanks, and said, "Take this and share it among yourselves; **18** for I tell you [that] from this time on I shall not drink of the fruit of the vine until the kingdom of God comes." **19** Then he took the bread, said the blessing, broke it, and gave it to them, saying, "This is my body, which will be given for you; do this in memory of me." **20** And likewise the cup after they had eaten, saying, "This cup is the new covenant in my blood, which will be shed for you.

21 "And yet behold, the hand of the one who is to betray me is with me on the table; **22** for the Son of Man indeed goes as it has been determined; but woe to that man by whom he is betrayed." **23** And they began to debate among themselves who among them would do such a deed.

24 Then an argument broke out among them about which of them should be regarded as the greatest. **25** He said to them, "The kings of the Gentiles lord it over them and those in authority over them are addressed as 'Benefactors'; **26** but among you it shall not be so. Rather, let the greatest among you be as the youngest, and the leader as the servant. **27** For who is greater: the one seated at table or the one who serves? Is it not the one seated at table? I am among you as the one who serves. **28** It is you who have stood by me in my trials; **29** and I confer a kingdom on you, just as my Father has conferred one on me, **30** that you may eat and drink at my table in my kingdom; and you will sit on thrones judging the twelve tribes of Israel."

We all have memories of some meals in our lives that were truly special. Certain dining experiences stand out because of an event being celebrated or the people we shared the meal with. Perhaps the food itself made the meal unforgettable. In this unit, we recall the most important meal in all of history! There are several reasons why this is so.

This Passover meal, like all previous Passover meals, celebrated God's protection of the Jewish people. Centuries earlier, the blood of the sacrificial lamb had saved the Israelites. The smearing of the lamb's blood on their doors had caused the Angel of Death to "pass over" their homes when they were enslaved in Egypt. This Passover meal was Jesus' last meal before He, the sacrificial Lamb, poured out His blood on the cross. In doing so, He freed us from the slavery of sin and death. During this meal, He gave us a way to share in His ultimate sacrifice of love. Depending on your belief, this allows us to remember Jesus in a very special way, or to actually partake of His true presence. In doing so, Jesus used words similar to Exodus 24:8 when Moses sealed the Old Covenant by sprinkling the blood of the sacrificial lamb on the Israelites at Mount Sinai. Here with His words, and later with His death and resurrection, Jesus initiated the New Covenant. Jesus' final meal, in which we are all invited to partake, is the prelude to the heavenly banquet.

Luke's account of the Last Supper contains a bit of controversy covered elsewhere by Mark and Matthew. Jesus was accustomed to mealtime controversy. Recall the woman with the ointment, the issue about cleansing rituals, and the man with dropsy, to mention several.

Earlier, on the way to Jerusalem, the disciples had argued about who among them was the greatest (Landmark 23). Jesus then taught the paradox of becoming childlike, humble, and a servant to others in order to be "great." Here Jesus continued this theme. The chosen ones are to serve others as Jesus had served. In doing so, spiritual greatness, not necessarily worldly greatness, would be rewarded. Jesus also gave His disciples the authority to serve others. With the metaphorical "thrones," Jesus empowered the disciples to be rulers of the church just as God gave Him the authority to be ruler of the Kingdom.

RACE CAR

Y̶ou have slowly and steadily walked with Jesus with the assistance of forty-two Landmarks. The forty-third Landmark will allow you to travel much faster. It is a car, but not just any car. It is a **race car**, but not just any **race car**. It is the famous **race car** 43 driven by the legendary "King of Racing," Richard Petty! Picture yourself walking out onto a racetrack. Waiting for you with engine rumbling is the blue and red **race car** 43. You climb in and get ready for the ride of your life. You and 43 are about to take a heart-pounding, hair-raising lap around the racetrack. The grandstands are full of race fans from around the world. They have traveled from far and wide to watch you circle the track. Buckle up! Landmark 43 is this famous **race car**.

Before stepping on the gas, you take a quick glance to the right. Standing where the passenger seat would be in other cars is a familiar ball of white fur, otherwise known as **Peter** Rabbit. You know **Peter** from Landmark 22 where he represented Peter's confession of faith. Here **Peter's** behavior is quite different. He is vigorously shaking his head and floppy ears back and forth as if to say, "No, no, no." **Peter** wants nothing to do with being in the race car while you are behind the wheel. He cannot believe he is in such a dangerous situation. He is **denying** himself the chance to take part in your fast lap around the track. After one last shake of the head, he hops through the open window and is gone. **Peter's** disbelief and strong **denial** of the opportunity to be your passenger represents a prediction Jesus made about Peter at the Lord's Supper. This is the unit when Peter's Denial Is Foretold.

PETER'S DENIAL IS FORETOLD

Mt 26:31–35

31 Then Jesus said to them, "This night all of you will have your faith in me shaken, for it is written:

'I will strike the shepherd,
and the sheep of the flock will be dispersed';

32 but after I have been raised up, I shall go before you to Galilee." **33** Peter said to him in reply, "Though all may have their faith in you shaken, mine will never be." **34** Jesus said to him, "Amen, I say to you, this very night before the cock crows, you will deny me three times." **35** Peter said to him, "Even though I should have to die with you, I will not deny you." And all the disciples spoke likewise.

Mk 14:27–31

27 Then Jesus said to them, "All of you will have your faith shaken, for it is written:

'I will strike the shepherd,
and the sheep will be dispersed.'

28 But after I have been raised up, I shall go before you to Galilee." **29** Peter said to him, "Even though all should have their faith shaken, mine will not be." **30** Then Jesus said to him, "Amen, I say to you, this very night before the cock crows twice you will deny me three times." **31** But he vehemently replied, "Even though I should have to die with you, I will not deny you." And they all spoke similarly.

Lk 22:31–38

31 "Simon, Simon, behold Satan has demanded to sift all of you like wheat, **32** but I have prayed that your own faith may not fail; and once you have turned back, you must strengthen your brothers." **33** He said to him, "Lord, I am prepared to go to prison and to die with you." **34** But he replied, "I tell you, Peter, before the cock crows this day, you will deny three times that you know me."

35 He said to them, "When I sent you forth without a money bag or a sack or sandals, were you in need of anything?" "No, nothing," they replied. **36** He said to them, "But now one who has a money bag should take it, and likewise a sack, and one who does not have a sword should sell his cloak and buy one. **37** For I tell you that this scripture must be fulfilled in me, namely, 'He was counted among the wicked'; and indeed what is written about me is coming to fulfillment." **38** Then they said, "Lord, look, there are two swords here." But he replied, "It is enough!"

Jn 13:36–38

36 Simon Peter said to him, "Master, where are you going?" Jesus answered [him], "Where I am going, you cannot follow me now, though you will follow later." 37 Peter said to him, "Master, why can't I follow you now? I will lay down my life for you." 38 Jesus answered, "Will you lay down your life for me? Amen, amen, I say to you, the cock will not crow before you deny me three times."

—————

Jesus and His disciples have just shared the Last Supper. Mark again served one of his "sandwiches." Jesus' final meal occurred between the foretelling of two betrayals, first Judas's and now Peter's. All four evangelists described the current prediction of denial. In this unit, Jesus made three predictions that would all soon occur.

Jesus first told the remaining eleven that they would flee in His hour of need. This prediction was made using the metaphor of a shepherd and his sheep. This prophecy taken from Zechariah 13:7 would soon play out in Gethsemane. The next prediction was probably not fully appreciated by the disciples until after it occurred. It was an amazing foretelling of hope and triumph. Jesus would rise from the dead and rejoin them in their old stomping grounds of Galilee! The scattered flock would reunite with their risen Shepherd. Jesus revealed that Peter, their leader, would deny Him not once, but three times that very night. Not surprisingly, Peter denied that he would deny.

Luke includes material in this unit not found in the other Gospels. Knowing that Peter would weaken and deny Him, Jesus prayed specifically for Peter. Jesus needed Peter to be a source of strength for the other disciples and to lead the new church through its infancy. Jesus predicted difficult times ahead for His followers, just as there had been for Him. However, the worst was yet to come. With Jesus' death, His disciples would no longer be able to literally follow Him from town to town. They would be able to follow His example and thereby attract other followers.

John mentioned that Peter would "follow later," perhaps a prediction of the martyr's death Peter would suffer. Jesus warned the disciples of future suffering by using the metaphor of "the sword." He tells us all of the spiritual battle we will face.

YOU ARE DISAPPOINTED THAT PETER denied himself the chance to ride with you. After he hops from the race car, you notice a piece of paper left behind on the floor. It appears to be a map of the track. Studying the map, you realize it shows **the way** around the high-banked oval track. Anyone could find their **way** around a closed oval racetrack! However, the map shows **the way** to negotiate the track the most efficiently. It shows **the way** to enter the turns. **The way** to handle the steep banks is indicated. **The way** to come down the straights is detailed. In short, the map shows **the way** to the fastest lap. You quickly memorize **the way**. This greatly boosts your confidence. This map that shows **the way** helps you recall the unit about how JESUS IS THE WAY.

JESUS IS THE WAY

Jn 14:1–14

1 "Do not let your hearts be troubled. You have faith in God; have faith also in me. 2 In my Father's house there are many dwelling places. If there were not, would I have told you that I am going to prepare a place for you? 3 And if I go and prepare a place for you, I will come back again and take you to myself, so that where I am you also may be. 4 Where [I] am going you know the way." 5 Thomas said to him, "Master, we do not know where you are going; how can we know the way?" 6 Jesus said to him, "I am the way and the truth and the life. No one comes to the Father except through me. 7 If you know me, then you will also know my Father. From now on you do know him and have seen him." 8 Philip said to him, "Master, show us the Father, and that will be enough for us." 9 Jesus said to him, "Have I been with you for so long a time and you still do not know me, Philip? Whoever has seen me has seen the Father. How can you say, 'Show us the Father'? 10 Do you not believe that I am in the Father and the Father is in me? The words that I speak to you I do not speak on my own. The Father who dwells in me is doing his works. 11 Believe me that I am in the Father and the Father is in me, or else, believe because of the works themselves. 12 Amen, amen, I say to you, whoever believes in me will do the works that I do, and will do greater ones than these, because I am going to the Father. 13 And whatever you ask in my name, I will do, so that the Father may be glorified in the Son. 14 If you ask anything of me in my name, I will do it."

This unit and the rest of the material associated with Landmark 43 is an after dinner discourse found only in John's Gospel. During the Last Supper with Jesus, His disciples were given a lot of disturbing information. The person to whom they had given their life was going away, and they could not continue to follow Him. They would soon all have their faith in Him shaken. Peter their leader would deny Him. Surely some words of encouragement were in order. They needed something they could hold on to when Jesus was no longer physically among them. Jesus began a much-needed pep talk.

After Jesus' death and resurrection, the disciples would need to maintain their faith in Him. It was this faith that would give them strength in the difficult days to come. Jesus emphasized the unity between Himself and God the Father. Jesus was the way to the Father. Today He is "The Way" to our dwelling place in the Father's house. We must continue to follow in His footsteps to our eternal dwelling place. Jesus provided the map. In a very real sense, Jesus is the map. He is "The Way." You can bet your life on it. Jesus is the way, the truth, and the life. Though the apostles may have felt lost, when they were looking at Jesus they were looking at their destination. They were looking at God. Jesus was, and continues to be, the living revelation of God.

YOU HAVE COMMITTED TO MEMORY the way you will drive around the track. Where will you store the map for safekeeping? Suddenly, a strong gust of **wind** answers your question. The **wind** blows the map out of your hands and out of the car. You watch as the **wind** carries the map straight up into the clear blue sky. Just as suddenly as the **wind** came, it is gone. All is calm, including you. Your pre-race jitters, like the map, have been swept away by the **wind**. The **wind**, which carried away the map, symbolizes the next unit. In Scripture, the Holy Spirit at times appears as a **wind**. The **wind** at the racetrack will help you recall Jesus' words at the Lord's Supper about THE PROMISE OF THE HOLY SPIRIT.

THE PROMISE OF THE HOLY SPIRIT

Jn 14:15–31

15 "If you love me, you will keep my commandments. **16** And I will ask the Father, and he will give you another Advocate to be with you always, **17** the Spirit of truth, which the world cannot accept, because it neither sees nor knows it. But you know it, because it remains with you, and will be in you. **18** I will not leave you orphans; I will come to you. **19** In a little while the world will no longer see me, but you will see me, because I live and you will live. **20** On that day you will realize that I am in my Father and you are in me and I in you. **21** Whoever has my commandments and observes them is the one who loves me. And whoever loves me will be loved by my Father, and I will love him and reveal myself to him." **22** Judas, not the Iscariot, said to him, "Master, [then] what happened that you will reveal yourself to us and not to the world?" **23** Jesus answered and said to him, "Whoever loves me will keep my word, and my Father will love him, and we will come to him and make our dwelling with him. **24** Whoever does not love me does not keep my words; yet the word you hear is not mine but that of the Father who sent me.

25 "I have told you this while I am with you. **26** The Advocate, the holy Spirit that the Father will send in my name—he will teach you everything and remind you of all that [I] told you. **27** Peace I leave with you; my peace I give to you. Not as the world gives do I give it to you. Do not let your hearts be troubled or afraid. **28** You heard me tell you, 'I am going away and I will come back to you.' If you loved me, you would rejoice that I am going to the Father; for the Father is greater than I. **29** And now I have told you this before it happens, so that when it happens you may believe. **30** I will no longer speak much with you, for the ruler of the world is coming. He has no power over me, **31** but the world must know that I love the Father and that I do just as the Father has commanded me. Get up, let us go."

In this discourse to the eleven after the Last Supper, Jesus made another important point, not once but twice. Those who love Him will keep His commandments. Jesus knew this would not be easy. He knew persecution would make it very difficult. Jesus knew that we would all need assistance, an advocate. His promise of the Holy Spirit was probably not fully appreciated by the apostles. They were still trying to understand that

Jesus would soon be taken from them. Later they would experience the indwelling of this precious gift. Their physical bodies would each become "a temple of the spirit."

The Holy Spirit will provide specific gifts. The Spirit will also be a source of strength in Jesus' absence. The Spirit will help us understand Jesus' teachings and be a source of new knowledge. What about peace and comfort? Once again the Holy Spirit will provide! In our efforts to keep the commandments, we will have an abundance of help. We are not orphans.

FINALLY, THE MUCH-ANTICIPATED ALL-OUT SPRINT around the track begins. You have a fast car, knowledge of the course, and an inner calm. You feel ready for anything. However, nothing could have prepared you for what is waiting in the first turn. Piled high from the infield to the top of the high-banked curve is a massive pile of **vines and branches**. How could such a collection of **vines and branches** have gotten onto the usually well-maintained track? Even more alarming is how the **vines and branches** could have gone unnoticed! You then realize the **vines and branches** must have been piled there purposely. Why? Perhaps to test your driving skills? You speed directly into the waiting **vines and branches**. You quickly pass through the pile, emerging with a tangle of **vines and branches** clinging to the car. Though your view is significantly obstructed, you push the accelerator and speed onward. This unexpected encounter with the **vines and branches** recalls the unit about THE VINE AND ITS BRANCHES.

THE VINE AND ITS BRANCHES

Jn 15:1–17

1 "I am the true vine, and my Father is the vine grower. 2 He takes away every branch in me that does not bear fruit, and everyone that does he prunes so that it bears more fruit. 3 You are already pruned because of the word that I spoke to you. 4 Remain in me, as I remain in you. Just as a branch cannot bear fruit on its own unless it remains on the vine, so neither can you unless you remain in me. 5 I am the vine, you are the branches. Whoever

remains in me and I in him will bear much fruit, because without me you can do nothing. **6** Anyone who does not remain in me will be thrown out like a branch and wither; people will gather them and throw them into a fire and they will be burned. **7** If you remain in me and my words remain in you, ask for whatever you want and it will be done for you. **8** By this is my Father glorified, that you bear much fruit and become my disciples. **9** As the Father loves me, so I also love you. Remain in my love. **10** If you keep my commandments, you will remain in my love, just as I have kept my Father's commandments and remain in his love.

11 "I have told you this so that my joy may be in you and your joy may be complete. **12** This is my commandment: love one another as I love you. **13** No one has greater love than this, to lay down one's life for one's friends. **14** You are my friends if you do what I command you. **15** I no longer call you slaves, because a slave does not know what his master is doing. I have called you friends, because I have told you everything I have heard from my Father. **16** It was not you who chose me, but I who chose you and appointed you to go and bear fruit that will remain, so that whatever you ask the Father in my name he may give you. **17** This I command you: love one another."

Jesus once again used everyday imagery from first-century Palestine in a dramatic teaching. Jesus is the vine providing life to us, the many branches. Without nourishment from the vine, the branches will not just be fruitless, they will be lifeless. We the branches will die without Jesus. We must do whatever is necessary to maintain a healthy connection to Him. We have heard in the teachings of John (Landmark 2) and in the parable of the weeds (Landmark 13) the fate of barren branches.

Jesus expressed His love for His disciples in terms that we cannot fully understand. He loves us as the Father loves Him, with a supernatural love. What an amazing love this must be. To remain in this love, Jesus reiterated the importance of keeping His commandments. He had just told the disciples in the previous unit that was how they were to show their love for Him. This is also the way we remain in the supernatural love Jesus has for us.

In Landmark 36, Jesus taught that the greatest commandment was to love God with our entire being. We show this love by keeping the other commandments and thus remain in His supernatural love for us. Of these other commandments, He reminded His disciples that loving one another as He loved them is essential. How do we do this? Jesus will soon give the greatest possible example.

YOU IMMEDIATELY LEARN THAT VINES and branches draped across your windshield dramatically increase the challenge of driving a race car. People from all around the world have come to watch you do just that. This is truly an international spectacle, so the show must go on. Unfortunately, your situation quickly deteriorates. You begin to swerve from one side of the track to the other. Cheering turns to jeering. You start to hear what sounds like yells of anger and words of **hatred**. When you scrape against the track wall, the crowd's response feels like the whole **world** has turned against you. The **hatred** coming from the crowd is palpable. Feeling more disappointed and frustrated than words can describe, you continue to slowly weave your way around the track. The international anger continues. The **hatred** of these people from around the **world** follows you, spreading like a wave through the stands. This **hatred** persists as your car finally limps across the finish line. This display of **hatred** is a powerful reminder of Jesus' words about THE WORLD'S HATRED.

THE WORLD'S HATRED

Jn 15:18–16:4

18 "If the world hates you, realize that it hated me first. **19** If you belonged to the world, the world would love its own; but because you do not belong to the world, and I have chosen you out of the world, the world hates you. **20** Remember the word I spoke to you, 'No slave is greater than his master.' If they persecuted me, they will also persecute you. If they kept my word, they will also keep yours. **21** And they will do all these things to you on account of my name, because they do not know the one who sent me. **22** If I had not come and spoken to them, they would have no sin; but as it is they have no excuse for their sin. **23** Whoever hates me also hates my Father. **24** If I had not done works among them that no one else ever did, they would not have sin; but as it is, they have seen and hated both me and my Father. **25** But in order that the word written in their law might be fulfilled, 'They hated me without cause.'

26 "When the Advocate comes whom I will send you from the Father, the Spirit of truth that proceeds from the Father, he will testify to me. **27** And you also testify, because you have been with me from the beginning.

1 "I have told you this so that you may not fall away. **2** They will expel you from the synagogues; in fact, the hour is coming when everyone who kills you will think he is offering worship to God. 3 They will do this because they have not known either the Father or me. 4 I have told you this so that when their hour comes you may remember that I told you.

"I did not tell you this from the beginning, because I was with you."

Jesus had some good news and some bad news. The bad news first. The world would dislike Jesus' disciples. Actually, it was worse; the world would hate those who belonged to Jesus and did not belong to the world. Jesus' followers would be treated as He was. The branches would share in the persecution of the vine. However, the persecutors would bear responsibility for their sins, for they had ignored both the words and works of Jesus.

The good news was that the coming Spirit would strengthen the persecuted in their times of trouble. This gift from the Father sent through the Son would help the disciples testify about Jesus. The Spirit also helps us bear witness that the disciples were right in following Jesus. The Spirit will be our Advocate in dealing with the hostility of a misguided world.

ALL YOU CAN THINK ABOUT as you bring the race car to a stop is how to make the quickest possible **departure**. You have never wanted to **depart** from any place so badly in your life. As you **depart** the vine-covered car, the yelling from the crowd is deafening. For safety, you keep your helmet on. This makes finding the nearest point of **departure** more difficult. You look about and finally see a nearby exit. That will be your point of **departure**. As you break into a run, the yelling from the crowd stops. The silence is more deafening than the yelling. Slowing to a walk, you **depart** in silence. This hasty **departure**, as the crowd goes from callous to calm, reminds you of the unit describing JESUS' DEPARTURE.

JESUS' DEPARTURE

Jn 16:5–33

5 "But now I am going to the one who sent me, and not one of you asks me, 'Where are you going?' **6** But because I told you this, grief has filled your hearts. **7** But I tell you the truth, it is better for you that I go. For if I do not go, the Advocate will not come to you. But if I go, I will send him to you. **8** And when he comes he will convict the world in regard to sin and righteousness and condemnation: **9** sin, because they do not believe in me; **10** righteousness, because I am going to the Father and you will no longer see me; **11** condemnation, because the ruler of this world has been condemned.

12 "I have much more to tell you, but you cannot bear it now. **13** But when he comes, the Spirit of truth, he will guide you to all truth. He will not speak on his own, but he will speak what he hears, and will declare to you the things that are coming. **14** He will glorify me, because he will take from what is mine and declare it to you. **15** Everything that the Father has is mine; for this reason I told you that he will take from what is mine and declare it to you.

16 "A little while and you will no longer see me, and again a little while later and you will see me." **17** So some of his disciples said to one another, "What does this mean that he is saying to us, 'A little while and you will not see me, and again a little while and you will see me,' and 'Because I am going to the Father'?" **18** So they said, "What is this 'little while' [of which he speaks]? We do not know what he means." **19** Jesus knew that they wanted to ask him, so he said to them, "Are you discussing with one another what I said, 'A little while and you will not see me, and again a little while and you will see me'? **20** Amen, amen, I say to you, you will weep and mourn, while the world rejoices; you will grieve, but your grief will become joy. **21** When a woman is in labor, she is in anguish because her hour has arrived; but when she has given birth to a child, she no longer remembers the pain because of her joy that a child has been born into the world. **22** So you also are now in anguish. But I will see you again, and your hearts will rejoice, and no one will take your joy away from you. **23** On that day you will not question me about anything. Amen, amen, I say to you, whatever you ask the Father in my name he will give you. **24** Until now you have not asked anything in my name; ask and you will receive, so that your joy may be complete.

25 "I have told you this in figures of speech. The hour is coming when I will no longer speak to you in figures but I will tell you clearly about the Father. **26** On that day you will ask in my name, and I do not tell you that I will ask the Father for you. **27** For the

Father himself loves you, because you have loved me and have come to believe that I came from God. **28** I came from the Father and have come into the world. Now I am leaving the world and going back to the Father." **29** His disciples said, "Now you are talking plainly, and not in any figure of speech. **30** Now we realize that you know everything and that you do not need to have anyone question you. Because of this we believe that you came from God." **31** Jesus answered them, "Do you believe now? **32** Behold, the hour is coming and has arrived when each of you will be scattered to his own home and you will leave me alone. But I am not alone, because the Father is with me. **33** I have told you this so that you might have peace in me. In the world you will have trouble, but take courage, I have conquered the world."

———————————

As Jesus' Last Supper with His disciples was ending, He repeated that He was going away. He was now more specific. Jesus was returning to the Father who had sent Him. With His death, resurrection, and departure, He will have completed the Father's divine plan. The disciples' task to preach this divine plan lay ahead. To assist them, they would have an Advocate. This Advocate would be "the Spirit of truth." This guiding Spirit would be a gift from the Father and the Son to the disciples, and to future generations. Through this Spirit, all can be led to the truth, which is Jesus Himself.

Jesus knew that His departure would be painful for those who loved Him. He likened it to the pain of a woman in labor, though He still gave them hope. Like the mother who rejoices when she holds her newborn child, the disciples would rejoice when they beheld the reborn Christ.

Jesus reiterated that He was going back to the Father from whence He came. In their enthusiasm, His flock of eleven confessed their faith, but in a few short hours the sheep would scatter, leaving the Shepherd alone with the wolves.

In concluding His final meal, Jesus did what He had previously taught His disciples to do. He prayed to His Father. Jesus began by emphasizing the relationship He had with the Father. He referred back to the first unit of the first Landmark, recalling their relationship before the world began. This relationship was more specifically a unity. To know Jesus is to know the Father, which is the way to eternal life. Jesus, who was sent by the Father and was one with the Father, offered to His Father the suffering and death He was about to endure. Jesus then prayed that the disciples He was leaving behind would be able to do the same, not necessarily to die an agonizing death, but to give their lives as a sacrifice for others.

AS YOU DEPART THROUGH THE gate, several people approach and ask why you are leaving so quickly. You say that the hatred of the crowd makes you feel unwelcome and afraid. These words are met with looks of disbelief. "What are you talking about? The crowd loves you!" They explain that you misunderstood the yelling. People were cheering your courage and bravery. Driving under those impossible conditions was respected and appreciated. What you thought were words of hatred were actually shouts of encouragement. Hearing this, you are overwhelmed with relief. Immediately, you fall to your knees and offer a **prayer** of thanksgiving. It is the most heartfelt **prayer** that you have ever prayed. After finishing the **prayer**, you rise to your feet and return to wave to the crowd. This **prayer** after your racing experience recalls the final unit associated with the 43 race car: THE PRAYER OF JESUS.

THE PRAYER OF JESUS

Jn 17:1–26

1 When Jesus had said this, he raised his eyes to heaven and said, "Father, the hour has come. Give glory to your son, so that your son may glorify you, 2 just as you gave him authority over all people, so that he may give eternal life to all you gave him. 3 Now this is eternal life, that they should know you, the only true God, and the one whom you sent, Jesus Christ. 4 I glorified you on earth by accomplishing the work that you gave me to do. 5 Now glorify me, Father, with you, with the glory that I had with you before the world began.

6 "I revealed your name to those whom you gave me out of the world. They belonged to you, and you gave them to me, and they have kept your word. 7 Now they know that everything you gave me is from you, 8 because the words you gave to me I have given to them, and they accepted them and truly understood that I came from you, and they have believed that you sent me. 9 I pray for them. I do not pray for the world but for the ones you have given me, because they are yours, 10 and everything of mine is yours and everything

of yours is mine, and I have been glorified in them. **11** And now I will no longer be in the world, but they are in the world, while I am coming to you. Holy Father, keep them in your name that you have given me, so that they may be one just as we are. **12** When I was with them I protected them in your name that you gave me, and I guarded them, and none of them was lost except the son of destruction, in order that the scripture might be fulfilled. **13** But now I am coming to you. I speak this in the world so that they may share my joy completely. **14** I gave them your word, and the world hated them, because they do not belong to the world any more than I belong to the world. **15** I do not ask that you take them out of the world but that you keep them from the evil one. **16** They do not belong to the world any more than I belong to the world. **17** Consecrate them in the truth. Your word is truth. **18** As you sent me into the world, so I sent them into the world. **19** And I consecrate myself for them, so that they also may be consecrated in truth.

20 "I pray not only for them, but also for those who will believe in me through their word, **21** so that they may all be one, as you, Father, are in me and I in you, that they also may be in us, that the world may believe that you sent me. **22** And I have given them the glory you gave me, so that they may be one, as we are one, **23** I in them and you in me, that they may be brought to perfection as one, that the world may know that you sent me, and that you loved them even as you loved me. **24** Father, they are your gift to me. I wish that where I am they also may be with me, that they may see my glory that you gave me, because you loved me before the foundation of the world. **25** Righteous Father, the world also does not know you, but I know you, and they know that you sent me. **26** I made known to them your name and I will make it known, that the love with which you loved me may be in them and I in them."

Jesus asked the Father to watch over and guide the disciples in their holy mission of spreading the Gospel. This request, combined with Jesus' future presence through the Holy Spirit, left the disciples and the church they would establish in good hands. The disciples, empowered by this Trinity of assistance, were to represent Jesus in the world after His death and resurrection. Disciples were to do Jesus' work in the world, but were not to be of the world.

Landmark 44:

FOOTBALL JERSEY

T he forty-fourth Landmark is the last one to be associated with a sport. In team sports, the individual athletes wear a team **jersey** or shirt. Each **jersey** bears a number to help distinguish one player from another. Sometimes an outstanding athlete's number is almost as well-known as their name. Some numbers are well-known because they have been worn by several great players. Such is the case with the number *44* in college football. Three of the greatest running backs in college football history all wore **jersey** number *44*. Amazingly, they all attended the same school; Jim Brown, Floyd Little, and Ernie Davis all carried the ball for Syracuse University while wearing an orange number *44* on their backs. As a result, the number *44* is often associated with football running backs. We will do the same. Imagine that you, no matter your size or skill level, are dressed in a football uniform. Your **jersey** number is *44*, of course. You are carrying a football and being chased by several very large, determined opponents. Hopefully, you can avoid being tackled! The forty-fourth Landmark is the **jersey** number *44*, which you are wearing.

You must avoid being tackled at all costs. Where can you run with the ball that your aggressive opponents would dare not follow? Running off the football field, you spot a nearby **garden**. Surely you will not be chased through the well-tended rows of this vegetable **garden**. As you enter the **garden**, your cleats lose traction. You lose your balance and fall face first into the tomatoes. Splat! The beautiful **garden** has taken a hit. Rolling over, you flatten a row of beans. The **garden** is becoming a shambles. As you regain your feet, sharp cleats puncture several potatoes and you fall again. You are now lying face up in the **garden**. Your opponents have now arrived at the edge of the **garden**. However, they, too, are on the ground. Your opponents are rolling in laughter at you and the disaster that was once a **garden**. This **garden** scene is a painful embarrassment, but it allows you to recall JESUS' AGONY IN THE GARDEN.

JESUS' AGONY IN THE GARDEN

Mt 26:36–46

36 Then Jesus came with them to a place called Gethsemane, and he said to his disciples, "Sit here while I go over there and pray." **37** He took along Peter and the two sons of Zebedee, and began to feel sorrow and distress. **38** Then he said to them, "My soul is sorrowful even to death. Remain here and keep watch with me." **39** He advanced a little and fell prostrate in prayer, saying, "My Father, if it is possible, let this cup pass from me; yet, not as I will, but as you will." **40** When he returned to his disciples he found them asleep. He said to Peter, "So you could not keep watch with me for one hour? **41** Watch and pray that you may not undergo the test. The spirit is willing, but the flesh is weak." **42** Withdrawing a second time, he prayed again, "My Father, if it is not possible that this cup pass without my drinking it, your will be done!" **43** Then he returned once more and found them asleep, for they could not keep their eyes open. **44** He left them and withdrew again and prayed a third time, saying the same thing again. **45** Then he returned to his disciples and said to them, "Are you still sleeping and taking your rest? Behold, the hour is at hand when the Son of Man is to be handed over to sinners. **46** Get up, let us go. Look, my betrayer is at hand."

Mk 14:32–42

32 Then they came to a place named Gethsemane, and he said to his disciples, "Sit here while I pray." **33** He took with him Peter, James, and John, and began to be troubled and distressed. **34** Then he said to them, "My soul is sorrowful even to death. Remain here and keep watch." **35** He advanced a little and fell to the ground and prayed that if it were possible the hour might pass by him; **36** he said, "Abba, Father, all things are possible to you. Take this cup away from me, but not what I will but what you will." **37** When he returned he found them asleep. He said to Peter, "Simon, are you asleep? Could you not keep watch for one hour? **38** Watch and pray that you may not undergo the test. The spirit is willing but the flesh is weak." **39** Withdrawing again, he prayed, saying the same thing. **40** Then he returned once more and found them asleep, for they could not keep their eyes open and did not know what to answer him. **41** He returned a third time and said to them, "Are you still sleeping and taking your rest? It is enough. The hour has come.

Behold, the Son of Man is to be handed over to sinners. **42** Get up, let us go. See, my betrayer is at hand."

Lk 22:39–46

39 Then going out he went, as was his custom, to the Mount of Olives, and the disciples followed him. **40** When he arrived at the place he said to them, "Pray that you may not undergo the test." **41** After withdrawing about a stone's throw from them and kneeling, he prayed, **42** saying, "Father, if you are willing, take this cup away from me; still, not my will but yours be done." **43** [And to strengthen him an angel from heaven appeared to him. **44** He was in such agony and he prayed so fervently that his sweat became like drops of blood falling on the ground.] **45** When he rose from prayer and returned to his disciples, he found them sleeping from grief. **46** He said to them, "Why are you sleeping? Get up and pray that you may not undergo the test."

Jesus was back in a familiar place. He and His disciples were in the Garden of Gethsemane on the Mount of Olives, just beyond the Jerusalem city walls. This visit was unlike any previous retreats to the garden. Jesus was about to endure several agonizing hours. This marks the beginning of Jesus' emotionally and physically painful death. The humanity of Jesus now struggled with accepting His fate. In a graphic example to us, through prayer Jesus came to terms with the Father's plan. Just as He had done before His first Galilean mission trip (Landmark 4), Jesus went off by Himself to pray. Spending quiet time with the Father, discerning and accepting His will in times of difficulty, is necessary for us all. Having a relationship in which we are comfortable with God as "Abba" will give us the strength to overcome all tests and temptations. Without a strong prayer life, we will certainly "fall asleep" in our relationship with Jesus. Though He was sorrowful and distressed, this prayer gave Jesus the strength to face His enemies and offer up His life as a sacrifice for all. Jesus knew this was not an easy example to follow. He knew firsthand that human flesh is weak. Thus, we must pray for the strength to overcome our physical desires and the temptations of this world. We pray to be in, but not of this world.

WHILE YOUR FOOTBALL OPPONENTS ARE laughing at your garden mishap, the owner of the garden is not amused. She has called the police.

An officer is now running toward you swinging a pair of handcuffs. This does not look good. Your wrists are still sore from your **arrest** at the wedding back in Landmark 3. The officer yells, "You are under **arrest** for inappropriate garden behavior." While still lying on the ground, you are cuffed and placed under **arrest**. You plead that there has been a mistake; you meant no harm. You are not some garden variety criminal! As you are helped to your feet, you are again told that you are under **arrest**. This rather harsh **arrest** helps you recall another **arrest**. This time it is not the **arrest** of John the Baptist, it is THE ARREST OF JESUS.

THE ARREST OF JESUS

Mt 26:47–56

47 While he was still speaking, Judas, one of the Twelve, arrived, accompanied by a large crowd, with swords and clubs, who had come from the chief priests and the elders of the people. **48** His betrayer had arranged a sign with them, saying, "The man I shall kiss is the one; arrest him." **49** Immediately he went over to Jesus and said, "Hail, Rabbi!" and he kissed him. **50** Jesus answered him, "Friend, do what you have come for." Then stepping forward they laid hands on Jesus and arrested him. **51** And behold, one of those who accompanied Jesus put his hand to his sword, drew it, and struck the high priest's servant, cutting off his ear. **52** Then Jesus said to him, "Put your sword back into its sheath, for all who take the sword will perish by the sword. **53** Do you think that I cannot call upon my Father and he will not provide me at this moment with more than twelve legions of angels? **54** But then how would the scriptures be fulfilled which say that it must come to pass in this way?" **55** At that hour Jesus said to the crowds, "Have you come out as against a robber, with swords and clubs to seize me? Day after day I sat teaching in the temple area, yet you did not arrest me. **56** But all this has come to pass that the writings of the prophets may be fulfilled." Then all the disciples left him and fled.

Mk 14:43–52

43 Then, while he was still speaking, Judas, one of the Twelve, arrived, accompanied by a crowd with swords and clubs who had come from the chief priests, the scribes, and the elders. **44** His betrayer had arranged a signal with them, saying, "The man I shall kiss is the one; arrest him and lead him away securely." **45** He came and immediately went over to him and said, "Rabbi." And he kissed him. **46** At this they laid hands on him and arrested him. **47** One of the bystanders drew his sword, struck the high priest's servant, and cut off his ear. **48** Jesus said to them in reply, "Have you come out as against a robber, with swords and clubs, to seize me? **49** Day after day I was with you teaching in the temple area, yet you did not arrest me; but that the scriptures may be fulfilled." **50** And they all left him and fled. **51** Now a young man followed him wearing nothing but a linen cloth about his body. They seized him, **52** but he left the cloth behind and ran off naked.

Lk 22:47–53

47 While he was still speaking, a crowd approached and in front was one of the Twelve, a man named Judas. He went up to Jesus to kiss him. **48** Jesus said to him, "Judas, are you betraying the Son of Man with a kiss?" **49** His disciples realized what was about to happen, and they asked, "Lord, shall we strike with a sword?" **50** And one of them struck the high priest's servant and cut off his right ear. **51** But Jesus said in reply, "Stop, no more of this!" Then he touched the servant's ear and healed him. **52** And Jesus said to the chief priests and temple guards and elders who had come for him, "Have you come out as against a robber, with swords and clubs? **53** Day after day I was with you in the temple area, and you did not seize me; but this is your hour, the time for the power of darkness."

Jn 18:1–12

1 When he had said this, Jesus went out with his disciples across the Kidron valley to where there was a garden, into which he and his disciples entered. **2** Judas his betrayer also knew the place, because Jesus had often met there with his disciples. **3** So Judas got a band of soldiers and guards from the chief priests and the Pharisees and went there with lanterns, torches, and weapons. **4** Jesus, knowing everything that was going to happen to him, went out and said to them, "Whom are you looking for?" **5** They answered him, "Jesus the Nazorean." He said to them, "I AM." Judas his betrayer was also with them. **6** When he said to them, "I AM," they turned away and fell to the ground. **7** So he again asked them, "Whom are you looking for?" They said, "Jesus the Nazorean." **8** Jesus answered, "I told you that I AM. So if you are looking for me, let these men go." **9** This was to fulfill what he had said, "I have not lost any of those you gave me." **10** Then Simon Peter, who had a sword, drew it, struck the high priest's slave, and cut off his right ear. The slave's name was Malchus. **11** Jesus said to Peter, "Put your sword into its scabbard. Shall I not drink the cup that the Father gave me?"

12 So the band of soldiers, the tribune, and the Jewish guards seized Jesus, bound him.

Up to this point, the Gospels have shown that Jesus was not the mighty warrior Messiah sent to free Israel from its earthly enemies. Nonetheless, the ignorant Jewish leaders dispatched a large force of armed soldiers, guards, and assorted others to arrest Jesus. They went to arrest the peaceful, loving Jesus who was willingly about to fulfill His mission to die for our sins. Ironically, this force was led by the cowardly Judas. This former apostle hypocritically identified Jesus with a kiss, a gesture of friendship.

John does not describe this lip service of betrayal. He told how Jesus boldly approached the horde. When Jesus identified Himself using the divine name (Ex 3:14), its power felled the armed soldiers and guards. In doing so, He allowed His disciples to go unharmed. This is certainly a better picture of the apostles than Matthew and Mark describe. They depict the frightened disciples fleeing in fear. They abandoned Jesus! However, before they ran off, an act of aggression occurred. A disciple (Peter, according to John) cut off an ear. It was not just any ear. It had been attached to the head of the high priest's servant. What was the high priest's servant doing there? Many believe his presence was symbolic of the high priest himself. According to the Hebrew Scripture, a man with a physical defect, such as a missing ear, was not able to serve as high priest. Thus the high priest who sent men to arrest Jesus was depicted as unfit for his office. Jesus rebuked the aggressor and preached nonviolence. Luke describes Jesus performing one last miracle with His healing touch. Jesus was preaching and healing even as He gave Himself over to a painful, violent death!

WHILE WALKING ALONG WITH THE arresting officer, your stomach begins to growl. It is almost dinnertime, and the prospect of a good meal seems slim. The officer reaches into his pocket and offers you an unusual snack. He has several **anise** fruits. These small, dry, green fruits are also called "**aniseed**," explains the officer. You have never tasted **aniseed**, but have heard that it tastes like licorice. The **anise** fruits certainly smell like licorice. You pop several **aniseeds** into your mouth and are immediately reminded of the taste of black licorice. You thank the officer for the **anise** fruits. The **anise** is a strong reminder of the unit when ANNAS QUESTIONS JESUS.

ANNAS QUESTIONS JESUS

Jn 18:13–14, 19–24

13 and brought him to Annas first. He was the father-in-law of Caiaphas, who was high priest that year. 14 It was Caiaphas who had counseled the Jews that it was better that one man should die rather than the people.

...

19 The high priest questioned Jesus about his disciples and about his doctrine. 20 Jesus answered him, "I have spoken publicly to the world. I have always taught in a synagogue or in the temple area where all the Jews gather, and in secret I have said nothing. 21 Why ask me? Ask those who heard me what I said to them. They know what I said." 22 When he had said this, one of the temple guards standing there struck Jesus and said, "Is this the way you answer the high priest?" 23 Jesus answered him, "If I have spoken wrongly, testify to the wrong; but if I have spoken rightly, why do you strike me?" 24 Then Annas sent him bound to Caiaphas the high priest.

Jesus now faced a series of questions and accusations before a motley crew of religious and political officials. Following His arrest, Jesus was first brought before Annas. Only John mentions this brief episode with the former high priest. Many at the time still considered Annas, rather than his son-in-law Caiaphas, to be the true high priest. He had been the official high priest in Jerusalem from AD 6–15, when the Romans "illegally" replaced him with Caiaphas.

Annas tried to discredit Jesus as a false prophet and even worse, a blasphemer. Jesus intimated that perhaps Annas already knew about His teachings. Jesus had hidden nothing. He had publicly proclaimed His good news throughout Galilee, Judea, and beyond. Many people had heard His radical message of love and forgiveness. Jesus suggested that perhaps Annas should question them. This response produced the first of many physical blows that Jesus would absorb over the next few hours. Annas had heard enough. Having no real authority, he passed Jesus on to His next inquisitors.

YOU THOUGHT THE POLICE OFFICER was going to take you to jail. It is a surprise to soon find yourself standing next to a large pile of **sand**. You cannot imagine why you are by the **sand** rather than in a cell. You soon find out. It is not pleasant. A cell would have been better than the **sand**. First, the officer buries your legs up to your knees. Clearly, you are going nowhere in a hurry. Then the unhappy gardener whose garden you recently terrorized appears. She is carrying a large box that she places by the sand pile a few feet from your buried legs. Uh oh! The box contains the tomatoes, beans, and potatoes you recently squashed. She dumps the damaged produce on the ground. The gardener then squeezes the juice from the now **sand**-covered produce over your head. It actually does not taste bad, though the **sand** is a bit gritty. Recall from Landmark 31 that *sand* is a soundalike for "Sanhedrin." This strange punishment in the **sand** is a vivid reminder of JESUS BEFORE THE SANHEDRIN.

JESUS BEFORE THE SANHEDRIN

Mt 26:57–68

57 Those who had arrested Jesus led him away to Caiaphas the high priest, where the scribes and the elders were assembled. **58** Peter was following him at a distance as far as the high priest's courtyard, and going inside he sat down with the servants to see the outcome. **59** The chief priests and the entire Sanhedrin kept trying to obtain false testimony against Jesus in order to put him to death, **60** but they found none, though many false witnesses came forward. Finally two came forward **61** who stated, "This man said, 'I can destroy the temple of God and within three days rebuild it.'" **62** The high priest rose and addressed him, "Have you no answer? What are these men testifying against you?" **63** But Jesus was silent. Then the high priest said to him, "I order you to tell us under oath before the living God whether you are the Messiah, the Son of God." **64** Jesus said to him in reply, "You have said so. But I tell you:

From now on you will see 'the Son of Man seated at the right hand of the Power'
and 'coming on the clouds of heaven.'"

65 Then the high priest tore his robes and said, "He has blasphemed! What further need have we of witnesses? You have now heard the blasphemy; **66** what is your opinion?" They said in reply,

"He deserves to die!" **67** Then they spat in his face and struck him, while some slapped him, **68** saying, "Prophesy for us, Messiah: who is it that struck you?"

Mk 14:53–65

53 They led Jesus away to the high priest, and all the chief priests and the elders and the scribes came together. **54** Peter followed him at a distance into the high priest's courtyard and was seated with the guards, warming himself at the fire. **55** The chief priests and the entire Sanhedrin kept trying to obtain testimony against Jesus in order to put him to death, but they found none. **56** Many gave false witness against him, but their testimony did not agree. **57** Some took the stand and testified falsely against him, alleging, **58** "We heard him say, 'I will destroy this temple made with hands and within three days I will build another not made with hands.'" **59** Even so their testimony did not agree. **60** The high priest rose before the assembly and questioned Jesus, saying, "Have you no answer? What are these men testifying against you?" **61** But he was silent and answered nothing. Again the high priest asked him and said to him, "Are you the Messiah, the son of the Blessed One?" **62** Then Jesus answered, "I am;

and 'you will see the Son of Man
seated at the right hand of the Power
and coming with the clouds of heaven.'"

63 At that the high priest tore his garments and said, "What further need have we of witnesses? **64** You have heard the blasphemy. What do you think?" They all condemned him as deserving to die. **65** Some began to spit on him. They blindfolded him and struck him and said to him, "Prophesy!" And the guards greeted him with blows.

Lk 22:63–71

63 The men who held Jesus in custody were ridiculing and beating him. **64** They blindfolded him and questioned him, saying, "Prophesy! Who is it that struck you?" **65** And they reviled him in saying many other things against him.

66 When day came the council of elders of the people met, both chief priests and scribes, and they brought him before their Sanhedrin. **67** They said, "If you are the Messiah, tell us," but he replied to them, "If I tell you, you will not believe, **68** and if I question, you will not respond. **69** But from this time on the Son of Man will be seated at the right hand of the power of God." **70** They all asked, "Are you then the Son of God?" He replied to them, "You say that I am." **71** Then they said, "What further need have we for testimony? We have heard it from his own mouth."

Jesus stood alone before the High Court of Jewish law. The Gospels vary as to the exact location of this "emergency" convening of the Sanhedrin. Matthew and Mark describe the "trial" at the home of the high priest instead of the normal meeting place adjacent to the temple. It was very early, an ungodly hour for the chief priest, high priests, scribes, and elders to leave their comfortable beds for a hastily called trial. They must have thought it important. Luke describes a later trial "when day came."

The members of the Sanhedrin must have been frustrated as a panel of "witnesses" came forth. The Sanhedrin was unable to coordinate a story that would allow them to seek help from their Roman enemies to "legally" put Jesus to death. Some testified about what they had heard Jesus say about the temple destruction (Landmark 37). Not only did their statements not agree, they had mistaken resurrection for construction! Jesus listened quietly, knowing the outcome of the charade being acted out before Him. The entire proceeding bore some resemblance to a trial that had been held many years earlier. Jeremiah had stood before Zedekiah and city officials who wanted him dead (Jer 38). Jeremiah had predicted the doom of Jerusalem.

Finally, Caiaphas chimed in. His initial question to Jesus regarding the allegations was met with loud silence. This surprising fulfillment of Psalm 38:13–15 likely increased Caiaphas's anger. He was not used to having his questions ignored. He then asked Jesus directly if He was the "Messiah." Though Caiaphas was the high priest, he did not understand the true meaning of his question. Jesus' response did not go over well. The answer was a combination of Daniel 7:13 and Psalm 110:1. It resulted in robe-ripping and the capital charge of blasphemy (Lev 24:16). By his actions, Caiaphas was actually breaking Jewish Law and invoking the wrath of God. Garment tearing was a no-no (Lev 10:6).

In Matthew and Mark, the Sanhedrin were a rowdy, aggressive bunch. They agreed that Jesus "deserved" to die. They also felt He deserved to be hit and spat upon. What incredible indignities the Son of God endured for us! The Sanhedrin had now done its job. They condemned Jesus, but legally only the Romans could carry out the execution. The high priest sent the true King to the Roman governor for this purpose.

Landmark 45:

STEEP HILL

A new Landmark is a very welcome sight, considering the predicament you were in at the end of Landmark 44. You are no longer buried in sand, but a difficult task lies ahead with Landmark 45. You are now standing at the bottom of a very steep hill. Actually, it is an extremely steep hill. It is not as tall as the mountain in Landmark 5, but it is much steeper. It is not an impossible ninety-degree climb, but it is half that. It is a hill that rises at a **45-degree** angle. You certainly have strong doubts about your ability to scale a **45-degree** slope. For most of the climb, you will have to be down on your hands and knees. Taking a deep breath, you prepare to take your first steps up the imposing challenge of this **steep 45-degree hill**. This **steep 45-degree hill** is Landmark 45.

You are not alone at the base of the steep 45-degree hill. **Peter** Rabbit has found his way here from the front seat of the 43 race car. **Peter** is now with you at the start of another challenging task. You would expect him to have no trouble hopping up this hill. You ask him to join you. Once again, he vigorously shakes his head from side to side. **Peter** again **denies** himself a chance to be with you. Trying to convince him to change his mind, you point out his strong and powerful legs. He **denies** that they are either strong or powerful. You remind him that he has probably hopped up this hill before. **Peter denies** this too. You are sad that **Peter** is in such **denial**, but realize that he has made his decision. Whereas the rabbit's **denial** in Landmark 43 represented the foretelling of **Peter's denial**, this episode at the base of the 45-degree hill recalls the actual occurrence of PETER'S DENIAL OF JESUS.

PETER'S DENIAL OF JESUS

Mt 26:69–75

69 Now Peter was sitting outside in the courtyard. One of the maids came over to him and said, "You too were with Jesus the Galilean." **70** But he denied it in front of everyone, saying, "I do not know what you are talking about!" **71** As he went out to the gate, another girl saw him and said to those who were there, "This man was with Jesus the Nazorean." **72** Again he denied it with an oath, "I do not know the man!" **73** A little later the bystanders came over and said to Peter, "Surely you too are one of them; even your speech gives you away." **74** At that he began to curse and to swear, "I do not know the man." And immediately a cock crowed. **75** Then Peter remembered the word that Jesus had spoken: "Before the cock crows you will deny me three times." He went out and began to weep bitterly.

Mk 14:66–72

66 While Peter was below in the courtyard, one of the high priest's maids came along. **67** Seeing Peter warming himself, she looked intently at him and said, "You too were with the Nazarene, Jesus." **68** But he denied it saying, "I neither know nor understand what you are talking about." So he went out into the outer court. [Then the cock crowed.] **69** The maid saw him and began again to say to the bystanders, "This man is one of them." **70** Once again he denied it. A little later the bystanders said to Peter once more, "Surely you are one of them; for you too are a Galilean." **71** He began to curse and to swear, "I do not know this man about whom you are talking." **72** And immediately a cock crowed a second time. Then Peter remembered the word that Jesus had said to him, "Before the cock crows twice you will deny me three times." He broke down and wept.

Lk 22:55–62

55 They lit a fire in the middle of the courtyard and sat around it, and Peter sat down with them. **56** When a maid saw him seated in the light, she looked intently at him and said, "This man too was with him." **57** But he denied it saying, "Woman, I do not know him." **58** A short while later someone else saw him and said, "You too are one of them"; but Peter answered, "My friend, I am not." **59** About an hour later, still another insisted, "Assuredly, this man too was with him, for he also is a Galilean." **60** But Peter said, "My friend, I do not know what you are talking about." Just as he was saying this, the cock crowed, **61** and the Lord turned and looked at Peter; and Peter remembered the word of the Lord, how he had said to him, "Before the cock crows today, you will deny me three times." **62** He went out and began to weep bitterly.

Jn 18:15–18, 25–27

15 Simon Peter and another disciple followed Jesus. Now the other disciple was known to the high priest, and he entered the courtyard of the high priest with Jesus. **16** But Peter stood at the gate outside. So the other disciple, the acquaintance of the high priest, went out and spoke to the gatekeeper and brought Peter in. **17** Then the maid who was the gatekeeper said to Peter, "You are not one of this man's disciples, are you?" He said, "I am not." **18** Now the slaves and the guards were standing around a charcoal fire that they had made, because it was cold, and were warming themselves. Peter was also standing there keeping warm.

...

25 Now Simon Peter was standing there keeping warm. And they said to him, "You are not one of his disciples, are you?" He denied it and said, "I am not." **26** One of the slaves of the high priest, a relative of the one whose ear Peter had cut off, said, "Didn't I see you in the garden with him?" **27** Again Peter denied it. And immediately the cock crowed.

All four Gospels describe the frightened and cowardly behavior of Peter. The leader of the Twelve (temporarily reduced to eleven) showed anything but leadership, fulfilling Jesus' prophecy at the Last Supper. Peter not only denied being a follower, he went so far as to say that he did not even know Jesus. He made his denials before a variety of people. He even denied Jesus to a relative of the now earless Malchus (Landmark 44), someone who had strong evidence of Peter's connection with Jesus. It was not a good night for Peter. Earlier he had fallen asleep three times while Jesus prayed in the garden. Now he denied Him three times. With each questioning, Peter's denial became more explicit and public. At 3:00 a.m., he was awakened to his frailty. As a horn sounded signaling the end of the third night watch ("cock crow"), tears of guilt and remorse began to flow. How these tears must have burned as he recalled Jesus' words at their last meal together. What a dramatic contrast in behavior between Jesus at His "trial" and Peter outside in the courtyard!

YOU BEGIN TO RETHINK YOUR plan to climb the steep hill. If a rabbit refuses to hop up this 45-degree hill, perhaps you should reconsider your ambitious goal. Your thoughts are suddenly and quite loudly interrupted. A small plane has just landed not far from the hill. You watch with some concern as the **pilot** jumps down from the cockpit. In a freshly pressed uniform and cap, the **pilot** comes striding toward you. When the **pilot** is just a few yards away, he says in a friendly voice "Hi, I'm a **pilot**. Do you need a lift?" Your first thought is, "I hope you are a **pilot** since you just landed a plane!" However, you respond to the **pilot** with a nod of the head, and say, "Yes, that would be great." You accept the **pilot's** offer to fly you to the top of the hill. The **pilot** leads you over to his little plane. This pleasant encounter with the **pilot** is quite different from the unit it represents: JESUS BEFORE PILATE.

||||||||||||||||||||||||||||||||||||||||||||||||||||||||||||||||||||||||||||||||||||||||||||||||||||||||||||||||||||||||||||||||||||

JESUS BEFORE PILATE

||||||||||||||||||||||||||||||||||||||||||||||||||||||||||||||||||||||||||||||||||||||||||||||||||||||||||||||||||||||||||||||||||||

Mt 27:1–2, 11–14

1 When it was morning, all the chief priests and the elders of the people took counsel against Jesus to put him to death. 2 They bound him, led him away, and handed him over to Pilate, the governor.
...

11 Now Jesus stood before the governor, and he questioned him, "Are you the king of the Jews?" Jesus said, "You say so." 12 And when he was accused by the chief priests and elders, he made no answer. 13 Then Pilate said to him, "Do you not hear how many things they are testifying against you?" 14 But he did not answer him one word, so that the governor was greatly amazed.

Mk 15:1–5

1 As soon as morning came, the chief priests with the elders and the scribes, that is, the whole Sanhedrin, held a council. They bound Jesus, led him away, and handed him over to Pilate. 2 Pilate questioned him, "Are you the king of the Jews?" He said to him in reply, "You say so." 3 The chief priests accused him of many things. 4 Again Pilate questioned him, "Have you no answer? See how many things they accuse you of." 5 Jesus gave him no further answer, so that Pilate was amazed.

Lk 23:1–5

1 Then the whole assembly of them arose and brought him before Pilate. 2 They brought charges against him, saying, "We found this man misleading our people; he opposes the payment of taxes to Caesar and maintains that he is the Messiah, a king." 3 Pilate asked him, "Are you the king of the Jews?" He said to him in reply, "You say so." 4 Pilate then addressed the chief priests and the crowds, "I find this man not guilty." 5 But they were adamant and said, "He is inciting the people with his teaching throughout all Judea, from Galilee where he began even to here."

Jn 18:28–38

28 Then they brought Jesus from Caiaphas to the praetorium. It was morning. And they themselves did not enter the praetorium, in order not to be defiled so that they could eat the Passover. 29 So Pilate came out to them and said, "What charge do you bring [against] this man?" 30 They answered and said to him, "If he were not a criminal, we would not have handed him over to you." 31 At this, Pilate said to them, "Take him yourselves, and judge him according to your law." The Jews answered him, "We do not have the right to execute anyone," 32 in order that the word of Jesus might be fulfilled that he said indicating the kind of death he would die. 33 So Pilate went back into the praetorium and summoned Jesus and said to him, "Are you the King of the Jews?" 34 Jesus answered, "Do you say this on your own or have others told you about me?" 35 Pilate answered, "I am not a Jew, am I? Your own nation and the chief priests handed you over to me. What have you done?" 36 Jesus answered, "My kingdom does not belong to this world. If my kingdom did belong to this world, my attendants [would] be fighting to keep me from being handed over to the Jews. But as it is, my kingdom is not here." 37 So Pilate said to him, "Then you are a king?" Jesus answered, "You say I am a king. For this I was born and for this I came into the world, to testify to the truth. Everyone who belongs to the truth listens to my voice." 38 Pilate said to him, "What is truth?"

Very few parents name their baby boy Judas. The same goes for the name Pilate. Both names are strongly associated with the death of Jesus. All four Gospels include Jesus' interrogation by Pilate, though his degree of involvement and culpability vary depending on the author. Who deserves the bulk of the blame for Jesus' death: the heavy-handed Romans, or the hard-hearted Jewish leadership?

For ten years, commencing in AD 26, Pontius Pilate was the Roman governor (or prefect) of Judea and nearby Idumea and Samaria. This harsh anti-Semitic tyrant ruled from his house in Caesarea Maritima on the Samaritan coast, some fifty miles from Jerusalem. He typically traveled to Jerusalem at the time of Passover. Pilate came not as a pilgrim, but as an enforcer, in case the large Jewish crowds became overly zealous. Thus he was now in the Praetorium, his residence in Jerusalem, where he had the opportunity to have an audience with Jesus.

In a spiritual sense, Jesus certainly was the "King of the Jews." As the Son of God sent to be the Messiah of the Jewish people and of all humanity, the term "King" seems to hardly do Him justice. Conversely, Jesus was anything but a political King. It was this latter false charge that brought Jesus before Pilate. It was the Prefect Pilate who had the earthly power to put the perfect Jesus to death.

The Jewish leaders were upset by what they perceived as Jesus' blasphemy. To the pagan Pilate, this would have been a trivial matter. However, a claim to be "King of the Jews" got his attention. Any political claim that might threaten Rome had to be dealt with and could be punishable by death.

Given the potential fate of Jesus, which Pilate believed he held in his hands, no wonder he was amazed at Jesus' response, or lack thereof. Jesus' silence in Mark and Matthew recalled the "suffering servant" described by Isaiah (53:7). His brief reply in Luke did not outright deny the charge, for in a greater sense Jesus was the "King of the Jews." However, He did not accept the political title. John goes further. He had Jesus educate Pilate (and us) about the otherworldly nature of His kingdom and His mission of truth. Pilate, like many others, did not appear to understand the meaning of the truth.

YOU ARE NOW ABOARD THE small plane with the pilot. There are also several musicians crammed into the tiny aircraft. You recognize them as the British metal band **Judas** Priest. They are busy rehearsing a song. You can immediately appreciate the talents of **Judas** Priest. You just wish they were not playing their loud music in such a small space. Since the flight with **Judas** Priest will be quite short, you decide to keep your thoughts to yourself. The pilot then asks you and each member of **Judas** Priest to fasten your seat belts, straighten the seats, and place all trays in their upright position. This surprising encounter with **Judas** Priest on the small plane

makes you think of another all too familiar **Judas** and the next unit: THE
DEATH OF JUDAS.

THE DEATH OF JUDAS

Mt 27:3–10

3 Then Judas, his betrayer, seeing that Jesus had been
condemned, deeply regretted what he had done. He returned the
thirty pieces of silver to the chief priests and elders, **4** saying,
"I have sinned in betraying innocent blood." They said, "What is
that to us? Look to it yourself." **5** Flinging the money into the
temple, he departed and went off and hanged himself. **6** The chief
priests gathered up the money, but said, "It is not lawful to deposit
this in the temple treasury, for it is the price of blood." **7** After
consultation, they used it to buy the potter's field as a burial place
for foreigners. **8** That is why that field even today is called the Field
of Blood. **9** Then was fulfilled what had been said through Jeremiah
the prophet, "And they took the thirty pieces of silver, the value of
a man with a price on his head, a price set by some of the Israelites,
10 and they paid it out for the potter's field just as the Lord had
commanded me."

Only Matthew mentions the suicide of Judas. In despair, after realizing what he had done, Judas hanged himself. Luke does describe Judas's
suicide in his book, The Acts of the Apostles (which follows the Gospel of
John in the New Testament). In Acts, Judas's "inner self" is exposed after
he falls from a height and "all his insides spill out" (Acts 1:18). Judas's
betrayal of "innocent blood" is perhaps the most infamous single act in all
of history. His name remains synonymous with betrayal and deceit.

Judas was the man who betrayed the Messiah. His action led to Jesus' arrest and eventual crucifixion. His behavior led to the fulfillment of
many prophecies. Judas did act of his own free will. He was not forced to
be the one to take the thirty pieces of silver. We, too, are not forced in our
own daily lives to betray our Lord, but we do. Let us not despair as Judas
did. We are granted forgiveness through repentance by a loving God. Ironically, the ultimate act of love, triggered by Judas's betrayal, makes this
forgiveness possible.

THE SMALL, CRAMPED PLANE FINALLY takes off. Within seconds, the plane is hovering over the top of the Landmark, the steep 45-degree hill. Unfortunately, the pilot announces that there is insufficient area on the summit to land the plane. You are informed in a rather matter-of-fact fashion that you must jump! Emphatically, you scream, "No way!" You insist that there must be another option. The pilot then offers a very bizarre alternative. "We could lower you down by your **hair**." "What, are you crazy?" you reply. The pilot very seriously explains that he will fly as low as is reasonably safe. Then, the musicians will each grab a handful of your **hair** and lower you to a safe jumping height. You shake your head in disagreement. It is too late. Your **hair** is being yanked from all directions. Before you can say another word, you are dangling from the plane by your **hair**. Almost instantly, you feel the pain of **hair** tearing from its follicles. Thud. You hit the ground, with a very bad **hair**cut. Since **hair** and Herod sound very similar, this painful episode involving your **hair** helps recall the unit JESUS BEFORE HEROD.

||||||||||||||||||||||||||||||||||||||||||||||||||||||||||||||||||||||||||||||||||||||||||||||||||||||||||||||||||||||||||||||||

JESUS BEFORE HEROD

||||||||||||||||||||||||||||||||||||||||||||||||||||||||||||||||||||||||||||||||||||||||||||||||||||||||||||||||||||||||||||||||

Lk 23:6–16

6 On hearing this Pilate asked if the man was a Galilean; **7** and upon learning that he was under Herod's jurisdiction, he sent him to Herod who was in Jerusalem at that time. **8** Herod was very glad to see Jesus; he had been wanting to see him for a long time, for he had heard about him and had been hoping to see him perform some sign. **9** He questioned him at length, but he gave him no answer. **10** The chief priests and scribes, meanwhile, stood by accusing him harshly. **11** [Even] Herod and his soldiers treated him contemptuously and mocked him, and after clothing him in resplendent garb, he sent him back to Pilate. **12** Herod and Pilate became friends that very day, even though they had been enemies formerly. **13** Pilate then summoned the chief priests, the rulers, and the people **14** and said to them, "You brought this man to me and accused him of inciting the people to revolt. I have conducted my investigation in your presence and have not found this man guilty of the charges you have brought against him, **15** nor did Herod, for he sent him back to us. So no capital crime has been committed by him. **16** Therefore I shall have him flogged and then release him."

Throughout the Gospels, Herod Antipas had been looming in the background. He briefly took center stage in the execution of John the Baptist. Early on, he wanted to meet Jesus, the teacher and miracle worker he had heard so much about. Later, he and other Jewish leaders conspired to kill Jesus, the blasphemous troublemaker who threatened his security. Now, thanks to Pilate, Herod had his opportunity. But the meeting did not go as Herod had hoped. Jesus, the Lamb soon to be slaughtered, was mute before the man He had previously called a "fox" (Landmark 28). Jesus truly was the silent, suffering servant described by Isaiah (53:7). Herod the Tetrarch was angered by the apparent insolence of this man being proclaimed as "King of the Jews." Herod, his cronies, and his soldiers mocked Jesus and His royal title. He then sent Jesus back to Pilate, his new partner in crime, to officially deliver the death sentence.

YOU ARE ON TOP OF the 45-degree hill, but you paid a very steep price. You are lying on the ground in pain with a mostly bare and bleeding scalp! Help is nowhere in sight. Yelling for help would be a waste of breath. You decide to write for help. There is no mail service on the hilltop, so you will write a **sentence** using stones. After gathering the stones, you plan to spell out the **sentence**, "Please help me" on the ground. Hopefully another plane will fly over and see the **sentence** on the ground below. After a few minutes, you have collected enough rocks to write the **sentence**. In your finest "stonemanship," you carefully lay out the rocks to form your cry for help. With the **sentence** complete, all you can do is sit and wait for assistance. This process of writing the **sentence** using rocks is the last unit of Landmark 45: JESUS IS SENTENCED TO DEATH.

JESUS IS SENTENCED TO DEATH

Mt 27:15–26

15 Now on the occasion of the feast the governor was accustomed to release to the crowd one prisoner whom they wished. **16** And at

that time they had a notorious prisoner called [Jesus] Barabbas.
17 So when they had assembled, Pilate said to them, "Which one
do you want me to release to you, [Jesus] Barabbas, or Jesus called
Messiah?" **18** For he knew that it was out of envy that they had
handed him over. **19** While he was still seated on the bench, his
wife sent him a message, "Have nothing to do with that righteous
man. I suffered much in a dream today because of him." **20** The
chief priests and the elders persuaded the crowds to ask for
Barabbas but to destroy Jesus. **21** The governor said to them in
reply, "Which of the two do you want me to release to you?" They
answered, "Barabbas!" **22** Pilate said to them, "Then what shall I do
with Jesus called Messiah?" They all said, "Let him be crucified!"
23 But he said, "Why? What evil has he done?" They only shouted
the louder, "Let him be crucified!" **24** When Pilate saw that he was
not succeeding at all, but that a riot was breaking out instead, he
took water and washed his hands in the sight of the crowd, saying,
"I am innocent of this man's blood. Look to it yourselves." **25** And
the whole people said in reply, "His blood be upon us and upon our
children." **26** Then he released Barabbas to them, but after he had
Jesus scourged, he handed him over to be crucified.

Mk 15:6–15

6 Now on the occasion of the feast he used to release to them
one prisoner whom they requested. **7** A man called Barabbas was
then in prison along with the rebels who had committed murder in
a rebellion. **8** The crowd came forward and began to ask him to do
for them as he was accustomed. **9** Pilate answered, "Do you want
me to release to you the king of the Jews?" **10** For he knew that it
was out of envy that the chief priests had handed him over. **11** But
the chief priests stirred up the crowd to have him release Barabbas
for them instead. **12** Pilate again said to them in reply, "Then what
[do you want] me to do with [the man you call] the king of the
Jews?" **13** They shouted again, "Crucify him." **14** Pilate said to
them, "Why? What evil has he done?" They only shouted the louder,
"Crucify him." **15** So Pilate, wishing to satisfy the crowd, released
Barabbas to them and, after he had Jesus scourged, handed him
over to be crucified.

Lk 23:18–25

18 But all together they shouted out, "Away with this man!
Release Barabbas to us." **19** (Now Barabbas had been imprisoned
for a rebellion that had taken place in the city and for murder.)
20 Again Pilate addressed them, still wishing to release Jesus,
21 but they continued their shouting, "Crucify him! Crucify him!"
22 Pilate addressed them a third time, "What evil has this man
done? I found him guilty of no capital crime. Therefore I shall have
him flogged and then release him." **23** With loud shouts, however,
they persisted in calling for his crucifixion, and their voices

prevailed. **24** The verdict of Pilate was that their demand should be granted. **25** So he released the man who had been imprisoned for rebellion and murder, for whom they asked, and he handed Jesus over to them to deal with as they wished.

Jn 18:38–40, 19:6-16

38 When he had said this, he again went out to the Jews and said to them, "I find no guilt in him. **39** But you have a custom that I release one prisoner to you at Passover. Do you want me to release to you the King of the Jews?" **40** They cried out again, "Not this one but Barabbas!" Now Barabbas was a revolutionary.

...

6 When the chief priests and the guards saw him they cried out, "Crucify him, crucify him!" Pilate said to them, "Take him yourselves and crucify him. I find no guilt in him." **7** The Jews answered, "We have a law, and according to that law he ought to die, because he made himself the Son of God." **8** Now when Pilate heard this statement, he became even more afraid, **9** and went back into the praetorium and said to Jesus, "Where are you from?" Jesus did not answer him. **10** So Pilate said to him, "Do you not speak to me? Do you not know that I have power to release you and I have power to crucify you?" **11** Jesus answered [him], "You would have no power over me if it had not been given to you from above. For this reason the one who handed me over to you has the greater sin." **12** Consequently, Pilate tried to release him; but the Jews cried out, "If you release him, you are not a Friend of Caesar. Everyone who makes himself a king opposes Caesar."

13 When Pilate heard these words he brought Jesus out and seated him on the judge's bench in the place called Stone Pavement, in Hebrew, Gabbatha. **14** It was preparation day for Passover, and it was about noon. And he said to the Jews, "Behold, your king!" **15** They cried out, "Take him away, take him away! Crucify him!" Pilate said to them, "Shall I crucify your king?" The chief priests answered, "We have no king but Caesar." **16** Then he handed him over to them to be crucified.

Jesus was back in the Praetorium to again meet with Pilate, who had the earthly power to sentence Jesus to death. Pilate wanted to release Jesus, so he offered the crowd the option of having Barabbas executed instead. Though his Aramaic name meant "Son of the Father," Barabbas was quite different from Jesus, the true Son of the Father. He was described as a "revolutionary" and a "murderer." Barabbas was certainly someone more dangerous to Rome than Jesus. It appears that Pilate had hoped that, given the choice between the two "Sons of the Father," the crowd would choose to free Jesus, their "King." Pilate's wife certainly hoped so.

Pilate had found Jesus innocent of a capital crime. Nonetheless, the crowd demanded crucifixion. This was a horrible death, reserved for the worst criminals. The people were given a free choice and chose Barabbas. Jesus would die so that we might live. Pilate lacked the backbone to stand up for his opinion about Jesus' innocence. Rather than using his authority to release Jesus as a free man, he ordered Him to be crucified.

Before being crucified, the true "Son of the Father" had to endure an excruciating flesh-shredding scourging. Tied to a pillar, our Savior was repeatedly struck with a leather whip studded with sharp shards of metal. Pilate poured out water to declare his own innocence; Jesus now began to pour out His blood to wash away our sins.

CHROMOSOME

The next Landmark is too small to see without the aid of a powerful microscope. It is found within all of the countless cells of our body. It contains the blueprints for life itself. It is a **chromosome**. There are forty-six **chromosomes** (twenty-three pairs) packed into the center of every cell. These tiny strands contain the DNA that encodes the instructions for life. The forty-sixth Landmark is one of these DNA-containing **chromosomes**.

Each chromosome contains many genes. Genes encode for various proteins that are composed of amino acids. Certain "**letters**" are used to denote the particular amino acid being coded for. The details of this are complex and unimportant for our journey. Just know that **letters** are used to denote different amino acids. Similarly, **letters** will be used to denote each of the units of this forty-sixth Landmark. In summary, the forty-sixth Landmark is one of the forty-six chromosomes in each cell of our body. **Letters** of the alphabet are used to denote the amino acids that are coded for by the DNA within each chromosome. The **letters** used in this Landmark will simply be the first five **letters** of the alphabet: A, B, C, D, and E, in that order. Note that the alphabet was used to help recall the content of the Sermon on the Mount. The letters here represent entire units.

A stands for **abuse**. This represents the unit that describes Jesus' ABUSE BY THE SOLDIERS.

ABUSE BY THE SOLDIERS

Mt 27:27–31

27 Then the soldiers of the governor took Jesus inside the praetorium and gathered the whole cohort around him. 28 They stripped off his clothes and threw a scarlet military cloak about him. 29 Weaving a crown out of thorns, they placed it on his head, and a reed in his right hand. And kneeling before him, they mocked him, saying, "Hail, King of the Jews!" 30 They spat upon him and took the reed and kept striking him on the head. 31 And when they had mocked him, they stripped him of the cloak, dressed him in his own clothes, and led him off to crucify him.

Mk 15:16–20

16 The soldiers led him away inside the palace, that is, the praetorium, and assembled the whole cohort. 17 They clothed him in purple and, weaving a crown of thorns, placed it on him. 18 They began to salute him with, "Hail, King of the Jews!" 19 and kept striking his head with a reed and spitting upon him. They knelt before him in homage. 20 And when they had mocked him, they stripped him of the purple cloak, dressed him in his own clothes, and led him out to crucify him.

Lk 22:63–65

63 The men who held Jesus in custody were ridiculing and beating him. 64 They blindfolded him and questioned him, saying, "Prophesy! Who is it that struck you?" 65 And they reviled him in saying many other things against him.

Jn 19:2–3

2 And the soldiers wove a crown out of thorns and placed it on his head, and clothed him in a purple cloak, 3 and they came to him and said, "Hail, King of the Jews!" And they struck him repeatedly.

The graphic scene of Jesus' treatment by the soldiers is disturbing. The physical and emotional abuse that had begun when Jesus was before the Sanhedrin continued. This is also one of the most ironic scenes in all of history. Jesus was mocked and crudely treated as an imperial impostor. In fact, He was truly the Son of God and the King of heaven and earth. The soldiers were striking, spitting upon, and painfully crowning their true

King. This King they treated so sinfully would soon save them from these and all their sins.

In John, this painful scene is woven into the trial itself. Matthew and Mark describe it after Pilate expressed his belief that Jesus was innocent, yet behaved as if Jesus was guilty. Pilate cleansed his hands but soiled his soul. The Jews who insisted on Jesus' crucifixion had done the same. Not only did they deny Jesus as their King, they denied their very identity as a people. Saying, "We have no king but Caesar" was a denial of their heritage, a denial of Yahweh!

B stands for **burden**. This represents the unit when Jesus bears THE BURDEN OF THE CROSS.

THE BURDEN OF THE CROSS

Mt 27:32

32 As they were going out, they met a Cyrenian named Simon; this man they pressed into service to carry his cross.

Mk 15:21

21 They pressed into service a passer-by, Simon, a Cyrenian, who was coming in from the country, the father of Alexander and Rufus, to carry his cross.

Lk 23:26–32

26 As they led him away they took hold of a certain Simon, a Cyrenian, who was coming in from the country; and after laying the cross on him, they made him carry it behind Jesus. 27 A large crowd of people followed Jesus, including many women who mourned and lamented him. 28 Jesus turned to them and said, "Daughters of Jerusalem, do not weep for me; weep instead for yourselves and for your children, 29 for indeed, the days are coming when people will say, 'Blessed are the barren, the wombs that never bore and the breasts that never nursed.' 30 At that time people will say to the mountains, 'Fall upon us!' and to the hills, 'Cover us!' 31 for if these things are done when the wood is green what will happen when it is dry?" 32 Now two others, both criminals, were led away with him to be executed.

Jn 19:16–17

16 So they took Jesus, **17** and carrying the cross himself he went out to what is called the Place of the Skull, in Hebrew, Golgotha.

Physically crushed and in severe pain, Jesus was burdened with the weighty crossbeam of the cross. How heavy it must have felt after the severe beating. How painful to know the hands struggling to hold the beam would soon be nailed to it. The flesh-torn shoulders supporting the beam would soon hang from it. His weary stumbling feet would soon be held tightly together by a single sharp spike. In this exhausted, weakened state, Jesus could have collapsed and died before arriving at Golgotha where the firmly planted vertical beam awaited. The Romans did not want such a premature death. Simon, from what is modern-day Libya, was pressed into service. His fresh legs and strong shoulders would ensure that a painful and humiliating crucifixion took place. Temporarily free of His burden, Jesus preached for the last time.

Luke emphasized the role of women more than the other evangelists. He described the encounter between the haggard Jesus and the distraught "daughters of Jerusalem." As Jesus walked to His death, He remained focused on the welfare of others. He again warned of the coming destruction of Jerusalem. The prophetic words of Hosea to the wayward Northern Kingdom of Israel (Hos 10:8) would soon apply to the people of Jerusalem. The need for repentance continued to be of utmost importance. Sin and rebellion are likened to sapping the lifeblood from wood. When the sap dries from green wood (Jerusalem), it burns easily. Jesus called for repentance at the outset of His Galilean ministry (Landmark 4) and did so until the end. Jesus also called for repentance when He had recently entered Jerusalem (Landmark 34). He now did so for the last time as He walked from the city to His death.

C stands for **crucifixion**. This represents THE CRUCIFIXION OF JESUS.

THE CRUCIFIXION OF JESUS

Mt 27:33–44

33 And when they came to a place called Golgotha (which means Place of the Skull), **34** they gave Jesus wine to drink mixed with gall. But when he had tasted it, he refused to drink. **35** After they had crucified him, they divided his garments by casting lots; **36** then they sat down and kept watch over him there. **37** And they placed over his head the written charge against him: This is Jesus, the King of the Jews. **38** Two revolutionaries were crucified with him, one on his right and the other on his left. **39** Those passing by reviled him, shaking their heads **40** and saying, "You who would destroy the temple and rebuild it in three days, save yourself, if you are the Son of God, [and] come down from the cross!" **41** Likewise the chief priests with the scribes and elders mocked him and said, **42** "He saved others; he cannot save himself. So he is the king of Israel! Let him come down from the cross now, and we will believe in him. **43** He trusted in God; let him deliver him now if he wants him. For he said, 'I am the Son of God.'" **44** The revolutionaries who were crucified with him also kept abusing him in the same way.

Mk 15:22–32

22 They brought him to the place of Golgotha (which is translated Place of the Skull). **23** They gave him wine drugged with myrrh, but he did not take it. **24** Then they crucified him and divided his garments by casting lots for them to see what each should take. **25** It was nine o'clock in the morning when they crucified him. **26** The inscription of the charge against him read, "The King of the Jews." **27** With him they crucified two revolutionaries, one on his right and one on his left. **[28] 29** Those passing by reviled him, shaking their heads and saying, "Aha! You who would destroy the temple and rebuild it in three days, **30** save yourself by coming down from the cross." **31** Likewise the chief priests, with the scribes, mocked him among themselves and said, "He saved others; he cannot save himself. **32** Let the Messiah, the King of Israel, come down now from the cross that we may see and believe." Those who were crucified with him also kept abusing him.

Lk 23:33–43

33 When they came to the place called the Skull, they crucified him and the criminals there, one on his right, the other on his left. **34** [Then Jesus said, "Father, forgive them, they know not what they do."] They divided his garments by casting lots. **35** The people stood by and watched; the rulers, meanwhile, sneered at him and said, "He saved others, let him save himself if he is the chosen one, the Messiah of God." **36** Even the soldiers jeered at him. As they approached to offer him wine **37** they called out, "If you are King of the Jews, save yourself." **38** Above him there was an inscription that read, "This is the King of the Jews."

39 Now one of the criminals hanging there reviled Jesus, saying, "Are you not the Messiah? Save yourself and us." **40** The other, however, rebuking him, said in reply, "Have you no fear of God, for you are subject to the same condemnation? **41** And indeed, we have been condemned justly, for the sentence we received corresponds to our crimes, but this man has done nothing criminal." **42** Then he said, "Jesus, remember me when you come into your kingdom." **43** He replied to him, "Amen, I say to you, today you will be with me in Paradise."

Jn 19:18–27

18 There they crucified him, and with him two others, one on either side, with Jesus in the middle. **19** Pilate also had an inscription written and put on the cross. It read, "Jesus the Nazorean, the King of the Jews." **20** Now many of the Jews read this inscription, because the place where Jesus was crucified was near the city; and it was written in Hebrew, Latin, and Greek. **21** So the chief priests of the Jews said to Pilate, "Do not write 'The King of the Jews,' but that he said, 'I am the King of the Jews.'" **22** Pilate answered, "What I have written, I have written." **23** When the soldiers had crucified Jesus, they took his clothes and divided them into four shares, a share for each soldier. They also took his tunic, but the tunic was seamless, woven in one piece from the top down. **24** So they said to one another, "Let's not tear it, but cast lots for it to see whose it will be," in order that the passage of scripture might be fulfilled [that says]:

"They divided my garments among them,
and for my vesture they cast lots."

This is what the soldiers did. **25** Standing by the cross of Jesus were his mother and his mother's sister, Mary the wife of Clopas, and Mary of Magdala. **26** When Jesus saw his mother and the disciple there whom he loved, he said to his mother, "Woman, behold, your son." **27** Then he said to the disciple, "Behold, your mother." And from that hour the disciple took her into his home.

———————

Crucifixion is painful to even think about. If the victim is a loved one, it becomes almost unthinkable. The fact that it happened to one who loves us beyond all understanding is something we must think about and try to understand.

Death by crucifixion inflicted maximum doses of physical and emotional pain. It was slow and agonizing. Death finally came due to eventual loss of blood or asphyxiation. All the while, the victim hung helpless and naked for all to see. A sign above the victim's head proclaimed the capital offense. The Son of God, though innocent, willingly endured all of this for us. Jesus even refused a drink of herbs and myrrh, which could have slightly numbed His pain.

All of the evangelists' descriptions of the actual crucifixion process are very stark. The nailing of Jesus' hands to the crosspiece, attaching it to the vertical piece, and then driving a spike through His feet is simply summarized as "they crucified Him." Much of what occurs next is described in Psalm 22 where the rejection of an innocent righteous man is described.

It seems that everyone had a chance to take a parting shot at Jesus as He hung helplessly, enduring a slow, painful death. His gasping for air and the falling drops of blood and sweat did not stop the taunts of those passing by. Jesus was sarcastically challenged by various groups to save Himself by coming down from the cross (the details vary among the evangelists). Just as Jesus refused the devil's temptations in the desert (Landmark 2), He remained on the cross, fulfilling the Father's purpose.

Luke describes one criminal rebuking the other for his harsh words to Jesus. He then testified to Jesus' innocence, but more importantly, he confessed his faith in Jesus' identity. Just as faith in Jesus was rewarded throughout His ministry, it was again rewarded as He was about to die.

This unit concludes with the heart-crushing scene of Jesus' mother at the foot of the cross. As a parent, what could be more devastating than to watch your child die in such a slow and tortuous way? Jesus continued to show His love by making preparations for her well-being.

D stands for **death**. This represents the unit describing THE DEATH OF JESUS.

THE DEATH OF JESUS

Mt 27:45–56

45 From noon onward, darkness came over the whole land until three in the afternoon. **46** And about three o'clock Jesus cried out in a loud voice, *"Eli, Eli, lema sabachthani?"* which means, "My God, my God, why have you forsaken me?" **47** Some of the bystanders who heard it said, "This one is calling for Elijah." **48** Immediately one of them ran to get a sponge; he soaked it in wine, and putting it on a reed, gave it to him to drink. **49** But the rest said, "Wait, let us see if Elijah comes to save him." **50** But Jesus cried out again in a loud voice, and gave up his spirit. **51** And behold, the veil of the sanctuary was torn in two from top to bottom. The earth quaked, rocks were split, **52** tombs were opened, and the bodies of many saints who had fallen asleep were raised. **53** And coming forth from their tombs after his resurrection, they entered the holy city and appeared to many. **54** The centurion and the men with him who were keeping watch over Jesus feared greatly when they saw the earthquake and all that was happening, and they said, "Truly, this was the Son of God!" **55** There were many women there, looking on from a distance, who had followed Jesus from Galilee, ministering to him. **56** Among them were Mary Magdalene and Mary the mother of James and Joseph, and the mother of the sons of Zebedee.

Mk 15:33–41

33 At noon darkness came over the whole land until three in the afternoon. **34** And at three o'clock Jesus cried out in a loud voice, *"Eloi, Eloi, lema sabachthani?"* which is translated, "My God, my God, why have you forsaken me?" **35** Some of the bystanders who heard it said, "Look, he is calling Elijah." **36** One of them ran, soaked a sponge with wine, put it on a reed, and gave it to him to drink, saying, "Wait, let us see if Elijah comes to take him down." **37** Jesus gave a loud cry and breathed his last. **38** The veil of the sanctuary was torn in two from top to bottom. **39** When the centurion who stood facing him saw how he breathed his last he said, "Truly this man was the Son of God!" **40** There were also women looking on from a distance. Among them were Mary Magdalene, Mary the mother of the younger James and of Joses, and Salome. **41** These women had followed him when he was in Galilee and ministered to him. There were also many other women who had come up with him to Jerusalem.

Lk 23:44–49

44 It was now about noon and darkness came over the whole land until three in the afternoon **45** because of an eclipse of the sun. Then the veil of the temple was torn down the middle. **46** Jesus cried out in a loud voice, "Father, into your hands I commend my spirit"; and when he had said this he breathed his last. **47** The centurion who witnessed what had happened glorified God and said, "This man was innocent beyond doubt." **48** When all the people who had gathered for this spectacle saw what had happened, they returned home beating their breasts; **49** but all his acquaintances stood at a distance, including the women who had followed him from Galilee and saw these events.

Jn 19:28–37

28 After this, aware that everything was now finished, in order that the scripture might be fulfilled, Jesus said, "I thirst." **29** There was a vessel filled with common wine. So they put a sponge soaked in wine on a sprig of hyssop and put it up to his mouth. **30** When Jesus had taken the wine, he said, "It is finished." And bowing his head, he handed over the spirit.

31 Now since it was preparation day, in order that the bodies might not remain on the cross on the sabbath, for the sabbath day of that week was a solemn one, the Jews asked Pilate that their legs be broken and they be taken down. **32** So the soldiers came and broke the legs of the first and then of the other one who was crucified with Jesus. **33** But when they came to Jesus and saw that he was already dead, they did not break his legs, **34** but one soldier thrust his lance into his side, and immediately blood and water flowed out. **35** An eyewitness has testified, and his testimony is true; he knows that he is speaking the truth, so that you also may [come to] believe. **36** For this happened so that the scripture passage might be fulfilled:

"Not a bone of it will be broken."

37 And again another passage says:

"They will look upon him whom they have pierced."

———

Jesus hung upon the cross, slowly dying, for six hours. For Him, it must have seemed like an eternity. Because of those few hours, we have the opportunity to spend eternity with Jesus. The evangelists' descriptions of perhaps the darkest few hours of human history are quite terse. For three of those six hours, it was literally dark. Luke describes a solar eclipse as being the cause. How fitting that the sun above became covered and failed to shine as the Son below, covered in blood, lost His life. Under the Old Covenant, darkness was associated with God's judgment (Ex 10:21–23— the ninth plague; Is 13:10–11—the oracle against Babylon; Amos 8:9—the day of the Lord). With Jesus' death, the darkness marked the dawning of a New Covenant and the possibility of salvation.

Jesus' last words as recorded in Matthew and Mark are another reference to Psalm 22, the prayer of a righteous suffering man who is eventually vindicated. Because of Jesus' human nature, He must have experienced feelings of utter abandonment and rejection. His cry out to His Father appeared to be words of despair. However, Jesus' final words in Luke, "Father, into your hands I commend my spirit," are certainly not. He remained the obedient Son to the end, trusting in the Father's plan. Jesus' life was not taken, but handed over as a willing sacrifice.

In John, just prior to His last words, Jesus mentioned His thirst. He who transformed water into fine wine was offered cheap wine, likely on a dirty sponge at the end of a stick. However, it was not just any stick. Hyssop had earlier been used to deliver another fluid. The Israelites used hyssop at the first Passover (Ex 12:22) to apply blood from a slain lamb to their doorposts. This alerted the Angel of Death to "pass over" them. Here death came to the Passover Lamb of God, though not before this reminder of God's earlier care for His chosen people. Now, through Jesus, we are all chosen.

The death of Jesus divided human history in two. This was symbolized by the veil in the temple sanctuary being torn. The place where only priests had been allowed was now open to all. The New Covenant and a new age in salvation history had begun. This was literally an earthshaking event.

After watching all that Jesus had endured for six hours and then experiencing nature's apocalyptic reaction, the centurion made his profession of faith. His words echoed those of the disciples in the boat after Jesus walked on the Sea of Galilee, "Truly, this was the Son of God!" It is ironic and sad that these words were spoken by a Roman soldier, a Gentile, while His closest friends were nowhere to be found. Fortunately, there were some faithful women willing to stay with Jesus to the end.

E stands for **entombed**. This represents Jesus being **entombed**, or THE BURIAL OF JESUS.

ENTOMBMENT (THE BURIAL OF JESUS)

Mt 27:57–61

57 When it was evening, there came a rich man from Arimathea named Joseph, who was himself a disciple of Jesus. **58** He went to Pilate and asked for the body of Jesus; then Pilate ordered it to be handed over. **59** Taking the body, Joseph wrapped it [in] clean linen **60** and laid it in his new tomb that he had hewn in the rock. Then he rolled a huge stone across the entrance to the tomb and departed. **61** But Mary Magdalene and the other Mary remained sitting there, facing the tomb.

Mk 15:42–47

42 When it was already evening, since it was the day of preparation, the day before the sabbath, **43** Joseph of Arimathea, a distinguished member of the council, who was himself awaiting the kingdom of God, came and courageously went to Pilate and asked for the body of Jesus. **44** Pilate was amazed that he was already dead. He summoned the centurion and asked him if Jesus had already died. **45** And when he learned of it from the centurion, he gave the body to Joseph. **46** Having bought a linen cloth, he took him down, wrapped him in the linen cloth and laid him in a tomb that had been hewn out of the rock. Then he rolled a stone against the entrance to the tomb. **47** Mary Magdalene and Mary the mother of Joses watched where he was laid.

Lk 23:50–56

50 Now there was a virtuous and righteous man named Joseph who, though he was a member of the council, **51** had not consented to their plan of action. He came from the Jewish town of Arimathea and was awaiting the kingdom of God. **52** He went to Pilate and asked for the body of Jesus. **53** After he had taken the body down, he wrapped it in a linen cloth and laid him in a rock-hewn tomb in which no one had yet been buried. **54** It was the day of preparation, and the sabbath was about to begin. **55** The women who had come from Galilee with him followed behind, and when they had seen the tomb and the way in which his body was laid in it, **56** they returned and prepared spices and perfumed oils. Then they rested on the sabbath according to the commandment.

Jn 19:38–42

38 After this, Joseph of Arimathea, secretly a disciple of Jesus for fear of the Jews, asked Pilate if he could remove the body of

Jesus. And Pilate permitted it. So he came and took his body.
39 Nicodemus, the one who had first come to him at night, also
came bringing a mixture of myrrh and aloes weighing about one
hundred pounds. **40** They took the body of Jesus and bound it with
burial cloths along with the spices, according to the Jewish burial
custom. **41** Now in the place where he had been crucified there
was a garden, and in the garden a new tomb, in which no one had
yet been buried. **42** So they laid Jesus there because of the Jewish
preparation day; for the tomb was close by.

Jesus was truly dead. His lungs stopped breathing, heart stopped
beating, nerves stopped firing, and body stopped moving. It all seemed to
be over. The prospect of a future without Jesus was overwhelming to His
followers. What would become of them? What would they do now?

The first task was to give Jesus a proper burial. There was not much
time. It was midafternoon. When the sun set in several hours, it would be
the Sabbath and the work of burying Jesus would be forbidden. Joseph,
from the nearby town of Arimathea, sprang into action. Another irony!
A member of the Sanhedrin responsible for condemning Jesus took the
initiative for His burial. Luke tells us that Joseph had not consented to
the Sanhedrin's decision. Further irony is supplied by John. He tells us
that Nicodemus, another Sanhedrin member, assisted Joseph. How fitting
that the man with whom Jesus discussed the idea of being "born again"
(Landmark 3) should participate in His burial.

Joseph used the tomb he had prepared for himself and his family. He
must have thought that someday his bones would lie in a box next to those
of Jesus. It was the custom to allow a body to decompose for a year or so
before placing the bones in an "ossuary" (bone box). First the body was
to be shrouded in linen, a material symbolizing immortality. Then Jesus'
body was to be anointed one last time. Due to the approaching darkness,
this final anointing would have to wait until the Sabbath was over.

Landmark 47:

747 AIRPLANE

R ecall that in Landmark 45 you had a very short flight on a small crowded plane. It is now time to board a much larger aircraft. Since you have arrived at the forty-seventh Landmark, it is fitting that the plane and the Landmark will be a huge **747 airplane**. Imagine standing on the runway being dwarfed by the massive plane. Though the **747 airplane** typically carries over four hundred passengers, today it will be just you and the crew. Mentally prepare yourself to climb aboard the **747** and have a smooth, relaxing flight!

On the runway while approaching the steps of the 747, you see a uniformed **guard** standing at attention. The **guard** is at the bottom of the stairway, ready to salute and greet you. Feeling presidential, you return the **guard's** salute. The **guard** is a tall, muscular man who appears stern. However, when you begin to converse with him he is quite friendly. You ask the **guard** who gave him this particular assignment. He responds that he is not at liberty to divulge that information. The **guard** does mention that he will do his best to keep you safe while onboard. You tell the **guard** that you are the only passenger. He smiles and says that should make his job of **guarding** you fairly easy. This encounter with the **guard** before boarding the 747 reminds you of the first unit to be associated with this Landmark: THE GUARD AT THE TOMB.

THE GUARD AT THE TOMB

Mt 27:62–66

62 The next day, the one following the day of preparation, the chief priests and the Pharisees gathered before Pilate 63 and said, "Sir, we remember that this impostor while still alive said, 'After

443

three days I will be raised up.' **64** Give orders, then, that the grave be secured until the third day, lest his disciples come and steal him and say to the people, 'He has been raised from the dead.' This last imposture would be worse than the first." **65** Pilate said to them, "The guard is yours; go secure it as best you can." **66** So they went and secured the tomb by fixing a seal to the stone and setting the guard.

The Pharisees continued to plot against Jesus even after He died upon the cross. They came to Pilate the next morning fearing that Jesus' disciples would try to make it appear that His earlier predictions had come true. Jesus had predicted His resurrection on three separate occasions (Landmarks 22, 23, and 33). The Pharisees also recalled His earlier words when they had sought a sign and Jesus spoke of Jonah's three-day burial in the belly of a whale (Landmark 20). The Pharisees wanted to prevent another "big fish" story. They knew that if Jesus' followers believed He had actually risen from the dead it would be the beginning of something big. They were right!

THE GUARD MOTIONS FOR YOU to climb the stairs and board the 747. You do so and take a seat. After getting settled, you excitedly await takeoff. The **rising** of the plane into the air has always been your favorite part about flying. The feeling you get when the plane **rises** from the ground is indescribable. This **rising** feeling always makes you envious of birds. The plane begins to move. It gradually increases its speed down the runway. The massive 747 begins to **rise** off the ground. Soon you have **risen** above the trees. A smile comes to your face as the plane continues to **rise** above the clouds. Several minutes later, the 747 levels off after **rising** to its cruising altitude. This description of the **rising** plane is a trigger to recall the infinitely more significant **rising** of Jesus from the dead: THE RESURRECTION.

THE RESURRECTION

Mt 28:1–7

1 After the sabbath, as the first day of the week was dawning, Mary Magdalene and the other Mary came to see the tomb. 2 And behold, there was a great earthquake; for an angel of the Lord descended from heaven, approached, rolled back the stone, and sat upon it. 3 His appearance was like lightning and his clothing was white as snow. 4 The guards were shaken with fear of him and became like dead men. 5 Then the angel said to the women in reply, "Do not be afraid! I know that you are seeking Jesus the crucified. 6 He is not here, for he has been raised just as he said. Come and see the place where he lay. 7 Then go quickly and tell his disciples, 'He has been raised from the dead, and he is going before you to Galilee; there you will see him.' Behold, I have told you."

Mk 16:1–8

1 When the sabbath was over, Mary Magdalene, Mary, the mother of James, and Salome bought spices so that they might go and anoint him. 2 Very early when the sun had risen, on the first day of the week, they came to the tomb. 3 They were saying to one another, "Who will roll back the stone for us from the entrance to the tomb?" 4 When they looked up, they saw that the stone had been rolled back; it was very large. 5 On entering the tomb they saw a young man sitting on the right side, clothed in a white robe, and they were utterly amazed. 6 He said to them, "Do not be amazed! You seek Jesus of Nazareth, the crucified. He has been raised; he is not here. Behold the place where they laid him. 7 But go and tell his disciples and Peter, 'He is going before you to Galilee; there you will see him, as he told you.'" 8 Then they went out and fled from the tomb, seized with trembling and bewilderment. They said nothing to anyone, for they were afraid.

Lk 24:1–12

1 But at daybreak on the first day of the week they took the spices they had prepared and went to the tomb. 2 They found the stone rolled away from the tomb; 3 but when they entered, they did not find the body of the Lord Jesus. 4 While they were puzzling over this, behold, two men in dazzling garments appeared to them. 5 They were terrified and bowed their faces to the ground. They said to them, "Why do you seek the living one among the dead? 6 He is not here, but he has been raised. Remember what he said to you while he was still in Galilee, 7 that the Son of Man must be handed over to sinners and be crucified, and rise on the third day." 8 And they remembered his words. 9 Then they returned from the tomb

and announced all these things to the eleven and to all the others.
10 The women were Mary Magdalene, Joanna, and Mary the mother
of James; the others who accompanied them also told this to the
apostles, 11 but their story seemed like nonsense and they did not
believe them. 12 But Peter got up and ran to the tomb, bent down,
and saw the burial cloths alone; then he went home amazed at what
had happened.

Jn 20:1–10

1 On the first day of the week, Mary of Magdala came to the tomb
early in the morning, while it was still dark, and saw the stone
removed from the tomb. 2 So she ran and went to Simon Peter and
to the other disciple whom Jesus loved, and told them, "They have
taken the Lord from the tomb, and we don't know where they put
him." 3 So Peter and the other disciple went out and came to the
tomb. 4 They both ran, but the other disciple ran faster than Peter
and arrived at the tomb first; 5 he bent down and saw the burial
cloths there, but did not go in. 6 When Simon Peter arrived after
him, he went into the tomb and saw the burial cloths there, 7 and
the cloth that had covered his head, not with the burial cloths but
rolled up in a separate place. 8 Then the other disciple also went in,
the one who had arrived at the tomb first, and he saw and believed.
9 For they did not yet understand the scripture that he had to rise
from the dead. 10 Then the disciples returned home.

You have covered a lot of ground since beginning your travels with
Jesus. You just witnessed His gruesome death and saw His burial in a
nearby cave. The hours between late Friday afternoon and early Sunday
morning were heart-wrenching for Jesus' disciples. Their Jesus was dead!

The accounts of the events of that Sunday morning vary considerably
between the four Gospels. Each writer describes the resurrection event
differently based on sources and purpose. However, the central event, in
fact the most important event in history, remained constant—Jesus had
truly been raised from the dead!

All of the evangelists begin with several of Jesus' devoted disciples
visiting the tomb early on that first Easter morning. Neither Peter, Andrew,
James, John, nor any of the other apostles were among them. They were
all women, the unsung, yet very important followers of Jesus. They were
the first to see the empty tomb and hear the glorious good news that Jesus
had risen. The heavenly messenger(s) must have been an incredible sight,
radiating dazzling light in a transfiguration-like display. The announce-

ment of the resurrection and the soon-to-occur appearances in Galilee surely flooded the women with many emotions. Faith, hope, joy, love, amazement, and excitement were all heaped upon their fear.

The Gospels vary significantly in describing the women's emotional reactions and responses to the news. In an upcoming unit, we will see how Matthew describes them. The women described in Mark remained too fearful to spread the good news, at least for the moment. It is widely believed that the Gospel of Mark in its original form ended here. The words of Mark that follow are thought to have been added by another writer(s) to provide more consistency with the other Gospel accounts. Many scholars believe that Mark did not feel it necessary to include post-resurrection appearances that his readers were already well aware of.

Luke continues to emphasize the important role of women. Their fear was overcome by joy and the need to tell about their risen Lord. The angels' words gave them insight into Jesus' earlier predictions of His resurrection. The women's report was confusing to all but Peter, who ran to the tomb to see for himself. The Gospel of John describes the actions of Peter and another disciple (perhaps John himself) on that Sunday morning. There is no mention of a heavenly messenger in the Gospel of John. That comes later.

Of the women in the resurrection accounts, Mary Magdalene is the only one specifically mentioned by all four evangelists. Thinking that Jesus' body had been stolen, Mary ran to inform Peter and John of the empty tomb. They, too, did not find a body, just the burial cloths. The positioning of these sacred linens indicated to them that the body had not been stolen. A robber would not have made the effort to neatly roll up a cloth. These valuable, expensive linens would have also been stolen.

YOU ARE NOW RELAXED IN your seat and on the verge of falling asleep. Feeling a light tap on your shoulder, you open your eyes. The guard apologizes for disturbing you but says he has some news to **report**. The guard begins his **report** by saying the plane is almost out of fuel. You are obviously concerned by this **report**. The guard clears his throat and continues. He next **reports** that the pilot is ill and can no longer fly the 747. Now you are alarmed. He concludes his **report** of unfortunate events by wishing you good luck and handing you a parachute. The guard's very disturbing

report concludes this Landmark by helping you recall the unit concerning THE REPORT OF THE GUARD.

THE REPORT OF THE GUARD

Mt 28:11–15

11 While they were going, some of the guard went into the city and told the chief priests all that had happened. 12 They assembled with the elders and took counsel; then they gave a large sum of money to the soldiers, 13 telling them, "You are to say, 'His disciples came by night and stole him while we were asleep.' 14 And if this gets to the ears of the governor, we will satisfy [him] and keep you out of trouble." 15 The soldiers took the money and did as they were instructed. And this story has circulated among the Jews to the present [day].

Recall that Matthew describes how the Jewish leaders went to Pilate requesting that guards be placed at Jesus' tomb. They wanted to prevent possible body-snatching disciples from perpetuating a resurrection hoax. When the fear-stricken guards reported what they had witnessed, it was the chief priests who orchestrated a hoax. In doing so, they probably paid the guards more than thirty pieces of silver to lie and say that they had been derelict in their duty. What must the chief priests have thought when they heard the guards report about the angel and that Jesus' body was gone, but that no one had taken it? Did they start to believe? Could they have been terribly wrong? Perhaps. However, the truth had to be suppressed at all costs!

Landmark 48:

A TREE

The anxiety-provoking experience in the 747 has left you mentally exhausted. Spotting a large **tree**, you decide to sit beneath its leafy branches and relax for a few minutes. While resting in the quiet shade, you soon begin to feel much calmer. It is then that you recall that Siddhartha Gautama (Buddha) found enlightenment while sitting under a **tree**. He sat beneath a Bodhi **tree** for forty-eight days. You certainly have no intention of spending the next forty-eight days under this **tree**. However, you need a forty-eighth Landmark. For Landmark 48, imagine yourself sitting peacefully under this **tree**.

Sitting under the tree was so relaxing that you fell asleep. You are startled awake when someone plops down next to you against the tree trunk. It is a tired-looking older woman with white hair. She is elegantly attired in a long, old-fashioned dress. She looks familiar. When she smiles, you recognize that it is **Mary** Washington. Recall that you played dominoes with her back in Landmark 28. **Mary** is now looking for her son George. You tell **Mary** that you have not seen him, but you would be glad to help her look. **Mary** says she has been searching for several days and needs to rest with you a bit longer under the tree. You tell **Mary** to rest as long as she would like and then you will help her find George. This second appearance of **Mary** Washington reminds you of Jesus' post-resurrection APPEARANCE TO MARY MAGDALENE.

APPEARANCE TO MARY MAGDALENE

Mt 28:8–10

8 Then they went away quickly from the tomb, fearful yet overjoyed, and ran to announce this to his disciples. **9** And behold, Jesus met them on their way and greeted them. They approached, embraced his feet, and did him homage. **10** Then Jesus said to them, "Do not be afraid. Go tell my brothers to go to Galilee, and there they will see me."

Mk 16:9–11

9 When he had risen, early on the first day of the week, he appeared first to Mary Magdalene, out of whom he had driven seven demons. **10** She went and told his companions who were mourning and weeping. **11** When they heard that he was alive and had been seen by her, they did not believe.

Jn 20:11–18

11 But Mary stayed outside the tomb weeping. And as she wept, she bent over into the tomb **12** and saw two angels in white sitting there, one at the head and one at the feet where the body of Jesus had been. **13** And they said to her, "Woman, why are you weeping?" She said to them, "They have taken my Lord, and I don't know where they laid him." **14** When she had said this, she turned around and saw Jesus there, but did not know it was Jesus. **15** Jesus said to her, "Woman, why are you weeping? Whom are you looking for?" She thought it was the gardener and said to him, "Sir, if you carried him away, tell me where you laid him, and I will take him." **16** Jesus said to her, "Mary!" She turned and said to him in Hebrew, "Rabbouni," which means Teacher. **17** Jesus said to her, "Stop holding on to me, for I have not yet ascended to the Father. But go to my brothers and tell them, 'I am going to my Father and your Father, to my God and your God.'" **18** Mary of Magdala went and announced to the disciples, "I have seen the Lord," and what he told her.

Mary Magdalene made several appearances throughout the Gospels, but none more significant than here. She and several other women were the first to see the empty tomb. She had the great privilege of being the first to see the risen Christ. In Mark, at the beginning of what is widely believed to be a later addition to this Gospel, Jesus appeared to Mary Magdalene, who had previously been "bewildered" and afraid to report finding an empty tomb. She had now seen the risen Lord and reported this to His grief-stricken "companions." In John, Mary did not immediately recognize Jesus. There must have been something different about the appearance of the risen Christ. Not only did Mary not immediately recognize the familiar face of Jesus, neither did other disciples in upcoming units. Jesus had not simply returned to life in His former body. He must have appeared in a different state until He ascended to His Father. John alludes to this when Jesus told Mary that He was no longer to be "held" in a physical sense. She was then instructed to be the first to spread the good news of His resurrection.

SOON MARY WASHINGTON TELLS YOU that she is ready to resume searching for her son George. She would like to continue down the same road she had been traveling. Mary has walked along this road for many miles and is obviously very tired. You wish you had some mode of transport to make her search less tiresome. As you both stand up, a very large, odd-looking bird saunters by. It is an **emu**! Where in the world is this big Australian bird going? You ask Mary if she would like to rest her legs and ride on the **emu**. She smiles and without hesitation jumps onto the unsuspecting **emu's** back. The **emu's** legs buckle, but quickly straighten. Mary seems eager to begin what is likely her first **emu** ride. The **emu** proceeds down the road with you following closely behind. *Emu* is a soundalike for **Emmaus**. This scene on the road with the **emu** is thus a reminder of another of Jesus' post-resurrection appearances: the appearance ON THE ROAD TO EMMAUS.

ON THE ROAD TO EMMAUS

Mk 16:12–13

12 After this he appeared in another form to two of them walking along on their way to the country. 13 They returned and told the others; but they did not believe them either.

13 Now that very day two of them were going to a village seven miles from Jerusalem called Emmaus, **14** and they were conversing about all the things that had occurred. **15** And it happened that while they were conversing and debating, Jesus himself drew near and walked with them, **16** but their eyes were prevented from recognizing him. **17** He asked them, "What are you discussing as you walk along?" They stopped, looking downcast. **18** One of them, named Cleopas, said to him in reply, "Are you the only visitor to Jerusalem who does not know of the things that have taken place there in these days?" **19** And he replied to them, "What sort of things?" They said to him, "The things that happened to Jesus the Nazarene, who was a prophet mighty in deed and word before God and all the people, **20** how our chief priests and rulers both handed him over to a sentence of death and crucified him. **21** But we were hoping that he would be the one to redeem Israel; and besides all this, it is now the third day since this took place. **22** Some women from our group, however, have astounded us: they were at the tomb early in the morning **23** and did not find his body; they came back and reported that they had indeed seen a vision of angels who announced that he was alive. **24** Then some of those with us went to the tomb and found things just as the women had described, but him they did not see." **25** And he said to them, "Oh, how foolish you are! How slow of heart to believe all that the prophets spoke! **26** Was it not necessary that the Messiah should suffer these things and enter into his glory?" **27** Then beginning with Moses and all the prophets, he interpreted to them what referred to him in all the scriptures. **28** As they approached the village to which they were going, he gave the impression that he was going on farther. **29** But they urged him, "Stay with us, for it is nearly evening and the day is almost over." So he went in to stay with them. **30** And it happened that, while he was with them at table, he took bread, said the blessing, broke it, and gave it to them. **31** With that their eyes were opened and they recognized him, but he vanished from their sight. **32** Then they said to each other, "Were not our hearts burning [within us] while he spoke to us on the way and opened the scriptures to us?" **33** So they set out at once and returned to Jerusalem where they found gathered together the eleven and those with them **34** who were saying, "The Lord has truly been raised and has appeared to Simon!" **35** Then the two recounted what had taken place on the way and how he was made known to them in the breaking of the bread.

Many disciples other than the chosen Twelve had traveled with Jesus at various times during His ministry. People came and went, walking portions of Jesus' journey to the cross. How sad these disciples must have been. They had believed that Jesus was the Messiah who would free them from Roman bondage. Their hopes and dreams died with Jesus on the cross. These men walking to Emmaus were two such disciples. The risen Jesus' appearance was different, but perhaps their lack of understanding contributed to their blindness to Jesus' identity when He joined them on the road. Though they still lacked faith, they did a good job of summarizing recent events. Jesus then put these events into perspective with a brief review of salvation history. Beginning with Moses, Jesus explained how He was in fact the Messiah, the fulfillment of Scripture.

After this explanation, Cleopas and his friend, though still ignorant, were hospitable. It was then, during the "breaking of the bread," that they received the gift of faith. Jesus revealed Himself to them. They could see that Jesus, who had died, was now sitting before them. He was the Bread of Life. When Jesus gave them the bread, they understood that He had been given by the Father to save and to nourish. Now on the "right road," the two wide-eyed disciples returned to Jerusalem to share their experience and faith.

YOU, WALKING NEXT TO MARY on the emu, are a strange sight! There has been no sign of George, so you continue on. In the distance, it seems there is a group of people sitting in the road. Drawing closer, you count a dozen people sitting at a large table that stretches across the width of the road. Now within earshot, you hear the words *guilty* and *innocent* being shouted angrily. It sounds as if this is a **jury** in the midst of deliberations. Upon arrival at the table, you are greeted with hostile stares. A woman at the table stands and asks, "Don't you know any better than to interrupt a **jury**?" You were right, this is a **jury**. You cannot help wondering why a **jury** is deliberating in the middle of a busy road. As if reading your mind, a tall, distinguished-looking man rises and says, "We the **jury** are on a busy road because we are deciding a case of drug trafficking." Recall from Landmark 34 that a **jury** represented Jerusalem. This encounter with another **jury** recalls JESUS' APPEARANCE IN JERUSALEM.

JESUS' APPEARANCE IN JERUSALEM

Mk 16:14

14 [But] later, as the eleven were at table, he appeared to them and rebuked them for their unbelief and hardness of heart because they had not believed those who saw him after he had been raised.

Lk 24:36–49

36 While they were still speaking about this, he stood in their midst and said to them, "Peace be with you." **37** But they were startled and terrified and thought that they were seeing a ghost. **38** Then he said to them, "Why are you troubled? And why do questions arise in your hearts? **39** Look at my hands and my feet, that it is I myself. Touch me and see, because a ghost does not have flesh and bones as you can see I have." **40** And as he said this, he showed them his hands and his feet. **41** While they were still incredulous for joy and were amazed, he asked them, "Have you anything here to eat?" **42** They gave him a piece of baked fish; **43** he took it and ate it in front of them.

44 He said to them, "These are my words that I spoke to you while I was still with you, that everything written about me in the law of Moses and in the prophets and psalms must be fulfilled." **45** Then he opened their minds to understand the scriptures. **46** And he said to them, "Thus it is written that the Messiah would suffer and rise from the dead on the third day **47** and that repentance, for the forgiveness of sins, would be preached in his name to all the nations, beginning from Jerusalem. **48** You are witnesses of these things. **49** And [behold] I am sending the promise of my Father upon you; but stay in the city until you are clothed with power from on high."

Jn 20:19–20

19 On the evening of that first day of the week, when the doors were locked, where the disciples were, for fear of the Jews, Jesus came and stood in their midst and said to them, "Peace be with you." **20** When he had said this, he showed them his hands and his side. The disciples rejoiced when they saw the Lord.

Jesus had made two post-resurrection appearances. First briefly to one woman, then more extensively to two men. The apostles (except Peter and John) had not believed Mary Magdalene. Perhaps the witnesses who had been on the road to Emmaus made more of an impression. Peter and

John, after seeing the empty tomb, had conveyed their findings. What were the disciples to believe?

The apostles, like those on the road to Emmaus, were not able to recognize the risen Christ. Initially in fear, they could not experience the peace that Jesus brings when we are aware of His presence in our lives. Jesus then literally allowed the stunned "not-yet believers" to feel His presence. The nail-scarred hands and feet and lance-gouged side did in fact belong to Jesus rather than some ghostly impostor. Jesus did appear to have been raised with a body that still bore the wounds of His earthly suffering. Risen from the dead, Jesus' body could no longer be called human. No human body could instantly disappear as Jesus had done at Emmaus, or pass through a door, as will happen in an upcoming unit.

Now that the apostles recognized Jesus, He renewed the table fellowship He had shared with them many times during His earthly ministry. They ate fish, a food Jesus had miraculously multiplied for many on two previous occasions. For dessert, Jesus provided a large portion of revelation. The disciples were able to understand how Jesus was the fulfillment of all of Scripture. Now graced with understanding, they would be able to continue Jesus' ministry. This would be a ministry to all nations, not just Israel. Jesus also reminded them that they would not be alone in this mission. The Holy Spirit, the gift from the Father, would soon come upon them.

THE DISTINGUISHED GENTLEMAN WHO EXPLAINED the jury's presence in the road looks very familiar. He also looks quite presidential. He appears to be the man who penned a historic document and founded an exceptional university. You think you may be speaking to **Thomas** Jefferson! You feel a need to ask, even though it would further delay the jury's work. "Sir, are you Mr. **Thomas** Jefferson?" He smiles, nods affirmatively, and says, "You can call me **Thomas**." He then looks at Mary Washington sitting on the emu and says, "Any friend of Mary's is a friend of mine." Mary responds by saying, "Hello, **Thomas**, have you seen George?" **Thomas** says he has not. You cannot believe you are on a first-name basis with **Thomas** Jefferson! You can't resist saying, "It's nice to meet you, **Thomas**." You do, however, manage to refrain from asking **Thomas** for his autograph. This memorable meeting with **Thomas** helps recall another of Jesus' post-resurrection appearances: JESUS' APPEARANCE TO THOMAS.

JESUS' APPEARANCE TO THOMAS

Jn 20:24–31

24 Thomas, called Didymus, one of the Twelve, was not with them when Jesus came. 25 So the other disciples said to him, "We have seen the Lord." But he said to them, "Unless I see the mark of the nails in his hands and put my finger into the nailmarks and put my hand into his side, I will not believe." 26 Now a week later his disciples were again inside and Thomas was with them. Jesus came, although the doors were locked, and stood in their midst and said, "Peace be with you." 27 Then he said to Thomas, "Put your finger here and see my hands, and bring your hand and put it into my side, and do not be unbelieving, but believe." 28 Thomas answered and said to him, "My Lord and my God!" 29 Jesus said to him, "Have you come to believe because you have seen me? Blessed are those who have not seen and have believed."

30 Now Jesus did many other signs in the presence of [his] disciples that are not written in this book. 31 But these are written that you may [come to] believe that Jesus is the Messiah, the Son of God, and that through this belief you may have life in his name.

Here the apostle Thomas plays the role of "everyman." At some point, we have all found ourselves at the wrong place at the wrong time. Imagine being one of the Twelve and finding yourself elsewhere when the risen Lord appeared to all of your brethren! Likewise, in times of trouble and disappointment, doubts about God and His very existence can creep in. How could a loving God "allow so many bad things to happen"? The absent Thomas is a metaphor for doubt. However, unlike us, Thomas was able to see and feel the sacred wounds as the other apostles had done a week earlier. Thomas immediately believed.

Living today, we are not able to have the experience that Thomas and the other apostles had. However, we do have many other opportunities to experience the risen Jesus in our lives. One way is through the Gospels. John explains that this was precisely why he had written his narrative, "so that we may believe that Jesus is the Messiah, the Son of God."

YOU AND MARY (STILL ATOP the emu) bid farewell to Thomas and the other members of the jury. Before you have gotten very far down the road, you hear Thomas yell, "Stop, come back!" You turn and see that he is not calling to you, Mary, or the emu. **Seven** members of the jury have left the table. These **seven** people are following you! Thomas continues to call for the **seven** to return. However, upon reaching you the **seven** declare in unison that they want to help search for George. Certainly **seven** additional sets of eyes will be helpful. You ask the **seven** why they are abandoning Thomas and the others. The **seven** mutter something about being Federalists. You don't really understand what they mean, but you are happy to have the **seven** come along. These **seven** people are a reminder of JESUS' APPEARANCE TO THE SEVEN.

JESUS' APPEARANCE TO THE SEVEN

Jn 21:1–14

1 After this, Jesus revealed himself again to his disciples at the Sea of Tiberias. He revealed himself in this way. **2** Together were Simon Peter, Thomas called Didymus, Nathanael from Cana in Galilee, Zebedee's sons, and two others of his disciples. **3** Simon Peter said to them, "I am going fishing." They said to him, "We also will come with you." So they went out and got into the boat, but that night they caught nothing. **4** When it was already dawn, Jesus was standing on the shore; but the disciples did not realize that it was Jesus. **5** Jesus said to them, "Children, have you caught anything to eat?" They answered him, "No." **6** So he said to them, "Cast the net over the right side of the boat and you will find something." So they cast it, and were not able to pull it in because of the number of fish. **7** So the disciple whom Jesus loved said to Peter, "It is the Lord." When Simon Peter heard that it was the Lord, he tucked in his garment, for he was lightly clad, and jumped into the sea. **8** The other disciples came in the boat, for they were not far from shore, only about a hundred yards, dragging the net with the fish. **9** When they climbed out on shore, they saw a charcoal fire with fish on it and bread. **10** Jesus said to them, "Bring some of the fish you just caught." **11** So Simon Peter went over and dragged the net ashore full of one hundred fifty-three large fish. Even though there were so many, the net was not torn. **12** Jesus said to them, "Come, have breakfast." And none of the disciples dared to ask him, "Who are you?" because they realized it was the Lord. **13** Jesus came over and took the bread and gave it to them, and in like manner the fish. **14** This was now the third time Jesus was revealed to his disciples after being raised from the dead.

This appearance of the risen Christ to the disciples should seem familiar. The scene has many similarities to the calling of the first disciples as told by Luke in Landmark 4. Now back at the Sea of Galilee, the seven were fishing at night. In the dark, while apart from Jesus, they were unable to catch any fish. Later, following His instructions, they were abundantly successful in their mission. Jesus showed concern for and participated in the efforts of His "children." Peter then found himself in a familiar place, in the water! Just as in Landmark 18, Peter took the plunge, unable to control his excitement in wanting to be closer to Jesus.

Back onshore, the seven were able to recognize Jesus, who had made the large catch possible. They likely recalled His earlier words, "From now on you will be catching men." They then broke bread with Jesus for the last time, there on the shore of the Sea of Galilee. Not coincidentally, they were back where their mission with Jesus had begun, and also where He had fed the masses (Landmark 18). They would soon be commissioned to do the same.

Landmark 49:

FORTY-NINER

You now come to the forty-ninth and final Landmark. It has been quite a journey walking with Jesus and seeing His earthly mission unfold step by step. Since this is the last of the forty-nine Landmarks, you decide to literally "go for the gold." You have never panned for gold before, so you will need some assistance. Who better to assist you than a **forty-niner**! A **forty-niner** was someone who participated in the California Gold Rush of 1849. As luck would have it, a grizzled older man carrying a pan is heading your way. He may be a good prospect! You ask him where you might locate a **forty-niner**. His gold tooth flashes when he says, "You're looking at one!" This rather disheveled fellow says he will be happy to help you find some gold. Reaching out to shake the **forty-niner's** hand, you express your appreciation. If the **forty-niner's** skills are as strong as his handshake, people will soon be calling you Midas! This friendly **forty-niner** will serve as the forty-ninth Landmark.

The forty-niner asks you to follow him. He tells you that prior to going to the river to pan for gold he has a chore to do at his nearby farm. This will be convenient since his farm is adjacent to the river. He explains that he needs to **feed his sheep**. As you and the forty-niner approach his farm, you see a hillside dotted with hundreds of sheep. He spends a significant amount of time each day **feeding sheep**. His land is barren, so he painstakingly **feeds his sheep** by hand. The forty-niner gives you bags of grass and clover and asks you to scatter them on the ground. Soon you discover that you actually enjoy **feeding the sheep**. When your bags are empty, the forty-niner says it is time to go for the gold. He will finish **feeding the sheep** later. This episode in the field recalls Jesus' conversation with Peter. Part of the conversation involves Jesus telling Peter to FEED MY SHEEP.

FEED MY SHEEP

Jn 21:15–19

15 When they had finished breakfast, Jesus said to Simon Peter, "Simon, son of John, do you love me more than these?" He said to him, "Yes, Lord, you know that I love you." He said to him, "Feed my lambs." **16** He then said to him a second time, "Simon, son of John, do you love me?" He said to him, "Yes, Lord, you know that I love you." He said to him, "Tend my sheep." **17** He said to him the third time, "Simon, son of John, do you love me?" Peter was distressed that he had said to him a third time, "Do you love me?" and he said to him, "Lord, you know everything; you know that I love you." [Jesus] said to him, "Feed my sheep. **18** Amen, amen, I say to you, when you were younger, you used to dress yourself and go where you wanted; but when you grow old, you will stretch out your hands, and someone else will dress you and lead you where you do not want to go." **19** He said this signifying by what kind of death he would glorify God. And when he had said this, he said to him, "Follow me."

Jesus had already forgiven the repentant Peter for his recent betrayal. Peter had seen the risen Lord at least twice in the company of others. It seemed right that Jesus would have a private audience with the man He had chosen to lead His church. Just as Peter had denied Jesus three times, he was given three opportunities to affirm his love for Jesus. With each affirmation, Jesus gave him the command to feed His sheep or lambs. This was something Peter would have ample opportunity to do as he shepherded the church through its infancy. Though Peter was the first to guide the church, there would be many who would follow in his footsteps. Jesus then foretold how the literal footsteps of Peter would end. Jesus' words seemed to indicate the martyr's death Peter would suffer. Peter was crucified in Rome some thirty years later. In the meantime, he obeyed Jesus' earlier and now current directive to "Follow Me."

YOU AND THE FORTY-NINER LEAVE the pasture of sheep and walk toward the river. One sheep has left the flock and is walking along beside the forty-niner. He explains, "This is Bella, my **beloved** sheep." She is his favorite, his "**beloved**." He goes on to explain that Bella is also **beloved** by his wife and children because of her sweet and gentle disposition. He tells you that some of the other sheep are jealous of Bella and her **beloved** status. You notice that Bella has a gold chain around her neck. Looking closer, you see the word *Beloved* engraved on a small nametag. No wonder the other sheep are jealous of this "**beloved**" beast! This encounter with the **beloved** sheep recalls the next unit about THE BELOVED DISCIPLE.

THE BELOVED DISCIPLE

Jn 21:20–25

20 Peter turned and saw the disciple following whom Jesus loved, the one who had also reclined upon his chest during the supper and had said, "Master, who is the one who will betray you?" 21 When Peter saw him, he said to Jesus, "Lord, what about him?" 22 Jesus said to him, "What if I want him to remain until I come? What concern is it of yours? You follow me." 23 So the word spread among the brothers that that disciple would not die. But Jesus had not told him that he would not die, just "What if I want him to remain until I come? [What concern is it of yours?]"

24 It is this disciple who testifies to these things and has written them, and we know that his testimony is true. 25 There are also many other things that Jesus did, but if these were to be described individually, I do not think the whole world would contain the books that would be written.

Peter's conversation with the risen Christ focused on another of the disciples with whom Jesus had a special relationship. It is John, the apostle (and evangelist) referred to as "the beloved disciple." Jesus had just said to Simon Peter, "Follow Me." Peter happened to turn and see John, who was literally "following" them. Jesus' next words were somewhat ambiguous. Some of the other disciples came to believe that they meant John would still be alive at Jesus' second coming. That, of course, was not the case. However, John's memory and spirit certainly stayed with his community long after his death.

John, the Gospel of the beloved disciple, concludes with his testimony to its truth. He had followed Jesus and lived through the events that he recorded. He did not describe all of the events that he had witnessed, but what he did describe is true. John began his Gospel talking about another John (the Baptist) who had come to give true testimony to the "light" so that all might believe. John ends his Gospel with the hope that his true testimony about Jesus will enlighten his readers so that they, too, will believe in Jesus who is "the light of the human race, the light (that) shines in the darkness."

SOON YOU, THE FORTY-NINER, AND Bella the beloved sheep arrive at the river. The forty-niner begins to explain the gold-panning process. Suddenly, he looks up and shouts "Eureka!" Coming down the river is the largest gold nugget that either of you have ever seen. It is the size of a **soccer ball**. You cannot begin to guess what a ball of gold the size of a **soccer ball** might weigh. The forty-niner braces himself to stop this mother of all nuggets from getting away. Unfortunately, it just bounces off of his leg. It is, in fact, a **soccer ball**. Some upstream prankster has painted a **soccer ball** gold. They had placed the **soccer ball** in the river hoping to fool someone into thinking they had made the discovery of a lifetime. Recall that Landmark 11 was a **soccer ball** because there are eleven players on a soccer team. Back then, a soccer ball represented the number *11*. It still does. This scene with the gold-painted **soccer ball** stands for the unit where JESUS COMMISSIONS THE ELEVEN.

JESUS COMMISSIONS THE ELEVEN

Mt 28:16–20

16 The eleven disciples went to Galilee, to the mountain to which Jesus had ordered them. **17** When they saw him, they worshiped, but they doubted. **18** Then Jesus approached and said to them, "All power in heaven and on earth has been given to me. **19** Go, therefore, and make disciples of all nations, baptizing them in the name of the Father, and of the Son, and of the holy Spirit, **20** teaching them to observe all that I have commanded you. And behold, I am with you always, until the end of the age."

Mk 16:15–18

15 He said to them, "Go into the whole world and proclaim the gospel to every creature. 16 Whoever believes and is baptized will be saved; whoever does not believe will be condemned. 17 These signs will accompany those who believe: in my name they will drive out demons, they will speak new languages. 18 They will pick up serpents [with their hands], and if they drink any deadly thing, it will not harm them. They will lay hands on the sick, and they will recover."

Jn 20:21–23

21 [Jesus] said to them again, "Peace be with you. As the Father has sent me, so I send you." 22 And when he had said this, he breathed on them and said to them, "Receive the holy Spirit. 23 Whose sins you forgive are forgiven them, and whose sins you retain are retained."

———————————

Jesus had been sent by the Father to die for our sins and to be raised in glory. This primary mission had been accomplished. His secondary purpose of calling and preparing apostles to carry on His presence in the world was about to conclude. The eleven were in Galilee, where the angel at the tomb had instructed them to gather. They were high on a mountaintop where Moses, Peter, James, and John could attest that important information was transmitted. It was here that Jesus summed up His purpose and gave final instructions before ascending to the Father. The disciples must have heard Jesus' final words with excitement, joy, sadness, and trepidation. He affirmed His relationship with the Father. Jesus reassured the eleven that the heavenly power that flowed through Him would also flow through them via the Holy Spirit. This power would enable them to baptize, to teach, and to forgive sins. This promise was symbolized by Jesus breathing on them. Jesus then commanded the eleven to go forth and do what He had done, to teach God's love and make disciples. Jesus' final words must have given them some comfort as they faced this monumental task. They would not be alone. Jesus, their friend, mentor, Son of God, and Messiah would be with them always.

THE FRUSTRATED FORTY-NINER IS NOW standing in the river holding a gold-painted soccer ball. You are not sure if he is laughing or crying.

You ask him to toss you the ball. Now holding the ball at arm's length, you prepare to kick the ball out of sight. As you release the ball, your leg swings forward and makes powerful contact with the "fool's gold." The ball immediately begins to **ascend**. As it **ascends** higher and higher, you and the forty-niner gaze upward. The ball has now **ascended** above the treetops. Much to your amazement, it continues to **ascend**. Soon the ball has **ascended** to the clouds. It continues its **ascension** and disappears into the clouds. You and the forty-niner are amazed by this **ascension**. This **ascension** of the soccer ball into the clouds and beyond brings you to the final unit of the journey: THE LORD'S ASCENSION.

THE LORD'S ASCENSION

Mk 16:19–20

19 So then the Lord Jesus, after he spoke to them, was taken up into heaven and took his seat at the right hand of God. **20** But they went forth and preached everywhere, while the Lord worked with them and confirmed the word through accompanying signs.

Lk 24:50–53

50 Then he led them [out] as far as Bethany, raised his hands, and blessed them. **51** As he blessed them he parted from them and was taken up to heaven. **52** They did him homage and then returned to Jerusalem with great joy, **53** and they were continually in the temple praising God.

The presence of Jesus on earth in human form ended with His Passion and death on Good Friday. It is now forty days later and time for the risen Christ to ascend to the Father. From the previous unit, as recounted by Matthew, it would seem that this occurred on the mountain in Galilee following Jesus' final instructions to the eleven. However, Matthew does not describe the ascension, nor does John. Mark does not mention a location, but implies Jesus was with the disciples in Jerusalem. Only Luke specifies the place, Bethany, about two miles east of Jerusalem.

God, our loving Father, had completed His plan of redemption through Jesus, His Son. The risen Christ had completed His instructions